Banking Performance and Socio Economic Development

Banking Performance and Socio Economic Development

Rajni Chaudhary

RANDOM
RANDOM PUBLICATIONS
NEW DELHI (INDIA)

Banking Performance and Socio Economic Development

ISBN 978-93-5111-940-1

Published in 2016 in India by

RANDOM PUBLICATIONS

4376-A/4B, Gali Murari Lal, Ansari Road
New Delhi-110 002
Phone : +9111-43580356, 011-23289044, 011-43142548
e-mail: sales@randompublications.com,
info@randompublications.com, randomexports@gmail.com

Reprinted 2025

Type Setting by : Friends Media, Delhi-110089
Printed at : Replika Press Pvt. Ltd.

Preface

Banks play an indispensable role in socio-economic development of the country. Analysis of a single bank group based performance and its relation with economic development is relatively unexplored area of research. The present book filled this gap.

Banking system has significant role in the economic development, historically. On one hand, banks give the security of savings for the general people, on the other hand, lend money to the entrepreneurs to start new businesses or expand their existing businesses, which ultimately create velocity of money and generation of employment within an economic territory. Modern banking system is involved in numerous financial services activities starting from lending money to exchange money nowadays.

The Indian banking system remained largely resilient to the economic turbulence of 2008-09. However, it highlighted the importance of responsible banking; focused more towards creating objectives parallel to the economic priorities. Hence, enhancing efficiency and productivity of banks with a strong risk management framework has been the objective of RBI from the past five years.

Amongst developing economics, India has a relatively deep financial system. Its financial depth is attributable in large to India's vast network of financial institution, particularly those focused on rural customers. The need to improve financial access to India's poor, the overwhelming majority of whom are concentrated in rural areas, motivated the establishment of a vast network of rural banks. Financial tools help entrepreneurs start and expand small businesses which are a source of local job creation, growth and poverty reduction. Rural banking has become a national and a government imperative in the last few years.

The book will enable public sector banks to act as better functioning entities. They will work in harmony and co-ordination with other banks and will maintain financial stability.

– Author

Contents

1

Banking Performance and Development: An Introduction

DEFINITION OF BANK

The definition of a bank varies from country to country. Under English common law, a banker is defined as a person who carries on the business of banking, which is specified as:

- Conducting current accounts for his customers
- Paying cheques drawn on him, and
- Collecting cheques for his customers.

In most common law jurisdictions there is a Bills of Exchange Act that codifies the law in relation to negotiable instruments, including cheques, and this Act contains a statutory definition of the term *banker*: *banker* includes a body of persons, whether incorporated or not, who carry on the business of banking'. Although this definition seems circular, it is actually functional, because it ensures that the legal basis for bank transactions such as cheques does not depend on how the bank is organized or regulated. The business of banking is in many English common law countries not defined by statute but by common law. In other English common law jurisdictions there are statutory definitions of the *business of banking* or *banking business*. When looking at these definitions it is important to keep in mind that they are defining the business of banking for the purposes of the legislation, and not necessarily in general. In particular, most of the definitions are from legislation that has the purposes of entry regulating and supervising banks rather than regulating the actual business of banking. However, in many cases the statutory definition closely mirrors the common law one.

Examples of statutory definitions:

- "Banking business" means the business of receiving money on current or deposit account, paying and collecting cheques drawn by or paid in by customers, the making of advances to customers, and includes such other business as the Authority may prescribe for the purposes of this Act; (Banking Act (Singapore), Section 2, Interpretation).

- "Banking business" means the business of either or both of the following:
- Receiving from the general public money on current, deposit, savings or other similar account repayable on demand or within less than [3 months]... or with a period of call or notice of less than that period;
- Paying or collecting checks drawn by or paid in by customers

Since the advent of EFTPOS (Electronic Funds Transfer at Point Of Sale), direct credit, direct debit and internet banking, the cheque has lost its primacy in most banking systems as a payment instrument. This has led legal theorists to suggest that the cheque based definition should be broadened to include financial institutions that conduct current accounts for customers and enable customers to pay and be paid by third parties, even if they do not pay and collect checks.

BANK PERFORMANCE

This study examines the relation between management ownership and firm performance for a sample of commercial bank holding companies. To measure bank performance, we use an economic measure: Stern Stewart and Co.'s *Economic Value Added* (EVA). Prior studies of firm ownership and performance have traditionally used accounting measures of corporate performance. Exceptions are Chen, Hexter, and Hu's and McConnell and Servaes, which use Tobin's *q* as a measure of performance, but which do not focus upon commercial banks. We find that, when an economic measure of performance is used, the relation between ownership and performance of commercial banks is not monotonic, but is significantly curvilinear.

This differs from the results of Pi and Timme. We also find that the question of whether or not the CEO also holds the title of chairman of the board has no impact on bank performance. We speculate that, in commercial banks, management entrenchment, as proposed in Morck, Shleifer and Vishny, may offset the effects predicted by the convergence-of-interest hypothesis of Jensen and Meckling. Jensen and Meckling's hypothesis suggests a uniformly positive relation between management ownership and the value of the firm. Jensen and Meckling propose that an inverse monotonic relation should exist between the ownermanager's control and agency costs, and that, as ownership increases, there is increased incentive for the ownermanager to maximize the value of the firm.

Berle and Means show that as firm size increases, ownership becomes diffused, thus leading to conflicts of interest between owners and managers. Jensen and Meckling and Berle and Means assume that the owner-manager is a single owner who has reduced his or her equity position in the firm. We know that in most circumstances this is not the case with the modern public corporation and management.

Therefore, it is this relation, the one between management ownership and bank performance that is examined. Principal/agent conflicts arise due to the separation of the ownership and the control of the corporation. Berle and Means emphasize that when control is distinct from ownership, those in control may deploy assets in ways that benefit those in control rather than owners.

Jensen and Meckling demonstrate that when the owner-manager sells equity in the firm to outsiders, and if both parties are utility maximizers, the owner-manager's interest will diverge from the new principals. Jensen and Meckling refer to this failure to maximize the welfare of the principal as residual loss, and feel it is likely to be the most important cost due to the principal/agent conflict. Morck, Shleifer, and Vishny propose another model in which increased ownership by the management leads to entrenchment, where the manager will indulge in non-value-maximizing behaviour.

However, management's self-indulgence is expected to be less than if he or she has control but no claim on the firm's cash flows. The entrenchment hypothesis predicts that the value of the firm will be less when management is free from checks on their control, and suggests that firm performance will decline as management ownership increases. Our findings of a significantly curvilinear relation between management ownership and firm value suggest that both the convergence-of-interest effect and the entrenchment effect are at work. Specifically, our results show that firm value increases, then declines, then increases with management ownership. The issue of management ownership and performance has been addressed extensively in the corporate literature, but has received little attention in the banking literature.

The corporate literature emphasizes the relation between management or insider ownership and the performance of the firm. These studies are important to this research because they indicate that a conflict exists as to whether control influences the performance of the firm. One study that does address control and bank performance is that of Pi and Timme. They investigate the principal/agent conflicts by examining variations in performance and the relations between performance, top management team and ownership structures, and the composition of the board of directors.

Their sample consists of large publicly traded US commercial banks. Their results suggest that top management team structure affects performance, and internal monitoring devices may not be an effective control. They find that when the CEO is also chairman of the board, principal/agent conflicts may be exacerbated because of the consolidation of the decision control processes. Their results indicate that when the CEO is also chairman, cost efficiency and return on assets are lower. Conversely, cost efficiency and return on assets are positively related to non-chairman-CEO ownership, and unrelated to institutional and large blockholders' ownership, and the proportion of inside directors. The next section explains the data and methodology. The third section presents the results, and the last section summarizes and concludes the study.

DATA AND METHODOLOGY

EVA

The sample consists of 100 bank holding companies obtained from the Stern Stewart and Co. 1997 database for year ending 1996. The EVA performance data were obtained from Stern Stewart and Co. The data required for calculating selected accounting measures were taken from COMPUSTAT, which was supplemented with information from the *Standard and Poor's Stock Guide*. EVA is defined as the current-period after-tax economic earnings net of the charge for the use of capital. The procedure for estimating EVA for each bank follows Uyemura, Kantor, and Pettit's methodology:

Equation:

EVA = NOPAT - Capital Charge

where NOPAT represents "net operating profits after-tax" and "Capital Charge" is the amount of capital multiplied by the cost of capital.

EVA differs form conventional earnings in two important ways. First, NOPAT reflects operational profits adjusted to minimize accounting conventions that misrepresent economic flows or that distort the proper matching of revenues and expenses. Second, EVA assumes that management must generate sufficient revenues to cover operating expenses, interest charges, and provide the return that shareholders require as compensation for assuming risks. Prior studies traditionally used *net income* (NI), *earnings per share* (EPS), *return on equity* (ROE), or *return on assets* (ROA); all are accounting measures of performance. None of these performance measures tells us how much management has increased shareholders wealth.

EVA can lead to management decisions that are different from those based on traditional measures. Traditional measures do not reflect risk and therefore promote behaviour that aims to maximize earnings or prevent the dilution of returns. Return or ratio measures do not accurately assess shareholder value creation; rather they only indicate average profitability. The advantage of EVA is that it is dollarbased and thus, EVA maximization correlates with wealth maximization. Uyemura, Kantor, and Pettit find that EVA has the strongest correlation with *market value added* (MVA).

To calculate EVA, we need NOPAT and the capital charge. NOPAT is the operational profits of the company restated in such a way that NI is adjusted to reflect the current economics of the business. Loan loss provisions, taxes, non-recurring events, and securities accounting are the four major adjustments that are the most common adjustments that are made when calculating EVA for banks. Capital is composed of shareholders' equity plus the following: loan loss reserves, other net deferred tax credits, non-recurring events, and unamortized securities gains or losses after taxes. This ensures that if an item is not considered a component of current operations that it will be capitalized and will be assessed a capital charge.

Ownership

Previous studies use Abrecht and Locker's *Corporate Data Exchange* (*CDE*). This data set contains principal stockholder ownership information of *Fortune 500* companies for year-end 1980, and is updated through May 1981 for holders of 5 per cent or more. For this study, ownership data were obtained from proxy statements for the year-end 1996. One of the problems with using current ownership data is availability. The *CDE Fortune 500* directory was published only once in 1981. However, ownership data is available from other sources. Anderson and Lee examine ownership data provided by four databases and proxy statements. They suggest that data collected from proxy statements are superior to data from other sources but can be expensive to acquire and time consuming to extract.

METHODOLOGY

We sought to extract certain measures of performance, ownership and control, and to determine which of the ownership or control measures was statistically significant as a predictor of performance. Because EVA is a function of a bank's size, we standardized it using year-end capital. Therefore, for performance, we used standardized measures of EVA. For measures of ownership and control, we constructed the following variables: CHM is a dummy variable, which takes on a value of 1 if the CEO is also the Chairman of the Board, and takes on a value of 0 otherwise.

TEN is the natural log of CEO tenure, expressed in years. AGE is the log of the age of the CEO. INS-BD is the log of the ratio of inside directors to total board members. INSIDE is the log of the ratio of insider ownership to total ownership. Finally, MAN is the log of the ratio of management ownership to total ownership. In order to test for possible non-linearity in the relation between management ownership and performance, we also constructed squared and cubed values of MAN. After constructing these variables for ownership and control, we looked at the correlation matrix, presented. Because of the high degree of collinearity between variables, we concluded that only CHM and MAN were sufficiently uncorrelated with the other variables to be included in our model. We therefore dropped all other variables, other than CHM and MAN, and included the squared and cubed values of MAN in order to test for possible non-linearity.

FORM OF GOVERNMENT REGULATION

Bank regulations are a form of government regulation which subject banks to certain requirements, restrictions and guidelines. This regulatory structure creates transparency between banking institutions and the individuals and corporations with whom they conduct business, among other things. Given the interconnectedness of the banking industry and the reliance that the national economy hold on banks, it is important for regulatory agencies to maintain control over the standardized practices of these institutions. Supporters of such regulation often hinge their arguments on the "too big to fail" notion.

This holds that many financial institutions hold too much control over the economy to fail without enormous consequences. This is the premise for government bailouts, in which federal financial assistance is provided to banks or other financial institutions who appear to be on the brink of collapse. The belief is that without this aid, the crippled banks would not only become bankrupt, but would create rippling effects throughout the economy. Others advocate deregulation, or free banking, whereby banks are given extended liberties as to how they operate the institution.

OBJECTIVES OF BANK REGULATION

The objectives of bank regulation, and the emphasis, vary between jurisdictions. The most common objectives are:

- Prudential—to reduce the level of risk to which bank creditors are exposed
- Systemic risk reduction—to reduce the risk of disruption resulting from adverse trading conditions for banks causing multiple or major bank failures
- Avoid misuse of banks—to reduce the risk of banks being used for criminal purposes, *e.g.* laundering the proceeds of crime
- To protect banking confidentiality
- Credit allocation—to direct credit to favoured sectors

GENERAL PRINCIPLES OF BANK REGULATION

Banking regulations can vary widely across nations and jurisdictions. This section of the article describes general principles of bank regulation throughout the world.

Minimum requirements

Requirements are imposed on banks in order to promote the objectives of the regulator. Often, these requirements are closely tied to the level of risk exposure for a certain sector of the bank. The most important minimum requirement in banking regulation is maintaining minimum capital ratios.

Supervisory review

Banks are required to be issued with a bank license by the regulator in order to carry on business as a bank, and the regulator supervises licenced banks for compliance with the requirements and responds to breaches of the requirements through obtaining undertakings, giving directions, imposing penalties or revoking the bank's licence.

Market discipline

The regulator requires banks to publicly disclose financial and other information, and depositors and other creditors are able to use this information to assess the level of risk and to make investment decisions. As a result of this, the bank is subject to market discipline and the regulator can also use market pricing information as an indicator of the bank's financial health.

ROLE OF BANKS

Money lending in one form or the other has evolved along with the history of the mankind. Even in the ancient times there are references to the moneylenders. Shakespeare also referred to 'Shylocks' who made unreasonable demands in case the loans were not repaid in time along with interest. Indian history is also replete with the instances referring to indigenous money lenders, Sahukars and Zamindars involved in the business of money lending by mortgaging the landed property of the borrowers. Towards the beginning of the twentieth century, with the onset of modern industry in the country, the need for government regulated banking system was felt.

The British government began to pay attention towards the need for an organised banking sector in the country and Reserve Bank of India was set up to regulate the formal banking sector in the country. But the growth of modern banking remained slow mainly due to lack of surplus capital in the Indian economic system at that point of time. Modern banking institutions came up only in big cities and industrial centres. The rural areas, representing vast majority of Indian society, remained dependent on the indigenous money lenders for their credit needs. Independence of the country heralded a new era in the growth of modern banking. Many new commercial banks came up in various parts of the country. As the modern banking network grew, the government began to realise that the banking sector was catering only to the needs of the well-to-do and the capitalists.

The interests of the poorer sections as well as those of the common man were being ignored. In 1969, Indian government took a historic decision to nationalise 14 biggest private commercial banks. A few more were nationalised after a couple of years. This resulted in transferring the ownership of these banks to the State and the Reserve Bank of India could then issue directions to these banks to fund the national programmes, the rural sector, the plan priorities and the priority sector at differential rate of interest.

This resulted in providing fillip the banking facilities to the rural areas, to the under-privileged and the downtrodden. It also resulted in financial inclusion of all categories of people in almost all the regions of the country. However, after almost two decades of bank nationalisation some new issues became contextual. The service standards of the public sector banks began to decline. Their profitability came down and the efficiency of the staff became suspect. Non-performing assets of these banks began to rise. The wheel of time had turned a full circle by early nineties and the government after the introduction of structural and economic reforms in the financial sector, allowed the setting up of new banks in the private sector. The new generation private banks have now established themselves in the system and have set new standards of service and efficiency. These banks have also given tough but healthy competition to the public sector banks.

MODERN DAY ROLE

Banking system and the Financial Institutions play very significant role in the economy. First and foremost is in the form of catering to the need of credit for all the sections of society. The modern economies in the world have developed primarily by making best use of the credit availability in their systems. An efficient banking system must cater to the needs of high end investors by making available high amounts of capital for big projects in the industrial, infrastructure and service sectors. At the same time, the medium and small ventures must also have credit available to them for new investment and expansion of the existing units. Rural sector in a country like India can grow only if cheaper credit is available to the farmers for their short and medium term needs. Credit availability for infrastructure sector is also extremely important.

The success of any financial system can be fathomed by finding out the availability of reliable and adequate credit for infrastructure projects. Fortunately, during the past about one decade there has been increased participation of the private sector in infrastructure projects. The banks and the financial institutions also cater to another important need of the society *i.e.* mopping up small savings at reasonable rates with several options.

The common man has the option to park his savings under a few alternatives, including the small savings schemes introduced by the government from time to time and in bank deposits in the form of savings accounts, recurring deposits and time deposits. Another option is to invest in the stocks or mutual funds. The banks and the financial institutions also perform certain new-age functions which could not be thought of a couple of decades ago. The facility of internet banking enables a consumer to access and operate his bank account without actually visiting the bank premises. The facility of ATMs and the credit/debit cards has revolutionised the choices available with the customers. The banks also serve as alternative gateways for making payments on account of income tax and online payment of various bills like the telephone, electricity and tax. The bank customers can also invest their funds in various stocks or mutual funds straight from their bank accounts. In the modern day economy, where people have no time to make these payments by standing in queue, the service provided by the banks is commendable. While the commercial banks cater to the banking needs of the people in the cities and towns, there is another category of banks that looks after the credit and banking needs of the people living in the rural areas, particularly the farmers. Regional Rural Banks (RRBs) have been sponsored by many commercial banks in several States. These banks, along with the cooperative banks, take care of the farmer-specific needs of credit and other banking facilities.

FUTURE

Till a few years ago, the government largely patro-nized the small savings schemes in which not only the interest rates were higher, but the income tax rebates and incentives were also in plenty. The bank deposits, on the other hand, did not entail such benefits. As a result, the small savings were the first choice of the investors. But for the last few years the trend has been reversed. The small savings, the bank deposits and the mutual funds have been brought at par for the purpose of incentives under the income tax.

Moreover, the interest rates in the small savings schemes are no longer higher than those offered by the banks. Banks today are free to determine their interest rates within the given limits prescribed by the RBI. It is now easier for the banks to open new branches. But the banking sector reforms are still not complete. A lot more is required to be done to revamp the public sector banks. Mergers and amalgamation is the next measure on the agenda of the government. The government is also preparing to disinvest some of its equity from the PSU banks. The option of allowing foreign direct investment beyond 50 per cent in the Indian banking sector has also been under consideration. Banks and financial intuitions have played major role in the economic development of the country and most of the credit- related schemes of the government to uplift the poorer and the under-privileged sections have been implemented through the banking sector. The role of the banks has been important, but it is going to be even more important in the future.

BANKING POLICY AND TRENDS

With liberalisation and growing integration of the Indian financial sector with the international market, the supervisory and regulatory role of RBI has become critical for the maintenance of financial stability. RBI has been continuously fine-tuning its regulatory and supervisory mechanism in recent years to match international standards.

Migration to new capital adequacy framework (Basel II) based on a three-pillar approach, namely, minimum capital requirements, supervisory review, and market discipline, involves implementation challenges for both RBI and banks. RBI has taken a number of initiatives to make migration to Basel II smoother. Banks have been advised to undertake a selfassessment of the existing risk management systems and to simultaneously initiate suitable measures to upgrade them to match international standards. Banks have also been asked to prepare a road map and to review the progress on a quarterly basis.

In its annual policy statement for 2004- 05, the RBI has carried forward initiatives aimed at improving prudential regulation and credit delivery, particularly to agriculture and the SSI sectors. The RBI has introduced higher provisioning requirement for NPAs included under 'doubtful for more than three years' category effective March 31, 2005. In order to contain risks arising from non-SLR portfolio of banks, the RBI has prohibited banks from investing in unrated non-SLR securities. Further, the RBI has indicated that with effect from January 1, 2005, only those banks, whose investment in unlisted non-SLR securities are within the prudential limit of 10 per cent of their total investment in non-SLR securities, will be allowed to make fresh investment in such securities up to the prudential limits.

FINANCIAL PERFORMANCE

During the year 2003-04, the banking sector witnessed strong growth in deposits and advances. Aggregate deposits of scheduled commercial banks (SCBs) grew by 17.5 per cent compared to 13.4 per cent in 2002-03. Credit and investments by SCBs increased by 15.3 per cent and 25.1 per cent, respectively in 2003-04 compared to 16.1 per cent and 23.3 per cent respectively in 2002-03. These developments coupled with a decline in gross NPAs enabled SCBs to improve their financial performance, despite a lower income growth consequent upon low interest rates. Ratio of net profits to total assets of SCBs improved marginally from 1.0 per cent to 1.1 per cent. Ratio of operating profits to total assets improved from 2.4 per cent in 2002-03 to 2.7 per cent in 2003-04 Total income of SCBs increased by 6.6 per cent to ₹ 1,83,767 crore in 2003-04 as compared to an increase of 14.0 per cent in 2002-03. The lower income growth was on account of lower growth of 2.4 per cent in interest income in 2003-04. Income growth in 2003-04 came mainly from other income, which increased by 25.5 per cent. Total expenditure of SCBs grew at a lower rate of 4.0 per cent in 2003-04 compared to 11.3 per cent in 2002-03.

The lower growth of total expenditure was entirely on account of a decline in interest expenditure from ₹ 93,596 crore in 2002-03 to ₹ 87,567 crore in 2003-04. As a proportion of total assets, interest expenditure declined from 5.5 per cent to 4.4 per cent. Expenditure on provisions and contingencies witnessed an increase of 28.8 per cent in 2003-04 on top of an increaes of 29.3 per cent in the previous year. The financial performance varied across bank groups.

Increase in the income of the SCBs varied from 2.4 per cent for old private sector banks to 8.1 per cent for foreign banks. The income of the public sector banks (PSBs) grew by 7.1 per cent in 2003-04. Among income, the growth of interest income was the highest for new private sector banks followed by old private banks, PSBs and foreign banks. The growth of other income was in sharp contrast with the growth in interest income.

Growth of other income was the highest in case of foreign banks and the lowest for the old private sector banks. Growth of expenditure was the highest in the case of foreign banks and lowest in the case of old private sector banks. Expenditure on interest declined for all bank groups, following the reduction in deposit rates. The decline in expenditure on interest was the highest for foreign banks (15.5 per cent) and lowest for old private sector banks (5.5 per cent) and PSBs (5.9 per cent). The ratio of net profits to total assets was the highest for foreign banks (1.7 per cent) followed by old private sector banks (1.2 per cent), PSBs (1.1 per cent), and new private sector banks (0.8 per cent).

The ratio of operating profits to total assets followed more or less a similar pattern with foreign banks performing the best (3.7 per cent), followed by PSBs (2.7 per cent), old private sector banks (2.6 per cent) and new private sector banks (2.0 per cent). There has been an overall improvement in the efficiency of SCBs as evident in the declining ratios for operating expenses to net total income (total income – interest expenditure). For SCBs as a whole the ratio declined from 53.0 per cent in 2001- 02 to 48.3 per cent in 2002-03 and further to 45.2 per cent in 2003-04.

Table. Working Reults of Scheduled Commercial Banks

Items	Public sector banks		Foreign banks		Old pvt. sector banks		New pvt. Sector banks		SCBs	
	2002-03	2003-04	2002-03	2003-04	2002-03	2003-04	2002-03	2003-04	2002-03	2003-04
					Rs. Crore					
A. Income	128464	137602	12034.6	13012	11279	11551	20567	21602	172345	183767
I) Interest Income	107232	109496	8958	8990	8920	9120	15633	16421	140742	144028
II) Other income	21232	28106	3076.95	4022	2359	2431	4934	5180.6	31603	39739
B. Expenditure	116169	121055	10210	10769	10047	10105	18843	19567.01	155270	161496
I) Interest expended	69853	65765	5055.01	4272	6327	5982	12361	11548	93596	87567
II) Intermediation cost	28895	32363	3251	3752	2147	2374	3774	5041	38067	43530
III) Provisions and contingenies	17422	22928	1904	2744	1573	1749	2708	2978	23607	30400
C. Operating profit (A-Bi-Bii)	29716	39475	3728	4987	2805	3196	4433	5013	40682	52671
D. Net profit (A-B)	12295	16546	1824	2243	1232	1446	1725	2035	17075	22271
E. Net interest income (Spread)	37379	43732	3903	4718	2593	3139	3272	4873	47146	56462
F. Total assets	1285411	1471428	116661	136316	104956	120700	192170	246576	1699198	1975020
					As per cent of total assets					
A. Income	10.0	9.4	10.3	9.5	10.7	9.6	10.7	8.8	10.1	9.3
I) Interest Income	8.3	7.4	7.7	6.6	8.5	7.6	8.1	6.7	8.3	7.3
II) Other income	1.7	1.9	2.6	3.0	2.2	2.0	2.6	2.1	1.9	2.0
B. Expenditure	9.0	8.2	8.8	7.9	9.6	8.4	9.8	7.9	9.1	8.2
I) Interest expended	5.4	4.5	4.3	3.1	6.0	5.0	6.4	4.7	5.5	4.4
II) Intermediation cost	2.2	2.2	2.8	2.8	2.0	2.0	2.0	2.0	2.2	2.2
III) Provisions and contingenies	1.4	1.6	1.6	2.0	1.5	1.4	1.4	1.2	1.4	1.5
C. Operating profit	2.3	2.7	3.2	3.7	2.7	2.6	2.3	2.0	2.4	2.7
D. Net profit (A-B)	1.0	1.1	1.6	1.6	1.2	1.2	0.9	0.8	1.0	1.1
E. Net interest income (Spread)	2.91	2.97	3.35	3.46	2.47	2.60	1.70	1.98	2.77	2.86
F. Total assets	1.0	1.1	1.6	1.6	1.2	1.2	0.9	0.8	1.0	1.1
Memo item										
1. Operating expenses as per cent of net income	49.3	45.0	46.6	42.9	43.4	42.6	46.0	50.1	48.3	45.2

The profitability of SCBs, though still high, showed a declining trend in the first half of 2004-05 on account of a fall in treasury income. The ratio of net profit to total assets (annualised) was lower at 1.1 per cent in the second quarter of 2004-05 compared to 1.3 per cent in the corresponding previous quarter.

INTEREST SPREAD

Increase in the net interest income or the interest spread, defined as the difference between interest income and interest expenses, of SCBs witnessed in recent years continued in 2003-04. Mainly on account of low interest expenditure, the spread increased by 19.8 per cent in 2003-04 compared to an increase of 19.5 per cent in 2002-03. The increase in the spread of private sector and foreign banks was sharper than that of PSBs.

The ratio of spread to total assets had increased for all bank groups in 2003-04. The ratio was the highest for foreign banks (3.46 per cent) followed by PSBs (2.97 per cent), old private sector banks (2.60 per cent) and new private sector banks (1.98 per cent). Interest spread is an important indicator of efficiency of banking operations.

The growth of spread in recent years clearly establishes that banks have not fully passed on the benefit of falling interest rates to their customers.

Despite the initiatives taken by the RBI, lending rates of banks have exhibited considerable downward rigidity. Net interest income (annualised) of SCBs as a proportion of total assets improved to 3.1 per cent in the second quarter of 2004-05 compared to 2.9 per cent in the corresponding quarter of last year.

NON-PERFORMING ASSETS OF THE BANKING SECTOR

There was a significant decline in the non-performing assets (NPAs) of SCBs in 2003-04, despite adoption of 90 day delinquency norm from March 31, 2004. The gross NPAs of SCBs declined from 4.0 per cent of total assets in 2002-03 to 3.3 per cent in 2003-04. The corresponding decline in net NPAs was from 1.9 per cent to 1.2 per cent.

Both gross NPAs and net NPAs declined in absolute terms. While the gross NPAs declined from ₹ 68,717 crore in 2002-03 to ₹ 64,787 crore in 2003-04, net NPAs declined from ₹ 32,670 crore to ₹ 24,617 crore in the same period. There was also a significant decline in the proportion of net NPAs to net advances from 4.4 per cent in 2002-03 to 2.9 per cent in 2003-04.

The significant decline in the net NPAs by 24.7 per cent in 2003-04 as compared to 8.1 per cent in 2002- 03 was mainly on account of higher provisions (up to 40.0 per cent) for NPAs made by SCBs. The decline in NPAs in 2003-04 was witnessed across all bank groups. The decline in net NPAs as a proportion of total assets was quite significant in the case of new private sector banks, followed by PSBs. The ratio of net NPAs to net advances of SCBs declined from 4.4 per cent in 2002-03 to 2.9 per cent in 2003-04.

Among the bank groups, old private sector banks had the highest ratio of net NPAs to net advances at 3.8 per cent followed by PSBs (3.0 per cent) new private sector banks (2.4 per cent) and foreign banks (1.5 per cent).

Table. Non-performing Assets of Scheduled Commercial Banks

Items	Gross NPAs (₹ Crore)			Percentage to gross Advances			Percentage to total assets		
	2001-02	2002-03	2003-04	2001-02	2002-03	2003-04	2001-02	2002-03	2003-04
Bank group									
1. Public Sector	56473	54090	51538	11.1	9.4	7.8	4.9	4.2	3.5
2. Private Sector	11662	11782	10355	9.6	8.1	5.8	4.4	4.0	2.8
3. Foreign	2726	2845	2894	5.4	5.3	4.6	2.4	2.4	2.1
4. SCBs(1+2+3)	70861	68717	64787	10.4	8.8	7.2	4.6	4.0	3.3
Items	**Net NPAs (₹ Crore)**			**Percentage to net Advances**			**Precentage to total assets**		
1. Public sector	27958	24867	18860	5.8	4.5	3.0	2.4	1.9	1.3
2. Private sector	6676	6882	4857	5.7	5.0	2.8	2.5	2.3	1.3
3. Foreign	920	921	900	1.9	1.8	1.5	0.8	0.8	0.7
4. SCBs(1+2+3)	35554	32670	24617	5.5	4.4	2.9	2.3	1.9	1.2

An analysis of NPAs by sec tors reveals that in 2003-04, advances to non-priority sectors accounted for bulk of the outstanding NPAs in the case of PSBs (51.24 per cent of total) and for private sector banks (75.30 per cent of total). While the share of NPAs in agriculture sector and SSIs of PSBs declined in 2003-04, the share of other priority sectors increased.

The share of loans to other priority sectors in priority sector lending also increased. Measures taken to reduce NPAs include reschedulement, restructuring at the bank level, corporate debt restructuring, and recovery through Lok Adalats, Civil Courts, and debt recovery tribunals and compromise settlements.

The recovery management received a major fillip with the enactment of the Securitisation and Reconstruction of Financial Assets and Enforcement of Security Interest (SARFAESI) Act, 2002 enabling banks to realise their dues without intervention of courts and tribunals. The Supreme Court in its judgement dated April 8, 2004, while upholding the constitutional validity of the Act, struck down section 17 (2) of the Act as unconstitutional and contrary to Article 14 of the Constitution of India.

The Government amended the relevant provisions of the Act to address the concerns expressed by the Supreme Court regarding a fair deal to borrowers through an ordinance dated November 11, 2004. It is been adjudicated.

The amount recovered was to ₹ 8,593 crore. Under the scheme of corporate debt restructuring introduced in 2001, the number of cases and value of assets restructured stood at 121 and ₹ 69,575 crore, respectively, as on December 31, 2004. Iron and steel, refinery, fertilizers and telecommunication sectors were the major beneficiaries of the scheme. These sectors accounted for more than two-third of the values of assets restructured. As credit information is crucial for the development of the financial system and for addressing the problems of NPAs, dissemination of credit information on suit-filed defaulters is being undertaken by the Credit Information Bureau of India Ltd. (CIBIL) from March 2003.

In its annual policy statement for 2004-05, the RBI advised banks and financial institutions to review the measures taken for furnishing credit information in respect of all borrowers to CIBIL. In its mid-term review, the RBI again urged the banks to make persistent efforts in obtaining consent from all the borrowers, in order to establish an efficient credit information system, which would help in enhancing the quality of credit decisions, improve the asset quality, and facilitate faster credit delivery.

CAPITAL ADEQUACY RATIO

The concept of minimum capital to risk weighted assets ratio (CRAR) has been developed to ensure that banks can absorb a reasonable level of losses. Application of minimum CRAR protects the interest of depositors and promotes stability and efficiency of the financial system.

At the end of March 31, 2004, CRAR of PSBs stood at 13.2 per cent, an improvement of 0.6 per centage point from the previous year. There was also an improvement in the CRAR of old private sector banks from 12.8 per cent in 2002-03 to 13.7 per cent in 2003-04. The CRAR of new private sector banks and foreign banks registered a decline in 2003-04.

For the SCBs as a whole the CRAR improved from 12.7 per cent in 2002-03 to 12.9 per cent in 2003-04. All the bank groups had CRAR above the minimum 9 per cent stipulated by the RBI. During the current year, there was further improvement in the CRAR of SCBs. The ratio in the first half of 2004-05 improved to 13.4 per cent as compared to 12.9 per cent at the end of 2003-04. Among the bank groups, a substantial improvement was witnessed in the case of new private sector banks from 10.2 per cent as at the end of 2003-04 to 13.5 per cent in the first half of 2004-05.

While PSBs and old private banks maintained the CRAR at almost the same level as in the previous year, the CRAR of foreign banks declined to 14.0 per cent in the first half of 2004-05 as compared to 15.0 per cent as at the end of 2003-04.

2

Performance and Efficiency of Indian Banking System

The Indian banking system remained largely resilient to the economic turbulence of 2008-09. However, it highlighted the importance of responsible banking; focused more towards creating objectives parallel to the economic priorities. Hence, enhancing efficiency and productivity of banks with a strong risk management framework has been the objective of RBI from the past five years. This five year time series assessment measures banking efficiency and productivity by tracking some of the key developments during FY07-11. The data required for the study was obtained from RBI and Indian Banks' Association (IBA).

The Indian banking system appears to be relatively well-placed in the global financial system as can be observed in Table 1 below. This can be attributed to the prudential supervision and the measures undertaken by the RBI in the past. The mixed bag opportunities offered in the global market are dealt with utmost care and planning, thus making the banking system robust and strong to stand global headwinds.

Countries	Regulatory Capital to Risk-Weighted Assets	Capital to Assets	Bank NPL to Total Loans	ROA	ROE
Australia	11.6	5.7	2.0	1.2	21.9
France	12.8	4.9	3.7	0.6	13.1
Greece	10.1	5.8	46.2	-2.1	-34.2
Italy	12.8	9.4	11.0	0.2	2.2
Singapore	16.0	8.6	1.2	1.1	11.2
United Kingdom	15.8	5.1	3.9	0.1	1.7
United States	15.3	11.2	4.1	1.2	6.8
Poland	13.1	7.7	8.2	1.3	16.6
Turkey	16.5	11.3	2.7	2.2	18.9
Russia	14.7	12.6	6.6	2.4	17.6
China	12.7	6.4	1.0	NA	NA
India	14.2	7.1	2.3	1.0	15.0
Malaysia	17.7	8.9	2.7	1.5	16.8
Thailand	14.7	10.5	2.9	1.2	12.0
Brazil	17.3	10.3	3.5	1.5	14.1

SOCIO-ECONOMIC RELEVANCE OF BANKS

STRONG ECONOMIC GROWTH PROPELS BANKING PERFORMANCE

India has grown significantly at 8.2 per cent CAGR from ' 35.6 trillion economy in FY07 to ' 48.9 trillion in FY11. Predominantly led by domestic demand, the Indian banking industry has played a significant role in the growth of Indian economy. Bank lending has grown at 21.4 per cent CAGR during 2007-2011 to ' 42.9 tn. As observed in the table below, bank credit consistently grew nearly 2.5 times more than the y-o-y GDP growth, demonstrating the inter-relation between the two. However, 2011 was an year of exception, where bank credit registered sharp growth despite consistent growth in GDP. Credit to GDP rose from 50.1 per cent in 2007 to 60.1 per cent in 2011; while deposits to GDP rose from 68.2 per cent in 2007 to 78.5 per cent in 2011. The immense contribution made by banks in the economy, highlights the need for a stable and risk free banking structure.

Particulars	2007	2008	2009	2010	2011
% Growth in GDP (factor cost)	9.6	9.3	6.7	8.4	8.4
% Growth in bank credit	28.1	22.3	17.5	16.9	21.5

DESPITE SIGNIFICANT PROGRESS, BANKING PENETRATION CONTINUES TO BE LOW COMPARED TO GLOBAL MARKETS

During the past five years, financial inclusion has been one of the core agenda of RBI with the introduction of Board-Approved Financial Inclusion Plans by banks. Indian banks are obligated towards financial inclusion *i.e.* taking banking products and services to the unbanked population. In India, the dispersion of banking services is fairly low compared to global markets. In FY11, about 61 per cent of population had access to a saving bank account while 19 per cent of population had debit cards and mere 1 per cent had credit cards. This epitomizes the unmet demand and the scope for expansion for the banks in India.

The average population per branch acts as a basic indicator of the penetration of banking services. It improved from 14,000 in 2009-10 to 13,466 in 2010-11 while population per ATM from 19,700 to 16,243 during the same period. Significant progress has been made in taking banking services to rural areas. Till the end of Mar 2011, villages that were covered under the various financial inclusion schemes almost doubled from 54,757 at Mar-10 to 99,840 at Mar-11. To further promote development, in June 2011, banks were suggested to assign at least 25 per cent of the total new branches to un-banked rural centres. The number of branches set up in un-banked centres has increased from 281 to 470 during the period FY10-FY11 but the population per bank branch is significantly higher than the national average in the North East, Eastern and Central Regions.

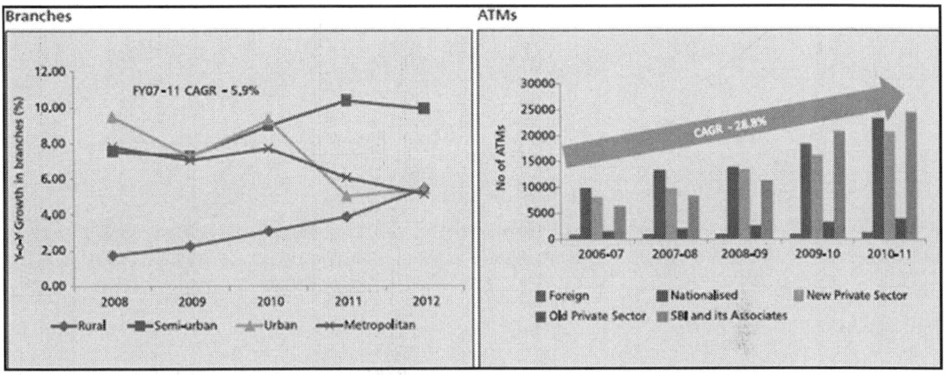

TECHNOLOGY – SUPPORTING FINANCIAL INCLUSION

Over the past five years, technology has been the backbone of the Indian banking system. It has not only simplified the banking process and service channels but has also strengthened financial inclusion initiatives taking banking services to the unbanked community of the country.

Historically, bank branches/offices have been the primary channel, supporting the core banking business; advances and deposits. However, with emergence of varied banking channels like internet banking, telebanking, ATM and mobile banking; branch banking seems to be losing steam, as visible in the y-o-y drop of deposit mobilization and credit off take specifically from bank branches in Table 3.

YoY growth (%)	2007	2008	2009	2010	2011
Deposits of Scheduled Commercial Banks per office (₹ lakh)	20.6	18.2	14.6	10.0	11.2
Credit of Scheduled Commercial Banks per office (₹ lakh)	24.8	16.9	12.2	10.2	14.9

Besides emergence of various banking channels, payments and settlement systems have also evolved over a period of time. Interestingly, modern day banking encompasses various payment systems involving paperless banking and facilitating speedy transfer of funds. The volume of transactions processed through NEFT/RTGS has witnessed more than 100 per cent CAGR over the last five years. According to RBI, in FY11, 40.9 per cent transactions were done electronically in FY11 compared to about 25 per cent in FY07. Since these electronic transactions are mostly high value in nature, this contributed to nearly 90 per cent in value. It was also observed that though the share of electronic transactions have increased significantly in value terms, paper based transactions still seem to dominate volumes with nearly 60 per cent share.

Mobile banking is also becoming increasingly popular across all parts of the country. Till FY11, it was offered by nearly 38 banks. Moreover, the regulator has permitted to facilitate mobile banking transactions without end-to-end encryption up to ‘ 5,000. With rising tele-density of nearly 33.79 per cent in 2011, the rural unbanked population represents a massive growth opportunity for Indian banks.

OPERATIONAL EFFICIENCY

Total assets of all SCBs increased at 20.0 per cent CAGR y-o-y from ‘ 34,599.6 bn to ‘ 71,835.2 bn during FY07-11, majorly driven by nearly 21 per cent growth in advances. During the same period, asset base of public banks (CAGR 21.4 per cent) grew more rapidly compared with other categories of banks primarily due to an upsurge in cash balance and advances. Owing to uncertain global environment and repercussions of financial crisis, the year FY10 witnessed come contraction. Return on Assets (ROA), an important indicator of profit generated from every unit of assets declined to 1.01 per cent in FY10. Asset growth also slowed down to 15 per cent during FY09-10 from an average 20 per cent growth observed each year. The total assets to GDP ratio (at current prices) escalated from 87.5 per cent in 2007 to 100.4 per cent in 2011.

Banking assets grew multifold in the last five years

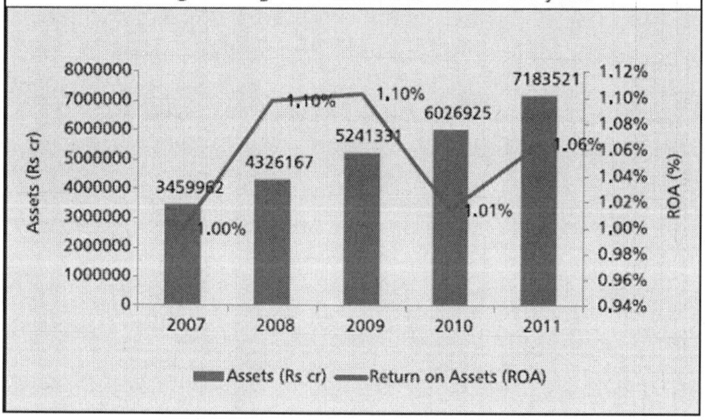

BOOMING ECONOMY: BANKING ON CREDIT GROWTH

Although the economy recovered from the recent financial turmoil, increased demand for credit and improved growth in deposits and capital enabled higher credit growth. Credit demand from sectors like infrastructure, telecom, power, SME led to a surge in bank credit portfolio. During FY07-11, credit growth of SCBs grew at 21.4 per cent CAGR. It exceeded RBI’s non-food credit growth target of 20 per cent for FY11, which was the trend observed in the past four years. The non-food credit noticed a CAGR of 19.6 per cent during FY07-11 with industry sector growing substantially at a CAGR of 23.7 per cent in FY07-11. (FY08-FY12 CAGR numbers are 11.9 per cent for food credit).The share of food credit in total bank credit declined from 2.5 per cent in FY07 to 1.72 per cent in FY11 and revived back to 1.87 per cent in FY12.

Y-o-Y growth trends in bank food & non-food credit					
Particulars	**Mar-08**	**Mar-09**	**Mar-10**	**Mar-11**	**Mar-12**
Food Credit Growth (%)	-4.6	2.6	6.6	32.0	27.3
Non-food Credit (%)	22.8	18.0	16.8	20.6	17.0

Since FY10, the share of non-food credit has moderated by 29 bps. Industrial credit which accounts for a large share in non-food credit moderated during this period, with corporates resorting to internal sources of financing and cheaper funds raised in the overseas market. Favorable interest rate differential between domestic and international markets and an appreciating domestic currency during this period made external commercial borrowings (ECBs) popular among corporates. Amongst the sectors that drive credit demand in the country, infrastructure sectors accounted for about 14.4 per cent (FY11) in the total non-food credit of SCBs. Demand for credit in this sector grew by an exceptional CAGR of 38.5 per cent, followed by cement and iron and steel sector that drove credit demand by 32 per cent and 26.5 per cent on a CAGR basis respectively. With emphasis on PPP for the infrastructure sector during this period, private companies have been the largest contributor to the propelling credit demand.

Y-o-Y Share of Core sectors in Gross Bank credit

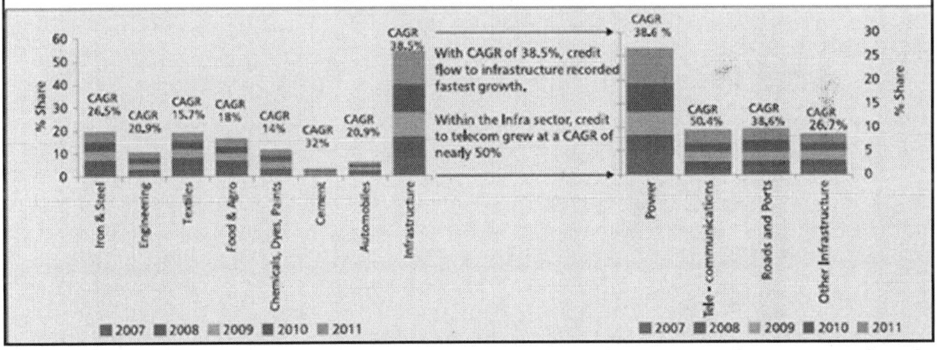

Credit off-take in the recent past has been far out-pacing expansion in deposits. Overall deposits of SCBs witnessed a CAGR of 20.1 per cent which emanated mainly from term deposits which grew at 20.6 per cent CAGR during FY07-11. Alternatively, CASA witnessed a slower CAGR of 19.2 per cent aggregating to ‘ 19,957.3 bn during the same period. Term deposit was highest for PSBs at 23.4 per cent in FY07-11. As per RBI, rapid credit growth without commensurate increase in deposits is not sustainable. Disproportionate growth in deposits compared to credit can be observed in the table below highlights inclination of banks towards borrowed funds. Increasing reliance on borrowed funds rather than deposits to fund businesses throws up liquidity and systematic risk to the overall health of banks in the long run. Given passive growth in deposits and improved credit off-take, CD ratio of SCBs improved from 73.5 per cent in FY07 to 76.5 per cent in FY11.

Credit – Deposit Growth Mismatch

Particulars	Unit	2007	2008	2009	2010	2011
Deposits	In ₹ Cr.	2696936	3320061	4063204	4746920	5616432
Advances	In ₹ Cr.	1981237	2476936	3000906	3496720	4298705
Credit Deposit Ratio	%	73.5	74.6	73.9	73.7	76.5

	2008	2009	2010	2011	2012
Credit Growth (%)	25.0	21.2	16.5	22.9	16.3
Deposits Growth (%)	23.1	22.4	16.8	18.3	14.0

MARGINS REMAIN INTACT, CURBING COSTS REMAINS CHALLENGING

Efficiency and productivity of banks cannot solely be judged on the basis of its sheer size and presence. With evolution in service offerings, diversification and rising risk management challenges, it is imperative to evaluate banking efficieny through excellence across all operational parameters like staff management and productivity, cost of operations and stability in profit margins.

The Indian banking sector appears to stable in terms of profit margins. High growth in advances translated into high growth in interest income (CAGR – 16.6 per cent), which resulted in a total income CAGR of 20.1 per cent during FY07-11 (reaching ‘ 5712.3 bn). PSBs continued to dominate the Indian banking industry with their share in total income which increased from 68.4 per cent to 72.5 per cent during FY07-11. However, private banks seem to have sustained margins better than PSBs by registering a maximum growth of 28.6 per cent during FY07-11. Overall net profit of SCB displayed a 22.5 per cent CAGR during the five year period of FY07-11.

Intermediation cost grew at a CAGR of 16.7 per cent, thereby taking the total expenditure to CAGR of 19.2 per cent in FY07-11. Employee expenses appeared to have weighed down margins significantly. During FY07-11, cost per employee registered a CAGR of 13.7 per cent with PSB registering a CAGR of 17 per cent.

In FY11 itself, cost per employee of PSBs grew 28.7 per cent, which occured due to wage revisions that included opening of pension option to existing and retired employees who had not opted for it earlier and enhancement in gratuity limits from ‘ 0.35 mn to ‘ 1.0 mn, following the amendment to Payment of Gratuity Act, 1972. Cost to Income ratio, a reflection of profitable fund deployment, moved up from 0.19 times since 2009 to 0.22 in 2011. Regulatory requirements like priority sector lending of atleast 40 per cent and SLR close to 25 per cent drag a considerbale amount of bank funds into low-yielding assets, contributing to high intermediation costs.

Profitablity & Efficiency Indicators of Indian Banks							
Parameters	**Indicators**	**Unit**	**2007**	**2008**	**2009**	**2010**	**2011**
Profitability	Business	In ₹ mn	46781730	57969970	70641100	82436400	99151370
	Net Interest Margin	%	7.4	7.9	8.1	7.4	7.4
	Cost of deposits	%	4.93	5.97	6.24	5.49	5.01
	Investment Deposit	%	35.3	35.4	35.7	36.4	34.1
Efficiency	Business/Employee	In ₹ Lakhs	522.9	638.3	750.4	867.6	987.4
	Profit/Employee	In ₹ lakhs	3.5	4.7	5.6	6.0	7.0
	Operating Cost/Employee	In ₹ Lakhs	7.4	8.5	9.5	10.5	12.3
	Operating Cost/Total Assets	%	1.9%	1.8%	1.7%	1.7%	1.7%
	Operating Cost/Total Income	%	0.24	0.21	0.19	0.20	0.22
	Return on advances	%	8.93	9.92	10.5	9.29	9.18
	Return on investments	%	7.19	7.33	7.01	6.54	6.79
	Return on Equity	%	14.2	13.5	14.3	13.3	13.8

STRENGTHENING GLOBAL PRESENCE

In the international frontier, Indian banks operating outside India have shown an increasing trend in the last five years. PSBs increased their operations abroad with a network of 112 offices in FY07 to 142 offices in FY11 while private sector banks doubled their network to 14 in FY11 (7 in FY07). Moreover, the total business of Indian banks registered a CAGR of 30.3 per cent during FY07-11. PSBs accounted for more than 80 per cent of the overall global business of SCBs.

Business of Indian banks abroad				
Particulars (In ₹ bn)	**Deposit**	**Advances**	**Investment**	**Total Assets**
FY07	913.1	1128.7	9509.8	34599.6
FY08	1056.4	1727.1	11761.6	43264.9
FY09	1451.5	2483.0	14495.5	52386.4
FY10	1756.8	2779.0	17290.1	60269.3
FY11	2249.1	3632.7	19160.5	71835.2

DEBT MANAGEMENT

Quality of bank asset has visibly improved for during the period 2007-2011, with standard assets consistently rising upwards, and moving from 97.3 per cent in FY07 to 97.7 per cent in FY11. During the same period; standard, substandard and doubtful assets have registered a CAGR of 22.5 per cent, 22 per cent and 8.4 per cent respectively. Doubtful assets registered highest growth of 37 per cent in 2010-11, reaching ‘ 447.7 bn.

RISING RISKS WITH GROWING EXPOSURE TO SENSITIVE SECTORS

Bank exposure to sensitive sectors registered CAGR of nearly 20 per cent during FY07-FY11, with capital market lending growing at the fastest rate of

35 per cent and real estate lending growing by almost 18 per cent on a CAGR basis.

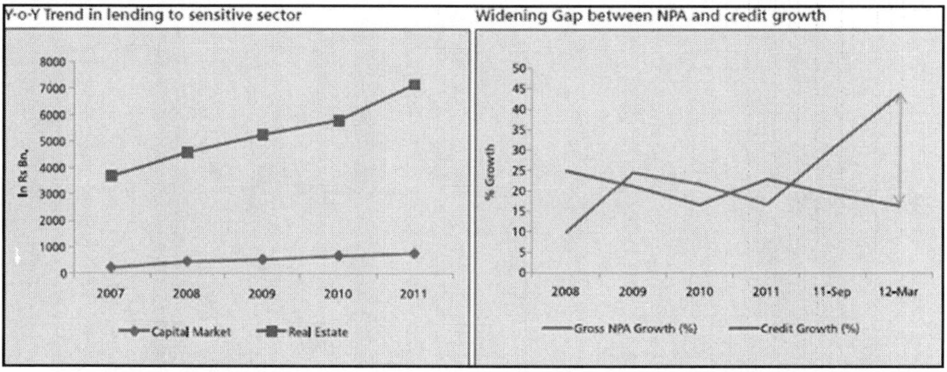

As per Financial Stability Report (June 2012), the gross NPA ratio of SCBs increased to 2.9 per cent as at end Mar 2012, as against 2.4 per cent at end of Mar 2011. A five year analysis unfolds a striking trend between the NPA levels and credit growth. Growth in NPAs outpaced credit growth during 2009-10 period, owing to global uncertainties, closely followed by a year long improvement in 2011. However, the scenario seems to have resurfaced the banking system with the widening gap between credit and NPA growth, thereby pressurizing asset quality.

In 2007, the movement of NPAs was favorable as the ratio of addition to NPAs was almost at the same level to the recovery of NPAs. From FY08, the ratio of addition to Gross NPAs surged higher, and the recovery of NPAs as a per cent of Gross NPAs declined. During FY10, the ratio of addition to Gross NPAs shot up sharply to 80 per cent, reinforcing concerns on asset quality. Furthermore, with slowing rate of recovery of NPAs, a 43 per cent CAGR in the total restructured loan assets during the above period raises further questions.

	2007	2008	2009	2010	2011	CAGR
Addition to NPA as a % of GNPA	52.1	61.6	76.8	80.3	74.8	68.3
Recovery as a % of GNPA	52.0	50.3	54.7	47.6	51.1	51.1

THE ROLE OF COMMERCIAL BANKS IN ECONOMIC DEVELOPMENT

Commercial banks are considered not merely as dealers in money but also the leaders in economic development. They are not only the store houses of the country's wealth but also the reservoirs of resources necessary for economic development. They play an important role in the economic development of a country. A well-developed banking system is essential for the economic development of a country. The "Industrial Revolution" in Europe in the 19th century would not have been possible without a sound system of commercial banking. In case of developing countries like India, the commercial banks are considered to be the backbone of the economy. Commercial banks can contribute to a country's economic development in the following ways:

ACCELERATING THE RATE OF CAPITAL FORMATION

Capital formation is the most important determinant of economic development. The basic problem of a developing economy is slow rate of capital formation. Banks promote capital formation. They encourage the habit of saving among people. They mobilise idle resources for production purposes. Economic development depends upon the diversion of economic resources from consumption to capital formation. Banks help in this direction by encouraging saving and mobilising them for productive uses.

PROVISION OF FINANCE AND CREDIT

Commercial banks are a very important source of finance and credit for industry and trade. Credit is a pillar of development. Credit lubricates all commerce and trade. Banks become the nerve centre of all commerce and trade. Banks are instruments for developing internal as well as external trade.

MONETISATION OF ECONOMY

An underdeveloped economy is characterised by the existence of a large non-monetised sector. The existence of this non-monetised sector is a hindrance in the economic development of the country. The banks, by opening branches in rural and backward areas can promote the process of monetisation (conversion of debt into money) in the economy.

INNOVATIONS

Innovations are an essential prerequisite for economic development. These innovations are mostly financed by bank credit in the developed countries. But in underdeveloped countries, entrepreneurs hesitate to invest in new ventures and undertake innovations largely due to lack of funds. Facilities of bank loans enable the entrepreneurs to step up their investment on innovational activities, adopt new methods of production and increase productive capacity of the economy.

IMPLEMENTATION OF MONETARY POLICY

Economic development need an appropriate monetary policy. But a well-developed banking is a necessary pre-condition for the effective implementation of the monetary policy. Control and regulation of credit by the monetary authority is not possible without the active co-operation of the banking system in the country.

ENCOURAGEMENT TO RIGHT TYPE OF INDUSTRIES

Banks generally provide financial resources to the right type of industries to secure the necessary material, machines and other inputs. In this way they influence the nature and volume of industrial production.

DEVELOPMENT OF AGRICULTURE

Underdeveloped economies are primarily agricultural economies. Majority of the population in these economies live in rural areas. Therefore, economic development in these economies requires the development of agriculture and small scale industries in rural areas. So far banks in underdeveloped countries have been paying more attention to trade and commerce and have almost neglected agriculture and industry. Banks must provide loans to agriculture for development and modernisation of agriculture. In recent years, the State Bank of India and other commercial banks are granting short term, medium-term and long term loans to agriculture and small-scale industries.

REGIONAL DEVELOPMENT

Banks can also play an important role in achieving balanced development in different regions of the country. They transfer surplus capital from the developed regions to the less developed regions, where it is scarce and most needed. This reallocation of funds between regions will promote economic development in underdeveloped areas of the country.

PROMOTE INDUSTRIAL DEVELOPMENT

Industrial development needs finance. In some countries, commercial banks encouraged industrial development by granting long-term loans also. Loan or credit is a pillar to development. In underdeveloped countries like India, commercial banks are granting short-term and medium-term loans to industries. They are also underwriting the issue of shares and debentures by industrial concerns. This helps industrial concerns to secure adequate capital for their establishment, expansion and modernisation.

Commercial banks are also helping manufacturers to secure machinery and equipment from foreign countries under installment system by guaranteeing deferred payments. Thus, banks promote or encourage industrial development.

PROMOTE COMMERCIAL VIRTUES

The businessmen are more afraid of a banker than a preacher. The businessmen should have certain business qualities like industry, forethought, honesty and punctuality. These qualities are called "commercial virtues" which are essential for rapid economic progress. The banker is in a better position to promote commercial virtues. Banks are called "public conservators of commercial virtues."

FULFILLMENT OF SOCIO-ECONOMIC OBJECTIVES

In recent years, commercial banks, particularly in developing countries, have been called upon to help achieve certain socio-economic objectives laid down by the state. For example, nationalised bank in India have framed special innovative schemes of credit to help small agriculturists, self-employed persons and retailers through loans and advances at concessional rates of interest. Banking is thus used to achieve the national policy objectives of reducing inequalities of income and wealth, removal of poverty and elimination of unemployment in the country.

Thus, banks in a developing country have to play a dynamic role. Economic development places heavy demand on the resources and ingenuity of the banking system. It has to respond to the multifarious economic needs of a developing country. Traditional views and methods may have to be discarded. "An Institution, such as the banking system, which touches and should touch the lives of millions, has necessarily to be inspired by a larger social purpose and has to sub serve national priorities and objectives." A well-developed banking system provides a firm and durable foundation for the economic development of the country.

BANK ON RURAL INDIA - WAY TO ECONOMIC DEVELOPMENT

The growth story of India is fascinating and interesting and unfolding the economy to the world with its vast presence of Human and Natural resources. India is the second most populous country of the globe with 1.20 billion and has become destination for quality workforce and potential market place for domestic and multinational companies. Today, India is one of the fastest growing economies amidst global uncertainties. Nonetheless, it is pertinent to note that the growth is not uniform across the sectors *viz.*, Agriculture, Industry and Service Sector, causing aberrations to the desired economic development process. The sectoral share of GDP since last two decades is as under:

GDP – Sectoral contribution (%)				
Year	**Agriculture**	**Industry**	**Services***	**Total**
1991	29.34	19.33	51.16	100
1996	14.46	28.02	57.24	100
2000	13.96	14.01	74.02	100
2006	17.26	20.12	62.62	100
2010	17.28	16.21	66.51	100
2012	13.72	13.75	72.53	100

Note:

*includes construction

It is evident from the above that India's growth is primarily driven by the services sector and its share has been growing year-on-year while the share of agriculture to GDP has declined from 29.34 per cent in 1991 to 13.72 per cent in 2012. Further, the growth rate registered in Agriculture Sector was 2.80 per cent only while industry and service sectors growth rate stood at 3.40 per cent and 8.90 per cent respectively during the year 2012. The trend clearly indicates that the economic development so far been largely limited to the urban population and is yet to widely percolate to the rural population.

ECONOMIC DEVELOPMENT - ROLE OF RURAL INDIA

India is known as country of villages and the agriculture and allied activities are the backbone for the economic development of the country. Agriculture Sector assumes vital importance since it provides livelihood to 3/4th of the country's population besides becoming significant source for raw material for many industries. Thus, agriculture is an important engine for economic growth of the country. Agriculture is a tradition which has shaped the culture and economic life of the people and therefore will continue to be central to all strategies on planned socio economic development of the country. Rapid growth of Agriculture is essential not only to achieve self-reliance but also to bring about equity in distribution of income and wealth resulting in reduction of poverty levels. In this context, it is worth to recapitulate the thoughts of first Prime Minister of India Sri.Pandit Jawaharlal Nehru "If Agriculture does not go right, nothing else will" which speaks the importance attached to the agriculture in those years.

RURAL ECONOMY - EMERGING TRENDS

Income Distribution Pattern

Though, the economic development achieved so far is mostly urban biased and with uneven distribution of wealth across the segments, improvement is seen in income levels of rural India especially in post reform era, is a positive factor and a trigger for hope for the future. Hitherto, Rural and Poverty are the synonyms but it is not so now, which is evident from the Rural Income patterns of various groups furnished here below:

Rural Income Patterns (%)					
Year	Upper	Upper Middle	Middle	Lower Middle	Lower
1995-96	2.1	3.1	8.6	29.0	57.2
2001-02	3.6	4.1	10.1	39.5	42.7
2005-06	5.2	5.0	13.8	43.5	32.5
2009-10	8.1	6.1	22.7	42.5	20.6

It is interesting to note that lower income segment has been gradually moving to Middle/Upper middle class in rural areas on account of the following factors.

- Considerable improvement is seen in agricultural productivity over the years due to adoption of better farm techniques. A series of good harvests on the back of favourable monsoons coupled with improved irrigation facilities and reasonable rise in procurement prices is also one of the reasons for shoring of income levels in rural India.

- Multiple occupations in rural household are a common feature on account of integration between Rural and Urban area resulting mobility of labour, capital, products and credit. As per NCAER report around 25 per cent of rural households solely depend on non-agriculture income.
- Government schemes like National Rural Employment Guarantee Scheme, which guarantees 100 days of employment to one member of every rural household, has provided employment opportunities and enabled the rural people to improve their income level.

Expenditure Pattern

As per NSSO data, the incremental consumption expenditure in urban is '2994 billion surprisingly the rural spending outpaced urban with '3750 billion in 2011-12 over 2009-10. Further noticeable shift in expenditure pattern of rural households is observed from traditional food items to non-food items *i.e.* Education, Housing, Cosmetics, and Entertainment etc. According to MART, rural India buys 46 per cent of soft drinks sold, 49 per cent of motorcycles and 59 per cent of cigarettes. Further, Rural markets account for 56 per cent of the total domestic Fast Moving Consumer Goods (FMCG) demand and 60 per cent of India's annual consumption of gold/jewelry is from rural India.

Literacy Rate

Till 1980s, the literacy rate in rural India was very low and it is too little among small/marginal farmers. Probably, that could be one of the principle reasons for them to have inseparable attachment to agricultural land as it is the primary source for their livelihood. However, of late, many changes have been taking place especially in the area of education in rural areas.As per census 2011, the literacy growth rate in rural area is higher (15.99 per cent) compared to urban areas (5.73 per cent), which clearly indicate that the rural population is keen to educate their children despite hardships. The literacy rate gap among rural-urban has been coming down over the years especially during the last two decades which is evident from the below table.

Rural Urban Literacy Rates 1951 to 2011 (%)

Period	Rural/Semi Urban	Urban / Metro	Total
1951	12.10	34.59	18.33
1961	22.50	54.40	28.30
1971	27.90	60.20	34.45
1981	36.00	67.20	43.57
1991	44.70	73.10	52.21
2001	59.40	80.30	65.38
2011	68.90	84.90	74.04

The increased literacy rate coupled with disguised unemployment in the farm sector has been forcing the rural masses to look for non-farm activities to supplement their family income.

CONTRACT FARMING

Contract Farming is gaining momentum. It is an agreement between a farmer and company for production and supply of agricultural/horticultural produce at a pre-determined price. It has the potential of combining small farmer efficiency, utilizing corporate management skills, providing assured markets and reducing transaction costs in the value chain by ensuring vertical integration. Contract farming is a win-win situation for both the parties and leads to building a platform for improvement of farm incomes, development of agro-processing andexpansion of rural economy. Corporates like Hidustan Lever, Pepsi Foods, Reliance, ITC, Cadbury, Rallies India, Mahindra's Shubhlabh, Tata Kisan Kendra, Godrej Aadhar and DSCL Haryali have emerged as new agribusiness supply chain models. The recent decision of Government permitting Foreign Direct Investment in Multi Brand Retail subject to states approval will go a long way to usher contract farming and big push to agro based activities in the ensuing years. Thus, contract farming as a strategy adopted by food processors is gaining prominence in India on account of steady progress in the economy, rising food demand, organized retail boom and an increasing shift towards branded food consumption.

White Revolution

India is one of the world's largest and fastest growing markets for Dairy products include milk, cheese, dahi and pro-biotic drinks etc., with annual turnover of above '20000 crore and growing at 7.5 per cent annually. Rural India has become destination for Dairy industry and majority of farm households rely on milk production to supplement their income. In view of the growing prominence of this sector, State Governments also initiated various steps to encourage dairy development by establishing the much-needed linkages between rural producers and urban consumers.

Blue Revolution

Of late, Aquaculture has emerged as an important and highly productive agriculture activity in the country. Today, India is pushing ahead with rapid increase of fish production (marine, brackish, fresh and Prawn), a boon to small farmers and contributing to the gross domestic product as well as exports.

Financial Inclusion

The banking industry has shown tremendous growth in volume and complexity during the last few decades. Despite making significant improvements in the areas relating to financial viability, profitability and competitiveness, there are concerns that banks have not been able to reach and bring vast segment of the population, especially the underprivileged sections of the society, into the fold of basic banking services.

Rural & Urban Banking at Glance					
Group	**Population (Crore)**	**Branches (in '000)**	**Per Branch Population**	**Share of Deposits**	**Share of Advances**
Rural	83 (68)	34 (37)	24	9%	8%
Urban	38 (32)	59 (63)	6	91%	92%
Total	121	93	13	100	100

Skewed distribution of bank branches is observed across population groups with 6000 per branch in urban areas and 24000 in Rural areas. Out of 6.4 lakh villages, the presence of bank branches with full-fledged services is available only in 34000 villages and recently another 73000 villages are covered under BC model. Still more than 5 lakh villages remain unbanked due to structural and operational issues such as infrastructure, distance, costs, viability etc. Though, rural India constitutes 68 per cent of country's population, its share to total deposits (9 per cent) and an advance (8 per cent) is abysmally low compared to urban counterpart.

Absence of banking services in villages is the cause to flourish informal financial markets which suffer from several imperfections such as high cost of credit at exploitative terms, loss of precious savings on account of fly-by-night operators, inordinate delays in effecting transfer of funds and settlement of accounts. Thus, the financial exclusion not only widens the 'Rich-Poor divide' but also leads to 'Social Exclusion'. As per Mckinsey Report published in Bancon 2011, only 41 per cent of rural households have access to savings bank accounts and 79 per cent rural households do not have access to credit facilities from formal sources. This fact reinforces the need for speedy implementation of "Financial Inclusion" initiatives with an objective to provide basic banking services at an affordable cost to the vast sections of disadvantaged and low income group. It means not only to extending banking facilities to rural people but also to provide at their convenient time and location. The increased infrastructure development across the country is blurring the geographical barriers and making the rural populace on par with the Urban. Hence, the entire gamut of banking in rural areas needs a relook as their needs are beyond traditional products like No Frill and Crop loans. Banks may look for alternate cost effective business models with appropriate structure to tap this segment.

Rural India – Banking Opportunities

There is a positive correlation between infrastructure development and aggregate agricultural productivity. Rural infrastructure such as irrigation water shed development, electrification, roads, markets, credit institutions, agriculture research and extension etc together plays key role in determining the improvement of productivity. In the recent years, the development of roads connecting to villages is one of the positive factors which eventually blurring the rural and urban divides to a greater extent. A quite revolution is taking place in rural India where economic growth is not just creating the rich but also providing ample opportunities to serve the financially excluded. Rural Banking is now a large opportunity and will be captured those who remove the current barriers of profitable scale. Rural financial services are the fastest growing segment on account of large untapped potential driven by the very low penetration in rural market. Today, only around 41 per cent of rural households have formal savings accounts and 20 per cent alone have access to credit from banking system. Hitherto, major share of bank credit flown to farm sector that too production loans. The presence of increased middle income group in rural area demands credit facilities on par with Urban people and providing ample opportunities to the banks to extend credit to non-farm sector also.

Farm Mechanization

Agricultural inflation has been consistently increasing due to demand supply gap and there is an imminent need to improve productivity by extensive use of farm mechanization. This invites major investments and it is an opportunity for banks to consider financing high tech agriculture production like agricultural biotechnology and farm mechanization besides continuing the traditional lending like production loans.

Agro Based Industries

The consumption boom is likely to lead to higher demand for food products *viz.*, milk, meat, eggs, fruits, vegetables, pulses etc., which warrants supply augmentation. This can be achieved through expanding farm production activities coupled with encouraging entrepreneurs to set up agro based industries. Next Generation belongs to the millions of Young Entrepreneurs of the country from hinter land. Setting up of agro based industries in rural areas will be beneficial to the owners as well as farmers since it addresses many logistic issues. Further, these industries usher employment opportunities in rural areas and supplement the income of the rural households.

Ware Housing

India is the world's largest producer of fruit and vegetables but it has been estimated that inadequate post-harvest storage and transportation cause losses of around 30-40 per cent of the produce every year. Construction of Rural Godowns, Cold Storage and setting up of agro process units not only helps the farmers to earn income besides providing employment opportunities to many in rural areas. However, this invites huge investments and the entrepreneurs look at Banks for required financial support and guidance.

Retail Banking

There is a spurt in middle class segment and it is expected to grow at accelerated pace in the ensuing years with distinct features *viz.*, Educated, Employable and Bankable. The declining dependency ratio and increased non-farm income source are the triggers for the increased flow of savings to the banking system and a demand for retail banking services. The demand for housing in rural area is on the rise over the years. Excepting weaker section housing, majority rural housing is being self-financed. There are ample opportunities for the banks to tap this segment. However, affordable housing is need of the hour; this would require a great deal of technological and financial innovation.

Education Loans

The increased literacy rate (from 12 per cent in 1951 to 69 per cent in 2011) among rural masses is a positive factor. The recent Government initiative *i.e.* waiver of entire interest on education loan during the study period to the students whose parental income is below '4.5 lakhs per annum, has made the education loan scheme more attractive and enabled the banks to improve retail lending. Further, it paves the way to strengthen the bondage with Gen-Y, a potential business segment for banks. The envisaged client expansion will lead to increased flow of savings to the banking system and a demand for retail banking services like housing loans, wealth management, insurance, asset management etc. It warrants revisiting the entire gamut of rural banking and looking for cost effective business models to reach the masses.

RURAL BANKING – DIVERSE BUSINESS MODELS

Today, the banking has become imperative to all the house-holds irrespective of their social and financial status and expects minimum financial services from the banking system. The recent Financial Inclusion initiatives of the Government *i.e.* provide access to banking services at all villages through Branch banking or Business Correspondent at affordable cost is going to transform the banking landscape to greater extent and it is an important business segment for banks. However, providing financial services to the poor, especially in rural areas, is both challenging and costly. The transaction costs have become one of the deterring factors to reach the un-banked by the banks. The stupendous task can be achievedby adopting Diverse Business Models.

BRANCH EXPANSION

Physical Branches

The penetration of banking in India is low compared to developed nations, which is evident from the presence of 5.40 lakh unbanked villages across the country. Branch banking continues to play significant role in business development despite increased adoption of Alternate Delivery Channels in the recent years. The road map of Indian Banks clearly indicates that BC model is going to be used in a big way to achieve the financial inclusion objective. However, banks need to open more number of brick and mortar branches especially in unbanked centers to cover the large population on one hand and branch network acts as service branch to route the transactions undertaken by BCs. Hence, branch network continued to grow in the ensuing years also.

Ultra Small Branches (Mobile Branches)

As part of liberalized Branch Authorization policy, RBI has granted general permission to domestic scheduled commercial banks to open satellite branches in unbanked areas where the population is below 50,000. It envisages the extension of banking facilities through one or two dedicated staff members who visit the identified village location on specified days. It is a cost effective model compared to physical branch model. A designated officer of the link branch shall visit the village on a prefixed date and time every week with a laptop with Virtual Private Network (VPS) connectivity to Core Banking Platform. The role of the visiting official is authorization of the accounts, balance enquiry, printing of account statements and recovery. However, the normal cash transactions will be done by the BC agent only.

Branch-in-a-Box

It is primarily a cost-effective, relocatable and pre-fabricated bank branch. It uses modern, broadband satellite technology for communication. This enhances customer convenience as it provides speedy access. It can also be used to test new markets, especially in areas with limited infrastructure where banking services are not readily available. It provides full transaction facilities to customers, including cash withdrawals and deposits, sales and service.

Alternate Delivery Channels

The residents of far-flung areas are unable to pay visit to branches located at distant places on account of resource constraints *viz.*, time, cost and opportunity.

Thus, it has become imperative for banks to reach out customers through a variety of technology driven delivery channels such as Micro ATMs, Bio-metric ATMs, Mobile ATMs, and Smart Cards etc., which are most cost effective compared to Brick and Mortar model. ATM has brought sea change in Indian Banking space with significant qualitative improvement in delivery of banking services and within short span the presence of ATMs are outnumbered the physical branch network.

Micro ATMs

Though there is considerable improvement in ATM network, the presence of ATMs in rural areas is very limited. Banks are not keen to install ATMs at Rural/Semi Urban centers on account of high investment and low transaction volume. In order to make the ATMs viable at these centers, there is a need to deploy low cost ATMs with basic features such as cash withdrawal and balance enquiry etc. It is convenient and cost effective to the customers compared to pay visit to the bank branch located at nearby center.

Biometric ATMs

The penetration of ATMs into Rural areas may not serve the envisaged purpose unless it is put to use by illiterates/semi-literates whose presence is predominant in unbanked areas. The existing ATMs are not put to use optimally by rural folk on account of PIN/Password related issues. Introduction of Biometric ATMs enable them to avail hassle-free services as these devices function on thumb print and recognize voice commands in vernacular language.

Mobile ATMs

In this model, ATM is installed in a vehicle, which would move to the pre-determined places at regular intervals to provide Door-step banking. These new breed of ATMs also have biometric authentication mechanisms like fingerprint verification and voice guided animated screens with touch enabled transactions. Mobile ATMs can undertake opening of accounts, which has immense benefit to the residents of unbanked centers.

White Label ATMs

The recent initiatives of the RBI and the Government is to allow white-label ATMs, permitting third-party service providers to set up more ATMs in off-premises areas, which include residential complexes, hospitals, tourist destinations, bus stops and railway stations. These ATMs would not belong to any bank in particular but will be owned as well as maintained by independent service providers. This initiative will enable the excluded segments to avail ATM services as at present majority ATMs are confined to Urban/Metro areas only. However, service provider levy charges which are to be either bear by the Bank or the customer.

Smart Cards

State Governments are actively looking at making pension payments and disbursals under Rural Employment Generation Programme using smart cards linked bank accounts. Smart card provides biometric authentication, which would help in reducing frauds and ensure identity of customers. In order to popularize smart cards, all agriculture short term loans and payment of social security schemes are to be dispensed through Smart Cards. All the above initiatives warrant the banks to invest substantial amounts in infrastructure besides recurring expenditure which adds cost to the customer where as the distribution of financial products and services at the lowest rung of the pyramid requires a low-cost model. High Operating Costs and Low Business Volume are the major constraints of the banks in extending banking services especially in remote rural and inaccessible areas through Branch Banking Model. To address this issue, RBI permitted the banks to make use the services of Business Correspondents to take banking to un-banked areas in a most cost effective manner.

BUSINESS CORRESPONDENT (BC) MODEL

Business Correspondent model using smart card and mobile technology is also an effective tool to reach the remote rural areas where alternate delivery channel mechanism is not feasible. This model enables greater rural outreach to improve the business volumes. RBI permitted the BCs to undertake basic banking services *viz.*, Collection/payment of small value deposits, disbursal of small value loan amounts, collection of loan installments, receipt and delivery of small value remittances and Sale of micro insurance/mutual fund products/ pension products/other third party products. Though, BC model has been gaining momentum since last two years, still desired results are not coming as the model is confronting the following issues and challenges, which need to be addressed on priority.

Operational Issues

Cash management is the biggest challenge as the major operations of BCs pertains to cash transactions. It entails interest costs as well as operational risks. Further, the beneficiaries of BC services are mostly illiterate and are susceptible to misguidance. At times, customers tend to perceive the BCs as banks. The success of the model crucially depend on the trust levels among customers, banks and BCs, which is possible through spread of financial awareness by conducting financial literacy programmes on an ongoing basis.

Viability

The viability of the BC model is the most critical issue which probably is one of the main reasons for not taking-off the model as envisaged. The transaction volume is not encouraging since many of the accounts opened are in dormant stage. Absence of sufficient business is causing concern to both BCs as well as banks; and in turn it is becoming difficult for BCs to continue operations on account of mismatch of revenues earned and costs incurred. Banks need to tweak the products and work with the BCs to design products that are suitable to the target market to make the model profitable. Further, to make the BC model viable, the funds pertaining to various government schemes are to be routed directly through the beneficiaries' bank accounts only.

MOBILE BANKING

Till recent years, Mobile/Cell phone used to be a status symbol or lifestyle product, and now it has become a necessity and inseparable with day-to-day life of the individuals irrespective of age, education and financial background. India accounts for about 1/4th of world's mobile market with 965 million and making inroads in to remote rural areas. The share of rural subscribers is around 35 per cent speaks growing potential of this segment. The reach of mobile to the remote areas and its usage by the common man has become order of the day. The swift growth in number of Mobile users and wider coverage of mobile phone networks has made this channel an important platform for extending banking services to customers. Mobile banking runs on Interbank Mobile Payment Service (IMPS) mode which enables the bank customers to have access to their bank accounts and carryout banking transactions including funds transfers across the banks using mobile phones independent of Branch/ Business Correspondents. M-wallet is the further extension of Mobile Banking and it acts like a pre-paid account operated through a mobile phone which can be used for small purchases, remittances, bill payments and cash withdrawals. Telecom players are playing significant role in taking this concept forward with strategic tie-ups with banks as service provider as well as business correspondents. As per the recent study, the cost effectiveness is one of the major advantages of the Mobile Banking, as the mobile based transaction cost is about 2 per cent of branch banking, 10 per cent of ATM and 50 per cent of the Internet banking. T-Banking: Today, we rarely come across a house without Television. It has become one of the cost effective modes to disseminate information and to provide entertainment to the public. Banks may make use of the existing cable network to extend banking services to vast segment using this mode as non-branch service delivery channel. However, this model yet to take a shape for pilot implementation.

CHALLENGES

Technology

Though, Mobile Banking is most cost effective compared to other channels to reach unbanked areas, all three stakeholders *viz.* the Telecom Operators, Banks and Merchants should work in tandem with suitable business model on robust technology platform to achieve the desired results.

Human Resources

The presence of full-fledged Brick and Mortar branches, newly introduced Ultra Small branches and Business Correspondents (BCs) are going to stay in rural India. However, the said delivery channels need to be handled by staff with positive attitude. The present recruitment policies of the banks signify the fact that majority of staff absorbed are from urban background and they are not keen to serve in rural areas, causing a hindrance for smooth banking operations in rural areas. At the same time the banking industry is in need of another 1.50 lakh additional manpower to serve the unbanked areas which is a major challenge.

Ironically, there are large numbers of rural young population with average academic background is eagerly waiting for employment opportunities. Similarly, Personnel handling BCs need to be trained further to enable them to help the customers in understanding the financial products and to take informed decisions. Achieving full scale financial inclusion, BCs also need to be adequately trained both on technology platform and banking domain knowledge. This issue needs to be addressed on priority by adopting suitable recruitment models to attract local talent. It is the time for the Banks, Government and Regulators to pay focused attention on the above issues and initiate necessary steps to bridge the gap through adopting appropriate recruitment policies for sustained growth of the banking industry.

Financial Literacy

In the above backdrop, major chunk of prospective customers are likely from unbanked/under banked population whose awareness towards banking services is limited. It warrants strategic initiatives from banks inviting investment in customer education through financial literacy and awareness programmes.

WAY FORWARD

Every household is bankable. Today around 100 million rural households are away from the banking system and their estimated average banking requirement is about 2 lakhs per household, which translates huge business (around '20 lakh crore) to the banking industry, almost two times of the existing business of rural bank branches of the country. Nonetheless, understanding the nuances of rural consumer behaviour, offering customized products, forging the right partnerships/collaborations and developing the appropriate business models and organization structure is the prerequisite for the banks to tap the vast potential of rural India. Mobile Banking has great potential to provide the banking facilities to people truly "anywhere" on account of easy adoptability, affordability and cost effectiveness compared to other delivery channels. Nevertheless, banks need to adopt multi-pronged approach *viz.*, Brick and Mortar Branches, Ultra Small Branches, ATMs and Business Correspondents, to reach the large number of unbanked population with diverse literacy, economic and social backgrounds across the geographies.

In the present scenario, no single channel is to be treated assubstitute to other channel; rather they are to be viewed as complement to each other. The expected burgeoning client base is really a daunting task for the banking industry to handle their diversified needs.

However, it is an opportunity to enhance the value of all stakeholders with improved business volumes. Banks need to adopt "High Volume – Low Margin" business model leveraging Technology and Human Capital to remain competitive in the present fierce dynamic environment. The initiatives of the policy makers, regulator and banks in this direction are going to transform the rural India in a big way. This decade definitely be an icon for Rural Banking and paves the way to achieve the long cherished dream of Inclusive Growth.

ROLE OF BANKS IN INDIAN ECONOMY

Banking system plays a very significant role in the economy of a country. It is central to a nation's economy as it caters to the needs of credit for all the sections of the society. Money-lending in one form or the other has evolved along with the history of mankind. Even in the ancient times, there are references to the money-lenders, in the form of sahukars and zamindars who lend money by mortgaging the land property of the borrowers.

Towards the beginning of the 20 century, with the onset of modern industry in our country, the need for government-regulated banking system was felt. The British government began to pay attention towards the need for an organized banking sector in the country and the Reserve Bank of India was set up to regulate the formal banking sector in the country. Ever since they were nationalized in 1969, banks have been playing a major role in the socio-economic life of the country. The have to act not only as purveyors of credit, but also as harbingers of social and economic development through a variety of enterprises, many of which may tiny and yet capable of generating productive energies.

India is not only the world's largest independent democracy, but also an emerging economic giant. Without a sound and effective banking system, no country can have a health economy. For the past three decades, India's banking system has several outstanding achievements to its credit. It is no longer confined to only the metropolitans, but have reached even to the remote corners of the country. This is one of the reasons of India's growth process.

Agriculture in India has a significant history and it is demographically the broadest economic sector and plays a significant role in the overall socio-economic fabric of India. Finance in agriculture is an important as development of technologies. A dynamic and growing agricultural sector needs adequate finance through banks to accelerate overall growth. Most of the credit-related schemes of the government to uplift the poorer and the under-privileged sections have been implemented through the banking sector. With the passing of the Reserve Bank of India Act 1934, there were improvements in agricultural credit. Earlier, the co-operative banks were the main institutional agencies providing finance to agriculture. But after nationalization of 14 major commercial banks, it was mandatory for them to provide finance to agriculture as a priority sector. Thus, agricultural credit acquired multi-agency dimension.

The government has allocated '10000 crore to the National Bank for Agriculture and Rural Development (NABARD) for refinancing Regional Rural Banks (RRBs) to disburse short term crop loans to small and marginal farmers. The short-term crop loans scheme offers credit to farmers at 7 per cent interest rate. Besides, in order to reduce post-harvest losses, farmers are eligible to get post-harvest loans up to six months at 4 per cent interest rate provided they keep their produce in warehouses. The rural sector in a country like India can growth only if cheaper credit is available to the farmers for their short-and medium-term loans. In addition, the farmers get loans for purchase of electric motors with pump, tractors and other machinery, digging wells or boring wells, purchase of dairy animals and for many other allied enterprises.

The Industrial Development Bank of India (IDBI) is the premier institution in India purveying financial assistance to the industrial sector projects. It provides direct financial assistance to the industrial concerns in the form of granting loans and advances, and purchasing or underwriting the issues of stocks, bonds or debentures. The creation of the Development Assistance Fund is the special of the IDBI. The Fund is used to provide assistance to those industries which are not able to obtain funds mainly because of heavy investment involved or low expected rate of returns. Assistance from the Fund requires the prior approval by the government. Apart from this, the IDBI even gives guidance to start a business.

In addition to the above traditional roles, banks also perform certain new age functions which could not be thought of a couple of decades ago. Today, the banking sector is one of the biggest service sectors in India. Availability of quality services is vital for the well-being of the economy.

The focus of banks has shifted from customer acquisition to customer retention. With the stepping in of information technology in the banking sector, the working strategy of the banking sector has been revolutionary changes. Various customer-oriented products like internet banking, ATM services, telebanking and electronic payment have lessened the workload of customers. The facility of internet banking enables a consumer to access and operate his bank account without actually visiting the bank premises.

The facility of ATMs and credit/debit cards has revolutionized the choices available with the customers. Banks also serve as alternative gateways for making payments on account of income-tax and online payment of various bills like the telephone, electricity and tax. In the modern-day economy where people have not time to make these payments by standing in queue, the services provided by banks are commendable.

To conclude, we can say that the modern economies of the world have developed primarily by making best use of the credit availability in their systems. India is on the march; far reaching socio-economic changes are taking place and Indian banks should come forward to play this role in the process. The role of banks has been important, but it is going to be even more important in the future.

3

Rural Banking and Economic Development

RURAL BANKING

Amongst developing economics, India has a relatively deep financial system. Its financial depth is attributable in large to India's vast network of financial institution, particularly those focused on rural customers. The need to improve financial access to India's poor, the overwhelming majority of whom are concentrated in rural areas, motivated the establishment of a vast network of rural banks. Financial tools help entrepreneurs start and expand small businesses which are a source of local job creation, growth and poverty reduction. Rural banking has become a national and a government imperative in the last few years.

The process of economic growth, especially when it is on high growth trajectory, must strive to encompass participation from all sections of society. Lack of access to finance for small farmers and weaker sections of the society has been recognized as a serious threat to economic progress especially in developing countries. Moreover, prolonged and persistent deprivation of banking services to a large segment of the population leads to a decline in investment and has the potential to fuel social tensions causing social exclusion. Access to finance, especially by the poor and vulnerable groups is a prerequisite for employment, economic growth, poverty reduction and social cohesion. This will be providing them an opportunity to have a bank account for saving as well as investment purposes and thereby facilitating them to break the chain of poverty.

However, while there is a growing awareness and agreement on the importance of rural banking, it is also important to appreciate that the objective of providing affordable access of suitable financial services to the financially excluded is to ensure 'economic development and progress of the financially excluded and that inclusion of the excluded' is only a means to an end and not the end in itself. Banks could play a major role in inclusive growth through financing of MSMEs, especially in rural and semi-urban centres in a big way.

Recognizing the contributory impact of the rural banking for achieving the inclusive growth, a series of efforts are being undertaken by the Government of India and Reserve Bank of India during the last few decades for greater inclusion. However, the seriousness of financial exclusion of poor was brought out in the report of National Sample Survey Organization (NSSO, 2005) based on which greater attention was focused on this aspect. While assessing the contributory factor for such exclusion, it was recognized that in spite of a large network of the institutional credit system, it has not been able to adequately penetrate the informal rural financial markets and the non-institutional sources continue to play a dominant role in purveying the credit needs of the people residing in rural areas. As a complementary persons have access to credit bears the fact that the exclusion is not only large, there is also a wide variation across regions, social groups and asset holdings. The poorer the group, the greater is the exclusion. The estimates of rural banking index revealed the wide variation in the status of rural banking was observed among the regions and districts with the regions and inadequate branch networking was observed to be one of the contributing factors for the greater exclusion. This situation called for appropriate institutional arrangements to bridge the gap between the existing bank branches and poor clients. Though several initiatives were undertaken for deepening and widening the process of providing financial services to the poor and vulnerable groups, in the recent periods, still there exists greater potential for qualitative and quantitative additions in the ongoing efforts.

OBJECTIVES OF RURAL BANKING

Rural Banking ensuring access to financial services and timely and adequate credit as needed by vulnerable groups such as weaker sections and low income groups at an affordable cost.

- Extending formal banking system among rural sector.
- Weaning them away from unorganized money markets and moneylenders.
- Equipping them with the confidence to make informed financial decisions.

Why is Rural Banking Important?

- Equitable growth is achievable only through the rural banking. There are hardly any instances of an economy transiting from an agrarian system in a post-industrial modern society without broad-based rural banking.
- Accessibility of public goods and services is a necessary condition of an open and efficient society. Banking services are like public goods, it is essential that the availability of banking services to the entire population is ensured.

- Financial access is essentially meant for the economically backward as it provides them opportunities to build savings, make investments and avail credit. Importantly, access to financial services also helps the poor insure themselves against income shocks and equips them to meet emergencies such as illness, death in the family or loss of employment. Needless to add, rural banking protects the poor from the clutches of the usurious moneylenders.
- It is now well understood with the experiences of FMCG companies, LIC, Microfinance companies that commerce with the poor is more viable and profitable, provided there is ability to do business with them. The availability of uncomplicated, small, affordable products can help bring low-income families into the formal financial sector. Taking into account their seasonal inflow of income from agricultural operations, migration from one place to another, and seasonal and irregular work availability and income, the existing financial system needs to be designed to suit their requirements. Mainstream financial institutions such as banks have an important role to play in this effort.
- Rural banking benefits banking sector in two ways. First, rural banking provides an avenue for bringing the savings of the poor into the formal financial intermediation system and channels them into investment. Second, the large amount of low- cost deposits offer banks an opportunity to reduce their dependence on bulk deposits and help them to better manage both liquidity risks and asset-liability mismatch.

INITIATIVES TOWARDS RURAL BANKING

The elements of rural banking focused in the recent initiatives by RBI includes, saving cum overdraft account, remittance facility, an access to credit through instruments like a general credit card. Performance of providing these services depends on the institutional network coverage of bank branches in the remote areas. The RBI had pursued the rural banking agenda more closely and now the banks have prepared plans in each and every State targeting 72,800 villages with the population of more than 2000 that are not covered by main stream financial institutions. Progress and issues in the implementation of the selected initiatives towards rural banking which are having direct bearing on micro finance sector progress.

Today, the banking has become imperative to all the households irrespective of their social and financial status and expects minimum financial services from the banking system. The recent rural banking initiatives of the Government, *i.e.* provide access to banking services at all villages through branch banking or business correspondent at affordable cost is going to transform the banking landscape to greater extent and it is an important business segment for banks. However, providing financial services to the poor, especially in rural areas, is both challenging and costly. The transaction costs have become one of the deterring factors to reach the un-banked by the banks. The stupendous task can be achieved by adopting following Initiatives:

Alternate Delivery Channels

The residents of far-flung areas are unable to pay visit to branches located at distant places on account of resource constraints *viz.*, time, cost and opportunity. Thus, it has become imperative for banks to reach out customers through a variety of technology driven delivery channels such as Micro ATMs, Bio-metric ATMs, Mobile ATMs, and Smart Cards etc., which are most cost effective compared to Brick and Mortar model. ATM has brought sea change in Indian banking space with significant qualitative improvement in delivery of banking services and within short span the presence of ATMs is outnumbered the physical branch network.

- *Micro ATMs*: Though there is considerable improvement in ATM network, the presence of ATMs in rural areas is very limited. Banks are not keen to install ATMs at Rural/Semi Urban centers on account of high investment and low transaction volume. In order to make the ATMs viable at these centers, there is a need to deploy low cost ATMs with basic features such as cash withdrawal and balance enquiry etc. It is convenient and cost effective to the customers compared to pay a visit to the bank branch located at nearby center.
- *Biometric ATMs*: The penetration of ATMs in Rural areas may not serve the envisaged purpose unless it is put to use by illiterate/semi-literate whose presence is predominant in unbanked areas. The existing ATMs are not put to use optimally by rural folk on account of PIN/Password related issues. Introduction of Biometric ATMs enable them to avail hassle-free services as these devices function on thumb print and recognize voice commands in vernacular language.
- *Mobile ATMs*: In this model, ATM is installed in a vehicle, which would move to the pre-determined places at regular intervals to provide doorstep banking. These new breeds of ATMs also have biometric authentication mechanisms like fingerprint verification and voice guided animated screens with touch enabled transactions. Mobile ATMs can undertake opening of accounts, which has immense benefit of the residents of unbanked centers.
- *White Label ATMs*: The recent initiatives of the RBI and the Government is to allow white-label ATMs, permitting third-party service providers to set up more ATMs in off-premises areas, which include residential complexes, hospitals, tourist destinations, bus stops and railway stations. These ATMs would not belong to any bank in

particular but will be owned as well as maintained by independent service providers. This initiative will enable the excluded segments to avail ATM services as at present majority ATMs are confined to Urban/Metro areas only. However, service provider levies charges which are to be either bear by the Bank or the customer.

- *Smart Cards*: State Governments are actively looking at making pension payments and disbursals under rural employment generation programme using smart cards linked bank accounts. Smart card provides biometric authentication, which would help in reducing frauds and ensure identity of customers. In order to popularize smart cards, all agriculture short term loans and payment of social security schemes are to be dispensed through Smart Cards.

All the above initiatives warrant the banks to invest substantial amounts in infrastructure besides recurring expenditure which adds cost to the customer whereas the distribution of financial products and services at the lowest rung of the pyramid requires a low-cost model. High Operating Costs and Low Business Volume are the major constraints of the banks in extending banking services especially in remote rural and inaccessible areas through Branch Banking Model. To address this issue, RBI permitted the banks to make use the services of Business Correspondents to take banking to un-banked areas in a most cost effective manner.

BUSINESS CORRESPONDENT (BC) MODEL

Business Correspondent model using smart card and mobile technology is also an effective tool to reach the remote rural areas where alternate delivery channel mechanism is not feasible. This model enables greater rural outreach to improve the business volumes. RBI has permitted the BCs to undertake basic banking services *viz.*, Collection/payment of small value deposits, disbursal of small value loan amounts, collection of loan installments, receipt and delivery of small value remittances and sale of micro insurance/mutual fund products/pension products/other third party products. Though, BC model has been gaining momentum since last two years, still desired results are not coming as the model is confronting the following issues and challenges, which need to be addressed on priority.

- *Operational Issues*: Cash management is the biggest challenge as the major operations of BCs pertains to cash transactions. It entails interest costs as well as operational risks. Further, the beneficiaries of BC services are mostly illiterate and are susceptible to misguidance. At times, customers tend to perceive the BCs as banks. The success of the model crucially depend on the trust levels among customers, banks and BCs, which is possible through spread of financial awareness by conducting financial literacy programmes on an ongoing basis.

- *Viability*: The viability of the BC model is the most critical issue which probably is one of the main reasons for not taking-off the model as envisaged. The transaction volume is not encouraging since many of the accounts opened are in dormant stage. Absence of sufficient business is causing concern to both BCs as well as banks; and in turn it is becoming difficult for BCs to continue operations on account of mismatch of revenues earned and costs incurred. Banks need to tweak the products and work with the BCs to design products that are suitable to the target market to make the model profitable. Further, to make the BC model viable, the funds pertaining to various government schemes are to be routed directly through the beneficiaries' bank accounts only.

BRANCH EXPANSION

- *Physical Branches*: The penetration of banking in India is low compared to developed nations, which is evident from the presence of 5.40 lakh unbanked villages across the country. Branch banking continues to play significant role in business development despite increased adoption of Alternate Delivery Channels in the recent years. The road map of Indian banks clearly indicates that BC model is going to be used in a big way to achieve the rural banking objective. However, banks need to open more number of brick and mortar branches especially in unbanked centers to cover the large population on one hand and branch network acts as service branch to route the transactions undertaken by BCs. Hence, branch network continued to grow in the ensuing years also.
- *Ultra Small Branches (Mobile Branches)*: As part of the liberalized branch authorisation policy, RBI has granted general permission to domestic scheduled commercial banks to open satellite branches in unbanked areas where the population is under 50,000. It envisages the extension of banking facilities through one or two dedicated staff members who visit the identified village location on specified days. It is a cost effective model compared to physical branch model. A designated officer of the link branch shall visit the village on a prefixed date and time every week with a laptop with Virtual Private Network (VPS) connectivity to Core Banking Platform. The role of the visiting official is authorization of the accounts, balance enquiry, printing of account statements and recovery. However, the normal cash transactions will be done by the BC agent only.
- *Branch-in-a-Box*: It is primarily a cost-effective, relocatable and pre-fabricated bank branch. It uses modern, broadband satellite technology for communication. This enhances customer convenience as it

provides speedy access. It can also be used to test new markets, especially in areas with limited infrastructure where banking services are not readily available. It provides full transaction facilities to customers, including cash withdrawals and deposits, sales and service.

NO FRILLS ACCOUNTS

Taking the view that access to a bank account can be considered a public good, in 2005, RBI directed all banks to offer at all branches the facility of 'No Frills' Account (NFA) to any person desirous of opening such an account. These accounts have nil or low minimum balances and charges and have limited facilities. As at the end of the year 2009-10, 74.4 million NFAs had been opened by the banking system. The impressive performance in terms of growth in number of NFA may not be contributory unless and otherwise, these accounts are considered to be active in operation. At the ground level, it was observed that most of the NFAs were non-operative and clients were not even aware of the terms of use of these accounts. There are certain barriers that inhibit the active operation of such accounts like the time and cost involved in reaching the nearest branch where the accounts have been opened. Concerted efforts by the implementing authorities by providing appropriate financial literacy with the innovations in use of technology will certainly improve the impact of these efforts to a greater extent.

RURAL BANK BRANCHES

In spite of the process of financial reforms in the country, the total number of bank branches of the scheduled commercial banks had increased from 60,220 branches in 1991 to 69,471 branches in 2006, at an annual rate of 0.96 per cent. While the number of bank offices in urban areas had increased from 25,014 branches in 1991 to 38,892 branches in 2006 at an annual rate of 2.99 per cent, the number of branches in rural areas had declined from 35,206 branches in 1991 to 30,579 branches in 2006 at annual rate of 0.93 per cent.

The influence of the declining trend of the bank branches in rural areas had been felt in marginalisation of the disadvantaged sections from accessing institutional credit, especially in the underdeveloped regions of the country. This has to some extent been offset by the SHG-Bank linkage programme, which provided credit to very poor people, especially poor rural women.

Credit flow vs. Productivity

Although credit for the agriculture sector has shown an impressive growth over a period of time between 1991-92 and 2005-06, no significant change in the value of output has been observed during this period. The relationship between the value of input and the value of output over the last decade has remained more or less the same with the output being less than five times the value of input. It is relevant to note that even at the highest level of production, credit forms around 11 per cent (in real term in 1993-94 prices) of the total output value. Thus, expecting credit with so little a share in the output value to have any significant impact on the output or productivity values may not be in order.

Emerging Challenges

There has been a long history of concern regarding rural credit. The increase in share of institutional credit has been rather slow. The dependence of small and marginal farmers is still very high on non-institutional sources. Besides, the developed regions have greater access to credit as compared with less developed regions. Therefore, the key issue now is how to ensure that rural credit from institutional sources achieves wider coverage and expands financial inclusion. As the credit-off-take depends on the willingness and ability of the person to avail of loans (which is a function of perceived returns to investments) and the willingness of the banker to lend (which is contingent on bank's perception and assessment of lending risk), there is a need to address the problems from both the supply side as also the demand side.

While distance from the bank branch, branch timings, cumbersome documentation and procedures, unsuitable products, communication and staff attitudes are some important supply side constraints, lack of awareness, low income/assets and small-sized loan demands are some of the demand side constraints. Further, large number of villages (more than 6 lakh villages), lack of infrastructure, vast geographical spread, high transaction costs and poor loan recovery are some other problems faced by banks. In the absence of any alternative, the poor and other weaker sections of rural society depend on the unorganized financial system, which utilizes local knowledge, offers credit for a wide variety of purposes and operates quite flexibly, though at high costs and as an exploitative relationship.

One strategy that has achieved great popularity and wide acceptance is that of micro finance. The banks need to involve micro-finance agencies and other financial intermediaries, as business opportunities. They must understand, recognise and streamline different activities like retail activities, service sector initiatives, and construction and rural housing that take place in the rural economy, in addition to financing agriculture. However, this needs innovations in risk assessment, reduction in transaction costs, search for new credit channels and the use of cheaper information technology. Technology is another option.

It can be a vital component in integrating strategies for achieving inclusive growth. Its use can be critical in building up a reliable credit information system and database on customers, reducing transaction costs and facilitating better pricing of risk, improving the efficiency of the financial system, and thereby increasing the access of un-banked rural people in an efficient manner. It can reduce the transaction costs sharply and time taken by banks in processing applications, maintaining accounts and disbursing loans. It has the potential to address the issues of outreach and credit delivery in rural areas, in a cost effective manner. But how the IT platform will provide a variety of financial services to the rural clients at affordable costs and in time needs to be examined.

Access to information is the key to ensure wider participation of all in the process of development. The challenge lies in ensuring easy flow of public information to rural citizens. The growing innovations in the use of information communication technologies have opened up a new era of information dissemination. Credit counseling, awareness creation and financial education regarding the benefits of financial inclusion are important for effective expansion of financial services in rural areas. To do this, banks may utilise the services of non-governmental organisations, village youth clubs, village Panchayats, farmer clubs and self-help groups into confidence.

Banks need to develop an array of financial products and services that are adapted to the needs of the majority of rural people at affordable prices. Interest rate is an important component of cost to agricultural producers and will become more important as backward and forward linkages are strengthened. As per the current interest rate policy of RBI, the interest rate on loans for the agriculture sector by commercial banks is linked to the size of the loan. While commercial banks have reduced their interest rates on crop loans up to ₹ 50,000 to 7 per cent, RRBs and cooperative banks, for various reasons, have not been able to bring down their rates of interest on lending to any appreciable extent. To ensure competitiveness of Indian agriculture produce in the world market, various Committees have suggested several measures of reducing cost of funds, transaction costs and the risk costs. Risk management is another option. While the farmers suffer from wide variety of risks like the climate risk, price risk, technology risk, etc., the bankers suffer from the problem of increasing non-performing assets and losses. These risks emanate from a host of factors including failure of investments, willful defaults, weather aberrations, improper appraisal of loans, diversion of funds, inadequate monitoring and follow up and inability to realize the securities available, are some of the cost drivers, which play a decisive role in determining the rates of interest charged by banks to ultimate borrowers in rural areas.

Therefore, if credit risk can be disaggregated into factors like failure of rainfall, price fluctuations, poor health and death of the borrower, these can be mitigated through non-credit financial products like insurance and derivatives. This could also facilitate the banks to provide credit at lower rates. On account of low levels of financial capacity as also awareness, risks affect lives and livelihood of the poor. Therefore, the risk management mechanisms should take into accounts the similarities and differences in the incidence of risks and seek to assist people to manage the consequences thereof. One possible risk management measure could be to enhance savings.

Creation of a large fund administered centrally or at each State level would be necessary to help people affected by calamities and disasters. The manner of contribution, mode of assistance, etc., could be designed to provide quick response to calamity-affected regions. Price hedging mechanisms to safeguard farmers from price risks would be needed. The gradual introduction of forward markets and future trading in select crops/commodities should be extended to all major crops in a phased manner. An enforcement mechanism whereby the suppliers of technology are made accountable for failure of technology, etc., could mitigate technology risks faced by the farmers.

Further, the infrastructure support, policy framework and technology could play an effective role in mitigating risks in financing to the rural sector. There is also a need for providing immediate relief at the time of disaster or natural calamity, smoothening the liquidity flow to ensure that consumption requirements are not unduly affected besides compensating people for loss of income, assets and livelihood. The rural Micro Finance Institutions (MFIs), which has emerged as a powerful tool for fighting poverty, may be made a part of the financial system for effective delivery of rural financial services.

The banks need to gear up their rural branches for facilitating bank linkages of SHGs where the programme has not shown satisfactory progress. The Business Correspondence models (MFIs, NGOs, etc.), as recommended by the Internal Group on Micro finance (Khan Committee), may also be put in place, which will increase banking outreach.

RURAL DEBT

Dependence of rural households on non-institutional sources of credit were as high as 92.8 per cent in the year 1951, just four years after India's independence which declined to 82.7 per cent in 1961 and further to 70.8 per cent in 1971 when cooperative credit institutions made their presence felt on the rural scene after acceptance and implementation of recommendations of the All India Rural Credit Survey Committee in 1954 and entry of major private sector banks after their nationalization in the year 1969.

Access of rural households to formal credit institutions sharply increased to 61.2 per cent in 1981 partly because of enabling measures initiated by the Reserve Bank to direct public sector banks towards rural lending and partly because of the establishment of Regional Rural Banks from the year 1975 onwards specifically to cater to the credit needs of rural poor households.

However, in the year 1991 there was only marginal increase in the institutional sources of credit from 61.2 per cent in 1981 to 64 per cent in 1991. While dependence of rural households on professional moneylenders in particular declined very significantly from 46.4 per cent in 1951 to 8.3 per cent in 1981, it again increased to 10.5 per cent in 1991. The role of agricultural money lenders had also declined progressively from 47 per cent in 1961 to 7.1

per cent in 1991. Commercial banks' performance was very spectacular between 1971 and 1981 but it showed little improvement in 1991. Cooperatives had shown good performance from 1961 to 1981 but its performance declined in 1991.

Doubling Farm Credit

The goal of Union Government, as announced by the Finance Minister in his Budget speech in 2004, to double the flow of farm credit in three years [2004-07] was achieved in two years. Actual flow of credit during the year 2006-07 is expected to exceed the target of ₹ 1,750,000 million set for the year by ₹ 150,000 million. During April to December 2006, around 5,337,000 new farmers, as against target of five million, were linked with the institutional credit system. For the year 2007-08, target of farm credit disbursement has been fixed at ₹ 2,250,000 million [28.6 per cent over target of 2006-07] and an addition of five million new farmer-borrowers. Following table exhibits banks' commitment, particularly of commercial banks and RRBs, to respond to Finance Minister's call to double the credit disbursements during 2004-07.

Total disbursements progressively increased from ₹ 620,450 million in 2001-02 to ₹ 1,574,800 million in the year 2005-06 reflecting rise by 153.8 per cent. Commercial banks and RRBs recorded phenomenal rise by 216 per cent and 189 per cent respectively as compared to 58 per cent by co-operatives. While there has been progressive rise in each successive year in case of cooperatives, commercial and regional rural banks, there has been spectacular increase during 2004-05 and 2005-06 in respect of commercial in the total disbursements of short-term and long-term credit progressively declined from 37.9 per cent in 2001-02 to 23.65 per cent in 2005-06 whereas that of commercial banks recorded progressive increase from 54.13 per cent to 67.41 per cent during the corresponding years. RRBs accounted for 7.82 per cent in 2001-02 which progressively rose to 9.91 per cent in 2004-05 but declined by one percentage point in the following year. Agriculture credit flow for the banking system as a whole during 2005-06 has surged to ₹ 1,804,860 million, reflecting 128 per cent of the target of ₹ 1,410,000 million that was set for that year data further revealed that proportion of short-term credit to enable farmers to conduct seasonal agricultural operations was around 63 per cent as against 37 per cent of long-term credit for investment purposes. Following table exhibits comparative performance among banks and within banks during nine months of 2005 and 2006.

Agriculture credit flow target for 2006-07 had been pegged at ₹ 1,750,000 million. However, for the fiscal year 2006-07, agriculture credit up to December 2006 stood at ₹ 1,493,430 million which represented a 25.38 per cent increase over the achievement of ₹ 1,191,150 million recorded in the same nine-month period in the previous year. Agriculture credit flow during April to December

2006 from public sector banks grew by 25.91 per cent to ₹ 868,650 million from ₹ 689,910 million during the corresponding period in the previous year. In case of private sector banks, it increased by 40.90 per cent to ₹ 141,340 million from ₹ 100,310 million. While cooperative banks recorded increase by 14.60 per cent from ₹ 289,470 million to ₹ 151,700 million. Share of public sector banks in the total disbursement during April-December'06 accounted for as high as 58 per cent followed by cooperative banks at 22 per cent where as RRBs and private sector banks had almost equal share of 10 per cent and 9 per cent respectively.

URBAN COOPERATIVE BANKS (UCB'S)

The Urban Cooperative Banks (UCB's) have made tremendous strides in the last decade. The Urban Cooperative Banks have come along way to occupy a distinctive place in the cooperative credit movement and being described as non-agricultural credit societies. It supplies credit needs of people residing in the urban areas having limited resources. They advance loans mostly to the small traders, artisans, salary earners and others on personal security.

Under the Banking Registration Act, the Urban Cooperative Banks' main purpose is banking, similar to other commercial banks. Their major activities are collection of deposits from members and non-members, to provide loans to members and weaker sections of the society, to provide lockers for safe custody of valuables, collection of endorsed bills, to provide facilities for training and education for employees, directors and to offer consultancy services to the customers.

Only recently, the RBI has classified the Urban Cooperative Banks as weak, sick and strong in terms of its growth and function, because they are not performing well now-a-days. The objective of UCB's is primarily to inculcate the habit of thrift, savings, mutual help, and aid leading to better socio-economic conditions of those joining it. Several Urban Cooperative Banks have been authorized to deal with the foreign exchange and maintain Non-Resident Indian (NRI) accounts.

PRIMARY AGRICULTURE AND RURAL DEVELOPMENT BANKS (PARDB'S)

The organizational structure of long-term cooperative Agricultural credit structure is not uniform all over the country. They have primary level organizations known as PARDB's. The primary level organizations advance loans to the borrowers for long-term purposes. The NABARD has come forward to render refinance assistance to PARDB's and State Cooperative Agriculture and Rural Development banks for financing different rural instrument transactions. They provide farm and non-farm loans to the borrower and they deal mainly with (i) Granting loans for improvement of loan and introduction of better methods of cultivation (ii) provide loans for minor irrigation schemes like small tube well, canals etc (ii) for land consolidation to secure efficient and economic cultivation (iv) loan for horticulture and social forestry (v) purchase of agricultural tools (vi) develop carts, biogas plants (viii) provide loan for other productive purposes as approved by NABARD.

DIVERSIFICATION OF LENDING OPERATIONS BY PARDB'S

There has been quantum increase of loan advance to the members during the past decade because members have shown interest in modern farming methods and techniques, therefore the demand for greater delivery of Agricultural farm loans and non-farm loans (Rural Non-farm sector). The PARDB's are diversifying their business operations considering the push factors and pull factors of lending operations. They have their diversification measures and policies tuned to the free market economy, hence their strategies and policies must be market-driven market-based *i.e.* oriented towards small scale Agro-Industries, Agro-Processing. Business Services, Marketing, Trade, Financial Services, Small Scale Business; In other words, there should be a paradigm shift from traditional sectoral approach to face the challenges posed by LPG's. A liberalized economic policy environment shall be a pre-condition for promoting intensification and extensification of banking business operations.

DOMESTIC LENDING

Lending is and remains one of the chief activities of KBC Bank, which is striving to achieve a balance between market share and profitability in its domestic lending activity. The bank's aim is to provide the most appropriate solutions for the financial needs of its customers by offering a broad range of short- and long-term credit, as well as leasing and factoring services. Where retail lending is concerned, KBC Bank aims to create standard products with straightforward pricing. A new risk-acceptance scoring system has been introduced for these small loans. This ensures rapid and uniform processing, which in turn has a positive impact on both costs and the bank's commercial position. Increasingly important as regards the more complex, commercial loans are customer-mindedness, flexibility, rapidity and expertise. Focusing on these aspects, the bank is investing in building up expertise in specific sectors or fields, enabling it as a lender to anticipate future developments earlier. In assessing credit applications, credit advisers and the officers responsible for the decision to lend are given maximum support by advisers specialized in various domains: real estate experts, environmental experts, business experts, government aid experts and legal experts.

DEPOSITS AND SAVINGS CERTIFICATES

Due to the persistently low interest rates on the market and the favourable stock market climate, the volume of savings reflected on the balance sheet has been under pressure for some years now, a trend that certainly persisted in 1998. However, investment funds were once again hugely popular.

PAYMENTS TRANSACTIONS

To facilitate the commercial operation of the branches, more and more administrative work is being shifted to head office. A major step in this respect was taken by extending the facility for the central processing of paper-based transfers to all branches. In spite of the rising proportion of automated transfers - which currently represent a rounded-off 53 per cent of the total - the number of paper-based transfers remains substantial. In 1998, KBC processed nearly 37 million.

LEASING AND FACTORING

KBC considers the breadth of its range of products and services to be a significant asset as far as corporate finance is concerned. The combination of various associated and subsidiary companies within a single, encompassing group and the synergy this creates makes it possible to tailor the offering to meet the customer's needs.

KBC Lease and KBC Autolease are a case in point, making KBC, as a Group, a major player on the leasing market, both as regards leasing in general and in automobile leasing.

MULTINATIONALS

The Multinationals Division met with mounting success in having KBC Bank selected as key banker by its customers. With a view to achieving quicker response times and guaranteeing a service better adapted to customer needs, the Multinationals Division opened new offices in Singapore and London.

REAL ESTATE ACTIVITIES

During 1998, the real estate lending and leasing portfolio continued to expand. The production of newly granted lines of credit was double the 1997 level. In terms of volume, 54 per cent of the portfolio concerns office buildings, 23 per cent is accounted for by residential buildings, 15 per cent has to do with retail outlets and 8 per cent is related to land. The immovables leasing portfolio also exhibited strong growth, with new real estate leasing contracts totalling over 4 billion BEF being concluded in 1998.

PROJECT FINANCE

Significant further progress was made in 1998 in developing the project finance business. KBC aims to be one of the leading international banks in this highly specialized business activity, and therefore provides world-wide coverage through a global team with operating units in Dublin, New York and Hong Kong.

STRATEGY FOR RURAL DEVELOPMENT

Despite significant advancement in industrial development, Indian economy is dependent on agrobased activities. Over 70per cent of the population living in rural areas is dependent on agriculture for livelihood. A majority of these families spend over 90per cent of their earnings on basic needs such as food, fuel and health care. Over 50per cent of the rural families who are not able to meet even these essential needs fall under the category of the poor. Thus, in an agrarian country like India, for improving the economic status of the population it is not enough to enhance the per capita GNP, but it is also necessary to ensure prosperity among the poor. Industrial development and adoption of modern technologies are likely to generate additional employment in urban areas and pay rich dividend to elite and rich investors. This in turn might widen the gap between the urban and rural as well as the rich and the poor, with respect to wealth accumulation, resulting in further hardship to the poor. Therefore, we need to address the problems of the poor to ensure social justice and better quality of life. Rural development also deserves priority for maintaining self sufficiency in food supply. Our food security is under severe threat because of the growing population. No doubt, India has tripled her food production over the last four decades, to reach the present level of 195 million tons/year. However, with over 1.8per cent annual birth rate, our growing population is bound to raise the annual demand for food to 250 million tons by 2010 A.D. As food security is a pre requisite for economic progress, agro based rural development deserves attention.

Fortunately, the Government of India has been giving top priority to rural development. However, in the absence of well planned development programmes and efficient delivery systems, most of these resources do not benefit the target groups. It has been reported that only 18per cent of the rural development budget reaches the target families, while the rest is wasted due to inefficient delivery systems or drained out. In the process of assisting the poor, a significant portion of the budget is spent on relief and subsidies. Poor families have received sympathy instead of motivation which has resulted in a dependency syndrome. As a result, most of the poor have lost confidence, initiative and entrepreneurship. The inputs and cash distributed for investment in development are being diverted for household consumption. In such a situation, free distribution of inputs may not help the rural poor any more.

The time is now ripe for a change in the strategy. The rural development programme should identify the problems of the poor and address the local needs, instead of forcing them to accept pre conceived plans. The participating families should take active part in the programme. There should be equal opportunity for the weaker sections of the society and women. The programme should facilitate sustainable management of natural resources and environmental protection and lead to better quality of life.

PROBLEMS OF THE POOR

Rural poor pass through series of problems which affect their survival and quality of life. These problems can be grouped into four broad categories namely livelihood, health, education and social development. These four components can be referred to as 4 A's 'Anna', 'Arogya', 'Akshar' and 'Acharan'. Problems such as scarcity of food, fodder, fuel, shelter, small holdings, poor crop yields, poor quality livestock, lack of irrigation, unemployment and underemployment affect the income generation and hence, fall in the category of livelihood problems.

Problems of livelihood are more serious and need immediate attention of the development agencies. The other problems are also serious and interrelated, but can be handled by the villagers, simultaneously with the livelihood programme. Health and education problems can be solved at a greater pace when the villagers start improving their livelihood. In the absence of assured livelihood, other development programmes may not sustain in the long run. Good moral values and commitment for upliftment of the community are also essential to ensure better quality of life.

SETTING THE PRIORITY

The problems of the rural poor throughout the country appear to be common. But the intensity of these problems vary widely and a few of them need to be addressed on priority. The cause of these problems also vary, due to the family size, employment status, ownership of various resources, socio economic background and religious beliefs. These restrictions need to be taken into consideration, while proposing suitable solutions for tackling the problems of rural development. Hence, basic data on the target community will be useful for planning the programme.

Baseline Data

The information needed for preparing a development plan are the nature of problems and their causes, resources available, type of technologies presently adopted and their capacity to absorb new activities for generating income.

Village level information on the following aspects will be useful for project formulation.

- Social background of the families: SC, ST, BC and poor and their employment status (men and women);
- Literacy status (men, women and children). Anganwadis, balwadis and school facilities;
- Land holding pattern with water resources, type of crops and levels of production (average yields) and inventory of livestock;
- Demand and supply of essential commodities such as fodder, fuel, food, agricultural commodities and per capita consumption;

- Prevailing diseases and community health problems, social problems, if any.

It is not feasible to conduct house to house survey in the initial stage as it is time consuming. Any survey without concrete project support may also demoralise the local population, who in turn may not cooperate in the future. Apart from the collection of secondary data, it is also advisable to conduct Rapid Rural Appraisal (RRA) and Participatory Rural Appraisal (PRA).

RRA can be carried out by a team of multidisciplinary specialists who can discuss with prominent people and office bearers of various organisations, local health officials, village sarpanch, school teachers, members of Youth and Women's clubs and cooperatives.

PRA involves discussion with various socio economic groups who can come up with their problems and possible solutions. It is an effective tool for identifying local problems and setting a priority for implementation.

DEVELOPMENT OF PROJECT PROPOSALS

Based on the local needs and available opportunities, it is preferable to prepare a project proposal for raising financial resources and implementation. The proposal should cover various aspects such as infrastructural needs, identification of the target groups and the activities to be undertaken. All these details can be systematically presented in the proposal.

Local Infrastructure

It is necessary to plan for various activities, identify the resources and manpower for proper management with time schedule and budgetary control. The community should be involved in project implementation right from the beginning. The domination of the implementing agencies may result in loss of initiatives among the beneficiaries. Subsequently, at the termination of the project, even the most successful projects may fail to sustain the programme due to inability of the local people. To avoid such a situation, formation of local organisations to implement the programme is helpful. It is not necessary in the initial stage to determine the type of the organisation to be established for implementing the project. The community can be mobilised through Self Help Groups (SHGs) to initiate the development activity. Subsequently, a formal organisation can be registered to manage the programme.

Apart from mobilising people, infrastructure is also necessary to organise input supply, finance, post production processing and marketing of the produce. In livelihood projects, realisation of benefits in the form of cash and kind is the indicator of success. Hence, market plays a very crucial role in sustaining the development programme. Marketing is a dynamic process which is influenced by demand and supply as well as information on new products and processes. Hence, the proposed infrastructure should also provide market information services required to enhance profits. For the success of any rural development programme, there is a need for a strong local organisation having a strong linkage with technology centres, financial institutions and marketing network. An ideal linkage of the local organisation with various institutions at various levels. Close relation with the Gram Panchayat and Gram Sabha is necessary, as most of the government sponsored development projects are implemented through the Gram Panchayat.

Target Groups

The development inputs in general consist of technology and resources. As there is no constraint in acquiring technology from various sources, it is neither feasible nor necessary to restrict the dissemination of technology. However, the poor who cannot mobilise adequate resources to adopt appropriate technologies need financial assistance as well.

It has been observed that the programmes focussed on the development of common properties and local infrastructures have mostly benefited the rich families. In the absence of assured support to weaker sections, the advantages of infrastructural development and technology transfer are enjoyed by the well to do and elite members of the society, while the illiterate and poor families lag behind. Hence, special attention on family based development programme can ensure the participation of the poor in development programmes.

Empowerment of women should cut across all these development activities, as women play a significant role in building the community. Although the women represent 50per cent of the population, they share an additional responsibility of bringing up their children. With empowerment of women, their drudgery will be reduced and they will be able to utilise their time effectively in shaping their children and family.

Programme Components

Establishing a good rapport with the local community before launching the development programme is helpful. However, livelihood programme may not be the correct entry point even among the poor communities.

The entry point activity should be such that a majority of the local population will be able to take part. In certain situations like post calamities, relief measures can be the best entry point. Health camps and drinking water resource development can also be considered for entry point activity.

Water is the lifeline of all human activities. Water is not only needed for survival but also for generating employment in rural areas. Therefore rural development projects involving water resources development may primarily aim at providing drinking water and subsequently for livestock and crop production.

The selection of villages for development can cover the entire area under a watershed. With the development of water resources, various income generation activities can be initiated. The strategy should be to conserve and make sustainable use of the denuded natural resources through appropriate technologies. Activities which provide employment at the doorsteps of local families particularly the women, deserve priority.

For successful economic development, the programme should focus on the following aspects:

- Equal distribution of natural resources, particularly water.
- Good extension network for transfer of technology.
- Infrastructure for timely distribution of inputs.
- Marketing network to procure, process and distribute the produce.

The development programme during the past few decades included free distribution of inputs to the poor. This however did not succeed in motivating the poor to take active part in development. Subsequently in 90's, many donor agencies changed their strategy and provided critical inputs in the form of loan. The response again was poor as the farmers were hesitant to avail loan, due to lack of confidence to generate adequate income and repay the loan. Therefore it is better to initiate the development programme with an aid component and subsequently encourage the families to avail of loans.

INCOME GENERATION ACTIVITIES

The opportunity for employment generation in rural areas can be grouped into on farm and off farm activities. Initially, the agro based activities cannot provide adequate opportunities for the landless. Subsequently, with optimum use of resources and enhanced productivity, demand for labour will rise and even the landless will have increased employment opportunities.

With improvement in agricultural production, job opportunities for ancillary services will also increase and the landless can take advantage of this situation. Nevertheless, land based activities have a serious limitation of maintaining the carrying capacity beyond a certain period. Hence, it is advisable to initiate the development programme through on farm and off farm activities, simultaneously.

While implementing the programme through a particular sector such as crop production, cattle breeding, forestry or kitchen garden or any such activities, it is necessary to estimate the expected benefits. The objective behind this analysis is to ensure that the families can earn adequate income to come out of poverty. If the development programme under implementation is not able to provide sufficient income to meet their basic needs, the beneficiaries may keep on looking for other opportunities, while ignoring the trickling benefits, from the project being implemented.

Therefore, the development strategy should aim at helping the rural families to come out of poverty by making use of the available resources and idle labour force. However, as the quality and quantity of natural resources owned by families within the community vary widely, their priorities also vary among the families. Therefore, it is preferable to undertake a micro level planning before undertaking various development activities. This planning should address all the problems of the families and the community.

CRITERIA FOR SELECTION OF LIVELIHOOD ACTIVITIES

In the absence of assured jobs in industries, self employment is the best alternative in rural areas. To enhance people's participation in rural development through self employment, priority should be given to the activities having the following criteria:

- Social acceptability of the participants;
- Easy availability of natural resources and external inputs;
- Local skill to operate the programme without depending on external technology;
- Ability of the participants to operate at low risk;
- Easy marketability of the produce;
- Economic viability and higher profitability;
- Short gestation period;
- Year round employment.

ASPECTS OF RURAL DEVELOPMENT

The essential aspects of rural development are as follows:

- Agricultural development constitutes the crucial aspect of rural development. Agricultural development is possible through the use of better seeds, adequate fertilizers, manures, and pesticides, adequate supply of water and effective implementation of land reform measures.
- By effecting changes in the socio-economic institutions, rural development seeks to change the socio-economic structure of the rural community.
- The effectiveness of the rural development programmes necessitates political non-interference. The persons associated with these programmes should be given adequate freedom to carry out their plans and programmes with undivided attention.
- The success of the rural development programmes depends on the co-operative orientation and attitude among the ruralites. The functioning of the co-operative societies goes a long way in improving the conditions of the vulnerable sections of the rural set-up.
- Rural development programmes demand the active participation of the ruralites. While formulating these programmes the opinions, attitudes, drives and interests of the rural people should be taken into account. Further, dedicated and committed village leaders should come forward to guide the masses for bringing about rural development.

INTEGRATED RURAL DEVELOPMENT

It is claimed that the concept of Integrated Rural Development was originally propounded by the World Bank. In India the concept was put forward in the year 1976 at the All-India Science Congress by C. Subramanyam, the then Finance Minister of India.

He viewed integrated rural development as "systematic, scientific and integrated use of all our natural resources and as a part of this process enabling every person to engage himself in a productive and socially useful occupation and earn an income that would meet at least the basic needs."

He holds the view that the use of natural resources is possible only through the application of science and technology. Further, proper application of science and technology results in the fulfilment of basic social needs.

G. Parthasarathy refers to four 'routes' in the context of integrated rural development: (i) the institutional route of Gunnar Myrdal, (ii) the 'New Economics' route, (iii) the Neo-Marxian route and (iv) the Gandhian route. V.K.R.V. Rao defines integrated rural development as "the optimum utilization of the natural and human resources of a given rural area for the enrichment of the quality of life of the population."

The concept of integrated rural development addresses itself to various rural problems like widespread poverty, unemployment, illiteracy, exploitation, inequitable distribution of land, poor health conditions *etc.* It signifies that various facets of rural development are integrally connected.

It is a holistic concept rather than a sequential one. K. Om Prakash and G. Satyanarayan rightly observe that integrated rural development embraces all the activities of enrichment and betterment of the overall quality of rural life through appropriate development of man power, resources, infrastructural facilities and provisions of minimum needs and livelihood. It has far-reaching socio-economic and political implications for the life of the ruralites.

INTEGRATED RURAL DEVELOPMENT APPROACH

The integrated development approach emphasis is the need of coordinating different agencies under a single management system of essential components (including education) required to get agricultural or rural development moving. The management system may be highly authoritarian credit may be designed to provide an important role for local people in planning, decision making and implementation of the programmers. The main emphasis is on rational development and coordination of all principal factors required for agricultural and rural development. The community development for agricultural India could not achieve the desired impact in increasing agricultural productions. As a solution to this situation the Intensive Agriculture District Programme (IADP) was launched in selected districts. The IADP used the integrated development approach in tackling the problem of rural development.

OBJECTIVES

In this Programme there was more emphasis on the package approach. In ten points included in the programme were:

- Adequate farm credit through strengthened cooperatives.
- Adequate supplies of fertilizers pesticides, improved seeds, implements and other essential production needs through strengthened service cooperatives.
- Price incentives to participating farmers through assured price agreements for rice, wheat and millet.
- Marketing arrangements and services to enable farmers to obtain a full market price for their marketed surplus.
- Intensive educational, technical and farm management assistance made available in every village.
- Participation of all interested farmers in farm planning for increased production.
- Village planning for increased production and village improvement programme by strengthening village organisations and leaderships.
- A public works programme using local labour and development works contributing directly to increased production.
- Analysis and evaluation of the programme from its inception and
- Coordination of all essential resources for maximum speed and effectiveness.

RURAL INFRASTRUCTURE DEVELOPMENT FUND

Rural infrastructure [both physical and institutional] such as irrigation, watershed development, rural electrification, roads, markets, credit institutions, rural literacy, agricultural research and extension etc. together play a key role in determining the agricultural output in India. For instance, irrigation infrastructure increases the land use intensity and cropping intensity, and provides incentives to farmers to use yield increasing inputs, and thus results in higher agricultural output. Rural electrification increases the energisation of pump-sets, which helps to increase the irrigated area using groundwater; the output of crops under groundwater irrigation is always higher than those under canal or tank irrigation, because of its better reliability and controllability. Rural road increase the diffusion of agricultural technology by improving access to markets, enhances more efficient allocation of resources, reduces the transaction costs as well as helps the farmers to realize better input and output prices. Improved road infrastructure also increases the transparent facility through which the rural farm households are able to get better health care, education, and credit facility. Rural-urban linkages are developed through road development, which also helps strengthening the backward and forward linkages in agricultural sector.

A classic study by Bhatia [1999] shows that, Indian states with highest rural infrastructure index [a composite measure for rural electrification, roads, transport, health, irrigation, farm credit, fertilizer, agricultural marketing, research and extension] such as Punjab, Haryana and Tamil Nadu have the highest food grain productivity per hectare and the states with lowest index such as Rajasthan, Bihar and Madhya Pradesh have lowest food grains productivity per hectare; the rural infrastructure explains about 68 per cent of the variability in the yield in different states; and 10 per cent improvement in rural infrastructure index in states with lower score would increase their food grains productivity by about 470 kg per hectare on an average. This study establishes a strong relationship between the level of rural infrastructure development and the level of agricultural output.

Using Indian state-level time-series data for 1957 to 1991, show that states with better initial endowments of physical and human infrastructure [towards the early 1960s] achieved higher rates of agricultural output growth than poorly endowed states; higher initial irrigation, higher initial literacy, and lower initial infant mortality, all contributed to higher long-term growth rates.

Using state level data for 1970-93 in Inida researches studied the relationship between government expenditure on agricultural research and development, irrigation, roads, education, power, soil and water conservation, rural development spending on agricultural growth and rural poverty. The study concludes that improved rural infrastructure and technology have all contribute3d to agricultural growth, but their impacts have varied by settings. Government expenditure on roads and R&D have by far the largest impact on poverty reduction and growth in agricultural productivity. Government spending on education has the third largest impact on rural poverty and productivity growth. Irrigation investment has had only modest impacts on growth in agricultural productivity and rural poverty reduction, even after allowing for trickle-down benefits.

The linkages between the Green Revolution technology package [irrigation, research and extension, improved varieties and fertilizer] and other rural infrastructure and agricultural output/ growth are well established by several researchers at All India level, state level, project/ scheme level, taluka/ sub-district level and village level. Likewise, studies using agro-ecological zones [AEZs] typology also provide further evidence on varied contribution of infrastructure to agricultural output growth in India.

A recent comprehensive study to better understand the linkages between rural infrastructure development and agricultural output using cross-sectional data for 256 districts in India drawn from 13 states at three time points [1970-71, 1980-81 and 1990-91] shows that the districts having value of agricultural output above the average are better placed in terms of rural infrastructure development [irrigation, road, literacy, school facility, rural electrification and fertilizer] than the other districts. NABARD in its annual exercise of preparing district-wise Potential Linked Credit Plans has been sharply focusing on the immediate needs for creating rural infrastructure having direct impact on increasing farm output and the sustainable development of farm sector. In order to supplement the efforts of the State Governments, at NABARD level Union Government has established Rural Infrastructure Development Fund [RIDF] which has yielded rich dividends. Following table exhibits the use of the fund in creating rural infrastructure from 1995-96 to 2005-06.

Commercial banks falling short of achieving priority sector/agricultural lending targets have since 1995-96 till 2005-06 deposited sum of ₹287,499.5 million with NABARD under Rural Infrastructure Development Fund at very reduced interest rate. NABARD has so far disbursed sum of ₹313,373.4 million to support 244,651 projects in various parts of the country. Types of projects supported relate to irrigation development, construction of rural bridges and roads, social sector and power generation etc. Share of irrigation development projects in terms of number was the highest at 36.7 per cent followed by social sector and rural roads, whereas in terms of amount disbursed irrigation development also accounted for as high as 34.3 per cent share followed by rural roads, rural bridge and social sector.

AREAS OF CONCERN

Rising Informal Debt

With the progressive institutionalization of rural credit system through adoption of multi-agency approach farmers' dependence on informal sources of credit sharply declined from 92.8 per cent in 1951 to 36 per cent in 1991. More importantly role of moneylenders [agricultural and professional] declined from 71.6 per cent to 17.1 per cent and that of banks [cooperatives and commercial] increased from 3.5 per cent to 55.3 per cent during the period. However, According to All India Debt and Investment Survey, the share of institutional credit appreciably declined to 57 per cent in 2001 from 64 per cent in 1991. Moreover, debt sourced from moneylenders [the very informal agents the institutionalization of credit was designed to replace] sharply increased in overall share of rural debt from nearly 18 per cent in 1991 to nearly 30 per cent in 2001.

According to recent Survey, a formal institutional credit provision in India now accounts for just 27 per cent of total cultivator debt, and that this reduces to just 20 per cent if data from the five States reporting the highest proportion of formal rural debt are removed. Moreover, nearly 90 per cent of households reporting no debt, either formal or informal are headed by small and marginal farmers. Intriguingly, Andhra Pradesh, the State with the highest concentration of SHGs, MFIs and banks, reports the highest proportion of rural non-institutional debt [nearly 73 per cent] and the highest proportion of rural moneylender debt [nearly 57 per cent] for all the States in India.

Table. Number of Projects and Amount Disbursed under RIDF during 1995-96 to 2005-06

Year	No. of Projects	Amount	Type of Projects	Number [%]	Amount [%]
1995-96	4,168	17,608.7	Irrigation	78,442	146,841.5
1996-97	8,334	23,979.5		[36.7%]	[34.3%]
1997-98	14,346	24,536	Rural Bridge	9,285	47,608.4
1998-99	6,172	24,280.0		(4.3%)	(11.1%)
1999-00	12,254	30,326.6	Rural Roads	43,857	144,935.7
2000-01	43.354	38.568.2		(20.5%)	(33.9%)
2001-02	24,987	37,568.2	Social Sector	67,995	38,718.4
2002-03	21,012	44.403.4		(31.7%)	(9.1%)
2003-04	19,605	33,874.8	Power Sector	717	12,943.7
2004-05	59,979	29,678.1		(0.3%)	(3.0%)
2005-06	30,440	8,070.8	Others	13,915(6.5%)	36,639.1 (8.6%)
Total	**244,651**	**313,373.4**	**Total**	**214,211 (100%)**	**427,686.8 (100%)**

NSSO'S FINDINGS

Findings of the National Sample Survery Organization revealed following.

1. At the All India level estimated number of rural households were 147.90 million of which 60.4 [89.35 million] were farmer households.
2. Of these farmer households 48.60 per cent [43.42 million] were reported to be indebted to either formal or informal or both sources of credit.
3. This implied that 51,4 per cent [45.93 million] farmer households were not indebted at all and 88 per cent of these excluded farmer households were either marginal farmers [less than one hectare] or small farmers [between 1-2 hectares.]
4. The incidence of indebtedness was 60 per cent in four States *viz*, Andhra Pradesh [82 per cent], Tamil Nadu [74.5 per cent], Pubjab [65.4 per cent] and Kerala [64.4 per cent]. However, Incidence of indebtedness was laower in States of Meghalaya [4.1 per cent], Arunchal Pradesh [5.9 per cent], Uttarakhand [7.2 per cent], Mizoram [23.6 per cent], Mnaipur [24.8 per cent] Jammu and Kashmir [31.8 per cent].
5. This indicated that incidence of indebtedness was relatively higher n agriculturally advanced States than that in agriculturally less developed States.

6. Ouit of 43.2 million indebted farmers 54 per cent [23.3 million] were indebted to formal sources.
7. Of the total farmer households [83.95million] coverage to formal sources.
8. More than 50 per cent of the indebted farmer households took loans for capital and current expenditure in farm business. Such loans accounted for 58.4 per cent of the outstanding loans.
9. The extent of farmer households not indebted to formal or informal sources of credit was more in the case of farmers with land holding of less than one hectare [55 per cent] than farmers with land holding of four hectares *and more [33 per cent].

WORLD BANK AND NCAER STUDY

The findings of the World Bank and the National Council of Applied Economic Research under the "Rural Financial Access Survey" conducted in States of Andhra Pradesh and Uttar Pradesh in 2003 also paints a very disheartening picture. The data reveal that

1. Only 21 per cent rural households had access to formal credit.
2. Small and Marginal farmers were in a relatively disadvantaged position as only 11.8 per cent of marginal farmers in Andhra Pradesh and 13.5 per cent in Uttar Pradesh secured loans from banks.
3. The time taken for loan clearance ranged from 24 to 33 weeks and loans were generally collateralized.

According to NSSO, rural poverty declined from 27.1 per cent to 21.1 per cent in 1999-2000 as against urban poverty at 23.6 per cent to 15.1 per cent respectively. This shows that rural areas have still very large number of households Below Poverty Line.

While these shocking finding are engaging the attention of the Government and Reserve Bank and further need immediate comprehensive research, broadly the factors contributing to this development are [i] percentage share of agriculture and allied sectors in the total Plan Outlay of Annual Budgets has sharply declined to below 6.0 during the 6th FYP [1980-85] and onwards from 11.3 and 16.4 in earlier FYPs.

[ii] while total investment in agriculture has been continuously declining to around 1.3 per cent and 2.2 per cent of the GDP, share of public sector investment has also declined from 33 per cent to 17.8 per cent during the period frm 1993-94 to 2004-05. [iii]rural infrastructure as pointed out in Annual District PLPs by NABARD has grossly been inadequate [iv] while commercial banks have financial resources which they have been deploying and their own limitation [v] Cooperative banks being leaders in the field of rural lending are very weak in all respects and are in the process of restructuring and being reapitalised.

RURAL ECONOMY

The Indian economy has been passing through the trajectory of high growth for several years. The overall Gross Domestic Product (GDP) is estimated to grow at 8.4 per cent, with the agriculture and allied sector projected to bounce back with 3.9 per cent growth during 2005-06. The Government has also been consolidating its fiscal position, creating a conducive climate for investment activities. Investment demand in the economy is picking up, reflecting the growing dynamism in the industrial sector.

The exports have also assumed vibrancy. Thus, the Indian economy as a whole is poised for still higher growth in the coming years. The Rural Economy in India is wholly agriculture based and it is of tremendous importance because it has vital supply and demand links with the other Indian industries. Agriculture is the main stay of the Indian economy, as it constitutes the backbone of rural India which inhabitants more than 70 per cent of total Indian population.

The fertility of the soil has augmented the success of agriculture in India. Further, Rural Economy in India has been playing an important role towards the overall economic growth and social growth of India. India has been predominantly an agriculture-based country and it was the only source of livelihood in ancient time. During prehistoric time when there was no currency system the India economy system followed barter system for trading *i.e.* the excess of agricultural produce were exchanged against other items. The agriculture produce and system in India are varied and thus offers a wide agricultural product portfolio.

Today, the rural economy in India and its subsequent productivity growth is predicated to a large extent upon the development of its 700-million strong rural population. The agricultural economy of India is drafted according to the needs of rural India since majority of the population lives in about 600,000 small villages. In India, agriculture accounts for almost 19 per cent of Indian gross domestic products (GDP). The rural section of Indian population is primarily engaged with agriculture, directly or indirectly. The Ministry of Agriculture, the Ministry of Rural Infrastructure, and the Planning Commission of India are the main governing bodies that formulate and implements the policy related to rural economy in India and its subsequent development for the overall growth of the Indian economy.

The main agricultural products that controls the fate of the Rural Economy in India are as follows:-

- *Food Grains*: Rice, Wheat, Pulses, Cereals, Corn, Maize, Rice Bran Extractions, Sorghum, Soy meal, Suji, Parmal, Lentils, Jowar, Bajra, Chick pea
- *Fruits and Nuts*: Cashew Kernels, Cashew Nut, Cashews, Almonds, Roasted Dry Fruits, Peanuts, Groundnut, Walnut Kernels, Walnuts, Indian Peanuts, HPS Groundnuts

- *Fruits*: Bananas, Beans, Cherry, Cucumbers, Dried Fruits, Dried Truffles, Carrots, Lemon, Mandarins, Mango steens, Meslin, Shallots, Apples, Asparagus, Grapes, Oranges, Gherkins, Turnips, Oranges, Papaya, Pineapple
- *Vegetables*: Potatoes, Bitter gourd, Stripe Gourd, Pumpkin, cauliflower, Cabbage, Tomato, Onion, Green Pepper, Drum Sticks, Lady's finger, Banana, Papaya, Spinach, Cucumber, Mushroom, Mushroom Spawn, Radiata
- *Seeds, Buds, Plantation and Related Products*: Basil Seed, Cumin seeds, Dill Seed, Buds, Celery Seed, Hybrid Seeds, Sesame Seeds, Sesbania Seed, Sunflower Seeds, Mustard Seeds, Oil Seeds, Plant Products, Plantation, Plants, Psyllium Seed, Fennel Seed, Fenugreek Seed, Herb Seeds, Tamarind Seed, Vegetable Seeds
- *Spices*: Black Pepper, Chilli Powder, Chillies, Cinnamon, Cloves, Coriander Powder, Cumin, Curry Powders, Dry Ginger, Dry Red Chilly, Cardamom, Anise, Salt, Onion Powder, Pepper, Fenugreek, Clove, Ginger, Turmeric, Turmeric Powder
- *Tea and Coffee:* Black Tea, Coffee, Coffee Beans, Darjeeling Teas, Assam Teas, Instant Coffee, Leaf Coffee, Leaf Tea, Packaged Tea, Green Tea, CTC Teas
- *Tobacco and Tobacco Products*: Beedi, Betel nut Leaves, Betel nut, Bidi Leaves, Chewing Tobacco, Cigarettes, Arecanut, Jarda, Scented Tobacco, Smoking Tobbacco, Snuff, Opium, Pan, Chatni, Pan Masala, Gutkazarda, Zafrani Zarda
- Cotton, Rubber, Jute etc.

No. The uneven growth will never help India to grow faster or help achieving the projected results. I support the PURA model of President A P J Abdul Kalam which calls for rural development and uplift of BPL with a social cause. Finance is still the biggest problem for development of rural economy despite it being innovative. People in the rural areas have no money and often tend to go for high-cost borrowings. No venture capitalists or funders have ever come forward to help those community with social obligations in mind.

Who lends the money to those poor people without collateral securities despite having the entrepreneurial capabilities, innovativeness, creativeness and hard working abilities? It is a pity to say that in few districts where I visited, villagers happened to be bonded labourers to big money launderers due to high cost borrowings which has never been a easy task to repay. The development of the Indian Rural Economy can be credited to the liberal policy of the Ministry of Rural Development, Government of India and the Planning Commission of India.

India is still an agriculture-based country and the agrarian sector contributes substantially to the GDP of India.

Around seventy per cent of the Indian population still depends on agriculture and allied areas for livelihood.

- Glimpses of Rural Economy of India
- A target of ₹ 225,000 crores for farm credit has been set for the financial year 2007-2008.
- 50 lakh new farmers have been brought under the banking system.
- Agricultural Insurance to facilitate agricultural loans to the farmer.
- Allocation for the Rural Infrastructure Development Fund to be increased substantially.
- In the financial year 2006-07, 35 projects were successfully completed.
- Additional irrigation of 900,000 hectares has been targeted in the financial year 2007 - 2008.
- For better farm yields modern farming techniques has been set up.
- Direct disbursement of subsidy to rural Indian farmers has been arranged through a pilot programme.

URBANIZATION AND RURAL ECONOMY

One should avoid following the straight jacketed approach followed by our smartest of all political leaders to comment on such issues. A 'Neta' (Perhaps we need to change the meaning of this word in Hindi dictionaries now) vouching for rural votes will say 'No' and someone vouching for urban votes will say 'Yes'.

An interesting and intriguing incident has been the downfall of BJP government, a government riding high on 'India Shining' campaign. The downfall has been associated with observations that BJP was concentrated on Urban India only. The truth of the analysis is evident form the fact that the campaign was in worded in English was pointed towards BJP's urban India approach. Ahem!

The Congress therefore followed their slogan as 'Aam Aadmi ki sarkar', worded in Hindi and worded for rural people. They made their huge plans {I have deliberately used the word 'Plans'} to associate with the rural people. Such developments may lead to conclude "Yes - urbanization has hindered the growth of rural people". In fact, I have also been to an extent convinced with this philosophy though I have thought that why concentrate on one side, why cannot both sides develop simultaneously.

1. A study of consumption in last 26 years reveals that an increase in Urban Household consumption of ₹ 100 leads to an increase of ₹ 39 in the rural household income. The driver of such increase is non-farm sector of rural economy such as manufacturing, construction and trade, hotels and restaurants.
2. During the last decade, the rural economy is estimated to have grown by 7.3 per cent as compared to 5.4 per cent of urban economy.

3. The rural economy is nearly as big as the urban. In 2000, the rural economy accounted for 49 per cent of the India's GDP.
4. Share of agriculture in Rural economy has dropped from 72 per cent in 1970s to 64 per cent in 1980s to 51 per cent in 2000
5. The rural-urban migration has fallen from 6.5 per cent in 1981 to 2.8 per cent in 2001.

The indications pointed by each point noted above leads to refute a number of myths such as rural people are suffering due to urbanisation; there is an India – C waiting to shine and many more - an encouraging realization!!!!

The major reason for this change, as noted by eminent researcher and economists is the growing and strengthening integration of the rural economy with the urban economy. Granted that logistics and supply chain for the route is no less than a shame for the progress we hope to achieve, yet the hope does exist. Perhaps an integration of the rural supply chains with the urban ones, steered by the boom in organised retail would provide the impetus to pass on the benefits lower down the pyramid. Just one problem though – Who will help Mayawati understand on the recent Reliance Fresh issues? Anyone ready to bell the cat?

Winds of Growth

There may finally be a silver lining to the gloomy economic picture prevailing in the country. Last week, there were economic forecasts from three important quarters that saw a better future for the country's economy in the current year. The Centre for Monitoring Indian Economy (CMIE) forecast a 6.3 per cent growth in real GDP in the current financial year against 5.2 per cent growth in GDP in the last fiscal.

Its forecast was quickly followed by estimates from the Reserve Bank of India (RBI) which saw the economy growing at over 6.5 per cent in FY2001-2002 and then the finance minister stated that he saw the economy turning around by the end of the calender year. In a nutshell, the picture for Indian economy appears to be brightening up as we go forward into the year.

However, the most remarkable feature of this improving economic outlook is that the growth is projected to come almost entirely from the agriculture sector. CMIE has forecast that growth in the agriculture production during the current year would be a whopping 9 per cent over the previous year. This would be almost the highest in the last seven years and comes after two consecutive years of shrinkage in agriculture sector.

Impact on Rural Economy

After having grown at over seven per cent annually during 1994 and 1997, India's GDP growth slowed down substantially because of the sharp fall in agricultural production and income. After an impressive 8.2 per cent rise in production in 1998-99, the pace of growth in the farm sector turned negative with output shrinking by 1.5 per cent in FY2000 and 4.5 per cent in FY2001.

This meant there was less disposable income generated in the rural areas and hence the demand pull from vast majority of population was absent. The last two years were marked by a drought in states like Gujarat, Maharashtra and Rajasthan which contribute significantly to domestic production and also account for substantial amount of consumer spending. With a pick up in income in these areas, the demand for goods and services is expected to pick up this year and that should contribute to the over all growth in economy.

Impact on Industry

Increased income in farm sector impacts the entire economy, however it has an almost immediate impact on some sectors like consumer durables and non-durables, tractors and motorcycles. There is also an increased demand for cement and steel from the resurgent housing sector. Heavy commercial vehicles too attract buying as transportation of goods picks up across the country and demand for services too is higher.

Therefore, the relationship between agricultural income and economic growth is almost direct. We expect FMCG companies, tractor manufacturers and motorcycle makers to feel an immediate pick up in demand once the kharif crop is harvested. This sentiment has already been reflected in the stock markets with the FMCG leader, Hindustan Lever attracting huge amount of buying by fund managers in expectation of a large top line growth this year.

We might also see a turnaround in the subdued sentiment in industries such as televisions, washing machines and refrigerators which have seen a fall in sales due to sluggish rural demand over the past two years. Higher demand for goods and services in rural areas necessitates increased movement of goods and hence a pick up in demand for commercial vehicles. This means increased demand in almost all sectors such as steel and engineering. Therefore, if the agriculture sector does grow at the projected 9 per cent this year, economy would receive a big boost by the end of the year.

Growth in Industry

The growth in industry suffers from poor demand in consumption as well as investments. Due to a decline in farm income over the past two years, demand from rural areas was poor and as result of this investment sentiment remains sluggish too. The situation can only reverse if consumption rises giving a boost to investment sentiment. However, as the impact of increased income in farm sector would be felt only from the end of the year, the growth in industrial production in expected to remain this year.

CMIE has projected that the growth in industrial production this year would be nearly 4.5 per cent, down from 5 per cent in the last financial year and the lowest level since 1998-99. The CMIE forecast notes that the index of industrial production (IIP) registered a growth of 5 per cent last year and 6.6 per cent in 1999-2000. While in April 2001 industrial production grew only 2.7 per cent and in May it was even lower at 1.9 per cent, the overall growth may be better as the impact of improved demand is felt later in the year. Morgan Stanley Dean Witter too has projected that the industrial activity will pick up in the second half of this calendar year and the IIP should be between 4 and 5 per cent for the year.

Gains from Rains

According to the CMIE study, the 2001 south west monsoon has been fairly widespread and intensive across most parts of the country. Between June 1 and June 27, 2001, as many as 29 out of the 35 meteorological sub-divisions in the country received excess to normal rains, covering almost 90 per cent of the gross cropped area. Out of this 75 per cent of the area received excess rains.

In comparison, in June 2000 only 72 per cent of the cropped area in 26 meteorological sub-divisions had received excess rains, the CMIE report states. Thus rains have not only been good they have also been evenly distributed leading to prospects of widespread growth. Rains have been particularly good for Eastern and Western UP, Haryana and Punjab, raising hopes of a huge demand rise in these states early net year. The only areas that have received deficient rainfall so far include Rayalseema in Andhra Pradesh, interiors of Karnataka and some parts of Tamil Nadu. Early and good rains have enthused farmers to go for kharif sowing operations ahead of the normal schedule. The CMIE report says that it expects kharif crop to be much better this year than the harvest of 2000.

Stocks to Watch

As we have stated earlier, the direct beneficiary of a surge in rural demand would be companies in the FMCG sector, like Hindustan Lever. HLL has seen a sluggish topline growth over the pat two years largely because of a slowdown in demand from rural areas. The company can be expected to capitalise heavily on a revival in farm income. The markets have already anticipated this and last week several prominent funds were buying into the counter. Infact, Hindustan Lever was one of the biggest gainers in the stock market index last week. Others that could gain too include Nirma, Colgate Palmolive, Britannia Industries and Tata Tea.

The other gainers could be tractor majors who have faced a sharp slump in demand over the past two years. The decline in farm income had forced a big slump in tractor sales. Tractors sales are almost first to be impacted by a change in farm income. We expect that tractor majors such as Punjab Tractors and Mahindra and Mahindra would be biggest beneficiaries of a look up in the prospects. Both the stocks, particularly, Mahindra and Mahindra, has taken a big hit in valuations due to the fall in sales. Both the companies are fundamentally sound and have very good management.

We could see a major re-rating of the industry in the coming months. Investors could watch out for these stocks. E also expect motorcycle sales to pick up and companies Hero Honda Motors could be the biggest gainers. While other two-wheeler makers should also see a pick up in demand, Hero Honda can outperform the market by a long margin. Other manufacturers of consumer durables like colour televisions, refrigerators and washing machines could also see a surge in demand driven by consumption in rural economy. Manufacturers such as Electrolux Kelvinator, Whirlpool and Voltas could see demand rising for their products. Electrolux and Whirlpool could be particularly fancied due to their large capacities and strong brand presnce.

A surge in rural economy would also mean more transportation needs, increased housing and larger demand for services. CMIE projects the growth in services at 7 per cent in the current year. We also expect commercial vehicle makers like Telco and Ashok Leyland to gain. Cement and steel could also see increased demand from a pick up in housing activity.

Overall, we may say that the worst may soon be over for the economy and things could begin to look much better from the second half of the year. Rural India is nothing but agriculture; and since agriculture has been growing at a mere 1.9 per cent since 1995-96, so is the rural economy. Therefore, per capita rural income has fallen in the recent past. "We have a dual economic structure in which a 1.9 per cent growth economy supports more than 60 per cent of the population, and a 7.3 per cent growth economy supports the remaining 40 per cent".

The rural-urban chasm is not only deep but also "has grown substantially over the past few years". For cell phones, other durables, consumer goods and services, penetrating the rural market will be limited by poverty and lack of growth, and that "companies might find themselves reaching saturation point much sooner than expected."

This gives a misleading picture of the economy, and would perhaps have been understandable if it had been a populist politician that had equated the rural economy with agriculture to say that two-third of India's population live on only 22 per cent of the country's income, while a third live in cities and lord over 78 per cent of the GDP.

Since April last year, we have constructed what is probably the most comprehensive picture of India's rural economy—a digitised database of economic, demographic, consumption data that has been extracted and harmonised across various sources, goes back over two decades, down to 530 districts. All the evidence that we have collected, processed and analysed tells us that rural is much more than agriculture. This is true not just for the present, but has been so for quite some time. In 1993-94, the Central Statistical Organisation conducted its last rural-urban classification of India's net domestic product (NDP, which is GDP minus depreciation).

It showed that rural India accounted for 54 per cent of the country's NDP, while agriculture contributed to 31 per cent of India's GDP. So, even if one were to account for depreciation, the rural economy of 1993-94 was quite a bit more than just agriculture, forestry and fishing. The share of rural economy is more or less the same seven years later. Our analysis shows that in 2000-01, out of India's NDP of ₹ 1,062,400 crore (₹ 10,624 billion) at constant 1993-94 prices, the share of rural India was 52 per cent.

This is how rural NDP played out in 2000-01: agriculture accounted for 46 per cent; industry took up another 21 per cent; and services 33 per cent. Between 1993-94 and 2000-01, rural NDP at constant prices grew at an average of 6.2 per cent per year. Since agriculture grew at around 2 per cent during this period, clearly the rural economy has been much more than just agriculture. There is a lot of other evidence as well that demonstrates the growth of non-agricultural activities throughout rural India. According to the Annual Survey of Industries, even in 1993-94, rural India accounted for 29 per cent of the country's organised manufacturing units; 30 per cent of its employees; 32 per cent of its output; and 30 per cent of its net value added. In 2000-01, over a rising base, rural India could speak of 36 per cent of organised manufacturing establishments, 38 per cent of its employees, 43 per cent of output; and 41 per cent of net value added.

Consider also the Census of India. In 1991, 30.6 per cent of rural households had permanent (or "pucca") houses. By 2001, this had risen to 41 per cent, over a base that was growing at 1.7 per cent a year. Between 1991 and 2001, households using LPG for cooking rose from 1 per cent to almost 6 per cent, with Himachal Pradesh leading at 22 per cent. In 2001, almost a fifth of rural households owned TV sets, and the rural regions of 10 states were significantly above the national average.

Between 1991 and 2001, the percentage of rural households with electricity connections rose from 30 per cent to 43.5 per cent and 11 states ranked well over the national rural average. In 2001, over 30 per cent of rural households kept their funds in banks or postal savings accounts. All this doesn't square up with the age-old image of rural India — that of highly indebted, underfed peasants ploughing handkerchief-sized fields under the blazing heat of the mid-day sun. That may be still be partly true of agriculture; but not of the rural economy. We won't inundate you with more evidence. Instead, let's make three points.

One, there's more to rural than just agriculture; it has a thriving and growing manufacturing and services sector. Two, between 1993-94 and 2000-

2001 per capita rural income grew at the same pace as urban income. The reason why total urban income was greater has much to do with higher population growth. Three, there is considerable pent-up demand for goods as well as services such as education, telecom, medical treatment and financial products.

Those in the top quartile of rural India have been discontinuously higher spenders than the average, spending at least ₹ 180,000 crore (₹ 1,800 billion) — NSS, 55th round — in 1999-2000, with expenditure patterns that are pretty similar to urban India. Consider this: services can't constitute 52 per cent of GDP on the rump of only the urban populace.

RECONSTRUCTION OF THE RURAL ECONOMY

Skill and enterprise will take them part of the journey. But they cannot bring back the lost prosperity unless the entire economy of the province, now severely deficit in several directions, is placed on stable foundations. In any programme of reconstruction, means of irrigation take the first place. Four-fifths of the new allottees had holdings even in West Punjab in the lowest grade of ten standard acres and less.

At least a third of the evacuee land in East Punjab and Pepsu has gone to the small rural traders from the predominantly Muslim districts of West Punjab. Many of them may take to the land, but theirs will continue to be an impoverished economy, for the call on their traditional skills cannot but be meagre. In virtue of the land held by them they have obtained land now, and this will give each of them a home and a location, but not as a general rule an adequate living.

Individuals from this group of settlers need assistance and encouragement to leave their families at home and to venture out into other parts of the country, where their intelligence and resourcefulness will enable them to build a new composite way of life intertwined with their interests in their own province. In this way they can re-establish themselves. Tenants from West Punjab as well as those who cultivated for large Muslim holders in East Punjab present another important problem of reconstruction.

Altogether, reduced holdings and poorer lands, a fall in the number of actual workers on the soil, insufficient irrigation facilities, slender capital resources, and the rise of tenant interests, combine to produce a picture of increasing economic pressure, which the land may not long sustain. If the stresses are not to overwhelm the social economy itseif, the end of the resettlement operations should be followed by a period of bold administrative action, reform in the management of land, and investment of capital on a scale sufficient to produce results. The migration has brought to

East Punjab a peasantry uncommonly rich in experience and progressive in outlook, whose record of achievement over sixty years of colonization is second to none in the world. In this and in the spirit of enterprise, which raised the western districts of the Punjab to the highest level of rural prosperity ever, reached in the long history of India lies perhaps the best hope of the future.

The East Punjab Government propose to replace the present system of temporary allotments of evacuee lands by a new system of allotments which will take account of the holdings of evacuees in West Punjab. The new allotments will not confer rights of ownership or permanent occupancy, but the possession of allottees will be maintained. Claims of allottees will be dealt with in accordance with decisions reached eventually regarding the treatment of evacuee property.

In the new scheme of allotments, land will be allotted only to those who, In West Punjab, were owners, occupancy tenants under the Punjab Tenancy Act, and tenants under the Colonization of Government Lands Act and to certain other classes of grantees and holders of land in West Punjab to be of equivalent areas, while in the case of larger holders there will be graded specified by Government. It is proposed to give to small holders allotments cuts.

The definition of the " Small Holders " and the details of the graded cuts will be determined when detailed information regarding the available areas in East Punjab and the East Punjab States, the areas held by the popu-lation to be settled in East Punjab and the East Punjab States, and other relevant information becomes available. It is intended to complete the new system of allotments in East Punjab and the East Punjab States, not later than the 31st May, 1948. Governments are, however, anxious to introduce the new scheme as early as may be feasible and steps to this end will be taken at once.

Arrangements for collecting complete information regarding the land available for allotment in East Punjab and the East Punjab States and the land abandoned by individual evacuees will be taken in hand without delay and it is hoped also to make arranagements on a reciprocal basis to secure Information from records of rights in West Punjab. To ensure accurate information an Ordinance will shortly be promulgated prescribing punishment lor false information regarding claims to land and action by way of forfeiture and otherwise in respect of allotments taken on false information.

Claims to land will be invited on a form to be prescribed by Government. Until the new system of allotments can be introduced, the present system of allotments will continue and allotments made to the present holders will be maintained subject to a complete scrutiny of existing allotments, cancel-lation of unauthorised and excessive allotments, dispossession from illicit occupation and such other adjustments as may be necessary Including ad-justments in the unit of allotment decided upon by Government. Government desires that kharif crops including sugar-cane and cotton should be sown to the maximum extent.

Accordingly they wish to assure the present allottees that in the event of their being otherwise dispossessed before the kharif crops have been harvested. Government will make arrange-ments for compensation after proper verification, through sharing of the crop or in some other appropriate manner. 7th February, 1948.

LAND CLAIMS PROCEDURE

The purpose of this chapter is to outline in some detail the steps taken and the instructions laid down from time to time in working on land claim' applications submitted by about half a million individuals. This description is given for two reasons. For several years it will be necessary for revenue officials to refer to papers con-nected with the allotment of land to displaced persons and to check whether the entries were according to the instructions and also, in some particulars, what the precise object of the various entries was. Secondly, the circumstances under which work on land claims was done during 1948 and 1949 imposed certain difficulties.

Not all the difficul-ties could be anticipated and, as the work proceeded, new problems arose. The experience gained in dealing with large numbers of claims to property and the errors which came to light in the course of this work should be recorded, so that when similar work is under-taken in other fields, mistakes and omissions can be avoided. It is possible in retrospect to distinguish between features, which arose from the nature of the task handled, and those, which were due to local or particular factors.

Inviting Land Claims

In the press note, which was issued on the 7th February, 1948 with the concurrence of the East Punjab States and the Government of India, the East Punjab Government announced its intention to invite claims to land abandoned by displaced persons. The East Punjab Refugee (Registration of Land Claims) Ordinance, 1948 was thereupon promulgated and corresponding legislation was introduced by the States of Patiala, Kapurthala. Nabha, Jind and Faridkot. The ordi-nance provided definitions of expressions such as "claim", "land", "land-holder", "refugee" and "registering officer". Claims were to be invited under the Ordinance from refugee landholders in respect of land situated in West Punjab, N.W.F.P., Sind, Baluchistan and States adjacent to these provinces, which had acceded to the Dominion of Pakistan, in other words, from displaced landholders from Western Pakistan.

The expression, "refugee" was defined in the Ordinance as:

- "A landholder in the territories now comprised in the Provinces of West Punjab, N.W.F.P., Sind or Baluchistan or in any State adjacent to any of the aforesaid Provinces and acceding to the Dominion of Pakistan, who has since the 1st day of March, 1947, abandoned or been made to abandon his land in the said territories on account of civil disturbances, or the fear of such disturbances, or the partition of the country."

This definition was amended by the legislature before passing the East Punjab Refugees (Registration of Land Claims) Act. 1948 to mean a—"landholder in the territories now comprised in the Province of West Punjab, or who or whose ancestor migrated as a colonist from the Punjab since 1901 to the Provinces of North-West Frontier Province, Sind or Baluchistan or to any State adja-cent to any of the aforesaid Provinces and acceding to the Dominion of Pakistan, and who has since the 1st day of March, 1947, abandoned or been made to abandon his land in the said territories on account of civil disturbances, or the fear of such disturbances, or the partition of the country." On the 7th April, 1948 the relative responsibilities of the Central and the Provincial Governments for the rehabilitation of dis-placed persons were considered in the Joint rehabilitation Board, in which both Governments were represented. *The record of pro-ceedings sets out the discussion and the decision in respect of settle-ment on evacuee land:*

> "After the East Punjab Government have made up their mind in re-gard to the refugees they are going to rehabilitate in the East Punjab and East Punjab States, the rehabilitation of the rest in the States of Bikaner, Bharatpur and Alwar will be the responsibility of the Centre. After some discussion, it was decided that the East Punjab Government will undertake the responsibility of rehabilitation in East Punjab and East Punjab States, of Sind. N.W.F.P., Bahawalpur and Baluchistan refugees who are of Punjabi extraction- Other refugees from Bahawalpur will be rehabilitated in Bikaner and else-where. Refugees from Sind, N.W.F.P. and Baluchistan who are not of Punjabi extraction will be rehabilitated outside East Punjab and East Punjab States, *e.g.*, Bharatpur, Alwar etc."

Penalties

No authentic records being available, it was felt that if severe penalties were provided, dishonesty in the submission of claims could be greatly reduced. The Ordinance provided rigorous imprisonment upto five years or fine upto ₹ 5000 or both as penalties for persons submitting false claims or a public servant abetting such an offence-In addition to these penalties, Deputy Commissioners were authorised to disqualify from allotment by an order passed in writing any person who has submitted a false claim and to cancel, either in whole or in part, any allotment which may have been made on the basis of a false claim. An appeal from such an order lies within thirty days to the Financial Commissioner whose decision is final and conclusive and cannot be called in question in any court.

The Claim Form

By rules made under the Ordinance, the East Punjab Govern-ment prescribed a form on which claims for land were to be submitted. The East

Punjab Government's form was used also in the States. The form was sold at the price of one anna. It was printed in Urdu, Punjabi and English. It provided for an affidavit by the applicant, signature or thumb-impression by one witness and attestation by a competent authority. The rules under the Ordinance prescribed competent authorities for the purpose of attest-ing affidavits on the land claim application.

Lacuna In the Form

For every district in which land was abandoned by a dis-placed person, one claim form was to be filled. Details of holdings in different villages of the same district were to be entered on one form. Subsequently, in actual work, since the particulars of land held by a person had to be verified and completed village by village, supplemen-tary land claim forms were prepared in the Land Claims Office.

Copying of extracts from claims which were frequently incomplete or badly written on such an extensive scale led to mistakes in supplemen-tary forms. Again, when it became necessary to consolidate into a single account, land held by an individual in different villages in more than one district, it was a serious handicap to have begun with claim forms on a district basis. Experience showed that the right course would have been to have obtained a separate form for each single village in which an individual held land along with a covering form giving particulars of all villages together, whether situated in one district or in several. The form did not specially provide space and directions for entering an applicant's address. This omission was soon noticed and the necessary instructions were issued to registering officers. Direc-tions to applicants for intimating changes in their addresses should also have been given. A column in the form asked for particulars of village, tehsil and district of origin from applicant who was colonists from different districts. The word "colonist" was not defined.

Gradually, in the course of land claims work, the word has come ⁱo mean not one necessarily who goes out from a particular district and "colonizes" land, but one who belongs to a particular district, whether of East Punjab or of West Punjab, who held land in another district. Since the claims of colonies from West Punjab were to be consolidated with their West Punjab districts and the claims of colonists from East Pun-jab and the States were to be sorted out for settlement in their parent districts, the column came to assume increasing importance. Incomplete information in this column led later to many difficulties in con-solidating individual accounts.

Arrangements for Registration

The Registration of Land Claims Ordinance provided for "registering officers," a term which included revenue officers within their jurisdiction, a Land Claims Officer at the central office and spe-cially appointed officials known as Assistant Land Claims Officers. Claims applications were to be presented under the rules to registering officers either in person or through recognised agents or they were to be sent by registered post. In the case of minors, applications had to be submitted by their next friends or guardians. An application sub-mitted by post unaccompanied by an affidavit not attested by a compe-tent authority was not to be entertained.

Arrangements for registration were made at the offices of tehsils and sub-tehsils throughout East Punjab and East Punjab States. Each tehsil carried its own classification number. A receipt was given for every claim received. Although the period 10th March, to the 31st March, 1948 was prescribed as the period for the registeration of land claims, the date was extended upto the 10th April, and even later small numbers of claims continued to arrive by post.

The work of registration was conducted satisfactorily. Nevertheless, it was felt that if more time had been given and claims had been written by trained hands there would have been a greater measure of accuracy.

Work in the Land Claims Office

The press note of the 7th February, 1948 had announced the intention of Government to complete the new system of allotment of land not later than the 31st May, 1948, but Government expressed its anxiety to introduce the new scheme as early as might be feasible and warning was given that the cultivation of the kharif crops including sugar-cane and cotton should not be allowed to suffer. Although not in theory, in actual practice this announcement reduced the period available for work in the central office to less than a month.

During the period available claims were tabulated at much pressure. Neces-sarily, the areas claimed to have been abandoned were included in the tabulation at their face value. The results of the tabulation left a general impression that there had been a certain degree of exaggera-tion in the claims and a number who did not hold land had claimed to be landholders. On the 14th May, 1948, Government felt bound to announce that without further steps for the verification of areas said to have been abandoned, the new scheme of land allotment announced in the press communique of the 7th February, 1948, would not be launched.

Verification of land Claims

At this stage there was no assurance that revenue records would be exchanged between the two Dominions. Correspondence on the subject had been inconclusive. There was a deep desire every-where to introduce a scheme of quasi-permanent allotment. It was decided to arrange for oral verification of claims. Verification took place at tehsils and sub-tehsils in East Punjab and East Punjab States between the 17th August, 1948, and the end of October, 1948. Centres were fixed at which the claims of individual villages of Western

Pakis-tan were verified. As a rule, a village was named against a particular centre if the largest number of claims of that village had been register-ed there. Brochures setting out the verification programmes in detail from the aspect of West Punjab districts as well as that of individual districts in East Punjab and East Punjab States were published. Addi-tional staff was recruited for the purpose and for the best part of two and a half months the energies of the revenue administration were employed on verification. For the first time an attempt was made to draw up lists of villages abandoned in Pakistan.

Without knowledge of hadbast numbers, following in many instances wrong names given by applicants, the lists contained errors, but these were gradually reduced. A form known as the parcha tasdiq was devised for recording the results of the verification. Verifying Officers were directed to read out to persons from any West Punjab village which was under verifi-cation the names of claimants as given in the claims and to ask lambardars and other persons present if they could give information concern-ing the area, the kind of soil or the nature of rights held by each individual in their village.

After clearing discrepancies as far as possible, Verifying Officers were to record in the parcha tasdiq their conclusions about the area, the kind of soil and the nature of rights possessed by each claimant.

In support of a claim, proof was to be considered in the following order of precedence:

- Entries in a jamabandi or other revenue record; or
- Entries and references in any registered document;
- Entries or references in other documents of unquestionable genuineness; and
- Oral evidence of reliable persons present at the verification.

Verifying Officers were also to record in the parcha tasdiq against each claimant whether he was personally present at the verification, whether he produced any documentary evidence, (if so. giving hrief description), and if a claimant was serving in the Defence Services, whether any relative had assisted in the verification of his claim. The assistance of non-officials was also sought in full measure. For displaced landholders residing outside East Punjab.

East Punjab States or Delhi, as well as for persons serving in the Defence Forces, personal attendance at verification was not suggested.

They were requested to give certain particulars and, among these, to answer the following questions:—

Do you want your allotment of land ?

- According to district, tehsil and residence of Pakistan ? or
- According to tehsil or district of origin ? or
- Along with landholders of one of the villages in which land was held. If so, name the village ? or
- According to the district and tehsil of present temporary allotment; or

- According to the village of present temporary allotment ? or
- In any other manner, which may be stated.

These questions were also included in the parcha tasdiq. The pre-ferences indicated by individuals were noted and considered later. But to an extraordinary degree applications giving new preferences or preferences stated with reference to particular villages poured in when the work of aIlotment was actually begun.

Where the object of invit-ing claims is to distribute any form of property, it is necessary to evolve In advance a suitable procedure for indication of wishes and preferences, which should then be treated as firm without repeated opportu-nity or permission to change; or to evolve a procedure which makes individual preferences largely unnecessary. The parcha tasdiq record proved on the whole a useful source of information in later work.

Exchange of Revenue Records

On the 1st July, 1948 arrangements were made between the West Punjab and the East Punjab Governments for preparation of copies of revenue records with a view to mutual exchange. Public opinion in the province, while appreciating the importance of exchange of records, was in favour of making such arrangements as would facilitate progress towards quasi-permanent allotment without being wholly dependent upon records which might be received in exchange.

The exchange of copies of revenue records between the two Govern-ments began on the 22nd November, 1948 and about two-thirds of the records due were received by the end of January. 1949. Thereafter, copies of jamabandis continued to be received at intervals in smaller numbers.

Analysis and tabulation of claims on the basis of the original Claim applications and the parcha tasdiq began in the '/curth week of November. 1948. In the first instance, as jamabandis were being received in driblets and it was not certain when the exchange would be completed, the analysis and tabulation of claims was carried out on the basis of material already available without recourse to details of individual holdings as given in jamabandis. The circumstances in which the work was done dictated the procedure which was adopted. Under other circumstances, work on individual claims may have been deferred until all the jamabandis were available, or all the effort might have been given to the preparation of accounts from jamabandis, the claims being considered later.

It was felt, however, that from the pre-liminary work on claims and the parcha tasdiq, it was possible and necessary to obtain a picture of the problem of resettlement as a whole, so that the main lines of policy could be drawn up. The desire to com-plete the quasi-permanent allotment by the end of May, 1949 hastened work on whatever material was available. The procedure followed was, therefore, to draw material from the claims and the parcha tasdiq, check area totals for villages of each tehsil whose jamabandis had been received by about the middle of January, 1949, apply certain correction factors and arrive at approximate figures of area abandoned in each tehsil and district of West Punjab.

Thus, there was a good deal of work connected with analysis and tabulation of claims which had to be done twice over, once before claims were verified against individual jambandi entries and, on the second occasion, after such verifications had taken place. Nevertheless the size of the problem and the policy issues on which decisions of Governments were called for became apparent six months earlier than they would have otherwise done. This led to clear and timely decisions which stood '" firm later in circumstances propitious to fundamental change.

THE PARCHA CLAIM

A form known as the parcha claim was devised in November, 1948 for extracting all information relevant to each individual's hold-ing and for working out various steps leading to the assessment and valuation of his total claim, and to the area due to him for allotment, and for recording the final orders of allotment. The parcha claim form is by far the most important document in the entire land resettlement operation and grasp of its details is essential. After its introduction most of the work centred upon its various columns. The parcha claim is divided into four parts. The first part, which may be described as preliminary, sets out general particulars such as the registration number of claim, name, father's name and caste, address, place of residence in Pakistan, details of origin and temporary allotment, wishes in the matter of allotment, details of co-sharers in the khewat, the nature of oral verification, if any, in the case of a landholder from outside West Punjab whether he is of Punjabi or of non-Punjabi extraction and finally, names of vil-lages in which the claimant held land.

The second part of the parcha claim comprises columns 1 to 12 and summarises the information given in' the original claim, in the parcha tasdiq and in other documents which may have been furnished by an individual with his claim. The second part thus ends with a find-ing concerning each person's area and rights upto the stage of oral verification. The third part of the parcha claim comprises columns 13 to 26. Columns 13 to 20 state the rights and details of area etc.

According to the jamabandi, if any received from the West Punjab Government. In columns 21 to 24 is entered the area abandoned by a person, as finally assessed on the basis of all the evidence available, against rights shown in columns 15 and 16. The extent of land, the classes of land and the rights abandoned by an individual being known, the next step is to value his claim. The value against each item in his claim is shown in column 25 of the third part of the parcha claim.

The fourth part of the parcha claim serves four purposes. It provides first a break-up of the claim of an individual according to different classes of land. For convenience of tabulation, seven cate-gories of land are adopted; namely, perennial nehri, other nehri, chahi and abi, barani, sailab, banjar jadid and qadim, and ghair mumkin.

Secondly, it has space for adding up the area abandoned by a person in different villages so as to give his total claim, there being a separate parcha claim in respect of each separate village in which land is held by an individual- In the third place, the total claim being stated in terms of standard acres and units, space is provided for indicating the net allotment due to an individual after application of cut- Finally, the particulars of the village and tehsil in which land is allotted in East Punjab or in the Patiala and East Punjab States Union is shown in this part of the parcha claim.

The Parcha Claim Number

Reference has been made earlier to the registration number carried by each claim based on the centre at which the claim has been registered. For facility of work it became necessary to evolve a new notation. Every parcha claim carries its own index number. For instance a parcha claim numbered JG 1|88|55 would mean that the claimant concerned is listed as No. 55 in the claimants' list of village hadbast No. 88 of tehsil Jhang, or a parcha claim numbered ML 7|435| EB25 would mean that the claimant concerned is listed as No. 25 in the village list of Chak 435|EB of tehsil Vehari of Multan district.

The first part of the parcha claim number indicates the tehsil, the second part the serial number of the village and the third part the serial number of the claimant in the West Punjab village list of claim-ants. It is necessary to have ready reference lists which would give against individual registra-tion numbers of claims according to centres of registration, the rele-vant parcha claim numbers.

The preparation of this directory is sche-duled to be undertaken after allotments have been completed. With-out such a directory it is necessary to know the name of the village and the tehsil in which an individual's land is situated before his claim can be located and other particulars ascertained.

The First Part of the Parcha Claim

A number of items in the first part of the parcha claim explain themselves, but a few require elucidation. The blank spaces at the head of the first part are for purposes of categorisation. Thus, parcha claims of defence personnel carried the letter ' D ' and of ex-defence personnel, the letters 'ED' wherever information was avail-able. Similarly, colonists would be linked with their districts of origin by means of descriptions such as C|JL, C|SL, C\RP, and indicating colonists of Jullundur, Sialkot and Rawalpindi respectively.

Categories of Verification

The nature of the verification to which a claim has been subjected is indicated briefly against the eighth item in the first part of the parcha claim.

Seven categories of verification were drawn up:

- In the presence of a claimant along with documentary evidence;
- In the absence of a claimant, but with documentary evidence;
- In the absence of a claimant and without documentary evidence;
- In the presence of a claimant;
- Unverified;
- False claim;
- Disputed claim.

Against the ninth item in the first part of the parcha claim, entry has to be made as to whether a claimant who had abandoned land outside West Punjab was of Punjabi or of non-Punjabi extraction, for claims of persons of non-Punjabi extraction abandoning land in Western Pakistan outside West Punjab are not eligible for allotment of land in East Punjab and East Punjab States. During the oral verification, verifying officers were asked to take special care to ascertain particulars of origin given by displaced persons from Bahawalpur, N.W.F.P., Sind and Baluchistan. If a displaced person from these areas claimed to hold agricultural land or to be the owner of a house anywhere in the Punjab such proof or attestation as might be possible were to be secured before accepting the claim.

It was not sufficient for an individual to state, for instance, that some generations ago his ancestors had gone from the Punjab to settle in the province or territory from which he had now come. The East Punjab Displaced Persons (Registration of Land Claims) Act provided, as has been noticed earlier, for registration of claims only from those dis-placed persons from N.W.F.P., Sind. Baluchistan and Bahawalpur who and whose ancestors had migrated as colonists from the Punjab since 1901.

The land claim form, however, which was issued under the Ordinance which preceded the Act, stated that claims to land were to be presented by " refugee landholders from West Punjab and Bahawalpur and by colonists who migrated from united Punjab to N.W.F.P., Sind or Bahawalpur or to any State adjacent to the province and acceding to Pakistan "- On this account a considerable amount of sort-ing was necessary in the claims of displaced persons from those areas.

The staff of the Land Claims Office was instructed not to depart from the finding on this question during the oral verification unless there were specific orders to the contrary. For instance, a claimant who had given only a vague description of his origin in the united Punjab, sometimes not even having indicated the name of his village of origin, was not to be accepted as being a person of Punjabi extraction without the orders in writing of a gazetted officer. Against the tenth item of the first part were to be entered the names of villages other than the one to which the parcha claim related in which a claimant was known to have held land.

These entries, for reasons, which have been explained earlier, frequently remained in-complete and much labour had to be given at a later stage to linking up each individual's claims relating to different villages.

Classification of Rights

In the second and third parts of the parcha claim, the important questions to be determined were the extent of area the classes of soil, and the rights held by an individual claimant. Without records rights were difficult to assess, and even with records the problem was by no means easy. Not all rights could be regarded as eligible for allotment in East Punjab and East Punjab States. For the assistance of staff, rights other than rights in 'shamilat' were divided into seven main categories with certain sub-categories as follows:

Category No. 1:

- Full ownership free of mortgage;
- Full ownership with mortgage with possession in favour of a non-Muslim;
- Full ownership with mortgage with possession In favour of a Muslim;

Explanations:

- In each sub-category there may be an occupancy tenant who may either be a Muslim or a non-Muslim.
- Land in which the same individual holds the rights of superior and inferior ownership is to be regarded as being under his full ownership.
- Malik Qabza is taken as full owner.

Category No. 2:

- Inferior ownership under a non-Muslim superior owner;
- Inferior ownership under a Muslim superior owner.

Explanations:

- An inferior owner may have an occupancy tenant who may be a Muslim or a non-Muslim;
- Rights of an occupancy tenant may be hem free of mortgage or may be mortgaged with possession in favour of a Muslim or in favour of a non-Muslim.

Category no. 3:

- Superior ownership with a non-Muslim as inferior owner;
- Superior ownership with a Muslim as inferior owner.

Category No. 4:

- Occupancy tenant under the Punjab Tenancy Act, 1887 with a non-Muslim as landlord;
- Occupancy tenant under the Punjab Tenancy Act, 1887 with a Muslim as a landlord.

Explanation:

Rights of an occupancy tenant may be held free of mortgage or under mortgage in favour of a non-Muslim or a Muslim.

Category No. 5:

- Grant or occupancy tenancy under the Punjab Colonization of Government Lands Act, 1912;
- Auction-purchase under the Punjab Colonization of Govern-ment Lands Act, 1912;
- Lease under the Punjab Colonization of Government Lands Act. 1912;
- Other rights under the Punjab Colonization of Government Lands Act, 1912;

Explanation

- In respect of land held as grantee or occupancy tenant or auction purchaser, details of installments paid to Gov-ernment or lease money paid and due were to be enter-ed in the parcha claim. In the case of leases, the period and other conditions were to be indicated.
- In (a) a grantee may be a non-occupancy tenant under the Punjab Colonization of Government Lands Act, 1912.

Category No. 6:

- Rights of mortgage with possession of land belonging to a non-Muslim;
- Rights of mortgage with possession of land belonging to a Muslim.

Explanation:

Rights of mortgage may pertain to land under full ownership or under inferior ownership or under occupancy rights.

Category No. 7:

- Rights of lease or mortgage for a limited period over land belonging to a non-Muslim;
- Rights of lease or mortgage for a limited period over land belonging to a Muslim.

The period of lease or mortgage with dates and particulars of the lands involved were to be indicated in the parcha claim.

Units of Area

In the second and third parts of the parcha claim area is to be shown in acres, kanal and marlas the karam being of 5 feet and six inches. Where different units of area are in vogue such as ghumaon 'higha and ghunta, these have to be converted, or where the karam is 'of a different size, the instructions given in nara 45 of the Punjab Land Records Manual have to be followed. Conversion is also necessary, for instance, when dealing with the Lower Chenab and Lower Jhelum Colonies where the 'killa is of 8 kanals and 18 marlas, while elsewhere it is equivalent to an acre. In certain parts of the Lahore District irrigated by the upper Bari Doab Canal, there are a variety of measures in use in different villages. These have to be ascertained carefully before conversion calculations are carried out, In Sind, 5 ghuntas make one kanal and 40 ghuntas make one acre. These strategies and programmes constitute the "five year plan", for the purpose of simplicity the measures undertaken have been categorized in broad groups and then elaborated upon. In the end, an ideal model of rural development, which is in contrast to the current model, is proposed.

The rural economy, as much as urban economy, is an integrated part of the overall Indian economy. Any talk of overall development without rural development, particularly in a country where three-quarters of people below the poverty line reside in rural areas, is flawed. Poverty is indeed a global issue. Its eradication is considered integral to humanity's quest for sustainable development. Reduction of poverty in India, is, therefore, vital for the attainment of international goals. Poverty alleviation has been one of the guiding principles of the planning process in India. This can be substantiated by the fact that anti-poverty programmes have been internalized in the (particularly the ninth) five-year plan. This article sheds light on the various "strategies and programmes" that form the instruments of the plan.

4

Structure and Structural Change in Indian Banking

BANKING IN INDIA

Banking has been known in India since time immemorial. It was initially only a system of money lending in which rates varied not according to the nature of the transaction, but in relation to the particular caste to which the borrower belonged. Deposit banking was practically unknown then. By the time the Europeans arrived, Indian banking houses had become more organized. Many among them had transregional connections across the subcontinent through an extensive network of Kothis or agencies. They financed other bankers, landlords, traders and princes and maintained close with the rulers of the princely states.

The British, who introduced a joint stock banking with limited liability in India, first set up through a charter the Bank of Bengal (after a brief period of infancy of three years at the Bank of Calcutta) in 1809 and followed it up by establishing the Bank of Bombay in 1840 and the Bank of Madras three years later. These three banks, which formed the highest tier of the apex banking system in British India, principally, finance internal trade and assisted the Company's Governments in the three presidencies to raise loans from time to time. They were also government bankers within the concerned presidencies. The position remained unaltered even for the Imperial Bank of India, which was created in 1921 by amalgamating the three presidency banks of Bengal, Bombay and Madras. Until the creation of the Reserve Bank of India in 1935, the Imperial Bank combined the functions of a commercial bank and a central bank. The Bank, thereafter, became a purely commercial bank and acquired a pre-eminent status in the Indian banking industry.

Innumerable private joint-stock banks under both European and Indian control also emerged during the 19th century, mainly to cater to the credit needs of the vast hinterland of the subcontinent. While some amongst them, like the Agra and United Services Bank and the Alliance Bank of Simla under European control, eventually collapsed owing to financial irregularities, there were many others under Indian management, especially in Bombay and Punjab, which succumbed during the banking crisis of 1913 and later in the 1930s and 1940s. It was these failures, which paved the way for the passing of the Banking Companies Act (later renamed as the Banking Regulation Act), in 1949. Quite a few of these private joint-stock banks, however survived and grew over the years, including the Allahabad Bank (1865) and the Punjab National Bank (1895) in the north, the Canara Bank (1906) and the Indian Bank (1907) in the south and the Bank of India (1906) and the Central Bank of India (1911) in the west.

The 19th century also witnessed the arrival of several exchange banks in India for financing the subcontinent's burgeoning foreign trade, which the three presidency banks and the Imperial Bank (until the establishment of the Reserve Bank), were rigorously excluded from engaging in. Such banks either chartered by the British Parliament or incorporated in Europe included the Chartered Bank of India, Australia and China, the Chartered Mercantile Bank of India, London and China, the Hongkong and Shanghai Banking Corporation, the Compote d' Escompte de Paris and so on.

Besides the above constituents of the formal sector of Indian banking, cooperative credit societies were also set up in the beginning of the 20th century and vested with the task of meeting the credit needs of the Indian peasantry. The progress in this regard was unfortunately sluggish, particularly outside the Bombay, Madras and Punjab provinces.

By the end of 1947, there were 654 scheduled, non-scheduled and exchange banks operating in the country with a network of 5009 offices and deposits and advances of ₹ 1153.45 crore and ₹ 520.299 crore respectively. The average population per bank office, though sharply reduced from about 8.5 lakh in 1916 to less than 70,000 in 1947, was still considerably high by international standards.

The almost total absence of banking facilities outside large towns or centres of trade, however, sadly left the vast majority of the rural masses in the clutches of the private creditor – the professional moneylender, the agriculturist moneylender and the trader. The committee of Direction of the All India Rural Credit Survey (AIRCS) constituted by the Reserve Bank to formulate a long-term policy for rural credit brought to focus the awful inadequacy of the banking system in providing rural credit, the Government's failure to strengthen the cooperative sector and the stranglehold of the moneylenders over the rural sector. The findings of the Committee revealed that the private creditor reigned 'supreme in the field of rural credit' accounting for more than 70 per cent of the total borrowings. The government, cooperatives and commercial banks together accounted for only 7.3 per cent. Perhaps more disturbing was the revelation that of this very little, the major part went to the bigger cultivators and only a minor fraction percolated down to the smaller cultivator.

Realizing that banks in India could not in the foreseeable future respond to the emergent needs of economic regeneration of rural areas, the Government decided to extend the concept of the state partnership to the important sector of commercial banking. On the recommendations of the AIRCS, the country's large commercial bank, the Imperial Bank, was nationalized for extending banking facilities, particularly to the rural and semi-urban areas in order to increase the flow of credit for both agriculture and small-scale industries and mobilize rural savings.

With the creation of the State Bank of India by an Act of Parliament on 1st July 1955, more than a quarter of the resources of the Indian banking system passed under the direct control of the state. Four years, later, the State Bank of India (Subsidiary Banks) Act was passed, enabling the State Bank to take over eight former State-associated banks as its subsidiaries.

The concept of banking underwent a sea change with the advent of the State Bank. A distinct shift in focus was evident – from security – oriented to need-based lending, from urban to rural banking, from class to mass banking and from activities that contributed essentially to the bank's commercial objectives to also those that largely served a social purpose. This transition from a primarily profit-seeking commercial bank to a great national institution with public responsibilities was however by no means an easy task. It became necessary for the Bank to reshape its organization and reset its tradition to make them sufficiently dynamically to suit the altered conditions. It also involved a re-orientation of the Bank's policies, a modification of its business methods and practices and a change of outlook on the part of its staff engaged at every level.

From its inception, the State Bank played a dual role with due 'regard being had to the public interest'. As a commercial bank, it continued to provide, as hitherto, finance to industry and trade. As a nationalized institution, it undertook several promotional and developmental activities by way of opening branches all over the country, including the remotest corners, evolving and implementing a special scheme for financing small-scale industries, extending financial accommodation to marketing and processing cooperative societies and fostering India's foreign trade.

The Bank succeeded in aligning itself with the planned economic development of the country and allocated credit according to the needs of the economy. Even before the Government had initiated measures under the scheme of social control in 1968, the State Bank had evolved schemes for all agricultural operations until the marketing of agricultural produce as also for mechanization and modernization of farms, provision of irrigation facilities and development of land. Innovative and well-planned strategies were also evolved as the bank's response to the main thrust of the Government on removing poverty and creating employment opportunities through accelerated economic development of the rural sector, with special emphasis on agricultural production, cottage industries, small industries, arts and crafts. Financial assistance to rural poor apart, an integrated view of the composite needs of the rural people covering economic, social and cultural areas was also evolved.

Besides setting up the State Bank of India, new institutions like the Industrial Finance Corporation of India (IFCI) (1948), the Agricultural Refinance Corporation (ARC) (1963), the Industrial Development Bank of India (IDBI) (1964) and the State Financial Corporations were also established for providing long-term finance to industry and agriculture.

Growing emphasis on agricultural, cottage and small-scale industrial development in the meantime, made it even more necessary that all the banks gear themselves to a more meaningful credit operation in India's hinterland. The Government thus initiated several measures under the scheme of social control in 1968 to secure a better alignment of banking policy with the needs of economic planning. Born out of persistent complaints of the deficiencies in the banking system, the basic postulate was 'to ensure that particular clients or groups of clients [were] not favoured in the matter of distribution of credit and whatever the character of the shareholding, its influence was neutralized in the constitution of the board of directors and in the actual credit decision taken at different levels of bank management'.

The National Credit Council set up in February 1968, to coordinate credit planning with economic planning and ensure allocation of credit to priority sectors, became the cornerstone of the social control scheme. From the position of mere purveyors of credit, especially to big industry and trading concerns, banks were hereafter encouraged to extend credit to agriculture and small-scale industries in a much larger measure as a matter of national responsibility. The same year, the Parliament also passed the banking Laws (Amendment) Bill seeking to reorient banking as a specialized profession. The amendment aimed, inter alia, at reconstituting the boards of directors of Indian commercial banks, appointing professional bankers and financial experts as full-time Chairmen and prohibiting loans and advances to directors and their concerns.

Soon after this, in February 1969, the Government appointed a banking commission under R.G. Saraiya, Chairman, Bombay State Cooperative Bank, to recommend, based on a comprehensive enquiry, changes in the structure, procedure and policy of the Indian banking system. Although the Commission made several recommendations relating to restructuring of commercial and cooperative banks, measures for widening their functional coverage, improving their operational efficiency, legislative reforms an area for further research and study, nothing much was done to implement them.

An event of far-reaching significance in the sphere of banking occurred in July 1969 when the Government of India promulgated an ordinance to nationalize major Indian scheduled banks with deposits of ₹ 50 crore and above, thereby ushering in a new phase of financial development. In a broadcast to the nation, Prime Minister Indira Gandhi observed-

"An institution such as the banking system, which touches – and should touch – the lives of millions, has necessarily to be inspired by a larger social purpose and has to subserve national priorities and objectives. That is why there has been widespread demand that the major banks should be not only socially controlled but also publicly owned."

The broad aims of nationalization as stated in the Preamble to the Act were ' to control the heights of the economy and to meet progressively and serve better the needs of development of the economy in conformity with national policy and objectives'. Nationalized banks were to ensure that the needs of productive efforts irrespective of the size and social status of the borrower and, in particular, those of farmers, small-scale industries and self-employed professional groups, were increasingly met. They were also to actively foster the growth of new and progressive entrepreneurs and create fresh opportunities for backward areas in different parts of the country. Besides widening the network of branches, particularly in the rural and semi-urban areas, banks were also to mobilize savings. Under the Lead Bank Scheme formulated thereafter, they were to act as pacesetters in providing integrated banking facilities at the districts allotted to them. Banks were also to be closely associated with credit linked poverty alleviation programmes (IRDP, SEPUP SEEUY, etc.) initiated from time to time.

In 1980, six more private banks with deposits of not less than ₹ 200 crore were nationalized. It was aimed 'to further control the heights of the economy, tom meet progressively and serve better the needs of the development of the economy, and to promote the welfare of the people in conformity with the policy of the State'. With this, the number of public sector banks increased to 28 including the State Bank and its seven associates, accounting at all for about 91 per cent of the total deposits and advances of commercial banks in the country. Banks in the private sector continued to exist, though only in the periphery of the industry.

Indian banking underwent a major structural transformation after the nationalization of banks. A phenomenal expansion of the branch network occurred, particularly in the hitherto under-banked rural areas. The Reserve Bank geared its branch licensing policy to the objectives of ensuring an expansion of offices both in unbanked centres and in under-banked states as well as in the urban and metropolitan centres. While the total number of commercial bank offices rose from 8,262 to as much as 60,294 between June 1969 and March 1990, the number of rural branches increased from 1,833 to 34,940 accounting for more than 57 per cent of the total compared with barely 22 per cent in 1969. The average population served by each bank office declined from 65,000 to about 12,000 during the same period.

There was also a massive qualitative change in the operations of the banking system as banks assumed a variety of new responsibilities in the area of social banking for which 'no procedures or guidelines in the history of modern banking existed elsewhere in the world'. The ratio of priority sector advances to net bank credit rose from 14 per cent by March 1990.

The phenomenal growth and development of the banking system during the 1970s and 1980s however rendered the system unwieldy. A complex structure of interest rates arising from economic and social concerns of providing concessional credit to certain sectors not only distorted the interest rate mechanism, but also adversely affected the viability and profitability of banks. Inability to gauge the importance of transparency, accountability and prudential norms in the operations of the banking system resulted in an increasing burden of non-performing assets (NPAs). Low operational efficiency, unhealthy balance sheets and unsatisfactory customer service further threatened the very stability of the financial system.

With the country facing a serious economic crisis partially due to a critical balance of payments situation, the Government in 1991 decided to initiate measures to stabilize the economy and simultaneously introduce structural reforms. The scheme of structural reforms was aimed at enhancing the productivity and efficiency of the economy as a whole and increasing global competitiveness. As a part of this, reforms based on the recommendations of the Narasimham Committee were also initiated in two phases in the financial sector to imbue it with operational flexibility and functional autonomy. Substantial reduction in pre-emptions in the form of reserve requirements, dismantling administered structure of interest rates, introduction of internationally accepted prudential norms relating to income recognition, asset classification, provisioning for bad debts and capital adequacy, granting licenses to new private sector banks, allowing a more liberal entry for foreign banks and permitting nationalized banks access to capital markets were some of the policy measures initiated in the first phase.

The second phase of reforms, aimed to strengthen the foundations of the banking system, saw guidelines being put in place for risk management systems in banks, initiation of risk-based supervision, etc., besides further strengthening prudential norms. A new framework for capital adequacy according to Basel II norms is now awaiting adoption by banks. New norms have also been evolved for recognizing the income of banks. All these measures have led to the strengthening of the Indian banking system making it one of the strongest in the region today.

The impact of the first phase of the financial sector reforms was felt within a few years. A marked improvement in the financial health of commercial banks was evident by the rise in operating and net profits and a decreasing tended in the percentage of NPAs. Most of the banks also succeeded in meeting the minimum capital adequacy ratio. The ongoing deregulation and liberalization of the financial markets have thrown up some challenges for banks in India. The most exciting among them has been the emergence of an increasingly competitive environment in the banking industry with the arrival of new domestic and foreign private players. Starting with the advantage of strong capitalisation, modern technology, lear network, and more importantly without any accumulated problems of the past, the new domestic entrants in particular were ambitious in their business targets and keen to expand their activities all over the county. Empowered with a model that ensures networking of branches with connection to a central processing centre for back office operations like account opening, loan maintenance, etc. and equipped with the ability to employ the best workforce in the market by offering attractive compensation packages, the new generation banks soon began to pose a stiff competition to public sector banks (PSBs).

In the face of this unprecedented onslaught, PSBs realized that in times to come, they would need to convert challenges into opportunities. The success obtained by private players through the networked model of banking prompted PSBs to embrace the same design. Today, not only are all PSBs fully computerized, some among them are also fully networked, while others are not far from accomplishing it. The seven Associate Banks of the State Bank Group are in fact the first PSBs to be fully networked in India.

In addition to computerization and networking, another major innovation that competition as encouraged in the banking industry is the popularization of alternative delivery channels like Automated Teller Machines (ATMs) and Internet Banking. These channels provide customers access to basic banking facilities round the clock and also help reduce operating costs of banks. Banks are also investing substantially in Information Technology to improve efficiency in their operations as also provide top class customer service.

The post-reform era has also witnessed a rapid growth of retail finance, which till recently was perhaps somewhat neglected as banks concentrated mostly in financing the manufacturing and agricultural sectors. With large manufacturing companies finding alternative and cheaper sources for funding their needs, banks have now turned to consumer finance in a big way. Retail finance today forms about a quarter of bank credit. The ready availability of bank credit has contributed in no small measure to the consumer boom that the economy has been witnessing of late including an upsurge in the housing and automobile sectors giving in turn a fillip to the real economy.

While the opening up of the Indian financial markets has provided enormous opportunities for banks to tap new areas of business, it has also posed an enormous challenge for the smaller banks to compete with the new entrants in terms of funds, base, technology and new products. With the further opening up of the Indian banking sector to foreign investors under the WTO agreement in April 2009, the smaller PSBs may well not be able to withstand the pressures on profitability for long. In order to overcome this, these banks would perhaps need to consolidate through amalgamations, as it the global phenomenon today.

Notwithstanding India's expanding economy and the phenomenal growth of bank credit in recent times, it is however lamentable that in India's countryside, about 58 per cent of farming households and 70 per cent of non-farming households still lack access to basic banking services. Banking penetration is in fact so low in India that bank deposits represent only 60 per cent of the GDP as compared to 190 per cent in China or 142 per cent in Japan. Despite the boom in the economy, economic disparities thus continue to grow in India with the rich becoming richer and the poor poorer. It is therefore imperative that a balance is struck between the demands of a market economy and the urgent needs of financial inclusion.

Drawing on Prof. C. K. Prahalad's much-publicized theory that 'the world's most exciting, fastest-growing new market is where you least expect it: at the bottom of the pyramid', Indian banks have increasingly begun to look for business among the rural poor. They are now working towards providing basic financial services to the villagers through a network of e-kiosks and agents – a business model that has been successfully tried in other developing economics. The day when a bouquet of financial services will be available to six lac Indian villages is perhaps not too far away.

The saga of Indian banking like most others has seen its vicissitudes. Its genre has not, however, changed much since the colonial days. Thanks to the booming global economy, expanding technology and changing mindsets, banking is now set to be transformed. Age-old processes and systems are about to be discarded as fresh rules are being framed. The age of 'disruptive technology' has already made its tentative foray. There is excitement in the air all around.

TRANSFORMING IN INDIAN BANKING

The significant transformation of the banking industry in India is clearly evident from the changes that have occurred in the financial markets, institutions and products. While deregulation has opened up new vistas for banks to augment revenues, it has entailed greater competition and consequently greater risks. Cross-border flows and entry of new products, particularly derivative instruments, have impacted significantly on the domestic banking sector, forcing banks to adjust the product mix, as also to effect rapid changes in their processes and operations in order to remain competitive to the globalised environment. These developments have facilitated greater choice for consumers, who have become more discerning and demanding compelling banks to offer a broader range of products through diverse distribution channels. The traditional face of banks as mere financial intermediaries has since altered and risk management has emerged as their defining attribute.

- Report on Trend and Progress of Banking in India 2001-02, Reserve Bank of India

It gives me great pleasure to deliver the valedictory address at the Bank Eonomists' Conference (BECON) 2002. We would like to thank the Corporation Bank and the Indian Banks' Association for giving me this opportunity. Over the years, the BECON has evolved as an important forum for intensive discussions on both contemporary and futuristic issues facing the Indian banking industry. This forum has served as an important platform for structured information-sharing among bankers, research analysts, credit rating agencies and other financial sector bodies. Currently, the most important factor shaping the world is globalisation. The benefits of globalisation have been well documented and are being increasingly recognised. Integration of domestic markets with international financial markets has been facilitated by tremendous advancement in information and communications technology. But, such an environment has also meant that a problem in one country can sometimes adversely impact one or more countries instantaneously, even if they are fundamentally strong.

There is a growing realisation that the ability of countries to conduct business across national borders and the ability to cope with the possible downside risks would depend, *inter alia*, on the soundness of the financial system. This has consequently meant the adoption of a strong and transparent, prudential, regulatory, supervisory, technological and institutional framework in the financial sector on par w®ith international best practices.

All this necessitates a transformation: a transformation in the mindset, a transformation in the business processes and finally, a transformation in knowledge management. This process is not a one shot affair; it needs to be appropriately phased in the least disruptive manner. The subject of the Conference is, therefore, very timely and appropriate and we would like to take this opportunity to congratulate the organisers for this theme.

As you would all appreciate, the banking and financial crises in recent years in emerging economies have demonstrated that, when things go wrong with the financial system, they can result in a severe economic downturn. Furthermore, banking crises often impose substantial costs on the exchequer, the incidence of which is ultimately borne by the taxpayer. The World Bank Annual Report (2002) has observed that the loss of US $1 trillion in banking crises in the 1980s and 1990s is equal to the total flow of official development assistance to developing countries from the 1950s to the present date. As a consequence, the focus of financial market reform in many emerging economies has been towards increasing efficiency while at the same time ensuring stability in financial markets.

From this perspective, financial sector reforms are essential in order to avoid such costs. It is, therefore, not surprising that financial market reform is at the forefront of public policy debate in recent years. The burgeoning literature on endogenous growth theory has come to recognise the crucial role of sound financial markets in promoting rapid economic growth and ensuring financial stability.

Indeed, it is by now widely documented that the structure of financial markets helps explain why some countries remain poor, while others grow richer. Financial sector reform, through the development of an efficient financial system, is thus perceived as a key element in raising countries out of their 'low level equilibrium trap'. As the World Bank Annual Report (2002) observes, 'a robust financial system is a precondition for a sound investment climate, growth and reduction of poverty'.

Financial sector reforms were initiated in India a decade ago with a view to improving efficiency in the process of financial intermediation, enhancing the effectiveness in the conduct of monetary policy and creating conditions for integration of the domestic financial sector with the global system. The first phase of reforms was guided by the recommendations of Narasimham Committee I. The approach was to ensure that 'the financial services industry operates on the basis of operational flexibility and functional autonomy with a view to enhancing efficiency, productivity and profitability'. The second phase, guided by Narasimham Committee II, focused on strengthening the foundations of the banking system and bringing about structural improvements. While there may be some concern over the pace and sequencing of reforms in the financial sector vis-à-vis the real sector, you will agree with me when I say that we have traversed a considerable distance since 1991. Reforms in the financial sector and their beneficial impact have been well documented and I will not attempt to repeat them here. The text of the Governor's inaugural address also covers at length important issues such as ownership, corporate governance, regulatory and supervisory issues and the like. I also see from the schedule that you have held intensive discussions on important issues related to corporate governance, reform of the capital structure (in the context of Basel II norms), retail banking, risk management technology, and human resources development, among others.

INTEREST RATE SCENARIO

The first important issue that I would like to highlight relates to interest rates. As a result of interest rate deregulation, the interest rate structure of banks is competitively determined in the market, barring a few exceptions. A major factor that has influenced the trend in interest rates is the sustained decline in the inflation rate in the recent period. Notwithstanding year-to-year fluctuations, there has been a distinct downward drift in the inflation rate during the second half of the 1990s, which is now at around half the level as compared with the first half of the 1990s. Both the popular measures of inflation - the

Wholesale Price Index (WPI) and the Consumer Price Index (CPI) – have shown a definite fall in the recent period.

For example, the WPI on an average basis has declined from an average of about 10.5 per cent per annum between 1990-91 to 1995-96 to about 5 per cent per annum over the last 5 years. A similar trend can be observed with regard to the Consumer Price Index for industrial workers. In the current year so far, inflation as measured by variations in WPI, has remained benign around 3 per cent despite the adverse effect of drought and uncertainty on account of oil prices. As the inflation rate has decelerated, it has also had a positive impact on inflationary expectations. This is clearly reflected in the downward trend in nominal interest rates.

For instance, the overnight call money rate has fallen sharply from about 13 per cent in August 2000 to the current levels of 5.5 per cent. Similarly, the 91-day Treasury Bill rate declined from 10.5 per cent to 5.4 per cent and the 364-day Treasury Bill rate from 10.9 per cent to 5.6 per cent over the same period.

The long-term interest rates too have declined. The yield on 10-Year government securities has declined from 11.5 per cent in August 2000 to the current levels of about 6.3 per cent. Similarly, interest rates on corporate paper have fallen significantly. For example, the interest rate on 5-Year AAA rated corporate paper has declined from 12 per cent in August 2000 to about 6.7 per cent currently.

The banks have also reduced their deposit rates. The term deposit rates of public sector banks over one year maturity have declined from a range of 8-10 per cent in August 2000 to 6-8 per cent now. This fall in the interest rates in the recent period has been in consonance with the monetary policy stance of a soft and a flexible interest rate regime. Despite the fall in deposit rates, depositors have received positive real interest rates of close to 2 per cent in the second half of the 1990s, which is much higher than the real return on deposits during the first half of the 1990s.

On the other hand, lending rates of banks have not come down as much. While banks have reduced their prime lending rates (PLRs) to some extent and are also extending sub-PLR loans, effective lending rates continue to remain high. It is estimated that the average lending rate of scheduled commercial banks has declined from a peak of about 17 per cent in 1995-96 to about 14 per cent by 2001-02. Hence, while nominal interest rates have come down, they have not fallen as much as the inflation rate. Consequently, the effective real lending rate continues to remain high. This development has adverse systemic implications, especially in a country like India where interest cost as a proportion of sales of corporates are much higher as compared to many emerging economies. A cross country comparison of interest rate trends during the 1990s provides some interesting insights. The average inflation rate in all these countries has come down during the second half of that decade (1997-2001) as compared to the first half. In line with this, the average money market interest rates and government securities yields have also come down in real terms in most of these countries. On the lending side, however, prime rates in some countries have not shown similar falls in real interest rates (UK, Germany, Japan, Thailand and Hungary). Thus, the Indian experience of sticky real lending rates is not unique. But, preliminary estimates do show a high correlation between government securities yields and real lending rate in Japan, India and Germany during the 1990s as a whole. Hence, the downward rigidity in lending rates in India as compared with the government securities rates during the second half of the 1990s does seem more surprising in this context. It would seem that changes in inflationary expectations take a little longer to adjust than inflation rates themselves. It would be rational for interest rates to be related to inflationary expectations, and in particular long-term interest rates. Therefore, bank economists have an important role of informing the management of appropriate inflationary expectations so that interest rates can be adjusted more systematically.

Understandably, there are certain rigidities in the overall interest rate structure in the economy that constrain banks from reducing their lending rates. These have been well documented in the earlier monetary and credit policy statements of the Reserve Bank. Subsequently, interest rates on small savings have also moved down and there is a commitment from the Government to link these rates with market related rates. The recovery environment has also improved. A related issue pertains to transparency in lending rates. Especially after the introduction of sub-PLR lending by banks, the spreads between the minimum and maximum lending rates seem to have widened. The Reserve Bank is making efforts to publish on its web site bank-wise information on the minimum and maximum lending rates. Our own internal exercises reveal that the concept of PLR may need to be reviewed in the current context. Perhaps, bank economists may like to study the international experience and come out with suggestions.

Lending to Small and Medium Enterprises

The problem arising out of high lending rates gets accentuated due to segmentation in the credit market. The large corporates are able to negotiate fine rates with banks and are able to bring down their overall interest costs. In addition, the large corporates have the option of accessing the international capital markets for funds. The burden of adjustment has, therefore, fallen on small and medium enterprises (SMEs), which have limited access to funds. The high interest rates paid by SMEs may not always be in accordance with their risk profile. It is clear that at present the Indian banking system is not fully equipped to promote small-scale enterprises around the country. The key issue is that banking institutions must be enabled to improve their credit assessment capabilities with regard to small-scale enterprises so that they can distinguish adequately between good and bad credit. Small-scale must not be equated with high risk. If the inflation rate is as low as 3 per cent and the interest rates charged to SMEs are much higher than normal good credit risk to large-sized industries, there is an implicit adverse selection in the credit appraisal process. Bank economists need to give focused attention to risk assessment to this sector so that there are no errors of high interest rate to low risk borrowers in the SME sector and vice-versa.

The provision for Credit Information Bureaus and better exchange of information on credit risk between banks and financial institutions is also necessary to enable these institutions to recognise higher risk without excessive costs. Furthermore, the cost of credit assessment of small and medium enterprises can be reduced by a focused recognition of clusters of like small-scale industries that exist around the country.

Such financial assistance programmes also need to be devised to provide assistance to those industries that are in the reserved list to enable them to expand and upgrade technology. This should be done both at the individual and group level. The focus of many such activities can be on the basis of industrial clusters so that economies of scale can be achieved both in financial assistance and in technology upgradation.

Very significant changes are also taking place in the agricultural sector. We can see the beginning of a much closer connection between primary producers, trade intermediaries, food processing entities, and eventual marketing of value added products. With the share of unprocessed foods falling, the real growth area in the agricultural sector is in value added food products such as meat, poultry, fish, vegetables, fruits and the like. There is an accelerating move of consumers to basic processed foods. These trends need to be studied carefully so that supporting policy changes and investments can be made. Banks should explore the feasibility of expanding substantially lending to these activities.

Apart from adequate quantum of credit at an affordable price, there are issues relating to provision of high processing costs and the attendant cumbersome paper work. There are lessons to be learnt from the experience of the Kisan Credit Card (KCC) Schemes and the Laghu Udhyami Credit Card Schemes to the agricultural and small entrepreneur borrowers. Surely, there is some scope for extending the benefits of hassle free credit facilities through similar innovative methods to other borrowers requiring credit limits of over ₹.2 lakh also.

It needs to be recognised that the SME sector has tremendous growth potential and accordingly pricing of loans to this sector should be at commensurate rates. Thus, there is need for realignment of interest rates among various segments of the financial market. As the financial market develops, ideally the interest rates on all types of debt instruments, both in the government and private sectors, and in the credit market should align in a relatively narrow band, reflecting realistic risk premia.

There have been some signals of industrial pick up during the last few months. For the four months from July to October 2002, on a point to point basis, the rise in index of industrial production (IIP) has been above 6 per cent. A major contribution to the high growth rates has been from the manufacturing sector. In use-based classification also, the capital goods sector has registered impressive growth rates of over 15 per cent and 12 per cent in September and October 2002 respectively. Most (14 out of 17) industry groups in the index have shown positive growth rates. The increase in non-food credit of scheduled commercial banks during the current financial year also appears to be commensurate with the IIP performance.

Nevertheless, banks have shown a marked preference for investments in government securities instead of pursuing their core activity of lending to commercial sector. At an aggregate level, the SLR holdings of banks are close to 39 per cent as compared to the regulatory prescription of 25 per cent. Even strong commercial banks seem to be voluntarily adopting 'narrow banking' in a bid to minimise credit risk while increasing profitability.

Such large investments in government securities well beyond the statutory requirement reflect dissipation of banking knowledge capital with regard to credit appraisals. The interest rate risk on investments in gilts need hardly be over emphasised. Further, the current focus of banks is bound to exact some heavy costs in terms of efficiency and credit availability. There is a danger of the link between liquidity, credit, money and economic activity being severed in the long run as a result of continued over-investment in government securities as a substitute for bank financing to the commercial sector.

At a time when the industry is showing signs of pick up, banks should make efforts to increase commercial lending. The need of the hour is revival of the manufacturing sector and financing of the new slew of activities allied to agricultural lending. Of course, this would require focused attention through specialised branches, sound credit appraisals, adoption of sophisticated risk management techniques, and better information sharing. The legal environment has also improved with the passing of the new act to regulate securitisation and reconstruction of financial assets and enforcement of security interest.

Revitalisation of Long-Term Financing

The development finance institutions (DFIs) were set up in the 1950s to provide medium and long-term finance to the private sector. Many of these institutions were sponsored by the Government. DFIs were expected to resolve long-term credit shortages and to acquire and disseminate skills necessary to assess projects and banks creditworthiness. DFIs were traditionally dependent on concessional sources of financing, guaranteed by Government.

On the asset side, they were predominantly engaged in term lending with banks financing working capital requirements. The post-reform period has altered the domain of the operations of DFIs both on the liabilities and assets sides. While DFIs started competing for funds at market rates of interest, their asset profile also shortened. On the other hand, banks have entered the domain of term lending. The current trend is of DFIs converting themselves into banks. In this context, the future of long-term lending acquires great importance. Finance theory suggests that banks can play an important role in corporate financing, especially in situations of asymmetric information, principal-agent problems, design of incentive compatible contracts and corporate governance issues. In their early stages of development, corporates are likely to rely on bank finance for working capital requirements. Bank financing is also likely to be predominant in an economy having a less-sophisticated legal framework. Considerations of lower transactions costs, efficient risk diversification, cost effective assessment, monitoring and renegotiation, etc., are likely to make firms more reliant on bank finance than on market based debt instruments.

International evidence on industrialised countries indicates that since the early 1970s, banks have played an important role in corporate financing. The benefits of a bank-based financial system vis-à-vis a market-based system were clearly noticeable particularly in the case of Japan, France and Italy. During this period, bank financing was equally important in other industrialised and developing countries, although equity finance has gained momentum in recent years.

This is a challenging area as financing of long-term projects involves commitment of large funds over long periods with the concomitant asset liability mismatches. The shift from a fixed to a floating interest rate regime, development of corporate debt market, introduction of derivatives instruments and further enabling changes in the regulatory and legal environment are likely to increase long-term financing by banks. Banks would need to think in terms of setting up special wings for term lending, development of consortia and syndication, and cooperation in assessment of projects. These are areas for further exploration by bank economists.

Non-Performing Possessions

One of the main constraints to the above issues that we have raised is the level of non-performing assets. As of March 31, 2002, the gross NPAs of scheduled commercial banks stood at ₹.71,000 crore, of which the NPAs of public sector banks constituted ₹.57,000 crore. The absolute amount of NPAs continues to be a major drag on the performance of banks. The large volume of NPAs reflects both an overhang of past dues and on-going problem of fresh accretion.

As we move towards the international norm of 90 days for recognition of loan impairment, there may be a temporary increase in crystalisation of NPAs in the banking sector.

There is, therefore, a need to bring about improvements in credit administration and management of credit risk. The Credit Information Bureau (CIB) should help in improving credit decisions by providing institutional mechanism for sharing of credit information on borrowers and potential borrowers among banks and financial institutions. The Reserve Bank modified the guidelines for compromise settlements of NPAs of the small sector to provide a simplified, non-discretionary and non-discriminatory mechanism. Banks should work out processes for settlement procedures and expedite quick recovery of NPAs.

The Securitisation and Reconstruction of Financial Assets and Enforcement of Security Interest Act, 2002 should help in cleansing the balance sheet of banks by facilitating foreclosure. The constitution of an Asset Reconstruction Company (ARC) is another channel to remove NPAs from the balance sheets of banks through the processes of securitisation of assets. The Reserve Bank has recently posted on its web site the draft of the directions on prudential norms proposed to be issued by it to securitisation companies/reconstruction companies. I hope despite the Christmas spirit and the Conference mood, experts would have studied the RBI proposals and sent their comments.

Risk Management in Interest

In the current interest rate environment, banks are finding it more profitable to invest in government securities. In 2001-02, trading profits of public sector banks more than doubled to ₹.5,999 crore from ₹.2,250 crore in 2000-01. The net profits of these banks during these two years were ₹.4,317 crore and ₹.8,301 crore respectively and this includes an additional ₹.1,365 crore and ₹.1,547 crore from forex operations. The Reserve Bank has been encouraging banks to be proactive in risk management. In this context, with a view to building up adequate reserves to guard against any possible reversal of interest rate environment in future, banks have been directed to maintain a certain level of Investment Fluctuation Reserve (IFR). The Reserve Bank is also taking a number of steps to develop further the derivatives market. As announced in the Mid-term review of monetary policy for 2002-03, a Working Group has been set up with representatives from the market to enlarge the avenues of managing interest rate risks for banks and other financial intermediaries as well as corporates in the rupee derivatives market.

Recently, the Reserve Bank has issued a guidance note on market risk management. The guidance note delineates the minimum requirements for a bank including approval levels and requirements for any exceptions, deviations or waivers. The note illustratively covers the responsibilities of risk management with regard to market risk management, the responsibilities of risk taking unit, the responsibilities of market risk manager, risk identification, risk monitoring, funding and liquidity, models of risk analysis, and risk reporting.

In a rapidly changing business environment, no business can afford to remain static. It is well understood that risk-taking is an integral part of any business enterprise. It is important that each bank needs to have in place the technical systems and management processes necessary to not only identify the risks associated with its activities, but also to effectively measure, monitor and control them. If Indian banks are to compete globally, the time is opportune for them to institute sound and robust risk management practices.

BANKING REFORM IN INDIA

Measured by share of deposits, 83 per cent of the banking business in India is in the hands of state or nationalized banks, which are banks that are owned by the government, in some, increasingly less clear-cut way. Moreover, even the non-nationalized banks are subject to extensive regulations on who they can lend to, in addition to the more standard prudential regulations.

Government control over banks has always had its fans, ranging from Lenin to Gerschenkron. While there are those who have emphasized the political importance of public control over banking, most arguments for nationalizing banks are based on the premise that profit maximizing lenders do not necessarily deliver credit where the social returns are the highest. The Indian government, when nationalizing all the larger Indian banks in 1969, argued that banking was "inspired by a larger social purpose" and must "sub serve national priorities and objectives such as rapid growth in agriculture, small industry and exports."

There is now a body of direct and indirect evidence showing that credit markets in developing countries often fail to deliver credit where its social product might be the highest, and both

- We thank the Reserve Bank of India, in particular Y.V. Reddy, R.B. Barman, and Abhiman Das, for generous assistance with technical and substantative issues. We also thank Abhiman Das for performing calculations which involved proprietary RBI data, as well as Saibal Ghosh and Petia Topalova for helpful comments. We are grateful to the staff of the public sector bank we study for allowing us access to their data. We gratefully acknowledge financial support from the Alfred P. Sloan Foundation.
- If nationalization succeeds in pushing credit into these sectors, as the Indian government claimed it would, it could indeed raise both equity and efficiency. The cross-country evidence on the impact of bank nationalization is not very encouraging. For example, find in a cross-country setting that govern-ment ownership of banks is negatively correlated with both financial development and economic growth.

- They interpret this as support for their view, which holds that the potential benefits of public ownership of banks, and public control over banks more generally, are swamped by the costs that come from the agency problems it creates: cronyism, leading to the deliberate misallocation of capital, bureaucratic lethargy, leading to less deliberate, but perhaps equally costly errors in the allocation of capital, as well as inefficiency in the process of mobilizing savings and transforming them into credit. Unfortunately the interpretation of this type of cross-country analysis is never easy, and never more so than the case of something like bank nationalization, which typically occurs as part of a package of other policies. For example, Bertrand et. al. study a 1985 banking deregulation in France, which gave banks much greater freedom to compete for clients.
- They find that deregulated banks respond more to profitability when making lending decisions. After the reform, firms that suffer a negative shock are much more likely to undertake restructuring measures, and there is more entry and exit in bank-dependent industries. Micro studies of the effect of bank nationalization are rare: an important exception is Mian who examines the privatization of a large public bank in Pakistan in 1991.
- He finds that the privatized bank does a better job both at choosing profitable clients and monitoring existing clients, than the commercial banks that remained public. Micro data from a nationalized bank to evaluate the effectiveness of the Indian banking system in delivering credit.
- The Indian financial system is characterized by under-lending in the sense that there are many firms that could earn large profits if they were given access to credit at the current market prices.

The work with the aim of using that evidence and evidence from other research by ourselves and others, to come to an assessment of the appropriate role of the Indian government vis a vis the banking sector. We first provide a very brief history of banking in India.

We begin by presenting evidence that there is substantial under-lending in India. To understand what role public ownership of banks may play in underlending, we identify differences between public and private banks in the sectoral allocation of credit between public and private banks. In particular, we focus on the question of whether being nationalized has made these banks more responsive to what the Indian government wants them to do. We report results, based on work by Cole showing that on many of the declared objectives of "social banking," the private banks were no less responsive than the comparable nationalized banks, with the exception of agricultural lending. Finally, the last sub-section compares the performance of public and private banks as financial intermediaries and concludes that the public banks have been less aggressive than private banks both in lending, in attracting deposits and in setting up branches, at least since 1990. We find that official lending policy is very rigid. Moreover, loan officers do not appear to use what little flexibility they have. We argue that the evidence suggests that bankers in the public sector have a preference for what we may call passive lending.

To understand why this is the case, we examine the incentives and constraints faced by public loan officers. We focus on whether vigilance activity impedes lending, and whether public sector banks prefer to lend to the government, rather than private firms. The penultimate part compares the performance of public and private banking in two other areas. First, we examine how nationalization of banks has affected the availability of bank branches in rural areas, and find that, if anything, nationalization appears to have inhibited the growth of rural branches. Second, we try to say something about the sensitive issue of NPAs and bailouts.

While the dataset we have now is rather sparse, it appears that the bailouts of the public banks have proved more expensive for the government, but once we control for differences in size between the public and private banks, it is less clear-cut. We conclude in a short discussion of the implications of these results for the future of banking reform. Background India has a long history of both public and private banking. Modern banking in India began in the 18th century, with the founding of the English Agency House in Calcutta and Bombay. In the first half of the 19th century, three Presidency banks were founded. After the 1860 introduction of limited liability, private banks began to appear, and foreign banks entered the market.

The beginning of the 20th century saw the introduction of joint stock banks. In 1935, the presidency banks were merged together to form the Imperial Bank of India, which was subsequently renamed the State Bank of India. Also that year, India's central bank, the Reserve Bank of India (RBI), began operation. Following independence, the RBI was given broad regulatory authority over commercial banks in India. In 1959, the State Bank of India acquired the state-owned banks of eight former princely states. Thus, by July 1969, approximately 31 per cent of scheduled bank branches throughout India were government controlled, as part of the State Bank of India. The post-war development strategy was in many ways a socialist one, and the Indian government felt that banks in private hands did not lend enough to those who needed it most.

In July 1969, the government nationalized all banks whose nationwide deposits were greater than ₹.500 million, resulting in the nationalization of 54 per cent more of the branches in India, and bringing the total number of branches under government control to 84 per cent. Prakesh Tandon, a former chairman of the Punjab National Bank (nationalized in 1969) describes the rationale for nationalization as follows: Many bank failures and crises over two centuries, and the damage they did under 'laissez faire' conditions; the needs of planned growth and equitable distribution of credit, which in privately owned banks was concentrated mainly on the controlling industrial houses and influential borrowers; the needs of growing small scale industry and farming regarding finance, equipment and inputs; from all these there emerged an inexorable demand for banking legislation, some government control and a central banking authority, adding up, in the final analysis, to social control and nationalization.

After nationalization, the breadth and scope of the Indian banking sector expanded at a rate perhaps unmatched by any other country. Indian banking has been remarkably successful at achieving mass participation. Between the time of the 1969 nationalizations and the present, over 58,000 bank branches were opened in India; these new branches, as of March 2003, had mobilized over 9 trillion Rupees in deposits, which represent the overwhelming majority of deposits in Indian banks. This rapid expansion is attributable to a policy which required banks to open four branches in unbanked locations for every branch opened in banked locations. Between 1969 and 1980, the number of private branches grew more quickly than public banks, and on April 1, 1980, they accounted for approximately 17.5 per cent of bank branches in India.

In April of 1980, the government undertook a second round of nationalization, placing under government control the six private banks whose nationwide deposits were above ₹ 2 billion, or a further 8 per cent of bank branches, leaving approximately 10 per cent of bank branches in private hands. The share of private bank branches stayed fairly constant between 1980 to 2000. Nationalized banks remained corporate entities, retaining most of their staff, with the exception of the board of directors, who were replaced by appointees of the central government.

The political appointments included representatives from the government, industry, agriculture, as well as the public. (Equity holders in the national bank were reimbursed at approximately par). Since 1980, has been no further nationalization, and indeed the trend appears to be reversing itself, as nationalized banks are issuing shares to the public, in what amounts to a step towards privatization. The considerable accomplishments of the Indian banking sector notwithstanding, advocates for privatization argue that privatization will lead to several substantial improvements.

Recently, the Indian banking sector has witnessed the introduction of several "new private banks," either newly founded, or created by previously extant financial institutions. The new private banks have grown quickly in the past few years, and one has grown to be the second largest bank in India. India has also seen the entry of over two dozen foreign banks since the commencement of financial reforms. While we believe both of these types of banks deserve study, our focus here is on the older private sector, and nationalized banks, since they represent the overwhelming majority of banking activity in India. The Indian banking sector has historically suffered from high intermediation costs, due in no small part to the staffing at public sector banks: as of March 2002, there were 1.17 crores of deposits per employee in nationalized banks, compared to 2.05 crores per employee in private sector banks. As with other government-run enterprises, corruption is a problem for public sector banks: in 1999, there were 1,916 cases which attracted attention from the Central Vigilance Commission.

While not all of these represent crimes, the investigations themselves may have a harmful effect, if bank officers fear that approving any risky loan will inevitably lead to scrutiny. Advocates for privatization also criticize public sector banking as unresponsive to credit needs. We use recent evidence on banking in India to shed light on the relative costs and benefits of nationalized banks. Throughout this exercise, it is important to bear in mind that the Indian banking sector is going through something like a transformation. Thus, it is potentially a dangerous time to evaluate its performance using historical data.

Under-lending therefore is a characteristic of the entire financial system: the firm has not been able to raise enough capital from the market as a whole. In other words, while as suggested, focus on the clients of a public sector bank, if these firms are getting too little credit from that bank, they should in theory have the option of going elsewhere for more credit. If they do not or cannot exercise this option, the market cannot be doing what, in its idealized form, we would have expected it to do. However, we know that the Indian financial system does not function as the ideal credit market might.

Most small or medium firms have a relationship with one bank, which they have built up over some time–they cannot expect to walk into another bank and get as much credit as they want. For that reason, their ability to finance investments they need to make does depend on the willingness of that one bank to finance them. In this sense the results we report might very well reflect the specificities of the public sector banks, or even the one bank that was kind enough to share its data with us, though given that it is seen as one of the best public sector banks, it seems unlikely that we would find much better results in other banks in its category.

On the other hand we do not have comparable data from any private bank and therefore cannot tell whether under-lending is as much of a problem for private banks. As suggested,, however, later report some results on the relative performance of public and private banks in terms of overall credit delivery Our identification of credit constrained firms is based on the following simple observation: if a firm that is not credit constrained is offered some extra credit at a rate below what it is paying on the market, then the best way to make use of the new loan must be to pay down the firm's current market borrowing, rather than to invest more. This is because, by the definition of not being credit constrained, any additional investment will drive the marginal product of capital below what the firm is paying on its market borrowing. It follows that a firm that is not facing any credit constraint will expand its investment in response to additional subsidized credit becoming available, only if it has no more market borrowing. By contrast, a firm that is credit constrained will always expand its investment to some extent. A corollary to this prediction is that for unconstrained firms, growth in revenue should be slower than the growth in subsidized credit. This is a direct consequence of the fact that firms are substituting subsidized credit for market borrowing. Therefore, if we do not see a gap in these growth rates, the firm must be credit constrained. Of course, revenue could increase slower than credit even for non-constrained firms, if the technology has declining marginal return to capital. These predictions are more robust than the traditional way of measuring credit constraints as the excess sensitivity of investment to cash flow.

Our approach inscribes itself in a literature that tries to identify specific shocks to wealth in order to identify credit constraints. In Banerjee and Duflo we test these predictions by taking advantage of a recent change in the so-called "priority sector" rules in India: all banks in India are required to lend at least 40 per cent of their net credit to the priority sector, which includes small scale industry (SSI), at an interest rate that is required to be no more than 4 percentage points their prime lending rate. If banks do not satisfy the priority sector target, they are required to lend money to specific government agencies at low rates of interest. In January, 1998, the limit on total investment in plants and machinery for a firm to be eligible for inclusion in the small scale industry category was raised from ₹ 6.5 million to ₹ 30 million.

Our empirical strategy focuses on the firms that became newly eligible for credit in this period, and uses firms that were always eligible for priority sector credit as a control. The evidence for under-lending Data: The data we use were obtained from one of the better-performing Indian public sector banks. We use data from the loan folders maintained by the bank on profit, sales, credit lines and utilization, and interest rates. The loan folders also report all numbers that the banker was required to calculate (*e.g.* his projection of the bank's future turnover, his calculation of the bank's credit needs, etc.) in order to determine the amount to be lent.

We have data on 253 firms (including 93 newly eligible firms). The data is available for the entire 1997 to 1999 period for 175 of these firms. We are in effect comparing how the outcomes change for the big firms after 1998, with how they change for the small firms. Since y is always a growth rate, this is, in effect, a triple difference–we can allow small firms and big firms to have different rates of growth, and the rate of growth to differ from year to year, but we assume that there would have been no differential changes in the rate of growth of small and large firms in 1998, absent the change in the priority sector regulation.

Using, respectively, the log of the credit limit and the log of next year's sales (or profit) in place of y in equation 1, we obtain the first stage and the reduced form of a regression of sales on credit, using the interaction BIG POST as an instrument for credit. As suggested, present the corresponding instrumental variable regressions. Results: The change in the regulation certainly had an impact on who got priority sector credit. The credit limit granted to firms below ₹ 6.5 million in plant and machinery (henceforth, small firms) grew by 11.1 per cent during 1997, while that granted to firms between ₹.6.5 million and ₹ 30 million (henceforth, big firms), grew by 5.4 per cent. In 1998, after the change in rules, small firms had 7.6 per cent growth while the big firms had 11.3 per cent growth. In 1999, both big and small firms had about the same growth, suggesting they had reached the new status quo.

This is confirmed when we estimate equation 1 using bank credit as the outcome. The coefficient of the interaction term BIG POST is 0.95, with a standard error of 0.033. Estimates the probability that a firm's credit limit was changed: the coefficient on BIG POST is close to zero and insignificant, suggesting that the reform did not affect which firm's limits was changed. This corresponds to the general observations that whether or not a firm's file is brought out for a change in limit has nothing to do with the needs of the firm, but respond to internal dynamics of the bank. As suggested, make use of this fact to partition the sample into two groups on the basis of whether there was a change in the credit limit or not: the sample where there was no change in limit can be used as a "placebo" group, where we can test our identification assumption.

Finally, column (3) gives the estimated impact of the reform on loan size for firms whose limit was changed: the coefficient of the interaction BIG POST is 0.27, with a standard error of 0.10. This increase in credit was not accompanied by a change in the rate of interest. It did not lead to reduction in the rate of utilization of the limits by the big firms (column (5)): the ratio of total turnover (the sum of all debts incurred during the year) to credit limit is not associated with the interaction BIG POST. The additional credit limit thus resulted in an increase in bank credit utilization by the firms.

The coefficient of the interaction BIG"POST in the sales equation, in the sample where the limit was increased, is 0.19, with a standard error of 0.11. By contrast, in the sample where there was no increase in limit, the interaction BIG POST is close to zero (0.007) and insignificant, which suggests that the sales result is not driven by a failure of the identification assumption. The coefficient of the interaction BIG POST is 0.27 in the credit regression, and 0.19 in the sales regression: thus, sales increased almost as fast as loans in response to the reform. This is an indication that there was little or no substitution of bank credit for non-bank credit as a result of the reform, and that firms are credit constrained. Additional evidence is provided in column

(2). We restrict the sample to firms which have a positive amount of borrowing from the market both before and after the reform, and thus have not completely substituted bank borrowing for market borrowing. In this sample as well, we obtain a positive and significant effect of the interaction BIG POST, indicating that these firms must be credit constrained. In column (3), we present the effect of the reform on profit. Because our dependent variable is the logarithm of profit, we can only estimate the impact on firms whose profits were positive. The effect is even bigger than that of sales: 0.54, with a standard error of 0.28.

Here again, we see no effect of the interaction BIG POST in the sample without a change in limit (line 2), which lends support to our identification assumption. The large effect on profit is not sufficient to establish the presence of credit constraints: even unconstrained firms should see profits increase when they gain access to subsidized credit, because they would substitute cheaper capital for more expensive capital. However, if firms were not expanding, we should not expect to see sales (column (1)) or costs (not reported) expand as well. Note that the coefficient is a lower bound of the effect of working capital on sales, because the reform should have led to some substitution of bank credit for market credit. The IV coefficient is 0.75, with a standard error of 0.37. The effect of working capital on sales is very close to 1, a result which would imply that there cannot be equilibrium without credit constraint. The IV estimate of the impact of bank credit on profit is 1.79, though again the sample is limited to firms with positive profits. This is substantially greater than, which suggests that the technology has a strong fixed cost component. However, these coefficients also allow us to estimate the effect of credit expansion on profits. We can use this estimate to get a sense of the average increase in profit caused by every rupee in loan.

The average loan is ₹ 8, 6800. Therefore, and increase of ₹ 1,000 in the loan corresponds to a 1.15 per cent increase in loans. Taking 1.79 as the estimate of the effect of the log increase in loan on log increase in profit, an increase of ₹ 1,000 in lending causes a 2 per cent increase in profit. At the mean profit (which is ₹ 36,700, this would correspond to an increase in profit of ₹ 756.13 A last piece of important evidence is whether big firms become more likely to default than small firms after the reform: the increase in profits (and sales) may otherwise reflect more risky strategies pursued by the large firms. In order to answer this question, we collected additional data on the firms based in the Mumbai region (138 firms, a bit over half the sample). In particular, we collected data on whether any of these firm's loan had become non-performing assets (NPA) in 1999, 2000 or 2001, or were NPA before 1999.

The number of NPAs is disturbingly large (consistent with the high rate of NPAs in Indian banks), but large and small firms are equally likely to have a non-performing loan: 7.7 per cent of the big firms and 7.29 per cent of the small firms (who were not already NPA), default on their loan in 2000 or 2001. Among the firms in Mumbai, 2.5 per cent of the large firms, and 5.96 per cent of the small firms had defaulted between 1996 and 1998. The fraction of firms that had defaulted thus increased a little bit more for large firms, but the difference is small, and not significant. The increase in credit did not cause an unusually large number of big firms to default. Default rate, and the higher cost of lending to the firms in the priority sector, is not sufficient to narrow significantly the gap between our estimate of the rate of returns to capital and the interest rate.

Using these estimates and our previous estimates of the cost of lending to small firms, we compute that the interest rate banks should charge to these firms is close to 22 per cent (rather than the 16 per cent they are charging on average). This means that the gap between the social marginal product of capital is at least 66 per cent. These results provide clear evidence of very substantial under-lending: some firms clearly can absorb much more capital at high rates of return. Moreover the firms in our sample are by Indian standards quite substantial: these are not the very small firms at the margins of the economy, where, even if the marginal product is high, the scope for expansion may be quite limited. These data do not tell us anything directly about the efficiency of allocation of capital across firms.

However, the IV estimate of the effect of loans on profit is strongly positive, while the OLS estimate is not different from zero. In other words, firms that have higher growth in loans do not generate faster growth in profits, suggesting that normally banks do not target loans enhancements to the most profitable firms. This is consistent with evidence reported in Dasgupta15, that the interest rate paid by firms and by implication the marginal product of capital varies enormously within the same sub-economy. It is also consistent with the more direct evidence in Banerjee and Munshi showing that there is very substantial variation in the productivity of capital in the knitted garment industry in Tirupur.

Furthermore, while we have no direct data on this point, banker's lore suggests that the firms that have relatively easy access to credit tend to be the bigger and longer established firms. The underprovision of credit to small-scale industry was one of the key reasons cited for nationalization in 1969: thus, it might in fact be the case that while the public sector banks provide relatively little credit to SSI firms, private banks are even worse. Bank Ownership and Sectoral Allocation of Credit An important rationale for the Indian bank nationalizations was to direct credit towards sectors the government thought were underserved, including small scale industry, as well as agriculture and backward areas.

Ownership was not the only means of directing credit: the Reserve Bank of India issued guidelines in 1974, indicating that both public and private sector banks must provide at least one-third of their aggregate advances to the priority sector by March 1979. In 1980, it was announced that this quota would be increased to 40 per cent by March 1985. Sub-targets were also specified for lending to agriculture and weaker sectors within the priority sector. Since public and private banks faced the same regulation, in this part we focus on how ownership affected credit allocation. The comparison of nationalized and private banks is never easy: banks that fail are often merged with healthy nationalized banks, which makes the comparison of nationalized banks and non-nationalized banks close to meaningless.

The Indian nationalization experience of 1980 represents a unique chance to learn about the relationship between bank ownership and bank lending behaviour. The 1980 nationalization took place according to a strict policy rule: all private banks whose deposits were a certain cutoff were nationalized. After 1980, the nationalized banks remained corporate entities, retaining most of their staff, though the board of directors was replaced by nominees of the Government of India. Both the banks that got nationalized under this rule and the banks that missed being nationalized, continued to operate in the same environment, and face the same regulations and therefore ought to be directly comparable.

Even this comparison between banks just nationalized and just not nationalized may be invalid, because policy rule means that banks nationalized in 1980 are larger than the banks that remained private. If size influences bank behaviour, it would be incorrect to attribute all differences between nationalized and private sector banks to nationalization. In this part, based on Cole, we adopt an approach in the spirit of regression discontinuity design, and compare banks that were just above the 1980 cutoff to those that were just below the 1980 cutoff, while control- ling for bank size in 1980. The idea behind this comparison is that the relationship between size and behaviour should not change dramatically around the cutoff, unless nationalization itself causes changes in bank behaviour.

This will allow for credible causal inference on the role of bank ownership on bank behaviour. In order to get a sense of the magnitude of lending differences among bank types, we first divide the banks into five groups, based on their size in 1980: State Bank of India and its affiliates, large nationalized banks (nationalized in 1969), "marginal" nationalized banks (nationalized in 1980), "marginal" private banks (relatively large, but just too small to be nationalized in 1980), and small private banks. Because the geographic districts in which banks are located vary (soil quality, rural population, etc.), and face different economic shocks, we focus here on comparing differential bank behaviour within each district. Our outcomes of interest include average loan size, residual interest rate, 20 and share of bank lending to the following areas: agriculture, rural credit, small scale industry, government credit, and "trade, transport and finance."

To estimate bank-group effects, we regress credit outcome variables for each bank group g in district d on D district dummy variables, and BG1..., BGG bank group dummy variables. The estimated bank group effects, ˆã1..., ˆãG give the average share each bank gives to each sector, after controlling for differences across districts. For example, the estimated ˆã for the average loan size from banks in the State Bank of India group is ₹ 56,190. Compared to the average loan size of the State Bank of India, nationalized banks gave slightly smaller loans (an average of 6,430 ₹ lower), while marginal nationalized banks gave slightly larger loans (the average was 8,350 ₹ greater), marginal private banks gave much larger loans (35,310 ₹ more), and small private banks gave loans much larger on average (58,500 ₹ more).

These results appear to confirm conventional wisdom that nationalized and public banks give smaller loans than private banks. The most informative comparison is between what we called the "marginal" nationalized and the "marginal" private bank, which were similar in size, but the former were nationalized while the latter weren't. Many of the differences between the marginal nationalized and the marginal private banks are large: the marginal private banks gave 5 percentage points less credit to agriculture than the marginal nationalized banks: given that the all-India share of credit to agriculture is 11 per cent, this difference is substantial.

The results also suggest that nationalization led to more credit to small scale industry (an increase of 2 percentage points relative to the private banks; India-wide small scale industry receives 9 per cent of total credit), four percentage points more credit to rural areas (compared to a national average of 12 per cent), and slightly more to government enterprises. These increases come at the expense of credit trade, transport, and finance (nationalized banks gave 6 per cent points less, compared to the national average share of 21 per cent).

The rural and government lending differences are significant at the 5 per cent level, while all others are significant at the one per cent level. While this is suggestive that private and public banks behave differently, the values in the table vary not only between marginal private and marginal nationalized banks, but across other bank groups as well. Thus, from this data alone, we cannot rule out the possibility that the difference in lending behaviour is attributable to bank size, rather than ownership.

To obtain an accurate measure of the impact of nationalization, we examine lending behaviour at the individual bank level, adopting a full-fledged regression-discontinuity approach. We first estimate bank effects analogous to the group effects estimated in equation (2), by replacing the Bank Group dummy indicators with individual bank dummy indicators, to obtain coefficients β 1... β B.

These coefficients tell us to what extent bank b behaves differently from other banks, after controlling for the characteristics of the districts in which each bank operates. We then regress the individual indicators bâ b on log deposits of the bank in 1980 (sizeb), an indicator variable (Natb),which takes the value of one when the size was larger than the cutoff and the bank therefore nationalized, and an interaction term. Banks are ordered by the size of their deposits in 1980, so that banks below the cutoff of 14.5 are private, while banks above were nationalized in 1980.21 Contrary to the results obtained by simple comparison of means, there does not appear to be any significant difference in lending to small-scale industry between public and private banks that are of similar size. That is, we cannot reject the hypothesis that nationali-zation had no effect on credit to small-scale industry. On the other hand, nationalization appears to have had the effect of lowering the amount of credit banks provide to trade, transport, and finance. Nationalization appears to have had a large effect on credit to agriculture.

There is a relationship between size in 1980 and lending to agriculture in 1992: larger banks lend more to agriculture. However, there is a visible break in the relationship at the nationalization cut-off: banks just above the cutoff lend substantially more to agriculture than banks, even after accounting for the effect of size. For example, for agriculture in 1992, the estimated break is.084, with a standard error of.029: the difference between nationalized and private banks is quite significant, both economically and statistically. The point estimates of the structural break confirm some of the differences, but suggest that others are merely functions of bank size. In particular, as measured by credit in 1992, nationalization had a causal effect on agricultural credit and rural credit, increasing each by about 8 percentage points.

These numbers are large, given that the set of all banks lent only 11 per cent of credit to agriculture and 12 per cent to rural areas. These results are significant at the 1 per cent level. Nationalization appears to have had no effect on the amount of credit banks lend to small scale industry, but caused a nine percentage point decrease in the credit banks issued to trade, transport and finance. Not surprisingly, we see that nationalized banks lend more to government-owned enterprises; the two-percentage point difference is particularly large in light of the fact credit to government borrowers represents only two per cent of bank credit. Public sector banks appear to lend at slightly lower interest rates, though the point estimate, seventy basis points, is not statistically significant. We also attempted to measure whether public sector banks gave more credit to industries that had been identified for support in various five-year plans after 1980, but found no evidence that these industries were favoured.

The differences between the nationalized and private banks seem to have decreased over time: in the 2000 data, the point estimate on agricultural lending drops from 8 to 5 points, on rural lending from 7 to 3 points, and on trade and transport and finance from -11 to -6 percentage points. In sum, bank ownership does seem to have had a limited impact on the government's ability to direct credit to specific sectors. Through the early 1990s, the credit environment in India was very tightly regulated.

The government set interest rates, required both public and private banks to issue 40 per cent of credit to the priority sector, and to meet specific sub-targets within the priority sector.

Nevertheless, banks controlled by the government provided substantially more credit to agriculture, rural areas, and the government, at the expense of credit to trade, transport, and finance. Though, surprisingly, there was no effect on credit to small scale industry. Lending differences shrunk over the 1990s, and in 2000 were about half of what they were in the early 1990s.

This might reflect the increasing dynamism of the private sector banks in the liberalized environment of the 1990s or the loosening grip of the government on the nationalized banks. To determine whether public ownership of banks inhibits financial intermediation, we again compare banks just above and just below the 1980 nationalization cut-off, using data from the Reserve Bank of India, for the period 1969 to 2000. We include the six, which were nationalized, which were not.

Since we have data from both the pre and post period, we adopt a difference-in-differences approach. Specifically, we regress the annual change in bank deposits, credit, and number of bank branches on a dummy for post nationalization, and a dummy for post-nationalization in a liberalized environment. We break the post-nationalization analysis up into two periods because the former period was characterized by continued financial repression, while substantial liberalization measures were implemented in the beginning of the 1990s. Public and private banks could well behave differently before and after liberalization. Because larger banks may grow at different rates than small banks, we include bank fixed effects (βi). The parameters of interest are $\gamma 1$ and $\gamma 2$, which capture the differential behaviour of nationalized banks after the nationalization. Standard errors are adjusted for auto-correlation within each bank. The results suggest that while the overall rate of growth in deposits and credit slowed substantially in the period 1980-1990 relative to the 1969-1979 period, there was no differential effect for nationalized and private banks. In the nineties, deposit and credit growth slowed further still. In this liberalized environment, deposits and credit of the nationalized banks slowed down more than the private banks: deposits grew 7.3 per cent slower, while credit grew 8.8 per cent less quickly. These results are significant at the ten and five per cent level, respectively.

The growth rate in bank branches generally tracked credit and deposits, though the decline after 1980 was more severe. While the growth rates for nationalized banks were slightly lower in both periods, the differences are not statistically significant. To answer the question of whether there was a significant difference between public and private banks prior to nationalization, were estimate equation, replacing the bank fixed effects with a nationalization dummy, and a control function $(Kb, 80) = \pi 1Kb,80 + \pi 2K2\ b,80$, which controls for the effect of 1980 log deposits of each bank in 1980 (denoted Kb,80). (These results are not reported, but are available from the authors).

The control function allows bank growth to depend on bank size, while the nationalization dummy will pick up any differences between the nationalized and non-nationalized banks that are not related to size. The estimates suggests that credit, deposit and number of branches grew at the same speed between 1969 and 1979 for banks that were going to be nationalized in 1980 and those that were not. The coefficients on the interaction terms remain negative, and are virtually unchanged from the specification. Thus, it is only after the 1980 nationalization that banks nationalized in 1980 started to grow more slowly.

These results provide some evidence that nationalization hindered the spread of intermediation in the 1990s, but not earlier. We look for features of public banks, examining both official lending policies, and other incentives faced by employees of public sector banks. Official Lending Policies While public sector banks in India are nominally independent entities, they are subject to intense regulation by the Reserve Bank of India (RBI). This includes rules about how much a bank should lend to individual borrowers–the so-called "maximum permissible bank finance."

Until 1997, the rule was based on the working capital gap, defined as the difference between the current assets of the firm and its total current liabilities excluding bank finance (other current liabilities). The presumption is that the current assets are illiquid in the very short run and therefore the firm needs to finance them. Trade credit is one source of finance, and what the firm cannot finance in this way constitutes the working capital gap. Firms were supposed to cover a part of this financing need, corresponding to no less than 25 per cent of the current assets, from equity.

The sum of all loans from the banking system was supposed not to exceed this amount. This definition of the maximum permissible bank finance applied to loans above ₹ 20 million. For loans below ₹.20 million, banks were supposed to calculate the limit based on the projected turnover of the firm. Projected turnover was to be determined by a loan officer in consultation with the client. The firm's financing need was estimated to be 25 per cent of the projected turnover and the bank was allowed to finance up to 80 per cent of what the firm needs, *i.e.* up to 20 per cent of the firm's projected turnover. The rest, amounting to at least 5 per cent of the projected turnover has again to be financed by long term resources available to the firm. In the middle of 1997, following the recommendation of the committee on financing of the small scale industries (the Nayak committee), the RBI decided to give each bank the flexibility to evolve its own lending policy, under the condition that it be made explicit.

Moreover the Nayak committee recommended that the turnover rule be used to calculate the lending limit for all loans under ₹ 40 millions. Given the freedom to choose the rule, different banks went for slightly different strategies.

The bank we studied adopted a policy which was, in effect, a mix between the now recommended turnover-based rule and the older rule based on the firm's asset position. First the limit on turnover basis was calculated as: min (0.20 Projected turnover, 0.25 Projected turnover " available margin). The available margin here is the financing available to the firm from long term sources (such as equity), and is calculated as Current Assets " Current Liabilities from the current balance sheet. In other words the presumption is that the firm has somehow managed to finance this gap in the current period and therefore should be able to do so in the future.

Therefore the bank only needs to finance the remaining amount. Note that if the firm had previously managed to get the bank to follow the turnover based rule exactly, its available margin would be precisely 5 per cent of turnover and the two amounts in 6 would be equal. The rule did not stop here. For all loans below ₹.40 million, the loan officer was supposed to use both equation 6 and the older rule represented by 5. The largest permissible limit on the loan was the maximum of these two numbers. Two comments about the nature of this rule are in order. First, this turnover based approach to working capital finance is relatively standard even in the USA.

However the view in the USA is that working capital finance is essentially financing inventories and is therefore backed by the value of the inventories. In India, the inventories do not seem to provide adequate security, as evidenced by the high rates of default. In such cases it may be much more important to pay attention to profitability, since profitable companies are less likely default. Second, in the USA the role of finding promising firms and promoting them is carried out, to a significant extent, by venture capitalists. In India the venture capital industry is still nascent and it will be a while before it can play the role that we expect of its US equivalent.

Therefore banks may have to be more pro-active in promoting promising firms. Following a rule that does not put any weight on profits may not be the way to favour the most promising firms: while the projected turnover calculation does favour faster growing firms, the loan officer is not allowed to project a growth rate greater than 15 per cent. This may be enough to meet the needs of a mature firm, but a small firm that is growing fast clearly needs much more than 15 per cent. It is important that the rules encourage the loan officers to lend more to companies on the basis of promise.

Actual Lending Policy

The lending policy statements give us the outside limits on what the banks can lend. There is nothing in the policies that stops them from lending less, though bankers are always enjoined to lend as much as possible in official documents. It is also possible, given that it is not clear how these rules are enforced, that the banks sometimes exceed the limits–it is, for example, often alleged that loan officers in public sector banks give out irresponsibly large loans to their friends and business associates. It is not even clear how one would necessarily know that banker had lent too much given that he is given the task of estimating expected turnover. Based on work by Banerjee and Duflo, we therefore look at the actual practice of lending in our sample of loans.

We use the same data source that was used in previous work by Banerjee and Duflo to look at what bankers actually do. Since we have data on current assets and other current liabilities, it is trivial to calculate the limit according to the traditional, working capital gap-based method of lending (henceforth LWC). We can also calculate the limit on turnover basis (henceforth LTB). The maximum of LTB and LWC is, according to the rules, the real limit on how much the banker can lend to the firm. Inertia and the fear of prosecution Since public sector banks are owned by the government, employees of the bank are treated by law as public servants, and thus subject to government anti-corruption legislation.

There is an impression among bankers that it is very easy to be charged with corruption, and that the law states that if any government functionary takes a decision which results in direct financial gain to a third party, the individual is prima facie guilty of corruption, and must prove her or his innocence. The executive director of a large public sector bank was quoted saying "Fear of prosecution for corruption hangs over every loan officer's head like the sword of Damocles." The Economic Times of India has attributed slowdowns in lending directly to vigilance activity. A working group on banking policy set up by the Reserve Bank of India, and chaired by M.S. Verma, noted: The [working group] observed that it has received representations from the managements and the unions of the banks complaining about the diffidence in taking credit decisions with which the banks are beset at present. This is due to investigations by outside agencies on the accountability of staff in respect of some of the Non Performing Assets. The group also noticed a marked reluctance at various level to take any credit decision."

In response to criticism from bankers, economists, and others, the Central Vigilance Commission (henceforth CVC), which is the body entrusted to investigate potential cases of fraud in the public sector, introduced in 1999 a special chapter of the vigilance manual, on vigilance in public sector banks. The language would probably not reassure anyone with experience working in a western bank. The manual reads, for example, that "every loss caused to the organization, either in pecuniary or non-pecuniary terms, need not necessarily become the subject matter of a vigilance enquiry... once a vigilance angle is evident, it becomes necessary to determine through an impartial investigation as to what went wrong and who is accountable for the same."

Interviews with public sector bankers revealed widespread concern: the legal proceedings surrounding charges of corruption can drag on for years, leaving individuals charged with corruption in an uncertain state. Even if an individual is exonerated, she may have been relieved of her duties, transferred, or passed over for promotion during the time of investigation. In theory (as well as practice), even one loan gone bad may be sufficient to start vigilance proceedings.

The possible penalties stand in stark contrast to rewards. While banks are constantly urged by the Reserve Bank of India to lend as much as possible, there are no explicit incentives for making good loans, or ways to penalize officers who make conservative decisions.

In effect, bankers are accountable to more than one authority –the loan officer's boss is one of them but central vigilance may be another, and the press may be yet another. In such circumstances, it may be very difficult to provide effective incentives. If this were the case, loan officers would prefer not to take new decisions. Simply renewing the loan without changing the amount is one easy way to avoid responsibility, especially if the original decision was someone else's (loan officers are frequently transferred). And when they do take a decision, making sure that they did not deviate enormously from the precedent, is a way of covering themselves against charges of wrong-doing or worse.

Not surprisingly, the Central Vigilance Commission disputes the claim that there is a "fear psychosis," and, to bolster their position, released in 2000 a "critical analysis" of vigilance activity in public sector banks in 1999. The analysis reveals that in 1999, the Central Vigilance Commission received 1916 references, 72 per cent of which were credit-related, recommending punishment in the majority of cases. Their 2000 report states "out of every 100 cases coming before it, the Commission would advice major penalty proceedings in 28 cases, minor penalty proceedings in 32 cases, and administrative warning/exoneration in 40 cases."

The author of the report, a CVC official, argued that this level of activity should not be enough to cause "fear psychoses": "These figures reveal that a person is not damned the moment his case is referred to the Commission... These statistics appear to indicate a very fair and objective approach on the part of the Commission to the cases that were referred to it." Based on work by Cole looks at whether there is any evidence for the so-called fear psychosis. The basic idea is simple: we ask whether bankers who are "close to" bankers who have been subject to CVC action, slow down lending in the aftermath of that particular CVC action.

Monthly credit data, by bank, were provided by the RBI. Data on frauds are naturally very difficult to come by. It is also the policy of the government of India to keep the data on vigilance activity confidential: while some aggregated statistics are published, they are too aggregated to be useful for econometric analysis. However, in 1998, in an effort increase the penalty for fraud through stigma, the government authorized the CVC to publish the name, position, employing bank, and punishment of individual officers of government agencies charged with major frauds. This list consists of eighty-seven officials in public sector banks between the years 1992 and 2001. While nature of the fraud with which they are charged is not known, we do know that approximately 72 per cent of frauds relate to illegal extension of credit, while the balance is classified as kite-flying or "other." Since our hypothesis is that vigilance results in a decrease in lending activity, the inclusion of spurious non-credit related vigilance activity should bias coefficients towards zero.

The first approach is to use bank level monthly lending data to estimate the effect of vigilance activity on lending, using the following equation, where yit is log credit extended by bank i in month t, ái is a bank fixed-effect, ât is a month fixed effect, and Di,t"k is an indicator variable for whether vigilance activity was reported by the CVC for bank i in month t-k. Standard errors reported are adjusted for serial correlation and heteroscedasticity. The basic idea is to compare the bank that was affected by the vigilance activity with other public sector banks, before and after the vigilance event.

Which event window to use is not immediately clear: the appropriate start date would most likely be the month in which it became known that vigilance proceedings were under way, or perhaps the date bankers learned of the judgement. The data published by the CVC give only the date at which the CVC provided advice on the case, and the date on which action was taken. Nor is it clear how long it should take before an effect appears, or for how long one would accept this effect to last. We therefore let the data decide, by estimating models which allow effects ranging from one month to four years.

CLASSIFICATION OF REFORMS

Reform measures can be classified into six categories namely a) measures meant for promotion of competition(b) measures meant for strengthening role of the market (c) prudential measures (d) legal measures (e) measures meant for strengthening supervision or supervisory measures and (f) measures relating technology.

Some of the reform measures were meant for strengthening of competition. They included grant of some operational autonomy to public sector banks, reduction of government stake to51 per cent of the total equity and permission to mobilize equity to the extent of 49 per cent from the market, adoption of transparent norms for the entry of private sector, foreign and joint venture banks, permission for foreign investment in the financial sector in the form of FDI as well as port-folio investment, permission to public sector banks to diversify product port-folio and business activities, road map for presence of foreign banks and guidelines for mergers and amalgamation of private sector banks and NBFCs with banks, issue of guidelines on ownership and governance in private sector banks, etc.

Reform measures initiated to strengthen the role of market forces included progressive reduction in SLR and CRR, market determined pricing of government securities, deregulation of interest rates with a few exceptions and increased transparency and disclosure standards to facilitate market discipline introduction of pure call money market, auction based repo-reverse repos for short term liquidity requirement, introduction of improved payment and settlement systems, etc. Prudential measures which have been implemented, covered, fulfillment of capital adequacy norms, new accounting, income recognition, provisioning and exposure norms. Measures initiated to strengthen risk weights to different categories of assets, norms on connected lending, credit concentration norms, application of market-to-market principle for investment port-folio and fixation of limits for deployment of funds in sensitive sectors and activities.

In addition, KYC guidelines, anti-money laundering standards, introduction of capital charge for market risk, higher graded provisioning for NPAs etc. were adopted for implementation. Institutional and legal measures introduced by way of supportives to banks to improve their performance in the area of recovery and asset quality up-gradation included setting up of Lok Adalats, debt recovery tribunal's asset reconstruction companies, settlement advisory committees, corporate debt restructuring mechanism, etc.

Enactment of SARFAESI At was another important measure initiated by the government. Setting up of CIBIL for the purpose of sharing credit information and establishment of clearing corporation of India (CCIL) to act as central counter party for facilitating payments and settlements systems relating to fixed income securities and money market instruments were also supportives extended to banks.

Certain supervisory measures were also initiated in the reform period. They were establishment of separate Board for Financial Supervision in RBI introduction of CAMELS supervisory rating system, recasting of the role of statutory auditors and increased internal control through strengthening of internal audit, strengthening of corporate governance etc. The technology related measures implemented were setting up of INFINET as the communication back bone for the financial sector introduction of negotiated dealing system for screen based trading in government securities and Real Time Gross Settlement System (RTGS).

CHANGES GALORE

Reforms have made significant impact on banks and their functioning. The following are the details of the banking transformation that took place as a result of impact of reforms:

Risk based management: There are various types of risk such as interest rate risk, credit risk, liquidity risk, market risk, operational risk, etc. Banks have started to give attention to all types of risks in their risk management strategies. The RBI has also shifted its focus to risk based supervision. Banks have adopted comprehensive risk management systems. Risk management systems spells out internationally accepted methods of risk measurement for various charge required for meeting prescribed capital charge required for meeting prescribed capital adequacy ratio. Banks have set up separate risk management departments charged with the task of risk management.

Risk management involves many challenges. These challenges include compliance with risk adjusted capital and capital ratios, as a key regulatory and supervisory tool, ensuring risk assessment by line of business, product or even individual customer for making risk profile comprehensive adoption of risk adjusted return on capital and return on risk adjusted capital for efficient portfolio management arranging for adequate IT initiatives for enabling comprehensive MIS and better risk based decision – support, adoption and implementation of better and prudent ALM system that would conform to the dictums of risk based supervisory system.

Acute competition: In post-reform era, competition between banks is constantly on the increase. The market for bank services and products has now became a buyers' market in respect of some products and services and the same will become a completely and universally buyers' market in the years to come. Competition has become acute consequent on the birth of new generation private sector banks. Because of competition now there is need to lay greater focus on product innovation backed by IT advancement and thrust on customization process of such products.

There is also need for greater focus on R&D initiatives and efforts. There is now increased focus on customer-orientation in all activities of banks. Because of competition banks are now giving greater attention to marketing of various products and services. Increase in competition may bring about further change in marketing strategy of banks, involving simulative analysis for clients, products and market segments with the help of sophisticated quantitative tools.

Change in Efficiency Parameters: In post-reform period, we find a complete change in efficiency parameters. To-day, what is important is strength of Balance Sheet. Return on assets, return on risk adjusted capital net interest margin, quality of assets, NPA percentage per employee business, per employee productivity proportion of low cost deposits are considered important to-day. Because of change inefficiency parameters there is now added emphasis on professionalism on the part of bank officers and staff and also on good corporate governance to increase customer satisfaction and enhance shareholder value. Banks will have to assume still tougher posture to recover NPAs and further reduce NPA percentage.

Universal Banking: As a result of reforms, the trend has been clearly towards universal banking. Now banks market credit cards, insurance products, mutual funds and even provide demat accounts and trading platform. There is no takers for narrow banking.

MERGERS AND ACQUISITIONS

In post-reform era, we have seen many mergers and acquisitions. New Bank of India, a nationalized bank and Negungadi Bank Ltd were merged with Punjab National Bank. Kashinath Seth Bank was merged with SBI in 1995-96. Barelley Corp bank and South Gujarat Local Area Bank were merged with Bank of Baroda. Times Bank and Centurion Bank of Punjab have been merged with HDFC Bank. Bank of Madura, ICICI Ltd and Sangli Bank have been merged with ICICI Bank. Sikkim Bank was merged with Union Bank of India in 1999-2000. Global Trust Bank was merged with Oriental Bank of Commerce; United Western Bank was merged with IDBI Bank. Ganesh Bank of Kuruvalwad was merged with Federal Bank in 2006. Lord Krishna Bank and Bank of Muscat SAOG were merged with Centurion Bank of Punjab.

Government of India encourages mergers as there is need for mergers to create larger and stronger banks and to bring about a new banking order. Mergers may be synergy-based mergers to derive economies of scale, market-driven mergers and mergers between banks and financial institutions including NBFCs in the interests of furthering universal banking. Mergers of public sector banks can also be done to create global banking institutions. Through the process of mergers, it is better to create 4 to 5 global banks, 10 to 15 national level players and remaining banks can be institutions, having regional character. We have seen even mergers of RRBs. State-wise and sponsor-bank wise mergers have brought about reduction in the number of RRBs from 196 to 98. Merger of South Gujarat Local Area Bank with Bank of Baroda has taken place in 2004.

IT INITIATIVES

In a post - reform era, there have been significant IT initiatives. In every bank, there has been stress on increased IT application and efforts are on to absorb latest technology is respect of all branches for greater customer conveniences right sizing manpower better MIS and internal control improved risk management, better ALM etc. Banks are striving hard to expand CBS to branches in a phased manner. Strategic alliance among banks in areas like, ATM sharing and funds transfer, etc. has been new developments in post-reform eta. Computerization of all branches including rural branches establishment of rural ATMs, etc. are expected in the days to come.

Focus on Concerns: Another development in post-reform period has been a shift in focus from size related issues to concerns in respect of productivity, efficiency profitability return on capital net interest margin return on assets etc. In the days to come, there will be greater stress on these concerns. This will result in adoption of still better and more prudent risk management system, better and more effective management of spreads and net interest margin through cost cutting product innovation, product-wise and business-line-wise cost, income and profitability analysis steps at an augmentation of fee-based income etc.

Towards Partial Privatisation: Moving towards partial privatization was a trend observed in port-reform period. Government stake in public sector bank stands reduced by 51 per cent from the original 100 per cent. It is possible that any new government coming to power in future may reduce stake to 33 per cent if there is adequate support for the same. When BIP led government was in power there was such a move, but the same was given up because of opposition from the left.

HRD Initiatives: In the post - reform era, there has been lot of human resource development initiatives. There is stress on objective manpower planning, adoption of scientific methods for evaluating the contributions of staff, etc. outsourcing of certain items of work is also a development in the post - reform period. Fresh recruitment of staff, including specialists is taking place in all banks. The performance linked reward system may also be implemented in public sector banks in the years ahead. Average age of staff in some public sector banks is high and this must be reduced by shedding of excessive inefficient staff aged beyond 50 and younger boys and girls with good educational background and IT skills must be recruited in their place.

There should be special courses for preparing bankers for tomorrow. National Institute of Bank Management (NIBM) has launched a post graduate programme in banking. This is meant for preparing bank officers. NIBM alone cannot meet the requirements of such trained officers in all banks. Hence, all management institutes may also start suitably designed post graduate programmers for preparing bank officers for tomorrow. MBA (finance) candidates coming out from management institutes have to be given training by banks in job specific skills. If management institutes have to be given training by banks in job specific skills. If management institutes launch programmers on the lines of the programme launched by NIBM, banks can recruit them and straight away put them on the job. This will save lot of time taken in providing job-specific training in banks.

Increased strength: On account of banking reforms, Indian banks have become relatively much stronger vis-à-vis their counterparts in other Asian countries in terms of range of loan products and services, range of deposit products, capital adequacy ratio, quality of assets, profitability and productivity and overall balance sheet strength. But, the banking sector will have to encounter new challenges particularly in the context Basel II norms that are being implemented and the creation of global brands, anti-money laundering standards and entry of foreign and new players. Standard and poor's analysis have shown that

Indian banking is ahead of China. Indonesia, Philippines and Vietnam. But, the banking sectors of Australia, New Zealand, Singapore, Hongkong, Japan, South Korea and Thailand are ahead of Indian banks. The study undertaken by Moody's Investor Service has revealed that Indian banking is qualitatively better than its counterparts even in developed countries like, Japan, Singapore and Australia. Indian banks have posted the highest return on equity compared to their Asian counter parts during the last four years. There has been a distinctly discernible improvement in the performance of Indian banks on various fronts.

But, the acquisition of a globally competitive size for Indian banks is a major challenge. Banks in other Asian countries, particularly in China are large in size compared to Indian banks. There will be a severe strain on capital on account of implementation of Basel II norms. The RBI has recently issued guidelines to banks on Pillar 2 of Basel II Framework. Pillar 2 deals with supervisory review process the objective of which is to ensure that banks have adequate capital to support all risks and also to encourage them to develop and use better risk management techniques for monitoring and managing their risks.

The RBI guidelines listed some risks that banks are generally exposed to, but which are not fully captured in the regulatory Capital to Risk Asset Ratio (CRAR), such as interest rate risk, credit concentration risk, liquidity risk, settlement risk and reputational risk among others. The RBI has asked banks to develop an Internal Capital Adequacy Assessment Process (ICAAP) commensurate with their size, level of complexity, risk profile an scope of operations. This would be in addition to calculation of regulatory capital requirement under Pillar I. The implementation of new norms and guidelines involves a new challenge for banks.

Acquisition of competitive advantage: The vision for a strong vibrant and globally competitive banking sector in India is based on achievement of competitive advantage the acquisition of which is possible only through stress on efficiency increase in productivity and improvement in profitability, up scaling of technological up gradation and continued improvement of overall balance sheet strength of banks. This would also require adoption of globally recognized best practices on the part of banks.

Facing the challenge of change in terms of range of products, delivery channels, process, culture, structure and overall capabilities would require key structural changes such as consolidation full implementation of real time gross settlement system at all branches, greater efficiency and higher productivity most effective risk management practices better credit management techniques to ensure improved credit quality good corporate governance better technology effective customer relationship management, focus on non-interest income improvement in human resource capabilities and increase in professionalism at all levels. Concentrated attention on these vital aspects can alone fetch competitive advantage.

PRODUCTIVITY

Business per employee of Indian banks increased from ₹ 5-4 million in 1992 to ₹ 163 million in 2004 and profit per employee rose from ₹ 20,000/- to ₹ 1,50,000/- in the same period. Also, business per branch increased from ₹109.9 million to ₹254.5 million in the above period. Measures of profitability *i.e.* return on assets and operating profit ratio and efficiency measures of net interest margin, operating profit to staff expense, operating cost ratio and staff expense ratio have to be improved. There is therefore need to increase business volumes by leveraging technology and down-sizing of staff strength to reduce cost of intermediation. All controllable costs must be reduced by banks.

RETAIL BANKING

This must continue to be an area of focus. Core banking solution must be expanded by all banks to cover all of their branches. Measuring and managing risk across a range of diverse business activities through integrated risk management requires devising a comprehensive integrated risk management framework. This requires urgent attention by all banks.

Banks to-day find it difficult to maintain the minimum required controls expected of them in a new complex and increasingly regulated business environment. The traditional audit and inspection provide assurance that control systems are adequate and function satisfactorily. But, audit and inspections are in fact, a post-mortem and the findings emerging there-from are only after the transactions may not cover all transactions are over. Also audit and inspections may not cover all transactions and many go un-noticed.

They are rarely able to check all transactions in a detailed manner for controls compliance. Therefore, there is a risk of even frauds remaining undetected. To assist in the efficient capture and evaluation of data sophisticated software tools need to be used for evaluation of disclosure controls and procedures and internal controls and supervision over financial reporting.

CORPORATE GOVERNANCE

Corporate governance is of crucial importance for banks. The corporate governance philosophy of banks has to be based on the pursuit of sound business ethics and strong professionalism that aligns the interests of all stakeholders and the society at large. It is therefore necessary to constantly strengthen the corporate governance mechanism in all banks.

Disclosure of reliable information facilitates market discipline, strengthens confidence and reduces the chances for rumours and creation of atmosphere of suspicion and misleading information that may bring about market instability. Indian accounting standards still lag behind global practices in many respects. This has to be addressed effectively at the earliest.

INNOVATIVE BUSINESS MODEL

The introduction of innovative business models and financial technologies the world over has received an impetus through slashing operating cost through higher labour productivity, innovation and business process re-engineering, further reduction of NPAs, micro planning, branch-centric profit planning, effective implementation of plans and monitoring of results CBS and market centric HRM policies and manpower planning. Very high average age of staff, requirement of new skills and talents, working in a computerized environment, foray into new and emerging areas require recruitment of new staff and specialists, extensive training, etc. Although 86 per cent of PSBs are fully computerized only 44 per cent are actually functioning under CBS platform. Covering all branches of all banks under CBS will be a challenge for banks.

Increased customer-orientation and customer focus, product innovation, greater use of multiple channels like ATMs internet and mobile banking, etc. efficient credit delivery besides building up sound financial are vital for banks for facing emerging challenges and obstacles.

Camping of Human Resource Management: Staff at banks irrespective of their functional domain needs to add value to acquire an extra cutting edge. Human resources policies and Human resource management should be revamped so as to convert human resource management from a support function to a strategic partner to the banking business. This must happen in all banks. It is, therefore, necessary to develop a proper recruitment strategy and ensure that it dovetails with identified objectives of banks and helps attract and retain talent through flexible compensation packages and an institutional mechanism of recognition and reward.

FINANCIAL INCLUSION:

There are abundant opportunities for intermediation and mobilisation of savings and extension of bank credit at the bottom of the pyramid. About 60 to 70 per cent of enterprises and individuals do not have access to basic financial services such as savings and credit. Hence, increased financial inclusion of all those who presently stand excluded is of paramount importance. Bank linkage with SHGs, financing of SMEs, rural artisans, rural non-farm activities, etc will be great business opportunities for banks. Emphasis on volume-led growth in competitive balance sheet size, shift of focus from interest income to non-interest income and from capital adequacy to capital efficiency, etc. are vital from the point of view of maintaining benchmarks of return on assets, return on owning funds, net NPAs, capital adequacy, cost to income ratio, net interest margin and intermediation cost.

In bracing for tomorrow a paradigm shift in bank financing through innovative mechanism such as, templates for assessing customer risk and pricing products and services credit scoring, ensuring availability and use of information etc are absolutely essential. Retail banking requires product development and differentiation innovation and business process re-engineering, micro-planning marketing prudent pricing customization technology upgradation home, electronic and mobile banking cost-reduction and cross selling. All these must be given adequate attention. Banking success requires imaginative strategic planning organizational restructuring streamlining and revamping of human resources management, etc.

Developing Immunity: Banks have to adopt and implement strategies to ensure immunity of their balance sheets from interest rate fluctuations by paying greater attention to non-interest income. Growing services sector and financial markets have created new avenues for fee based income. Merchant banking international trade, funds transfer, payment and settlements, consultancy services financial derivatives utility service etc opened up new income sources for banks. But, what is required is a total transition from branch banking to virtual banking, market segmentation to customer-profitability and these are real challenges for banks. Many new challenges may also crop up in the years ahead.

Areas of continues challenge: The areas of continued challenge for banks would be risk management, full implementation of Basel II norms, achievement of full and meaningful financial inclusion an availment of rural business opportunities and opportunities at the bottom of the pyramid, rural credit delivery system, enhancing customer satisfaction, technology upgradation on a continual basis, expansion of CBS platform to all branches including rural branches, further reduction of NPAs reducing intermediation cost increasing non-interest income and fee based income for improving profitability staff involvement in all bank functions, revamping of human resource management – increasing volumes of business despite competition from other banks and other dis-in-termedition sources and participative and strategic planning.

As all the existing and future challenges have to be faced through staff banks have to give top priority to revamping of human resources management and development of human resources. Development of human resources through training, inducing participation and full involvement of all staff in bank functions and activities etc are very vital. Streamlining of audit and inspection, strict internal control and house-keeping, improved risk management, increasing capital efficiency and mobiisation of fresh equity from time to time, asset-liability management and balance sheet management are real challenges, requiring utmost attention.

Ensuring optimum performance: Developing concern for results and performance on the part of entire personnel in banks is a vital requirement. This too will be a challenge. Future of banks will depend on their alertness, operational and capital efficiency, customer orientation and standard of service creation of larger and larger volumes of performing assets, attainment of optimum levels of productivity profitability and overall performance. Future of banks hinges on these and also on their ability to build up large volumes of quality assets with lesser capital charge thereon that perform on an enduring basis. Ensuring optimum performance of each manager, officer and staff will be crucial. Only those banks which are pro-active and which respond quickly to changing customer needs and changing environment and which give adequate attention to the above issues alone can successfully face the future challenges, perform well and grow as strong, vibrant, efficient and sound financial institutions.

5

Social Systems Theory: Applying Knowledge Management to E-Banking

So far in this chapter we have argued for a systems-based KM approach to e-banking, bringing together the social and technical elements of the domain in order to better balance the technology and human elements of e-banking systems. We begin building a perception of these as systems informed directly by social theory, in order to further enhance their foundation. In the study of social systems, where the key to the functioning of the system is human activity, functionalist views are therefore questioned. Experimentation is of limited value in such systems: the utility of problem solving, functionalist techniques, is diminished when dealing with ill-defined, highly complex human activity systems.

As a result, 'softer' methods of approaching the issues are seen to be of value. Social systems are therefore where the reductionist, functionalist approach meets its most severe challenges, and where systems views are seen to be of increasing relevance. Social science involves increasing complexity; a complexity which derives from the systemic nature of the objects of study and the introduction of human activity. The limitations of functionalism are demonstrated in the study of social systems, where predictive models may be seen to have only limited value. Social action does not lend itself to study by reductionist methods, but is determined by the meaning that individuals attribute to their actions.

This brings the discussion back to the functionalist - interpretivist debate, but now, with the support of social theory, this debate can be taken further and a foundation developed for e-banking. This is the direction which has been pursued by part of the systems movement, from its origins in the so called Singer/ Churchman/ Ackoff school, through to present day systems thinkers. Jackson has shown how the soft methods of Ackoff, Checkland and Churchman all adhere to some degree to the assumptions of the interpretative paradigm, and identifies a third position which distinguishes hard, soft and emancipatory systems thinking. The argument is for a pluralist approach, which sees the strengths and weaknesses in each of the three areas and argues that each one must be respected for those strengths and weaknesses. All of this is mirrored in e-banking, where the argument, which from a Habermasian perspective is seen as a critical social problem, is wrongly cast within the sociology of regulation. E-banking is best perceived from a radical humanist perspective. Seen from social theory, for example, the concept of an e-banking system consisting of only the computer element might be seen as excessively functionalist, though perhaps with some evidence of interpretative analysis. But interpretative approaches alone would be seen as insufficient to deal with the complexity of human interaction, which critical social theory, whilst addressing the functionalist and interpretivist, also signals progression to a more radical approach. Much work in this area has already been undertaken in the management science domain, and it is from here that further support will be sought in formulating an alternative framework for e-banking.

CRITICAL SOCIAL THEORY: THE THEORETICAL UNDERPINNING

Critical social theory can be traced from the work of Kant, through Marx and the Frankfurt School. The two most widely accepted modern theorists are Foucault and Habermas, and it is to the latter that management science turned in the 1980s in order to develop a more human-centred view of its domain. CSoT applied to the field of e-banking is appealing for its denial of a grounding in solely natural scientific principles. Seen through a scientific framework, e-banking appears as objective: the same for all involved since it is independent of human perception. CSoT refutes this, seeing our understanding of the world as determined by *a priori* conditions which are uncritically accepted. Critical theory seeks to expose these, and thereby release human beings from their 'false consciousness' to a position from which true potentiality can be attained. An alternative to the current functionalist and interpretivist approaches to e-banking may be found in developments based on the work of Habermas, in particular his theory of knowledge constitutive interests.

Table. The Theory of Knowledge Constitutive Interests

Knowledge Constitutive Interest	Basis of Human Interest	Underlying Paradigm	Methodological Approach
Technical (Control)	Labour (Instrumental action)	Functionalist	Empiricism Rule-based
Practical (Understanding)	Communicative Interaction	Interpretative	Hermeneutics Human-Centred
Emancipatory (Freedom) intent	Authority (Power)	Radical/Critical	Critique Human-Centred with critical

Habermas' three cognitive interests, technical, practical, and emancipatory, are identified in labour, interaction and power, and provide conditions for the three sciences, empirical/analytic, hermeneutic, and critical. The empirical/analytic, served by the natural sciences, is therefore seen as satisfying only the technical interest. Since, as has been argued, traditional approaches to e-banking might be seen as having their roots in the natural sciences, or at best in an interpretative ontology, they appear from a Habermasian perspective as an insufficient basis for e-banking. What is needed in addition is critical science to deal with issues of power and domination, serving the emancipatory interest. From these roots came the development, in the domain of management science, of critical systems thinking.

CRITICAL SYSTEMS THINKING

Critical systems thinking (CST), it is argued, accepts the contribution of both hard and soft approaches, and, through critique, enhances awareness of the circumstances in which such approaches can be properly employed. The pragmatism of functionalist approaches and the lack of theoretical reflection in interpretivism allow CST to expose both as special cases with limited domains of application. The value of CST to e-banking can be demonstrated through the Burrell and Morgan grid. Burrell and Morgan's work, together with contributions from Oliga, may be interpreted as shown in Figure.

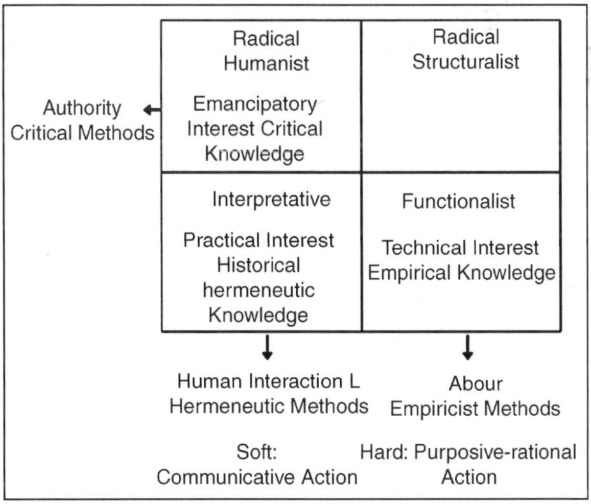

Fig. The Social Validity of Hard, Soft and Critical Approaches

This perspective further supports the view that traditional views of e-banking largely emerge as serving the technical interest, focusing on purposive-rational action. The alternative, evident in this domain since the 1970s but still limited in acceptance, is the service of the practical interest from the interpretative paradigm, relying on the communication of perceptions and consensus forming. The key to the value of critical systems thinking to e-banking rests on the value of an approach based on critical pluralist method.

THE SYSTEM OF SYSTEMS METHODOLOGIES

A convenient starting point is to be found in the work of Jackson and Keys and the 'system of systems methodologies'.

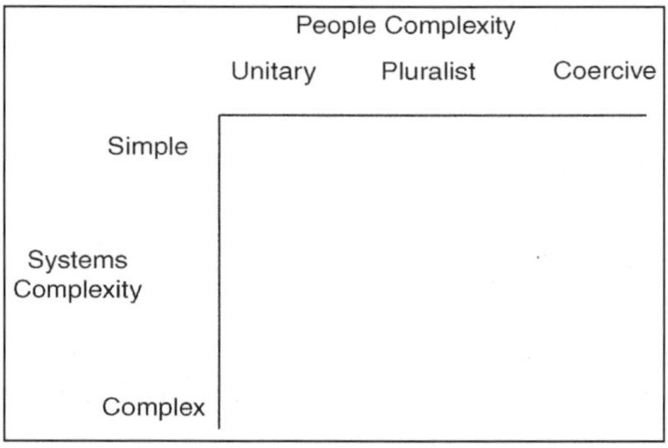

Fig. The System of System Methodologies

The SOSM is used as the basis for an argument that organisational intervention can be understood through determination of the problem contexts within which it is conducted. The SOSM is therefore, first and foremost, a problem context classification, through which it is argued that problem contexts can be categorised according to the extent to which they exhibit a 'people complexity', from unitary to coercive, and a 'systems complexity', from simple to complex. So, for example, a 'problem' may be seen as 'simple-unitary': 'simple' in the sense that it has few elements and few interactions between elements; 'unitary' in terms of people complexity in that there is only one agreed viewpoint.

Such 'problems', it is argued, do not require discussion, and can be 'solved' using hard, scientific, 'design-based' methods. By contrast, a 'complex-coercive' context not only exhibits system characteristics of high complexity but also cannot be progressed until the power issues (hence high 'people complexity') dominating the context are resolved.

In use, this problem context classification forms a basis for determining the methodology to be used in the intervention. So, for example, a 'simple-unitary' problem context will demand the use of a methodology which focuses on design issues, and does not seek to address multiple viewpoints, since these are seen not to exist within the context identified. For e-banking, our earlier analysis would seem to place it at complex – pluralist/ coercive on this classification.

TOTAL SYSTEMS INTERVENTION AND THE COMPLEMENTARIST FRAMEWORK

In the early development of total systems intervention (TSI), the paradigm position taken by the SOSM was core to the approaches recommended. That is to say, it was accepted that different problem contexts 'inhabited' different paradigms, and further that communication across paradigms was difficult if not impossible. So, for example, a problem context characterised by high levels of disagreement among participants, in which debate might be seen as a way forward, might prove difficult to combine with a requirement to produce a technical system, where focus is on design, and agreement as to means and ends is typically assumed.

Whilst 'paradigm incommensurability' was the normal view in these approaches, a way out of the problem, which was proposed through Habermas' theory of knowledge constitutive interests. In essence, this theory was that, at a fundamental level, human beings, in carrying out any task, seek to satisfy three interests: technical, practical and emancipatory. If this could be shown to be so, then the incommensurability of paradigms becomes a human construction, rather than something fundamental to human activity, and by acceding to approaches which take account of Habermas' interest constitution theory, such incommensurability could be overcome.

By the early 1990s, the most comprehensive attempt at applying this theory to organisations was undertaken through total systems intervention, where 'complementarism' was promoted as a way forward, enabling methodologies from different paradigms to be used together in a single intervention, applied to the same problem situation. Total systems intervention (TSI), offered a 'critical complementarist' approach which was seen to be capable of resolving both the theoretical and practical difficulties. This Habermasian perspective sees the functionalist view of organisations as an insufficient basis, serving only the technical interest.

What is needed in addition is social science, to service the practical (hermeneutic) interest in achieving communication and consensus, together with critical science to deal with issues of power and domination, serving the emancipatory interest.

Critique is applied in a Kantian sense, aiming to:

- Free participants from purely instrumental reason;
- Enable practical reason, to examine and re-examine assumptions made; and
- Inform the choice and mix of methodologies in relation to the changing nature of the problem contexts and the strengths and weaknesses of the available methodologies.

TSI is iterative and recursive. Iteration implies that the process is continuous, rather than a start-end method. The TSI ideology explicitly recognises the part played by both technical and human activities in organisations, and the extent to which human interpretation may in some instances so distort the so called 'real world' that study of the latter may become meaningless.

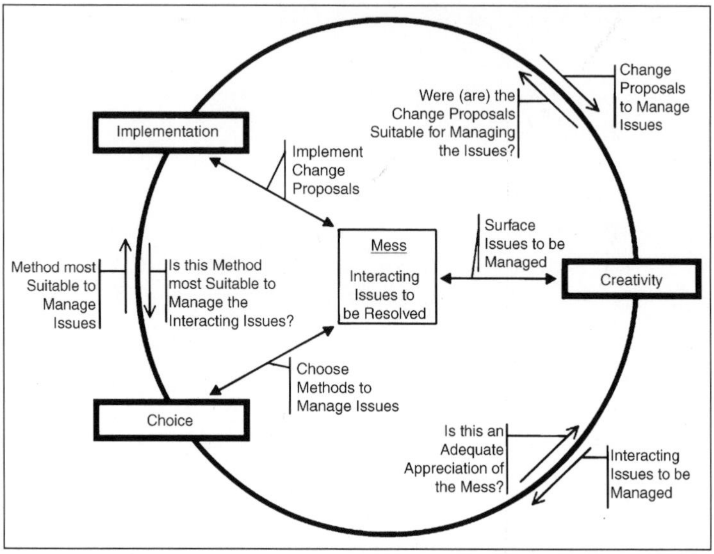

Fig. The Process of Total Systems Intervention(TSI)

TSI provides a critical framework within which choice and implementation of methodologies in an intervention can be managed pluralistically. The problem context is viewed as a 'mess' within which creativity is used to surface the issues to be managed; reflection on creativity then seeks to critically determine whether an adequate appreciation of the 'mess' has been gained. Originally, the SOSM was used to inform methodological choice. Latterly, it has been recommended that this be replaced by the complementarist framework.

In this, first metaphor is used to determine whether the key concern is one of design (technical), debate (practical) or disimprisonment (emancipation); then a methodology or mix of methodologies may be chosen to address the problem context, with critical reflection on whether these methodologies are indeed the most suitable being carried out prior to implementation.

THE CREATIVE DESIGN OF METHODS

Midgley and Ulrich focus on boundary critique as the key to mixing methods. Boundary critique has a long history, but it is from Ulrich and Midgley that the recommendation to critically challenge what should or should not be considered part of any system is drawn. Midgley's approach is to begin with a boundary definition which is accepted as arbitrary, and progress by " ... looking for grey areas in which marginal elements lie that are neither fully included in, nor excluded from, the system definition." The critical choices made at the boundary are of truth and rightness: truth being represented by questions of what is, and rightness by questions of what ought to be. Critical assessment of the system boundary should be undertaken by a representative sample of participants in the system.

Typically, an arbitrary system definition is presented for discussion in, for example, a brainstorming session. Critique can be informed by a combination of Midgley's and Ulrich's approaches to boundary critique: Midgley's approach to examining what is in the margin for elements which support the secondary boundary or the primary boundary; Ulrich's approach to challenging system boundaries through twelve 'critically heuristic boundary questions' which address issues of motivation, power, knowledge and legitimisation for an example of the use of boundary critique). Boundary critique has led to Midgley's promotion of the creative design of methods which was originally conceived as an improvement to SOSM, but is now promoted as addressing issues which SOSM deals with insufficiently.

For example, whilst SOSM promotes the idea that there is only one interpretation of each method, creative design of methods sees methods as subject to multiple interpretations. Also, importantly, Midgley argues that SOSM restricts boundary judgement to simple coercive problem contexts, whereas it is a primary concern of creative design of methods to free up boundary judgement for use in all contexts. Applying the creative design of methods requires that the interventionist maintain a multiplicity of participant viewpoints, together with the potential mix of methods or parts of methods required to address them, within an ongoing critical framework. The boundaries must be critically challenged throughout an intervention, and the approach will be continually changing in response to this and participant feedback.

DIVERSITY MANAGEMENT

Flood and Romm promote diversity management and triple loop learning as an improved way to deal with mixing methods. In essence, triple loop learning is seen as a way to manage the diversity of methodologies and theories available, in addressing the diversity of issues to be found in organisational intervention. In application, diversity management is about managing design, debate, and might-right issues, and so is a complementarist approach to the perceived hard, soft and critical factors which Flood and Romm see as pervading organisational problem contexts. The overall objective of diversity management might be seen as the enhancement of emancipatory practice.

CRITICAL SYSTEMS PRACTICE

In his most recent work, Jackson continues to promote critical pluralism, but now sees this in terms of developing TSI into critical systems practice. Pluralism in the use of methodology is advocated: ".. to make the best use of the methodologies, methods, models and techniques ... to tackle diverse and difficult problem situations while ... ensuring their continual improvement through research". This pluralism must: encourage flexibility in the use of methodologies, enabling practitioners to decompose approaches and tailor them, within a critical framework; encourage paradigm diversity: using methodologies from different paradigms in the same intervention. What is clear in Jackson's recommendations is his view that it is no longer possible to rely on Habermas, but, rather, pluralism calls for a meta-methodology, for which Jackson lays out nine "constitutive rules".

This "critical systems meta-methodology" is seen by Jackson as a "structured way of thinking which understands and respects the uniqueness of the functionalists, interpretative, emancipatory and post-modern theoretical rationales, and draws upon them to improve real-world problem situations." It is recommended that methods for enhancing creativity are applied, at least, from these perspectives, and that methodologies are used as appropriate. Critical systems practice, Jackson recommends, should be embedded within a systems and action research approach; should ensure a pluralism of 'clients', theoretical and methodological pluralism, pluralism in the modes of representation employed, and pluralism in the facilitation process; and should be sensitive to the organisational context in which it is operating.

Further, the claim to be using a generic system methodology, according to the particular theoretical rationale it is designed to serve, must be justified according to the principles and guidelines established for the use of each generic systems methodology. In essence, critical systems practice calls for an improved version of TSI, but it is as yet unclear how these ideas are to be applied. In essence, a set of constitutive rules are provided, but a framework within which these might be operationalised is not given.

CRITICAL PLURALISM

In critical pluralism, Mingers promotes what he sees to be missing in critical approaches to the use of a mix of methodologies: multi-paradigm multimethodology. From a discussion of current dilemmas in critical systems thinking, Mingers promotes emphasis on engagement with agents in a social context as the basis for his approach. The focus, he suggests, should be on the relationship between three notional systems seen to form the multimethodological context: the problem content system, or real world situation of concern; the intellectual resources system, or available theories and methodologies; and the intervention system, or agents undertaking the intervention.

In theoretical terms, the work is strongly grounded on Habermas' theory of communicative action but with the added consideration of knowledge being linked to power. Mingers uses this thinking to develop a framework for mapping methodologies against the four phases of appreciation, analysis, assessment and action, based on Habermas' three worlds. The actual process of critical multimethodology, he argues, "will be a continual cycle of reflection, judgement, and action".

PRAGMATIC PLURALISM

Taket and White offer pragmatic pluralism as a means of mixing methods from an essentially postmodernist perspective. Their approach is strongly grounded theoretically, with the suggestion that guidelines, examples, stories and metaphors are of more value than prescribed frameworks for action. The approach is expressly holistic, and sees pluralism as a means of addressing diversity. Pluralism, they argue, should be applied to the roles of the interventionist, modes of representation, and the nature of the client.

It is explicit that work with the disempowered should be seen as fundamental within any intervention context. In application, it is argued that, in any intervention, there will be multiple rationalities to be managed, and that, whilst guidelines may be offered for addressing these, there is little to be gained from a prescriptive approach. The approach is therefore largely left open to the practitioner, who should follow a strategy of mix and match, operationalising what feels good in accordance with the guidelines provided: the interventionist should recognise differences in methodologies and match these with variety in the local context. Triangulation, the use of parts of methodologies in combination, a flexible and adaptive stance, and critical reflection, are all fundamental to the application of this approach. This completes the review of perspectives on KM.

DISCUSSION AND CRITIQUE

Each of the approaches has in common the aim of addressing diverse problem contexts with a diversity of methods. The system of systems methodologies originally presented an approach to matching problem context to methodologies seen to be applicable to that context, and was expressly based on Habermas' theory of knowledge constitutive interests (KCI). Total systems intervention initially operationalised SOSM into a process for intervention, similarly based on KCI; arguably, diversity management has continued this theme, being essentially an improved application of KCI.

With the creative design of methods came an approach which sought to develop the ideas of SOSM and TSI, enabling the use of parts of methodologies, synthesised to address a unique problem context, within an expressly critical framework. The creative design of methods also introduced the idea of a basis in Habermas' theories of communicative action, rather than the theory of knowledge constitutive interests. The recent critical systems practice advocated by Jackson also moves away from KCI, recommending instead that any claim to be using a methodology according to its theoretical rationale must be justified "according to the principles and guidelines established for the use of each ... methodology."

In this, Jackson might be seen as returning to the need to recognise the distinctive background and theory of each methodology. Pragmatic pluralism draws on a very broad theoretical range, but much is premised on critical social theory. Finally, critical pluralism provides a framework for intervention grounded on Habermas' theory of communicative action.

If we seek to summarise much of the work in KM in terms of theoretical development, the primary basis is to be found in critical social theory, with the main theories being applied in determining intervention approaches having been Habermas' theory of knowledge constitutive interests, and his theory of communicative action. Of these, communicative action seems the most promising arena in which to ground future development of the domain, and to apply KM to e-banking.

A FUTURE FOR KNOWLEDGE MANAGEMENT AND E-BANKING

The ability to communicate by use of language is something that human beings bring to the world by nature of their existence: that is to say, it is not developed empirically, but is a priori. To the extent that any theoretical position can be grounded on such an a priori ability, then such a position may be seen as fundamental to us as communicative human actors. In so far as communication, at least partially, may be oriented towards mutual understanding, it might be argued as the foundation of knowledge creation and sharing.

In these terms, knowledge is not reducible to the properties of an objective world, but can be defined both objectively and according to the a priori concepts that the knowing subject brings to the act of perception. This knowing subject, being social, mediates all knowledge through social action and experience: subject and object are linked in the acts of cognition and social interaction, and the so-called subjective and objective 'paradigms' may be represented as just a convenient tool for understanding, which has been accorded too much primacy as a form of reality. Rather, then, than relying on the concept of paradigms, this concept, and particularly the idea of paradigm incommensura-bility, should be opened up to challenge.

Consider the so-called subjective/ objective dichotomy. According to the paradigm argument, viewed from an epistemological perspective, one who sees a problem context as positivistic, and seeks, for example, a technological solution, will be unable to communicate and share knowledge with another who views the same problem context as existing in the views and opinions of those participants involved in and affected by the system of concern.

There are at least two fundamental difficulties with this:

1. It contradicts common human practice, and, dare it be suggested, common sense. Human participants in social groups commonly combine technical ('positivistic') and interpretative ('anti-positivistic') activity, seemingly denying the paradigm incommensurability thesis from an epistemological standpoint.
2. Theoretically, the paradigm incommensurability view seems to have

dubious support. At its most basic level, it derives from the idea that technical, scientific, functionalist activity cannot be conducted together with interpretivistic, subjective activity. But if, theoretically, subjective and objective are inseparable, paradigm incommensurability becomes much less compelling.

In essence, then, it is the argument of this chapter that these difficulties disappear once a scientific basis for our thinking is denied. For example, suppose science is seen as just one form of knowledge, which in any case is simply a convenient human perception of how the world works. Now, all human endeavour becomes mediated through subjective understanding, and the paradigms as impenetrable barriers disappear. So, the problem of interest constitution theory being no longer defensible is resolved, since it is no longer being relied on.

However, this problem has been replaced with another, which may be stated as follows:

- Accepting all human actions as mediated through subjective understanding leads to the possibility of a basis for KM in the universal characteristics of language.
- The dichotomy between subject and object has gone, and with it, paradigm incommensurability.
- Organisational intervention is recast as an entirely communicative issue. For example, the so-called technical interest of knowledge constitution theory becomes instead an question of how technology may further enable human interaction, all within a framework of human intercommunication.
- The difficulty which now arises is essentially a practical one, of how to incorporate these ideas into e-banking practice.

Work by Habermas on communicative action presents a universal theory of language which suggests that all language is oriented towards three fundamental validity claims: truth, rightness and sincerity. What is most compelling about this theory, however, is that all three validity claims are communicatively mediated.

This viewpoint is most radically seen in respect of the truth claim, where it is proposed that such a claim results not from the content of descriptive statements, but from the Wittgenstinian approach casting them as arising in language games which are linked to culture: truth claims are socially contextual.

'Truth', can therefore be assessed by reference to communi-cation. Rightness is about norms of behaviour, which are culturally relevant, and are therefore to be determined by reference to that which is acceptable to those involved and affected in the system of concern as a cultural group. Finally, sincerity is about the speaker's internal world: his/her internal subjectivity.

These ideas can now be taken forward to provide a KM approach to e-banking which is theoretically grounded, and closer to that which is experienced in action.

TECHNOLOGIES DEVELOPMENT IN MOBILE BANKING

Some banks are making significant investments in mobile systems to deliver a range of types of business value, from increased efficiency and cost reduction, to improved operational effectiveness and customer service to provide a competitive advantage. A factor that has contributed to this development has been the extended availability and capacity of mobile communications infrastructure around the world. The number of types of mobile devices has been increasing rapidly and the functionality available has also improved.

The shrinking costs of data transmission and, due to the intense competition from suppliers, the reduced costs of devices have catalysed the distribution of mobile technologies and amplified the growth of the worldwide mobile market. In those countries where traditional telecommunication infrastructure is not well developed, mobile technologies is transforming accessibility to the Internet based services. Mobile banking may be described as the newest channel in electronic banking to provide a convenient way of performing banking transaction using mobile phones or other mobile devices.

The potential for mobile banking may be far greater than typical desk-top access, as there are several times more mobile phone users than online PC users. Increasingly "mobile life styles" may also fuel the growth of anywhere, anytime applications. There are two main types of technologies available for use in mobile Banking: Wireless Application Protocol (WAP) and Wireless Internet Gateway (WIG). WAP is an application environment and set of communication protocols for wireless devices designed to enable manufacturer, vendor, and platform independent access to the Internet and advanced telephony services. WIG is a Short Message Service (SMS)-based service, in which a menu of available banking options is initially downloaded from the bank to the phone device.

This enables users to browse bank accounts and conduct other banking related tasks. Mobile banking was offered in the UK by the banks such as The Woolwich during early 2000s, but it failed to achieve a critical mass of users. The same story has been repeated in many other counties with mixed results.

The main hurdle in development of mobile banking is low consumer adoption due to a number of factors discussed below:

- *Internet connectivity costs*: Although connection costs from mobile phones is steadily declining it is still high enough in many countries to deter customers from using their mobiles for applications such as e-banking.

- *Difficult user interface*: Human Computer Interface (HCI) issues are a key factor in mobile technology acceptance. HCI includes the use and context of computers, human characteristics, computer systems and interface architecture, and the development process. A general rule is that the easier and more adoptable the interface, the greater is the user acceptance. HCI issues in mobile working are different in the mobile working context than in the traditional office environment. Kristoffersen identifies three key elements that define mobile work contexts and explain how they differ from the office setting:
  - Users' hands are often used to manipulate physical objects, as opposed to users in the traditional office setting, whose hands are safely and ergonomically placed on the keyboard.
  - Users may be involved in tasks ("outside the computer") that demand a high level of visual attention (to avoid danger as well as monitor progress), as opposed to the traditional office setting where a large degree of visual attention is usually directed at the computer.
  - Attention span of a mobile device user is much shorter than a desktop computer user so design of mobile systems interfaces need to be much simpler with very limited amounts of text. Systems navigation needs to be very easy too.
  - Methods to ease the burden of input and spread the requirements of processing output over all the human senses, while still maintaining data integrity are of importance
  - Speech and handwriting recognition are two growing forms of input. The benefits of speech recognition include minimal user attention input, direct system entry, remote microphone capabilities, and faster speed of operation compared to other competing input methods. These technologies need to be incorporated into mobile devices to improve the user's interface.
- *Lack of awareness amongst customers*: Many banking customers are not even aware of availability of mobile banking or associated benefits. As with other technologies, awareness increases with time and needs considerable promotional efforts.
- *Limitations in functionality of mobile devices*: Mobile technologies are still dogged by limitations such as limited battery life, unreliable network connections, volatile access points, risk of data loss, portability, and location discovery. Even in the developed world, until recently, wireless communications were very limited with regards to functionality of devices and speed of communications. Constraints such as screen size, memory, and storage capabilities as well as data transfer rates averaging 14.4 Kilo Bytes Per Second (KBPS), limited

the amount of data that could be both displayed and accessed. These limitations are still one of the biggest barriers to the adoption of mobile working in many countries.

- *Accessibility issues*: High speed public Internet access is offering opportunities to get and stay connected in more locations. Today, hotels that cater to business travellers frequently offer in-room high speed Internet access. As these high speed access networks ramp up, mobile applications are growing in popularity. It may take several years to reach that 'always connected' goal, and connectivity in less populous areas will lag behind high tech corridors.
- *Security concerns*: Mobile technology still suffers from questionable security. So it may not be suitable for transfer of highly confidential financial information. Mobile devices are increasingly becoming a target for virus writers, hackers, and short message service (SMS) spammers. Tower Group's research, over 200 mobile phone viruses have been identified since phones have been able to support PC-like applications such as e mail, instant messaging and Web browsing, and the number is doubling every six months. The resulting disruption of service and data theft can cause many problems for consumers, including lost revenues and customer dissatisfaction for mobile operators. However, the greatest loss may be absorbed by banks providing mobile access, as in almost all cases of fraud banks suffers from the losses. This factor may be making many banks hesitant in providing mobile banking. To be successful in mobile banking the industry must develop an ability to effectively contain the malware problems to a level that is at least on part with that of the existing Internet channels.
- *Organisational changes*: To offer mobile banking many organizations will need to change their business processes, ways in which information is provided and accessed, working practices and work relationships, working styles and most important of all, changes in roles, responsibilities and management structures. It may be a manageable task in some organizations but a very difficult one in others'.
- *Small number of choices (only a few banks offer mobile banking)*: There are a bewildering number of options when it comes to providing mobile banking. It is possible to spend anything from a few thousand to several millions of pounds on any combination of mobile hardware, software and networks without realising many real benefits. With falling prices of mobile technology one may perceive that mobile working is cheap to implement. However, it is important to remember that technology costs are only a small proportion of the likely total

costs. As a rule of thumb, these costs account for 30 per cent of a typical mobile project, with the remaining 70 per cent including items such as training, maintenance, security, management and integration (Flood date?). This implies that the real cost of mobile working could be much greater than promised savings.

- *Technology overload*: The proliferation of personal information devices such as home computers, mobile phones and digital organizers, coupled with the rise of new media such as e-mail and the World Wide Web, have forever altered the way in which information consumers work and play. These fragmented information channels often result in inefficient working patterns as users switch from device to device and between different media which may result in mobile savvy customers unable to use their devices for day to day tasks such as e-banking.

To promote adoption, customers need to be made aware of the advantages mobile banking offers over other channels. Customers should be provided with opportunities to try out mobile banking or see demonstrations, maybe at branches or through electronic media, of how this channel operates. This would raise awareness, and give people a better understanding of mobile banking options. In addition, services being offered should be widely advertised to the target market, such as young people who tend to be early adopters of innovative services. Perceptions of risk, as with many innovations need to be addressed by limiting customers' liability and implementation of latest security technologies. New versions of WAP use encrypted digital signature to enhance security.

The functionality and user interface of mobile devices is improving all the time whereas the cost of Internet connectivity in the developed world is decreasing. These developments mean that the prospects of widespread mobile banking adoption now looks brighter than ever. An example of a mobile phone banking system is reported by Geach. Named M-pessa, the system is developed by mobile phone operator Safaricom in Kenya. It was launched to improve the efficiency of Microfinance by using mobile technology to make financial transactions cheaper, quicker and accessible to much wider population than currently was the case. M-Pessa is a fully operational service available to phone users in Kenya.

The ideas and systems were adopted from South Korea and proved to be especially useful for people with no access to banking or Internet through their computers. Basically, M-pessa is a financial services application installed on a mobile phone. A new generation SIM card is needed with M-pessa software embedded. Upgrades to older SIM cards are available free of charge and works on most mobile phone sets so users don't have to buy a new handset to access it.

Financial services available at present include:

- Person to person (P2P) transfers
- Individual to business transfers
- Cash withdrawals at the registered outlets
- Receipt or payment of loans
- Balances in real time and ordering of statements.

All of which are executed by SMS text message. The transfer facility works in a similar way to PayPal. An area where M-pessa differs from PayPal is that Pay- Pal requires users to have a bank account or credit card to transfer funds to their PayPal account and to obtain the funds on withdrawal from the PayPal account. Arguably, M-pessa could therefore, be better in terms of increased commercial transactions as people without any account or card such as under 18s could use it to make purchases. In the case of M-pessa, a customer must have an account with Safaricom in which to pay cash into initially.

The customer then selects the option he/she wants, for example 'Send Cash' and enters the phone number for the individual or business that they wish to transfer the funds to. The amount is then entered followed by the user's PIN. A message appears asking for confirmation; by selecting 'OK' an SMS will be sent to M-pessa. Soon after that the customer will then receive an SMS from M-pessa confirming that the funds have been sent, and a code for the recipient to use. The recipient will also receive an SMS stating they have been sent funds from the names person/business. To withdraw cash the recipient needs to go to the nearest registered outlet with the code that the funds sender sends directly to the individual, and identification.

The transfer process would take just a few hours in most cases. This or a similar system can easily be implemented in advanced countries such as the UK, US or Australia. The registered outlet could be a post office, a bank, a mobile phone retailer or a local grocery shop. The main advantage is that no access to a bank is needed by either party; all that is needed is traditional cash to pay into the service provider's (such as Safaricom) account. by the person wishing to send the funds. This means that service would be especially useful for people without a local bank or without a bank account at all. The Mpessa technology is therefore, a viable alternative to the traditional financial system. M-pessa provides fairly low cost service in Kenya. Benefits for businesses are that the potential customer base is increased by providing another means of payment and an easy access to funds that for some people currently do not exist. This has the potential, therefore, to help maintain and increase trade in local shops – a much needed respite for them from increasing competitive pressures from supermarkets. Security of such a system could be a problem.

The mobile phone itself could be stolen, potentially allowing the thief to transfer or withdraw funds. The phone could be hacked into, akin to what is done in desktop environments. In the case of a stolen phone the built in PIN and authentication provisions of M-pessa should mean that provided these security details are not held with the phone the thief should not have the chance to use the phone for fraudulent purposes. Extra security could come from CCTV at the registered outlets or phone can be blocked by the network providers. Anti-virus software could also be provided to financial service users at low cost to counter the threat of hacking and viruses. Recent trends suggest that, with the arrival of more functionality and user friendliness in mobile technologies, these technologies might be ready for the delivery of financial services. Riivari's research on mobile banking found that mobile banking is accelerating around Europe and beyond. Laforet and Li's research on mobile and Internet banking claimed that younger consumers were more interested in online and mobile banking than older consumers, and use of mobile banking amongst this segment is growing fast.

To cash in on improved prospects, at least in the developed world, some banks such as Citibank in the US have re-introduced the mobile (or wireless device as they call it) banking. This new service will allow mobile phone or other wireless devices such as BlackBerry users to enter a six digit pin to access a wide range of financial services. Experiments are also underway, mainly in Japan, Norway and US, to turn these mobile devices into payment tools. Often called 'Contactless Payments' it involves swiping an enabled mobile phone near a point-of-sale terminal to make payments which could be a bill or purchase of goods. These efforts to develop such systems often have support from credit card vendors who are looking for new ways to make payment processes more convenient.

6

Fractional Reserve Banking

Fractional-reserve banking is a form of banking where banks maintain reserves (of cash and coin or deposits at the central bank) that are only a fraction of the customer's deposits. Funds deposited into a bank are mostly lent out, and a bank keeps only a fraction (called the reserve ratio) of the quantity of deposits as reserves. Some of the funds lent out are subsequently deposited with another bank, increasing deposits at that second bank and allowing further lending. As most bank deposits are treated as money in their own right, fractional reserve banking increases the money supply, and banks are said to create money. Due to the prevalence of fractional reserve banking, the broad money supply of most countries is a multiple larger than the amount of base money created by the country's central bank. That multiple (called the money multiplier) is determined by the reserve requirement or other financial ratio requirements imposed by financial regulators, and by the excess reserves kept by commercial banks. Central banks generally mandate reserve requirements that require banks to keep a minimum fraction of their demand deposits as cash reserves.

This both limits the amount of money creation that occurs in the commercial banking system, and ensures that banks have enough ready cash to meet normal demand for withdrawals. Problems can arise, however, when depositors seek withdrawal of a large proportion of deposits at the same time; this can cause a bank run or, when problems are extreme and widespread, a systemic crisis. To mitigate this risk, the governments of most countries (usually acting through the central bank) regulate and oversee commercial banks, provide deposit insurance and act as lender of last resort to commercial banks. Fractional-reserve banking is the most common form of banking and is practiced in almost all countries. Although Islamic banking prohibits the making of profit from interest on debt, a form of fractional-reserve banking is still evident in most Islamic countries.

HISTORY

Savers looking to keep their valuables in safekeeping depositories deposited gold coins and silver coins at goldsmiths, receiving in turn a note for their deposit. Once these notes became a trusted medium of exchange an early form of paper money was born, in the form of the goldsmiths' notes. As the notes were used directly in trade, the goldsmiths observed that people would not usually redeem all their notes at the same time, and they saw the opportunity to invest their coin reserves in interest-bearing loans and bills.

This generated income for the goldsmiths but left them with more notes on issue than reserves with which to pay them. A process was started that altered the role of the goldsmiths from passive guardians of bullion, charging fees for safe storage, to interest-paying and interest-earning banks. Thus fractional-reserve banking was born. However, if creditors (note holders of gold originally deposited) lost faith in the ability of a bank to redeem (pay) their notes, many would try to redeem their notes at the same time. If in response a bank could not raise enough funds by calling in loans or selling bills, it either went into insolvency or defaulted on its notes.

Such a situation is called a *bank run* and caused the demise of many early banks. Repeated bank failures and financial crises led to the creation of central banks – public institutions that have the authority to regulate commercial banks, impose reserve requirements, and act as lender-of-last-resort if a bank runs low on liquidity. The emergence of central banks mitigated the dangers associated with fractional reserve banking. From about 1991 a consensus had emerged within developed economies about the optimum design of monetary policy. In essence central bankers gave up attempts to directly control the amount of money in the economy and instead moved to indirect means by targeting interest rates. This consensus is criticized by some economists.

Reason for Existence

Fractional reserve banking allows people to invest their money, without losing the ability to use it on demand. Since most people do not need to use all their money all the time, banks lend out that money, to generate profit for themselves. Thus, banks can act as financial intermediaries — facilitating the investment of savers' funds. Full reserve banking, on the other hand, does not allow any money in such demand deposits to be invested (since all of the money would be locked up in reserves) and less liquid investments (such as stocks, bonds and time deposits) lock up a lender's money for a time, making it unavailable for the lender to use. According to mainstream economic theory, regulated fractional-reserve banking also benefits the economy by providing regulators with powerful tools for manipulating the money supply and interest rates, which many see as essential to a healthy economy.

HOW IT WORKS

The nature of modern banking is such that the cash reserves at the bank available to repay demand deposits need only be a fraction of the demand deposits owed to depositors. In most legal systems, a demand deposit at a bank (*e.g.*, a checking or savings account) is considered a loan to the bank (instead of a bailment) repayable on demand, that the bank can use to finance its investments in loans and interest bearing securities.

Banks make a profit based on the difference between the interest they charge on the loans they make, and the interest they pay to their depositors (aggregately called the net interest margin (NIM)). Since a bank lends out most of the money deposited, keeping only a fraction of the total as reserves, it necessarily has less money than the account balances of its depositors.

The main reason customers deposit funds at a bank is to store savings in the form of a demand claim on the bank. Depositors still have a claim to full repayment of their funds on demand even though most of the funds have already been invested by the bank in interest bearing loans and securities. Holders of demand deposits can withdraw all of their deposits at any time. If all the depositors of a bank did so at the same time a bank run would occur, and the bank would likely collapse.

Due to the practice of central banking, this is a rare event today, as central banks usually guarantee the deposits at commercial banks, and act as lender of last resort when there is a run on a bank. However, there have been some recent bank runs: the Northern Rock crisis of 2007 in the United Kingdom is an example.

The collapse of Washington Mutual bank in September 2008, the largest bank failure in history, was preceded by a "silent run" on the bank, where depositors removed vast sums of money from the bank through electronic transfer. However, in these cases, the banks proved to have been insolvent at the time of the run. Thus, these bank runs merely precipitated failures that were inevitable in any case.

In the absence of crises that trigger bank runs, fractional-reserve banking usually functions smoothly because at any one time relatively few depositors will make cash withdrawals simultaneously compared to the total amount on deposit, and a cash reserve can be maintained as a buffer to deal with the normal cash demands from depositors seeking withdrawals. In addition, in a normal economic environment, cash is steadily being introduced into the economy by the central bank, and new funds are steadily being deposited into the commercial banks. However, if a bank is experiencing a financial crisis, and net redemption demands are unusually large over a period of time, the bank will run low on cash reserves and will be forced to raise additional funds to avoid running out of reserves and defaulting on its obligations.

A bank can raise funds from additional borrowings (*e.g.*, by borrowing from the money market or using lines of credit held with other banks), or by selling assets, or by calling in short-term loans. If creditors are afraid that the bank is running out of cash or is insolvent, they have an incentive to redeem their deposits as soon as possible before other depositors access the remaining cash reserves before they do, triggering a cascading crisis that can result in a full-scale bank run.

As an example for a very simple idea of how the fractional reserve system can work if there is only one bank, for a Reserve Fraction of 10 per cent, a bank can turn a $1000 deposit of "M0" money, into $18,997 of "M1" money. Ignoring interest and fees, which makes banks even more profitable, this is how a bank can copy 90 per cent of "M0" money to make "M1" money, where in this example the money loaned out is simply re-deposited in the bank and loaned out again, and so on, that is how the $18,997 "M1" money comes from the $1000 of "M0" money. Banks do this by accumulating loans and deposits (effectively multiplying) the "M0" supply to make a larger "M1" supply.

Banks can collect interest on the spread of the higher loan interest from the lower deposit interests. Return On Investment (ROI) for a bank is theoretically infinite considering the bank is using none of its own money, if one excludes the cost of setting up and maintaining the accounting system.

WHAT IS MONEY?

Money is not necessarily legal currency (notes and coins). Money is any asset (or assets) that the public in general accepts as capable of performing certain functions (the functions of money). The social agreement (or acceptance) is the most important requirement. Money is believed to improve economic efficiency and social welfare.

- *Barter:* Barter is the direct exchange of commodities without the use of money (exchanging commodities for commodities). Barter is less efficient than monetary exchange (selling one commodity for money and buying another using that money). The exchange is not possible unless there is a "double coincidence of wants" (*i.e.*, the wants of the two parties match exactly), a condition not easy to satisfy. Time and other real costs of completing a transaction (transaction cost) are therefore higher with barter. There are other difficulties with barter as well.
- *The Functions of Money:* Money fulfills three basic functions as:
  1. A medium of exchange (as payment for goods and services);
  2. A unit of account (as a yardstick for measuring value or price); and
  3. A store of value (as an asset in terms of which the storage of wealth is possible).

As a generally acceptable medium of exchange, money is perfectly liquid and eliminates the need for a double coincidence of wants. The ease with which an asset can be converted into a medium of exchange is called liquidity. The suggestion that money must be designated as legal tender is not appropriate since the confidence of the public, not government enforcement, ultimately decides which assets will be used as money. Transaction costs can be lowered by using media of transaction such as traveller's cheques or credit cards. The medium of exchange function does not imply the store of value function, as there other interest rate-bearing assets than money (or cash) which may function better as stores of value.

MONETARY STANDARDS

A society's monetary standard is the basis of its monetary arrangements and includes rules, regulations, and customs regarding the issue and use of money. Broadly, two monetary standards are found in history: commodity standards and fiat-money standards. Under a commodity standard the monetary unit is defined as a commodity such as gold (a physical asset) in a specified quantity and often quality.

The physical commodity itself, or minted coins made from it or papers convertible into the commodity, were used as circulating media (actually used in transactions). Under a fiat-money standard (paper-money standard), the circulating media are the legal tender (notes and coins whose monetary worth is determined and guaranteed by the taxing and borrowing powers of the government), and have virtually no commodity value. No monetary standard is perfect, but fiat-money standards have become more popular and widespread.

GOLD STANDARD

Gold has been the commodity most often used as money. Many countries have used versions of a gold standard in which the exchange rate is fixed to the price of gold. Canada had a gold standard from 1854 to 1914 and from 1926 to 1931. Before 1914, many countries in the West were on a classical gold standard according to which their currencies were convertible into gold on demand. Under this system, the price of gold was fixed and exchange rate fluctuations were limited.

In a pure gold standard circulating notes are fully (100 per cent) backed by gold. The ability of governments and monetary authorities to manipulate the money supply (the power of discretionary monetary policy) is very limited, and hence it is easy to maintain price stability. However, the limited power of monetary policy and other inflexibilities under a pure gold standard may exacerbate economic problems in a recession.

- *Bimetallism:* A monetary system based on two metals, such as gold and silver, is called bimetallism. The exchange rate between the two metals is fixed. Changes in the relative market value of the two metals can lead to the operation of Gresham's Law, which states that "Bad money drives good money out of circulation."
- *Canada's Early Paper Money:* Canada's early experience with paper-

money standards (for example, when playing cards and pieces of cardboard were used as circulating media) were not happy, in particular when the paper money was not fully backed by redemptions. Under the paper standard known as Army Bills, the circulating media were redeemed in full. Prior to Confederation in 1867 the private notes issued by private banks were believed to be the best way to satisfy the need for money. Circulating coins appeared only in 1858. By 1866 provincial notes were introduced. Government effectively had monopoly over small denomination notes while the private banks circulated larger denomination notes. Following Confederation, dominion notes replaced provincial notes, and the first Bank Act was introduced. In the mid 1930s the Bank of Canada was created, and the Bank of Canada notes replaced the dominion notes and private bank notes.

- *Fiat Money and Central Banks:* As the adoption of fiat-money standards became widespread in the twentieth century, the importance of central banks increased. A central bank (*e.g.*, Bank of Canada) is a national bank which is owned by the public sector and is responsible for the conduct of monetary policy. It acts as the banker for the federal (central) government, and entertains a certain degree of independence from the government.

MEASURING THE MONEY SUPPLY IN ECONOMY

The amount of money available in the economy is called the money supply or money stock. Money may include many assets other than currency in circulation (notes and coins), and therefore, the measurement of its supply is not simple.

Some Helpful Concepts of Money

- *Types of Banks and Deposits:* Banks are a group of deposit-taking financial institutions which include chartered banks (*e.g.*, Bank of Montreal, Bank of Nova Scotia), and near banks such as trust companies and credit unions. Depositors lend their funds to the banks Therefore, the deposits are assets to the depositor and liabilities to the institution.

  The deposits are of four types:

  1. Current accounts and personal chequing accounts;
  2. Savings deposits;
  3. Term deposits; and
  4. Money market mutual funds.
- *Cheques and Cheque Clearing:* A cheque is a written order for a bank to transfer a specific amount of funds from the writer's account to

someone else. In a system of many banks, a large number of transactions are done every day using cheques which require the transfer of funds between the banks and changes in the balances of accounts. In Canada this is done by the Canadian Payments Association, which operates an automated cheque-clearing system (a clearing house). Computer technology has increased the speed of cheque clearing, but at all times some cheques are in transit. As a result, the double counting of money held by financial institutions is unavoidable. Therefore, an estimate called private sector float is used to adjust for the amount of double counting.

Definitions of the Money Supply

Empirical definitions used in Canada, from the narrowest to the broadest, are listed below:

1. Currency in Circulation, *i.e.*, the notes and coins outside the banking system.
2. M1. The currency in circulation plus current, demand, and personal chequing accounts at chartered banks, net of the private sector float.
3. M2. M1 plus non-personal notice deposits and personal savings deposits at chartered banks.
4. M2+. M2 plus notice and term deposits at near banks, generally at trust and mortgage loan companies.
5. M3. M2 plus non-personal fixed-term deposits at chartered banks plus the Canadian dollar value of foreign currency deposits of residents booked in Canada.

Some Possible Refinements: Still broader measures of the money supply may be constructed which include some liquid assets such as Canada Savings Bonds, unused portions of credit card balances, and consumer or residential mortgage credit. Each of the money supply definitions measures the aggregate value of many different types of assets. Divisia Indexes have been developed to take into account the degree of liquidity of different assets included in the definitions of money supply.

Why So Many Monetary Aggregates? The link between the money supply and key macro aggregates such as GDP and price level has evolved over time because of financial innovations and deregulation. In response to new developments in the financial sector and the economy, the Bank of Canada has introduced a series of monetary aggregates. These aggregates are crucial variables in the analysis of economic performance and monetary policy effectiveness.

Seasonal Adjustment: Seasonal adjustments, calculated to smooth seasonal variations of money supply aggregates, are less necessary as we move from narrow to broad definitions.

INFLATION AND SOCIAL WELFARE

Inflation is an increase in the general level of prices. Inflation reduces the purchasing power (real value) of money and decreases social welfare through a redistribution of income and other harmful effects. Social costs result because inflation upsets the debtor-creditor relationship; influences the government revenue motive for inflation; creates a deadweight loss for society; leads to the additional cost of distinguishing nominal from real magnitudes; increases menu costs, poses problems for accounting in historical and current values; and generates uncertainty associated with higher and volatile prices.

THE BASIC FUNCTION OF MONEY

The basic function of money is to enable buying to be separated from selling, thus permitting trade to take place without the so-called double coincidence of barter. In principle, credit could perform this function, but before extending credit, the seller would want to know about the prospects of repayment. That requires much more information about the buyer and imposes costs of information and verification that the use of money avoids.

If a person has something to sell and wants something else in return, the use of money avoids the need to search for someone able and willing to make the desired exchange of items. The person can sell the surplus item for general purchasing power — that is, "money" — to anyone who wants to buy it and then use the proceeds to buy the desired item from anyone who wants to sell it.

The importance of this function of money is dramatically illustrated by the experience of Germany just after World War II, when paper money was rendered largely useless because of price controls that were enforced effectively by the American, French, and British armies of occupation. Money rapidly lost its value. People were unwilling to exchange real goods for depreciating currency.

They had to resort to barter or to inefficient money substitutes. Price controls reduced incentives to produce. The result was to cut total output of the economy in half. The German "economic miracle" just after 1948 reflected partly a currency reform by the occupation authorities that replaced depreciating money with money of stable value and, at the same time, eliminated all price controls, thereby permitting a money economy to replace a barter economy.

Separation of the act of sale from the act of purchase requires the existence of something that will be generally accepted in payment — this is the "medium of exchange" function of money. But there must also be something that can serve as a temporary store of purchasing power, in which the seller holds the proceeds in the interim between the first sale and the subsequent purchase, or from which the buyer can extract the general purchasing power with which to pay for what is bought. This is the "asset" function of money.

VARIETIES OF MONEY

Anything can serve as money that habit or social convention and successful experience endow with the quality of general acceptability, and a variety of items have so served — from the wampum (beads made from shells) of American Indians to cowries (brightly coloured shells) in India, to whales' teeth among the Fijians, to tobacco among early colonists in North America, to large stone disks on the Pacific island of Yap, to cigarettes and liquor in post-World War II Germany. The wide use of cattle as money in primitive times survives in the word pecuniary, which comes from the Latin *pecus*, meaning cattle.

Metallic Money

The use of metals as money has occurred throughout history. As Aristotle observed, the various necessities of life are not easily carried about, and hence people agreed to employ in their dealings with each other something that was intrinsically useful and easily applicable to the purposes of life, for example, iron, silver, and the like. The value of the metal was at first measured by size and weight but, in time, governments or sovereigns put a stamp upon it, to save the trouble of weighing and to make the value known at sight.

The use of metal for money can be traced back to Babylon more than 3000 years before the birth of Christ, but there were earlier standards. Standardisation and certification in the form of coinage, as referred to by Aristotle, did not occur except perhaps in isolated instances until the 7th century. Historians generally assign to Croesus, King of Lydia, a state in Anatolia, priority in using coined money. The first coins were made of electrum, a natural mixture of gold and silver, and were crude, bean-shaped ingots bearing a primitive punchmark certifying to either weight or fineness, or both.

The use of coins enabled payment to be by "tale," or count, rather than weight, greatly facilitating commerce. But this in turn encouraged clipping (shaving off tiny slivers from the sides or edges of coins) and sweating (shaking a bunch of coins together in a leather bag and collecting the dust that was thereby knocked off) in the hope of passing on the lighter coin at its face value. Gresham's law (that "bad money drives out good" when there is a fixed rate of exchange between them) came into operation, and heavy, good coins were held for their metallic value, while light coins were passed on to others.

The coins became lighter and lighter, and prices higher and higher. Then payment by weight would be resumed for large transactions, and there would be pressure for recoinage. These particular defects were largely ended by the "milling" of coins (making serrations around the circumference of a coin), which began in the late 17th century. A more serious matter was the attempt by the sovereign to benefit from the monopoly of coinage. In this respect, Greek and Roman experience offers an interesting contrast.

Though Solon, on taking office in Athens in 594 BC, did institute a partial debasement of the currency, for the next four centuries, until the absorption of Greece into the Roman Empire, the Athenian *drachma* had an almost constant silver content (67 grains of fine silver until Alexander, 65 grains thereafter) and became the standard coin of trade in Greece and in much of Asia and Europe as well. Even after the Roman conquest, the *drachma* continued to be minted and widely used.

The Roman experience was very different. Not long after the silver *denarius*, patterned after the Greek *drachma*, was introduced in about 212 BC, the prior copper coinage (*aes*, or *libra*) began to be debased until, by the time the empire began, its weight had been reduced from one pound to half an ounce. The silver *denarius* and the gold *aureus* (introduced about 87 BC) suffered only minor debasement until the time of Nero (54 BC), when almost continuous tampering with the coinage began.

The metal content of the gold and silver coins was reduced, and the proportion of alloy was increased to three-fourths or more of its weight. Debasement in Rome (as ever since) used the state's profit from money creation to cover its inability or unwillingness to finance its expenditures through explicit taxes. But the debasement in turn raised prices, worsened Rome's economic situation and contributed to the collapse of the empire.

History of Paper Money

The history of money shows repeated innovations that changed the objects used as money. Carrying large sums in gold, silver, or other metal was inconvenient and risked loss or theft. China was the first to use paper money, more than 1000 years ago. By the late 18th and early 19th centuries, paper money and bank notes spread widely. The bulk of the money in use came to consist not of actual gold or silver but of fiduciary money — promises to pay specified amounts of gold and silver.

These promises were initially issued by individuals or companies as bank notes or as the transferable book entries that came to be called deposits. Although deposits and bank notes began as claims to gold or silver on deposit at a bank or with a merchant, this later changed. Knowing that everyone would not claim his or her balance at once, the bank or merchant could issue more claims to the gold and silver than the amount held in safekeeping. It could invest the difference or lend it at interest. In periods of distress, when borrowers did not repay their loans or in case of overissue, the bank might fail.

Gradually, the government assumed a supervisory role. It specified legal tender, defining the type of payment that legally discharged a debt when offered to the creditor and that could be used to pay taxes. It set the weight of coins and their metallic composition. Later, it replaced fiduciary paper money promising to pay gold or silver with fiat paper money — that is, notes that are issued on the "fiat" of the sovereign government, are specified to be so many dollars or pounds, or yen, and are legal tender but are not promises to pay something else.

The first large-scale issue in a Western country occurred in France in the early 18th century. The French revolutionary government issued paper money in the form of assignats from 1789 to 1796. The American colonies and later the Continental Congress issued bills of credit that could be used in making payments. These early experiments gave fiat money a deservedly bad name. The money was overissued, and prices rose drastically until the money became worthless or was redeemed in metallic money (or promises to pay metallic money) at a small fraction of its initial value.

Subsequent issues of fiat money in the major countries during the 19th century were temporary departures from a metallic standard. In Great Britain, for example, the government suspended payment of gold for the outstanding bank notes during the Napoleonic Wars (1797-1815). To finance the war, the government issued fiat paper money. Prices in Great Britain doubled as a result, and gold coin and bullion became more expensive in terms of paper. To restore the gold standard at the former gold price, the government deflated the price level by reducing the quantity of money. In 1821, the gold standard was restored. Similarly, in the United States during the Civil War, the government suspended convertibility of Union currency (greenbacks) into specie, and resumption did not occur until 1879. At its peak in 1864, the greenback price of gold, nominally equivalent to $100, reached more than $250.

Episodes of this kind, repeated in many countries, convinced the public that war brings inflation, and the aftermath of war brings deflation and depression. This sequence is not inevitable. It reflected nineteenth century experience under metallic money standards. Typically, wars required increased government spending and budget deficits. Governments suspended the metallic (gold) standard and financed their deficits by borrowing and printing paper money. Prices rose. The end of wartime spending and inflation left the price of gold far above its pre-war value. To restore the metallic standard at the prewar price of gold in paper money, prices quoted in paper money had to fall. The alternative was to accept the increased price of gold in paper money by devaluing the currency. After World War I, Great Britain and the United States deflated, but many other countries devalued their currencies against gold. After World War II, all major countries accepted the higher price level and most devalued to avoid deflation and depression.

Since the cost of producing paper money is far below its exchange value, forgery is common. The development of copying machines made forgery easier, necessitating changes in paper, use of metallic strips and other devices to make forgery more difficult. The use of machines to identify, count, or change currency increases the need for tests to identify genuine currency.

MONEY CREATION

Modern central banking allows banks to practice fractional reserve banking with inter-bank business transactions with a reduced risk of bankruptcy. The process of fractional-reserve banking expands the money supply of the economy but also increases the risk that a bank cannot meet its depositor withdrawals.

Though not a mainstream economic belief, a number of central bankers, monetary economists, and text books, have said that banks create money by 'extending credit', where banks obligate themselves to borrowers, and then later manage whatever liabilities this creates for them, where if the central bank targets interest rates, it must supply base money on demand to meet the banks reserve requirements, *after* the banks have begun the lending process and that rather than deposits leading to loans, causality is reversed, and loans lead to deposits.

There are two types of money in a fractional-reserve banking system operating with a central bank:

1. *Central bank money:* Money created or adopted by the central bank regardless of its form -- precious metals, commodity certificates, banknotes, coins, electronic money loaned to commercial banks, or anything else the central bank chooses as its form of money
2. *Commercial bank money:* Demand deposits in the commercial banking system; sometimes referred to as chequebook money

When a deposit of central bank money is made at a commercial bank, the central bank money is removed from circulation and added to the commercial banks' reserves (it is no longer counted as part of M1 money supply). Simultaneously, an equal amount of new commercial bank money is created in the form of bank deposits. When a loan is made by the commercial bank (which keeps only a fraction of the central bank money as reserves), using the central bank money from the commercial bank's reserves, the m1 money supply expands by the size of the loan. This process is called deposit multiplication.

Example of Deposit Multiplication

The mainstream economics relending model of how loans are funded and how the money supply is affected. It also shows how central bank money is used to create commercial bank money from an initial deposit of $100 of central bank money. In the example, the initial deposit is lent out 10 times with a fractional-reserve rate of 20 per cent to ultimately create $500 of commercial bank money. Each successive bank involved in this process creates new commercial bank money on a diminishing portion of the original deposit of central bank money. This is because banks only lend out a portion of the central bank money deposited, in order to fulfill reserve requirements and to ensure that they always have enough reserves on hand to meet normal transaction demands.

The relending model begins when an initial $100 deposit of central bank money is made into Bank A. Bank A takes 20 per cent of it, or $20, and sets it aside as reserves, and then loans out the remaining 80 per cent, or $80. At this point, the money supply actually totals $180, not $100, because the bank has loaned out $80 of the central bank money, kept $20 of central bank money in reserve (not part of the money supply), and substituted a newly created $100 IOU claim for the depositor that *acts equivalently to and can be implicitly redeemed for* central bank money (the depositor can transfer it to another account, write a check on it, demand his cash back, etc.). These claims by depositors on banks are termed *demand deposits* or *commercial bank money* and are simply recorded in a bank's accounts as a liability (specifically, an IOU to the depositor). From a depositor's perspective, commercial bank money is equivalent to central bank money – it is impossible to tell the two forms of money apart unless a bank run occurs (at which time everyone wants central bank money).

At this point in the relending model, Bank A now only has $20 of central bank money on its books. The loan recipient is holding $80 in central bank money, but he soon spends the $80. The receiver of that $80 then deposits it into Bank B. Bank B is now in the same situation as Bank A started with, except it has a deposit of $80 of central bank money instead of $100. Similar to Bank A, Bank B sets aside 20 per cent of that $80, or $16, as reserves and lends out the remaining $64, increasing money supply by $64. As the process continues, more commercial bank money is created. To simplify the table, a different bank is used for each deposit. In the real world, the money a bank lends may end up in the same bank so that it then has more money to lend out.

Individual Bank	**Amount Deposited**	**Lent Out**	**Reserves**
A	100	80	20
B	80	64	16
C	64	51.20	12.80
D	51.20	40.96	10.24
E	40.96	32.77	8.19
F	32.77	26.21	6.55
G	26.21	20.97	5.24
H	20.97	16.78	4.19
I	16.78	13.42	3.36
J	13.42	10.74	2.68
K	10.74		
			Total Reserves:
			89.26
	Total Amount of Deposits:	Total Amount Lent Out:	Total Reserves + Last Amount Deposited:
	457.05	357.05	100

The expansion of \$100 of central bank money through fractional-reserve lending with a 20 per cent reserve rate. \$400 of commercial bank money is created virtually through loans. Although no new money was physically created in addition to the initial \$100 deposit, new commercial bank money is created through loans. The 2 boxes marked in red show the location of the original \$100 deposit throughout the entire process. The total reserves plus the last deposit (or last loan, whichever is last) will always equal the original amount, which in this case is \$100. As this process continues, more commercial bank money is created. The amounts in each step decrease towards a limit. If a graph is made showing the accumulation of deposits, one can see that the graph is curved and approaches a limit. This limit is the maximum amount of money that can be created with a given reserve rate. When the reserve rate is 20 per cent, the maximum amount of total deposits that can be created is \$500 and the maximum increase in the money supply is \$400. For an individual bank, the deposit is considered a *liability* whereas the loan it gives out and the reserves are considered *assets*. Deposits will always be equal to loans plus a bank's reserves, since loans and reserves are created from deposits. This is the basis for a bank's *balance sheet*. Fractional reserve banking allows the money supply to expand or contract. Generally the expansion or contraction of the money supply is dictated by the balance between the rate of new loans being created and the rate of existing loans being repaid or defaulted on.

The balance between these two rates can be influenced to some degree by actions of the central bank. This table gives an outline of the makeup of money supplies worldwide. Most of the money in any given money supply consists of commercial bank money. The value of commercial bank money is based on the fact that it can be exchanged freely at a bank for central bank money. The actual increase in the money supply through this process may be lower, as (at each step) banks may choose to hold reserves in excess of the statutory minimum, borrowers may let some funds sit idle, and some members of the public may choose to hold cash, and there also may be delays or frictions in the lending process. Government regulations may also be used to limit the money creation process by preventing banks from giving out loans even though the reserve requirements have been fulfilled.

Money multiplier

The most common mechanism used to measure this increase in the money supply is typically called the money multiplier. It calculates the maximum amount of money that an initial deposit can be expanded to with a given reserve ratio.

Formula

The money multiplier, m, is the inverse of the reserve requirement, R:

$$m = \frac{1}{R}$$

Example:

For example, with the reserve ratio of 20 per cent, this reserve ratio, *R*, can also be expressed as a fraction:

$$R = \frac{1}{5}$$

So then the money multiplier, *m*, will be calculated as:

$$m = \frac{1}{1/5} = 5$$

This number is multiplied by the initial deposit to show the maximum amount of money it can be expanded to. The money creation process is also affected by the currency drain ratio (the propensity of the public to hold banknotes rather than deposit them with a commercial bank), and the safety reserve ratio (excess reserves beyond the legal requirement that commercial banks voluntarily hold—usually a small amount). Data for "excess" reserves and vault cash are published regularly by the Federal Reserve in the United States.

In practice, the actual money multiplier varies over time, and may be substantially lower than the theoretical maximum. Confusingly there are many different "money multipliers", some referring to ratios of rates of change of different money measures and others referring to ratios of absolute values of money measures.

Reserve requirements

The modern mainstream view of reserve requirements is that they are intended to prevent banks from:

- Generating too much money by making too many loans against the narrow money deposit base;
- Having a shortage of cash when large deposits are withdrawn (although the reserve is thought to be a legal minimum, it is understood that in a crisis or bank run, reserves may be made available on a temporary basis).

In practice, some central banks do not require reserves to be held, and in some countries that do, such as the USA and the EU they are not required to be held during the day when the banks are lending, and banks can borrow from other banks at near the central bank policy rate to ensure they have the necessary amount of required reserves by the close of business. *Required* reserves are therefore considered by some central bankers, monetary economists and textbooks to only play a very small role in limiting money creation in these countries. Most commentators agree however, that they help the banks have sufficient supplies of highly liquid assets, so that the system operates in an orderly fashion and maintains public confidence.

The UK for example, which does not have required reserves, does have requirements that the banks keep a certain amount of cash, and in Australia while there are no reserve requirements, there *are* a variety of requirements to ensure the banks have a stabilising ratio of liquid assets, such as deposits held with local banks.

Individual countries adhere to varying required reserve ratios which have changed over time. In addition to reserve requirements, there are other required financial ratios that affect the amount of loans that a bank can fund. The capital requirement ratio is perhaps the most important of these other required ratios. When there are no mandatory reserve requirements, which are considered by some mainstream economists to restrict lending, the capital requirement ratio acts to prevent an infinite amount of bank lending.

Alternative views

Theories of *endogenous money* date to the 19th century, and were described by Joseph Schumpeter, and later the post-Keynesians. Endogenous money theory states that the supply of money is credit-driven and determined endogenously by the demand for bank loans, rather than exogenously by monetary authorities.

Charles Goodhart worked for many years to encourage a different approach to money supply analysis and said the base money multiplier model was "such an incomplete way of describing the process of the determination of the stock of money that it amounts to misinstruction" Ten years later he said: "Almost all those who have worked in a [central bank] believe that this view is totally mistaken; in particular, it ignores the implications of several of the crucial institutional features of a modern commercial banking system...". Goodhart has characterized the money stock as a dependent endogenous variable. In 1994, Mervyn King said that the causation between money and demand is a contentious issue, because although textbooks assume that money is exogenous, in the United Kingdom money is endogenous, as the Bank of England provides base money on demand and broad money is created by the banking system.

Seth B. Carpenter and Selva Demiralp concluded the simple textbook base money multiplier is implausible in the United States.

MONEY SUPPLIES AROUND THE WORLD

Fractional-reserve banking determines the relationship between the amount of central bank money (currency) in the official money supply statistics and the total money supply. Most of the money in these systems is commercial bank money. Fractional reserve banking involves the issuance and creation of commercial bank money, which increases the money supply through the deposit creation multiplier. The issue of money through the banking system is a mechanism of monetary transmission, which a central bank can influence indirectly by raising or lowering interest rates (although banking regulations may also be adjusted to influence the money supply, depending on the circumstances).

REGULATION

Because the nature of fractional-reserve banking involves the possibility of bank runs, central banks have been created throughout the world to address these problems.

Central banks

Government controls and bank regulations related to fractional-reserve banking have generally been used to impose restrictive requirements on note issue and deposit taking on the one hand, and to provide relief from bankruptcy and creditor claims, and/or protect creditors with government funds, when banks defaulted on the other hand.

Such measures have included:

- Minimum required reserve ratios (RRRs)
- Minimum capital ratios
- Government bond deposit requirements for note issue
- 100 per cent Marginal Reserve requirements for note issue, such as the Bank Charter Act 1844 (UK)
- Sanction on bank defaults and protection from creditors for many months or even years, and
- Central bank support for distressed banks, and government guarantee funds for notes and deposits, both to counteract bank runs and to protect bank creditors.

MONETARY THEORY OF CREDIT

Credit theories of money, also called debt theories of money are concerned with the relationship between credit and money. Proponents of these theories, such as Alfred Mitchell-Innes, will sometimes emphasize that credit and debt are the same thing, seen from different points of view. Proponents assert that the essential nature of money is credit (debt), at least in eras where money is not backed by a commodity such as gold. Two common strands of thought within these theories are the idea that money originated as a unit of account for debt, and the position that money creation involves the simultaneous creation of money and debt. Some proponents of credit theories of money argue that money is best understood as debt even in systems often understood as usingcommodity money. Others hold that money equates to credit only in a system based on fiat money, where they argue that all forms of money including cash can be considered as forms of credit money. The first formal *Credit theory of money* arose in the 19th century. Anthropologist David Graeber has argued that for most of human history, money has been widely understood to represent debt, though he concedes that even prior to the modern era, there have been several periods where rival theories like Metallism have held sway.

Schumpeter made a useful distinction between the "monetary theory of credit" and the "credit theory of money". The first sees private "credit money" as only a temporary substitute for "real money"—possibly a "natural" money that is free of social relations. Final settlement must take place in real money, which is the ultimate unit of account, store of value, and means of payment. Exchanges might take place based on credit, but credit expansion is strictly constrained by the quantity of real money.

Ultimately, only the quantity of real money matters so far as economic activity is concerned. Most modern macroeconomic theory is based on the concept of a deposit multiplier that links the quantity of privately created money (mostly, bank deposits) to the quantity of high powered money, HPM. This is the modern equivalent to what Schumpeter called the monetary theory of credit, and Friedman (or Karl Brunner) is a good representative. The real money that is the basis of deposit expansion should be controlled, preferably by a rule that will make modern fiat money operate more like the metallic money of the hypothesised past.

The credit theory of money, by contrast, emphasizes that credit normally expands to allow economic activity to grow. This new credit creates new claims on HPM even as it leads to new production. However, because there is a clearing system that cancels claims and debits without use of HPM, credit is not merely a temporary substitute for HPM. Schumpeter does not deny the role played by HPM as an ultimate means of settlement, he simply denies that it is required for most final settlements.

Like Schumpeter, Innes focused on credit and the clearing system, mocking the view that "in modern days a money-saving device has been introduced called *credit* and that, before this device was known all purchases were paid for in cash, in other words in coins." Instead, he argued "careful investigation shows that the precise reverse is true". Rather than selling in exchange for "some intermediate commodity called the 'medium of exchange'", a sale is really "the exchange of a commodity for a credit". Innes called this the "primitive law of commerce": "The constant creation of credits and debts, and their extinction by being cancelled against one another, forms the whole mechanism of commerce..." He explains:

By buying we become debtors and by selling we become creditors, and being all both buyers and sellers we are all debtors and creditors. As debtor we can compel our creditor to cancel our obligation to him by handing to him his own acknowlegment [sic] of a debt to an equivalent amount which he, in his turn, has incurred. The market, then, is not viewed as the place where goods are exchanged, but rather as a clearinghouse for debts and credits: credits and debits are the focus, not market exchange. Indeed, Innes rejected the typical analysis of the medieval village fairs, arguing that these were first developed to settle debts, with retail trade later developing as a sideline to the clearing house trade. Even if Innes goes too far in this claim, it is useful in emphasizing debts and credits and clearing as primary, with trade in goods and services of subsidiary interest—one of the ways in which one becomes a debtor or creditor (or clears debts). Innes viewed the creditor-debtor relation (not the barter exchange) as the fundamental social relation lying behind money's veil. Further, there is no "natural" relation-free money that lies behind the credits and debts. Indeed, for Innes even HPM, including gold coins, is credit money—for reasons discussed in the next section.

The credit approach as advanced by Innes and Schumpeter provides a more useful vision of monetary operations of a capitalist, "market", economy than does the orthodox view of money serving as a lubricating medium of exchange. The monetary production economy as described by Marx, Veblen, and Keynes is dominated by a complex web of financial relations that were characterised by Minsky as "money now for money later" propositions. Money is not a veil that should be stripped away to observe the essential characteristics of the "market economy". Rather, the money of account and those credit-debt relations are the key institutional relations of the capitalist economy.

THE STATE THEORY OF MONEY

Now, however, the problems of metallism and the idea of money as credit, and in turn the functional finance implications, are well understood. Besides the contributions of Knapp and Innes to these areas, what did they think about private credit money creation? There is, given their focus on metallism and other issues of the time, relatively little on private money creation in their work.

The past century, as mentioned, has seen the development of more or less a full understanding of the implications of the ideas of Knapp and Innes. However, there have been numerous relatively small crises in the past century (just since the 1980s: Savings and Loan in the US, the Japanese asset price bubble, LCTM, banking crises in Finland, Sweden, Asia, Russia, Argentina, Ecuador, Uruguay, and throughout Europe) and two massive economic crises that have had much or most of their basis in the private credit money creation realm of the economy.

In other words, although a great deal of the suboptimal performance (sustained unemployment, lack of investment in infrastructure, education, and health care) has been due to a failure to understand and apply readily implementable state money and functional finance insights, there has also been another major source of economic suffering, resulting from the non-state-money side of the economy. The worldwide private credit money system has caused untold suffering and misery for millions.

State Money and Approach

Goodhart (1998) makes a useful distinction between the metalist, orthodox, approach and the chartalist—or state money—approach. The latter emphasizes that money evolves not from a pre-money market system but rather from the "penal system" based on the ancient practice of wergild. Hence, it highlights the important role played by "authorities" in the origins and evolution of money. More specifically, the state (or any other authority able to impose an obligation) imposes a liability in the form of a generalised, social unit of account—a money—used for measuring the obligation.

This does not require the pre-existence of markets, and, indeed, almost certainly predates them (as discussed above). Once the authorities can levy such obligations, they can name what fulfills the obligations by denominating in a social unit of account those things that can be delivered, in other words, by pricing them. This resolves the conundrum faced by methodological individualists and emphasizes the social nature of money and markets—which did not spring from the minds of individual utility maximizers, but rather were both socially created.

Note that the state can—in theory—choose anything to function as the "money thing" denominated in the money of account: "Validity by proclamation is not bound to any material" and the material can be changed to any other so long as the state announces a conversion rate. In practice, the state needs to choose something that cannot be readily counterfeited. The state chooses the unit, names the thing accepted in payment of obligations to itself, and (eventually) issues the money-thing it accepts.

In (almost) all modern developed nations, the state accepts the currency issued by the treasury (in the US, coins), plus notes issued by the central bank (Federal Reserve notes in the US), plus bank reserves (again, liabilities of the central bank)—together, HPM. The material from which the money thing issued by the state is produced is not important (whether it is gold, base metal, paper, or even digitised numbers at the central bank). No matter what it is made of, the state must announce its nominal value (that is to say, the value at which the money-thing is accepted in meeting obligations to the state) and accept it in payments made to the state.

The state money approach might appear to be inconsistent with the credit money approach described in the previous section because it is not obvious that state money represents a credit/debt relation. Indeed, some critics of the state money approach imagine that markets operating on the basis of private credits and debits denominated in a money of account pre-existed the state or authorities. The state is then supposed to have inserted itself into the private money system, taxing and borrowing the *private credit money* for use in public expenditures. The state's own money initially consists of "commodity money"—precious metal coins whose value is determined by embodied bullion—*not* a credit money. Later, somehow, the state manages to dupe the public into accepting "fiat money" that is neither fish (debt) nor fowl (precious metal). Again, close control over the issue of intrinsically valueless state money is necessary to prevent inflation or hyperinflation.

In contrast, Innes insisted that when the state spends, it becomes a debtor (as he said, "by buying we become debtors") as it issues state money. Hence, even state money is credit money, however, as we will see, it is a special kind of credit, "redeemed by taxation". For the government, a dollar is a promise to 'pay', a promise to 'satisfy', a promise to 'redeem,' just as all other money is. Innes argued that even on a gold standard it is not gold that government promises to pay:

It is true that all the government paper money is convertible into gold coin, but redemption of paper issues in gold coin is not redemption at all, but merely the exchange of one form of obligation for another of an identical nature.

Whether the government's IOU is printed on paper or on a gold coin, it is indebted just the same. What, then, is the nature of the government's IOU? This brings us to the "very nature of credit throughout the world", which is "the right of the holder of the credit (the creditor) to hand back to the issuer of the debt (the debtor) the latter's acknowledgment or obligation".

The holder of a coin or certificate has the absolute right to pay any debt due to the government by tendering that coin or certificate, and it is this right and nothing else which gives them their value. It is immaterial whether or not the right is conveyed by statute, or even whether there may be a statute law defining the nature of a coin or certificate otherwise.

Hence, we can integrate the state money and credit money approaches through the recognition of the "very nature of credit", which is that the issuer must accept its own IOUs when presented (as when bank notes are returned to the issuing bank for redemption if conversion is promised, or to pay a debt owed to the issuing bank).

What, then, is special about government? The government's credit "usually ranks in any given city slightly higher than does the money of a banker outside the city, not at all because it represents gold, but merely because the financial operations of the government are so extensive that government money is required everywhere for the discharge of taxes or other obligations to the government."

The special characteristic of government money, then, is that it is "redeemable by the mechanism of taxation": "[I]t is the tax which imparts to the obligation its 'value'.... A dollar of money is a dollar, not because of the material of which it is made, but because of the dollar of tax which is imposed to redeem it". This tax liability is imposed by the government on a sufficient proportion of the population that there is a nearly universal demand for the government's own liabilities—which are necessary to pay taxes.

By contrast, orthodox economists accept a "metalist" position, arguing that until recently, the value of the government's money was determined by the gold used in producing coins or by the gold backing paper notes. However, in spite of the attention paid to the gold standard, it was actually in place for only a short period. Typically, the money-thing issued by the authorities was not gold-money nor was there any promise to convert the money-thing to gold.

Indeed, as Innes insisted, throughout most of Europe's history, the money-thing issued by the state was the hazelwood tally stick: "This is well seen in medieval England, where the regular method used by the government for paying a creditor was by 'raising a tally' on the Customs or on some other revenue getting department, that is to say by giving to the creditor as an acknowledment of indebtedness a wooden tally." Other money-things included clay tablets, leather and base metal coins, and paper certificates. Why would the population accept otherwise "worthless" sticks, clay, base metal, leather, or paper? Because these were evidence of the state's liabilities that it would accept in payment of taxes and other debts owed to itself. The key power of the state was its ability to impose taxes: "[t]he government by law obliges certain selected persons to become its debtors.... This procedure is called levying a tax, and the persons thus forced into the position of debtors to the government must in theory seek out the holders of the tallies or other instrument acknowledging a debt due by the government." Contrary to orthodox thinking, then, the desirability of the money-thing issued by the state was not generally determined by intrinsic value, but by the nominal value set by the state at its own pay offices.

Nor was the government's money forced onto the public through legal tender laws. It is certainly true that governments often do adopt legal tender laws, but these are difficult to enforce and hence often ineffective. The power of government to impose a tax and to name what will be accepted in tax payment is sufficient, and certainly trumps legal tender laws.

Once the state has created the unit of account and named what can be delivered to fulfill obligations to the state, it has generated the necessary preconditions for development of markets. As Innes argued, credits and debts probably preceded markets, and indeed, created the need for markets. The quintessential debt is the tax obligation, which then creates the incentive for private credits and debts and then for markets—because those without the means of paying taxes could use markets to obtain those means. Evidence from Babylonia suggests that early authorities set prices for each of the most important products and services—perhaps those accepted to meet obligations to the authorities. Once prices in money were established, it was a short technical leap to creation of markets. This stands orthodoxy on its head by reversing the order: first money and prices, then markets and money-things (rather than barter-based markets and relative prices, and then numeraire money and nominal prices). The next step was the recognition by the authority that it could issue the money-thing to purchase the mix it desired, then receive the same money-thing in the tax payments by subjects/citizens. This would further the development of markets because those with tax liabilities but without the goods and services the authority wished to buy would have to produce for market to obtain the means of paying obligations to the state.

There need not be any conflict between credit money and state money approaches. The state provides the unit of account in which private credits and debts are denominated. The state denominates tax liabilities in that same money unit, and names what can be delivered in tax payment. The modern state issues HPM—its liability that is accepted in tax payment—as it spends. The private sector not only uses HPM for tax payment, but also for net clearing of private debts. The state even accepts some private liabilities in payments to the state, although ultimate clearing takes place in the state's HPM. In the next section we turn to the endogenous money approach, and a more detailed look at the role played by HPM in net clearing.

The Endogenous Money Move Towards

Beginning in the early 1970s there has been a revival of the endogenous money approach that had been followed by the Banking School of the early 19th century as well as by Marx several decades later. (It could be argued that most economists before WWII accepted some version of endogenous money, and that the exogenous approach gained dominance only with the development of the neo-classical synthesis. See Wray 1990.) This culminated in the "horizontalist" approach to money advanced by Moore (1988) that emphasizes the non-discretionary nature of reserves. This effectively reverses the "deposit multiplier" of the money and banking textbooks, arguing that "loans make deposits" and "deposits make reserves".

The focus is on the private decisions made by banks and their customers, which determine the supply of loans and deposits, hence, the supply of credit money that "endogenously" expands to meet the needs of trade. The central bank can only "exogenously" set the short-term interest rate (federal funds rate in the US, repo rate in the UK) at which it supplies reserves "horizontally" on demand to banks. Finally, the endogenous money approach rejects even long-run neutrality of money, arguing that the creation of money is tied to the fundamental processes of a capitalist economy, thus, money *always* matters. These points are all well-established in the Post Keynesian literature and do not require further elaboration here.

The links between the endogenous money approach and the credit money approach discussed above should be obvious. The difference is really one of emphasis, with the endogenous money approach focusing more upon bank and central bank decision-making and interactions, while the credit approach has been more interested in identifying the nature of credit/debt relations. The fundamental property of all credit, according to Innes, is that its issuer must accept it; the endogenous money equivalent is the Banking School reflux principle: excess bank deposits return to banks to retire loans.

There certainly is no conflict between the endogenous money emphasis on the monetary role played by bank liabilities and the credit money claim that bank money is debt. The endogenous money approach also recognises that today's HPM is the debt of the government (treasury and central bank), although it is not clear that all followers of this approach would agree with Innes that all money—even gold coin—is debt.

What has largely been neglected in the endogenous money literature is the role of the state and the impact of fiscal operations on banks and the central bank. At least in the horizontalist version, the role of the state is limited to the central bank's ability to set the overnight interest rate, which requires that it passively accommodate bank demand for reserves. Indeed, the index to Moore's 1988 book does not even list entries for fiscal policy, treasury, or taxes, and discussion of the connection between fiscal and monetary policy is limited to a brief argument that governments in the Third World are generally biased towards low interest rates because they are typically the largest borrower in any economy.

By implication, government is seen to be in the same position as any other economic agent, financing its spending either by running down deposit balances, or through borrowing from financial institutions. Hence, relations between the state money approach and the endogenous money approach remain relatively unclear. It is somewhat surprising that fiscal effects on reserves are largely ignored in the endogenous money literature, because these are potentially many times larger than the quantities of reserves added or drained by central bank operations. Some of those who adopt the endogenous money approach have even argued that central bank behaviour should be analysed separately from fiscal operations, as the central bank is formally independent of the treasury in many nations.

In reality, however, the central bank's desire to set and hit overnight rate targets means that it cannot be independent of the treasury—in the sense that any undesired impact of fiscal operations on banking system reserves must be immediately and completely offset by central bank operations. All else equal, treasury spending leads to a credit to banking system reserves while tax payments lead to a debit, thus, treasury deficits lead to net credits. In practice, daily operations of the treasury would almost always generate either net credits or net debits even if the budget were balanced over the course of the year for the simple reason that tax payments on any given day would differ from government spending on that day. Hence, the treasury and central bank have created complex procedures that allow them to closely coordinate activities to minimize effects on reserves. These reserve effects of fiscal operations have been a central concern of the Chartalist literature.

None of this really requires revision of the horizontalist, or more generally the endogenous money, approach that is consistent with both the credit and the state money approaches. According to the state money approach, the state chooses the unit of account (the dollar, for example) in which the privately-issued credit moneys are denominated. The state also chooses which moneys it will accept in payment of taxes. In modern sovereign nations with their own domestic, floating, currencies, this is always an inconvertible, high powered, money (liabilities of the treasury and central bank). Private banks help in clearing between the government and the private sector, since most taxes are "paid" using bank accounts and most recipients of treasury checks deposit them into private banks.

In these operations, the private banks act as intermediaries making payments to the government on behalf of their depositors, and crediting depositors with government payments. The central bank and treasury then coordinate activities to offset undesired impacts on bank reserves, allowing the central bank to exogenously set and hit the overnight rate target. The high powered money accepted by the state in such countries is always a credit money, a liability of the treasury or central bank, and hence operates according to Innes' fundamental law of credit—or the law of reflux cited by the followers of the endogenous money approach. That is to say, state liabilities (HPM) are destroyed when they return to the state, mostly in tax payments or bond purchases by the non-government sector.

Still, we are left with a question: must an endogenous money approach adopt a chartalist, or state money, approach? An endogenous money approach could possibly locate the origins of money in barter, or in a primordial "free market" economy free from government intrusion (as in Parguez and Seccareccia 2003). As discussed above, it is not so important to finally uncover the "true" origins of money, but rather, to explicate the "nature" of money.

The question is whether a hypothesised stateless but monetary economy sheds any important light on the nature of the modern money we use. Does it help us to understand the "horizontal" monetary policy of modern central banks? Does it reveal the social relations important to the operation of modern capitalist economies? Is our understanding enhanced by presuming that the money of account originated from the spontaneous adoption by individuals of a numeraire to denominate their private credits and debits? In my view, the notion that private credit monies are denominated in a chartalist, national, unit of account is far more illuminating. Further, there is a "pyramidal" monetary hierarchy that rules clearing—most private clearing of accounts takes place on the balance sheets of banks, while banks use the central bank for ultimate, or net, clearing. All of this is in terms of the national currency. Finally, the central bank is the ultimate clearer for private-government transactions. While all credit money—even that issued by the treasury and central bank—represents a liability, this does not put all liabilities on an equal playing field. Further, as almost all liabilities in any given sovereign nation are denominated in the national currency, it becomes possible to clear accounts in that currency using liabilities high in the debt pyramid. At the same time, it becomes desirable to *hold* these liabilities for clearing. If such a hierarchy is important, then starting analysis without a treasury or central bank is deficient.

Today only the *sovereign* government can impose liabilities on others. This puts it in a privileged position because it can create a demand for its own liabilities simply by requiring that taxpayers must deliver government liabilities in payment of taxes. It can also enact legal tender laws and legal reserve requirements to try to provide further privilege to treasury and central bank liabilities.

Finally, the modern state is, of course, a very large entity—hence an important purchaser of output and source of income—which makes its liabilities ubiquitous. Still, if the state did not impose tax liabilities in its currency and require ultimate payments to itself in the form of its treasury and central bank liabilities, it is difficult to believe that its sheer size and its legal tender laws alone would be sufficient to guarantee its current spot at the top of the money hierarchy.

Perhaps the more significant and contentious point concerns the implication of the state money approach for government budgetary issues. As Lerner (1943, 1947) recognised, the "money as a creature of the state" approach leads logically to a "functional finance" view of state budgeting. Because the state spends by emitting its own liability, it does not need tax revenue or the proceeds from borrowing in order to spend. Thus, the first principle of functional finance is that the state should increase taxes only if the public's income were too high (threatening inflation).

The second principle is that the state should "borrow" (sell bonds) only if "it is desirable that the public should have less money and more government bonds." We will return to these points later but it is important to note how the state money approach conflicts with the conventional "government budget constraint" (GBC) notion, according to which state spending must be "financed" by tax revenues, borrowing, or "printing money". In reality, the GBC is nothing but an ex post identity that conflates the state's financial situation with that of a household. In any case, there is certainly nothing within the horizontalist or endogenous money approaches that requires a GBC approach to government finance. Indeed, it is a fundamental proposition of horizontalism that central bank provision of its own liabilities is limited only by demand—it can potentially supply reserves without limit. The state money approach simply extends that to the treasury—so long as state liabilities are demanded, they can be supplied by the state (central bank plus treasury). In the US, the Federal Reserve (Fed) is, like the treasury, ultimately a "creature of Congress", and notwithstanding various claims about the desirability of the independence of the central bank, this is a typical arrangement in most developed nations. Leaving aside the logical impossibility of central bank "independence" from its treasury (since hitting overnight rate targets requires cooperation between treasury and central bank), the law-making body can direct its central bank to accommodate the treasury's spending as necessary. (Indeed, if it did not, treasury checks could "bounce".) While a GBC holds ex post as an accounting identity, it is not an operational constraint on treasury spending.

In practice, once the central bank has met all the demand for bank reserves by crediting reserves as the treasury spends, additional treasury spending places downward pressure on the overnight rate, forcing bond sales (by the central bank and/or the treasury) to drain excess reserves and keep overnight rates on target. While it might appear that the bond sales "finance" the treasury spending, in reality, bond sales logically are made after the spending takes place, and are undertaken to mop up the excess reserves that would push overnight rates below target.

We, thus, return to the second principle of functional finance: bonds should be sold only if the private sector holds more HPM than desired, a situation that is manifested by overnight rates falling below target. Hence, the functional finance approach is ultimately consistent with the endogenous money approach that insists that reserves are non-discretionary, indeed, the second principle of functional finance can be seen as a corollary of horizontalism—that bond sales are undertaken only to drain excess reserves. Thus, bond sales, even by the treasury, are non-discretionary and permit the central bank to exogenously hit interest rate targets.

Finally, note that both Keynesians and Institutionalists insist that *at the aggregate level,* saving does not finance investment, rather, that investment spending creates saving flows. In the expanded model, investment plus government spending *injections* determine aggregate saving plus taxes *leakages*; or investment plus the budget deficit creates an equivalent amount of saving. There is thus a link between endogenous money and the recognition that saving does not finance investment, rather, expansion of loans finances increased spending (of any type).

Just as saving (a leakage) cannot finance investment (an injection), neither can taxes (a leakage) finance government spending (an injection) nor can saving (a leakage) finance a budget deficit (a net injection) because logically the injections must come first to generate the income that is then lost through the leakages. Careful analysis of balance sheets (a record of stocks that accumulate flows) strengthens the argument that taxes cannot provide a prior source of finance of government spending. While both investment and saving can take place on the balance sheets of the private sector, in the form of private credit money, both government spending and taxes must ultimately involve the balance sheets of the government sector (treasury and central bank).

It is not possible for taxpayers and their banks to clear accounts with the government in HPM unless there is a mechanism for advance provision of the HPM to be used in clearing. Government spending is the primary source of HPM, although government (treasury, central bank, or other agents of government) can also lend HPM, purchase assets from the private sector, or provide HPM through transfer payments. Hence, Lerner's functional finance and chartalist approaches (or, money as a creature of the state approach) are consistent with the usual Keynesian and Institutionalist views of the temporal relation between injections and leakages: the state must spend its liabilities into existence before they can be redeemed in taxation.

As Lerner argued, the purpose of government bond sales is not to borrow reserves (the government's own IOU), but to offer an interest-earning alternative to undesired reserves that would otherwise drive the overnight rate towards zero.

Note that if the central bank paid interest on excess reserves, the treasury would never need to sell bonds because the overnight interest rate could never fall below the rate paid by the central bank on excess reserves. Note also that in spite of the widespread belief that government deficits push up interest rates, they actually reduce the overnight rate to zero unless the treasury and central bank coordinate efforts to drain the resulting excess reserves. (For many years the overnight interest rate in Japan has been kept at zero, in spite of government deficits that reached 8 per cent of GDP, merely by keeping some excess reserves in the banking system.) On the other hand, budget surpluses drain reserves, causing a shortage that drives up the overnight rate unless the central bank and treasury buy and/or retire government debt. Needless to say, orthodoxy has got the interest rate effects of government budgets exactly backwards.

LIQUIDITY MANAGEMENT

Liquidity management operations in 2004-05 had to cope with the sharp increase in reserve money in the previous year emanating largely from build-up of excess cash balances by commercial banks towards the end of the year, particularly in the last week of March, 2004. Another problem in liquidity management in the current year was the carry forward of excess liquidity amounting to ₹.81,000 crore from the previous year. The Government and the

RBI have been taking appropriate steps to address the concerns emanating from large capital flows. The RBI has been moderating the impact of capital flows through open market sale of Government securities held by it and through repo operations under the LAF.

The depletion of the stock of Government securities held by the RBI from ₹.1,16,444 crore at end-March, 2003 to ₹.44, 217 crore at end-March, 2004 constrained the OMOs of the RBI.

As reported in the Economic Survey 2003-04, MSS was introduced effective April 1, 2004 to augment the stock of Government securities held by the RBI. The ceiling of ₹.60,000 crore fixed for raising treasury bills and dated securities under MSS for the year 2004-05 was raised to ₹.80,000 crore on August 26, 2004, when the amount raised under MSS crossed the threshold limit of ₹.50,000 crore. Liquidity absorption through MSS was ₹ 54,499 crore as on January 28, 2005. The RBI had put in place a revised LAF scheme effective March 29, 2004 consisting of i) 7-day fixed rate reverse repo conducted daily, and ii) overnight fixed rate reverse repo conducted daily on weekdays, and iii) repo auction on overnight basis at a fixed rate and gradual phasing out of the extant 14-day repo.

In its mid-term review of the annual policy statement for 2004-05 (October 26, 2004), the RBI introduced further changes in the LAF scheme to enhance its effectiveness and to facilitate liquidity management in a flexible manner. These changes relate to operating LAF scheme with overnight fixed rate repo and reverse repo and discontinuation of 7-day and 14-day reverse repo from November 1, 2004. The RBI increased the fixed reverse repo rate by 25 basis points to 4.75 per cent from October 27, 2004. The spread between reverse repo and repo rates was reduced from 150 basis points to 125 basis points from October 27, 2004 to maintain the fixed repo rate unchanged at 6.0 per cent.

The interest rate on eligible CRR balances was de-linked from the Bank Rate and was reduced to 3.5 per cent. With the operationalisation of MSS, the daily volumes under LAF have come down drastically. Though RBI has been absorbing liquidity under MSS and LAF to address the problem of overhang of liquidity, there have been occasions in recent months when RBI injected liquidity through the LAF window, indicating situations of occasional strains in liquidity in the banking system on account of a significant increase in domestic credit.

The outstanding occasional injection of liquidity touched a peak of ₹.17,235 crore on November 18, 2004. Excess liquidity sterilised as on January 28, 2005 was about ₹ 69,259 crore, with ₹ 54,499 crore sterilised under MSS and ₹ 14,760 crore absorbed under LAF. In addition, surplus balances in the Central Government account with the RBI also helped in sterilising excess liquidity from time to time.

LIQUIDITY AND CAPITAL MANAGEMENT FOR A BANK

To avoid defaulting on its obligations, the bank must maintain a minimal reserve ratio that it fixes in accordance with, notably, regulations and its liabilities. In practice this means that the bank sets a reserve ratio target and responds when the actual ratio falls below the target.

Such response can be, for instance:

- Selling or redeeming other assets, or securitization of illiquid assets,
- Restricting investment in new loans,
- Borrowing funds (whether repayable on demand or at a fixed maturity),
- Issuing additional capital instruments, or
- Reducing dividends.

Because different funding options have different costs, and differ in reliability, banks maintain a stock of low cost and reliable sources of liquidity such as:

- Demand deposits with other banks
- High quality marketable debt securities
- Committed lines of credit with other banks

As with reserves, other sources of liquidity are managed with targets. The ability of the bank to borrow money reliably and economically is crucial, which is why confidence in the bank's creditworthiness is important to its liquidity. This means that the bank needs to maintain adequate capitalisation and to effectively control its exposures to risk in order to continue its operations. If creditors doubt the bank's assets are worth more than its liabilities, all demand creditors have an incentive to demand payment immediately, a situation known as a run on the bank.

Contemporary bank management methods for liquidity are based on maturity analysis of all the bank's assets and liabilities (off balance sheet exposures may also be included). Assets and liabilities are put into residual contractual maturity buckets such as 'on demand', 'less than 1 month', '2–3 months' etc. These residual contractual maturities may be adjusted to account for expected counter party behaviour such as early loan repayments due to borrowers refinancing and expected renewals of term deposits to give forecast cash flows.

This analysis highlights any large future net outflows of cash and enables the bank to respond before they occur. Scenario analysis may also be conducted, depicting scenarios including stress scenarios such as a bank-specific crisis.

Risk and Prudential Regulation

In a fractional-reserve banking system, in the event of a bank run, the demand depositors and note holders would attempt to withdraw more money than the bank has in reserves, causing the bank to suffer a liquidity crisis and, ultimately, to perhaps default.

In the event of a default, the bank would need to liquidate assets and the creditors of the bank would suffer a loss if the proceeds were insufficient to pay its liabilities. Since public deposits are payable on demand, liquidation may require selling assets quickly and potentially in large enough quantities to affect the price of those assets.

An otherwise solvent bank (whose assets are worth more than its liabilities) may be made insolvent by a bank run. This problem potentially exists for any corporation with debt or liabilities, but is more critical for banks as they rely upon public deposits (which may be redeemable upon demand). Although an initial analysis of a bank run and default points to the bank's inability to liquidate or sell assets (*i.e.* because the fraction of assets not held in the form of liquid reserves are held in less liquid investments such as loans), a more full analysis indicates that depositors will cause a bank run only when they have a genuine fear of loss of capital, and that banks with a strong risk adjusted capital ratio should be able to liquidate assets and obtain other sources of finance to avoid default.

For this reason, fractional-reserve banks have every reason to maintain their liquidity, even at the cost of selling assets at heavy discounts and obtaining finance at high cost, during a bank run (to avoid a total loss for the contributors of the bank's capital, the shareholders).

Many governments have enforced or established deposit insurance systems in order to protect depositors from the event of bank defaults and to help maintain public confidence in the fractional-reserve system. Responses to the problem of financial risk described above include:

- Proponents of prudential regulation, such as minimum capital ratios, minimum reserve ratios, central bank or other regulatory supervision, and compulsory note and deposit insurance;
- Proponents of free banking, who believe that banking should be open to free entry and competition, and that the self-interest of debtors, creditors and shareholders should result in effective risk management; and,
- Withdrawal restrictions: some bank accounts may place a limit on daily cash withdrawals and may require a notice period for very large withdrawals. Banking laws in some countries may allow restrictions to be placed on withdrawals under certain circumstances, although these restrictions may rarely, if ever, be used;
- Opponents of fractional reserve banking who insist that notes and demand deposits be 100 per cent reserved.

Example of a Bank Balance Sheet and Financial Ratios

An example of fractional reserve banking, and the calculation of the reserve ratio is shown in the balance sheet below:

Table. ANZ National Bank Limited
Balance Sheet as at 30 September 2007

Assets	NZ$m	Liabilities	NZ$m
Cash	201	Demand Deposits	25482
Balance with Central Bank	2809	Term Deposits and other borrowings	35231
Other Liquid Assets	1797	Due to Other Financial Institutions	3170
Due from other Financial Institutions	3563	Derivative financial instruments	4924
Trading Securities	1887	Payables and other liabilities	1351
Derivative financial instruments	4771	Provisions	165
Available for sale assets	48	Bonds and Notes	14607
Net loans and advances	87878	Related Party Funding	2775
Shares in controlled entities	206	[subordinated] Loan Capital	2062
Current Tax Assets	112	Total Liabilities	99084
Other assets	1045	Share Capital	5943
Deferred Tax Assets	11	[revaluation] Reserves	83
Premises and Equipment	232	Retained profits	2667
Goodwill and other intangibles	3297	Total Equity	8703
Total Assets	107787	Total Liabilities plus Net Worth	107787

In this example the cash reserves held by the bank is $3010m ($201m currency + $2809m held at central bank) and the demand liabilities of the bank are $25482m, for a cash reserve ratio of 11.81 per cent.

Other Financial Ratios

The key financial ratio used to analyze fractional-reserve banks is the cash reserve ratio, which is the ratio of cash reserves to demand deposits. However, other important financial ratios are also used to analyze the bank's liquidity, financial strength, profitability etc.

For example the ANZ National Bank Limited balance sheet above gives the following financial ratios:

The cash reserve ratio is $3010m/$25482m, *i.e.* 11.81 per cent.

The liquid assets reserve ratio is ($201m+$2809m+$1797m)/$25482m, *i.e.* 18.86 per cent.

The equity capital ratio is $8703m/107787m, *i.e.* 8.07 per cent.

The tangible equity ratio is ($8703m-$3297m)/107787m, *i.e.* 5.02 per cent

The total capital ratio is ($8703m+$2062m)/$107787m, *i.e.* 9.99 per cent.

It is very important how the term 'reserves' is defined for calculating the reserve ratio, as different definitions give different results. Other important financial ratios may require analysis of disclosures in other parts of the bank's financial statements. In particular, for liquidity risk, disclosures are incorporated into a note to the financial statements that provides maturity analysis of the bank's assets and liabilities and an explanation of how the bank manages its liquidity. Critics of fractional reserve banking have argued one or more of the following: that it is unstable, that it exacerbates business cycles, that it causes inflation, or that it leads to environmental degradation. “The Federal Reserve Idea was doubtless right; if it had not been, it could not have been established. But it has been manipulated. It has not been a ‘federal’ reserve; it has been a private reserve.

It has been operated in the interest of bankers and not of everyone in general. Capable of being used to carry the country gradually back to a natural flow of business and to a natural level of prices, it was used to bludgeon business at a critical time and to bludgeon it in such a way that money-lenders profited when producers suffered. If that is the fact, there is no American banker but will say that the method was wrong; economically wrong, logically wrong, commercially wrong, if not criminally wrong. Today the Federal Reserve boasts of its own reserve as if that were a sign of national economic health. With the country struggling to live, the Federal Reserve ought to be low, not high. The height which the reserve has reached is a measure of the depth of the country’s depression. If the Federal Reserve would let out a part of that flood of money — a high financial authority suggests that less than 10 per cent would do it — it would be like an infusion of blood into the nation’s veins.”—Henry Ford.

7

Performance Development in Internet Banking

Internet is a vast network of individual computers and computer networks connected to and communicate with each other using the same communication protocol — TCP/IP (Transmission Control Protocol/ Internet Protocol). When two or more computers are connected a network is created; connecting two or more networks create 'internet-work' or Internet. The Internet, as commonly understood, is the largest example of such a system. Internet is often and aptly described as 'Information Superhighway', a means to reach innumerable potential destinations.

The destination can be any one of the connected networks and host computers. Internet has evolved to its present state out of a US Department of Defence project ARPANet (Advanced Research Project Administration Network), developed in the late- 1960s and early -1970s as an experiment in wide area networking. A major perceived advantage of ARPANet was that the network would continue to operate even if a segment of it is lost or destroyed since its operation did not depend on operation of any single computer.

Though originally designed as a defence network, over the years it was used predominantly in areas of scientific research and communication. By the 1980s, it moved out of Pentagon's control and more independent networks from US and outside got connected to it. In 1986, the US National Science Foundation (NSF) established a national network based on ARPA protocol using commercial telephone lines for connectivity. The NSFNet was accessible by a much larger scientific community, commercial networks and general users and the number of host computers grew rapidly. Eventually, NSFNet became the framework of today's Internet. ARPANet was officially decommissioned in 1990. It has become possible for innumerable computers operating on different platforms to communicate with each other over Internet because they adopt the same communication protocol, *viz*, TCP/IP.

The latter, which stands for 'Transmission Control Protocol/ Internet Protocol', is a set of rules which define how computers communicate with each other. In order to access Internet one must have an account in a host computer, set up by any one of the ISPs (Internet Service Providers). The accounts can be SLIP (Serial Line Internet Protocol) or PPP (Point to Point Protocol) account. These accounts allow creating temporary TCP/IP sessions with the host, thereby allowing the computer to join the Internet and directly establish communication with any other computer in the Internet. Through this type of connection, the client computer does not merely act as a remote terminal of the host, but can run whatever programmes are available on the web.

It can also run several programmes simultaneously, subject to limitations of speed and memory of the client computer and modem. TCP/IP protocol uses a unique addressing scheme through which each computer on the network is identified. TCP/ IP protocol is insecure because data packets flowing through TCP/ IP networks are not normally encrypted. Thus, any one who interrupts communication between two machines will have a clear view of the data, passwords and the like.

This has been addressed through Secured Socket Layer(SSL), a Transport Layer Security (TLS) system which involves an encrypted session between the client browser and the web server. FTP or File Transfer Protocol is a mechanism for transferring files between computers on the Internet. It is possible to transfer a file to and from a computer (ftp site) without having an account in that machine. Any organization intending to make available to public its documents would normally set up a ftp site from which any one can access the documents for download. Certain ftp sites are available to validated users with an account ID and password.

E-MAIL

The most common and basic use of Internet is the exchange of e-mail (electronic mail). It is an extremely powerful and revolutionary result of Internet, which has facilitated almost instantaneous communication with people in any part of the globe. With enhancements like attachment of documents, audio, video and voice mail, this segment of Internet is fast expanding as the most used communication medium for the whole world. Many web sites offer e-mail as a free facility to individuals. Many corporates have interfaced their private networks with Internet in order to make their e mail accessible from outside their corporate network.

WORLD WIDE WEB (WWW)

Internet encompasses any electronic communication between computers using TCP/IP protocol, such as e-mail, file transfers etc. WWW is a segment of Internet, which uses Hyper Text Markup Language (HTML) to link together files containing text, rich text, sound, graphics, video etc. and offers a very convenient means of navigating through the net. It uses hypertext transfer protocol (HTTP) for communication between computers. Web documents can contain links to other related documents and so on, in a tree like structure.

The person browsing one document can access any other linked page. The web documents and the web browsers which are the application programmes to access them, are designed to be platform independent. Thus any web document can be accessed irrespective of the platform of the computer accessing the document and that of the host computer. The programmeming capabilities and platform independence of Java and Java applets have further enriched the web.

The 'point and click' method of browsing is extremely simple for any lay user of the net. In fact, the introduction of web since early 1990 has made Internet an extremely popular medium and its use in business has been enhanced dramatically. The next in the HTML genre is the Extensible Markup Language (XML), which allows automated two-way information flow between data stores and browser screens. XML documents provide both the raw content of data and the data structure and is projected by its proponents as taking the web technology beyond the limits of HTML.

WIRELESS APPLICATION PROTOCOL (WAP)

WAP is the latest industry standard which provides wireless access to Internet through handheld devices like a cellular telephone. This is an open standard promoted by WAP forum and has been adopted by world's all major handset manufacturers. WAP is supplemented by Wireless Application Environment (WAE), which provides industry wise standard for developing applications and services for wireless communication networks.

This is based on WWW technology and provides for application for small screens, with interactive capabilities and adequate security. Wireless Transaction Protocol (WTP), which is the equivalent of TCP, sets the communication rules and Wireless Transport Layer Security (WTLS) provides the required security by encrypting all the session data. WAP is set to revolutionize the commercial use of net.

ADVANTAGES OF INTERNET BANKING

The advantages of Internet banking are obvious. Business people can access their personal and business account information while saving a trip to the bank. You can check your balance whenever you need to, even if the bank is closed. Not only that, but you can pay your bills online as well, which saves both time and money on postage. Another advantage of Internet banking is the ability to easily compare services offered by different banks. You can buy financial products and apply for loans online, and in doing so, you can compare your options to ensure that you get the best possible services. You can even buy insurance online through Internet banking services. Stocks and bonds and other investments can be managed with online banking from your home or office independent of a financial intermediary like a stockbroker. The number one tip for banking online is to be very aware of Internet banking security. Identity theft is a real and growing problem today. As such, you need to be highly protective of your personal account information whenever doing transactions online. Make sure you never give personal information out over the Internet unless you are connected to a secure site.

Also, store your access information in a secure place. Routinely check your computer for spy ware and viruses, protecting your identity this way as well. Anther important security feature you will want to make sure is in place with your online bank is encryption. Verify that the banking portal has high-end encryption software in place. If not, it might be advisable to choose a different banking option. You can verify this by looking for the graphic, which is usually located at the bottom right of the browser that signifies the encryption is in place. Another tip about Internet banking is to remember that some procedures are still affected by the business hours of the bank. Even if you transfer a balance at 8:00 PM, it may not show up on your account until the next business day. Plan your transactions accordingly if you are working on a tight budget. Use the Internet to shop for the best banking options. Check interest rates on loans and savings accounts online. The Internet can be a great tool in helping you secure the best possible banking services to meet your needs. The history of Internet banking has come a long way over the last six years, and it is only going to get better! Get connected to Internet banking today. You can be in complete control of your finances with the click of a mouse!

Internet Opens New Vistas for Indian Banks

Indian banks have a chequered history. The British legacy left behind a host of large and small privately-held banks. The late 60s saw the nationalisation of banks, leading to the emergence of the public sector banks. The 90s saw the banking industry embracing technology in a massive way, led in particular by the new private banks and MNC banks. Among these series of technology innovations, Internet banking for the retail segment is a recent phenomenon that has generated a lot of interest in the Indian banking industry. Private and foreign banks have been the early adopters while the PSU banks are also beginning to latch on to the bandwagon. As per IDC estimates, the total number of registered users for Internet banking in India is over two million.

India has a little less than a million active Internet banking users. And though this is just 0.096 per cent of the total population, it represents 15 per cent of the India's Internet user population. Thus indicating that the concept of Internet banking is surely catching on. Impressive as these figures might be, the truth is that India lags behind other countries in Internet banking. In the US, the number of commercial banks with transactional web sites is 1,275 or

12 per cent of the total number of banks. Of these, seven could be called 'virtual banks.' Ten traditional banks have established Internet branches or divisions that operate under a unique brand name. At present, in the US approximately 78 per cent of all commercial banks with assets more than $5 billion, 43 per cent of banks with $500 million to $5 billion in assets, and 10 per cent of banks under $500 million in assets have transactional web sites. From the Asian market experience, it is clear that Internet banking is here to stay and will be a major channel to acquire and service customers. Markets like Korea and Singapore have nearly 10 per cent of their population banking over the Internet. Though, these markets are way ahead of India both in terms of Internet penetration and online banking penetration, India is a big potential market and is fast catching up with its Asian counterparts.

Technology Innovations and PSU Lethargy

As in all forms of technology innovations, PSU banks have remained laggards in the race for adopting Internet banking practices. There are very few nationalised banks like State Bank of India, Bank of Baroda, Allahabad Bank, Syndicate Bank and Bank of India, that offer Internet banking services. Some others like Union Bank of India, Canara Bank and Punjab National Bank are on the verge of doing so. SBI's Internet banking initiative, launched in July 2001, is in fact doing quite well and has over 18,000 registered customers across 150 branches. The enthusiastic response has encouraged the SBI management to extend the service to an additional 500 branches. But despite positive news like this, PSU banks still have a lot of catching up to do on the Internet banking services front. DD Krishnamoorthy, deputy general manager, information technology, Bank of India says that the primary reason preventing PSU banks from introducing online banking services, has been the absence of a legal framework to back up, and regulate Internet banking operations in the country. Though the Information Technology Act 2000 attempted to address a number of e-commerce regulatory issues, he feels that there still are several grey areas which have neither been spelt out properly, nor have the courts suggested workable modes of implementation.

Though Internet banking is only an extension of traditional banking services, there are several instances which contradict the legal framework for this banking in India provided by a set of enactments like the Banking Regulations Act, 1949, the Reserve Bank of India Act, 1934 and the Foreign Exchange Management Act, 1999. However, not many are willing to buy the argument that it's the lack of regulations that is preventing the PSU banks from taking the Internet plunge. Says an industry analyst, "More than a lack of regulatory framework, it is lack of zeal and a mindset attuned towards resisting any new technology that is holding back the nationalised banks. On top of this, the highly politicised unions are also an impediment as they feel that Internet banking would expose the low productive levels of the workforce." The average customer profile of PSU banks is also comfortable with the traditional banking system and is not too keen on adopting an online model. Typically, most PSU banks have the majority of their customer base in the smaller cities or towns and even in remote villages.

Even in bigger cities, a large proportion of their customers are either senior citizens or at least 50+ who have a natural aversion towards adopting new technology. This not the case with private or MNC banks, where the clientele is mostly urban-based falling in the 20-40 age group and who have a higher exposure to technology. Even the IDC survey seems to confirm this premise. Among the elite Internet banking users, that is, those customers who belong to Socio-Economic Class A1 (SEC A1) in the top five cities, it has been found that people access their account through the Internet once every week. Similarly users visit their ATM centre on an average of two times per week. The workplace happens to be the most favoured place to access Internet for banking purposes. The home comes a close second while cybercafes take the third place. ATM in the close vicinity to the office is the most preferred place among users for banking.

Insignificant Internet Banking

In contrast, Indian banks have an insignificant Internet banking record. ICICI Bank kicked off online banking way back in 1996 and a host of other banks soon followed suit. But even for the Internet as a whole, 1996 to 1998 marked the adoption phase, while usage increased only in 1999—due to lower ISP online charges, increased PC penetration and a tech-friendly atmosphere. Reveals Anup Bagchi, head, Internet Banking, ICICI Bank, "We had launched the Internet banking service even before the RBI had formulated its guidelines. Fortunately, as it was a comparatively new concept, the regulating authorities were extremely cooperative with us." After ICICI, Citibank, IndusInd Bank and HDFC Bank and Timesbank (now part of HDFC Bank), were the early ones to bite the technology bullet in 1999. Says C N Ram, head, information technology, HDFC Bank, "Our vision was very clear, we were not enamoured by the concept of Internet banking but looked at it more as an add-on service which our customers should gradually adopt." In line with this strategy, initially the Net banking facility was provided in order to meet the information requirements of the customers and gradually it ventured into fund transfers and third party transfers.

Though adoption of Internet banking by Indian banks and their customers would not set the Arabian Sea on fire, no one can deny the obvious benefits that this service offers. Costs of banking service through the Internet amount to a fraction of the costs through conventional methods. Industry estimates assume teller cost at Re 1 per transaction, ATM transaction costs at Re 0.45, phone banking at Re 0.35, debit cards at Re 0.20 and Internet banking at Re 0.10 per transaction. Says V K Ramani, president, information technology, UTI Bank, another of the early adopters, "No wonder, the cost-conscious banks in the country are now actively considering using the Internet as a channel for providing services. People were sceptical about even ATM at the beginning, but look how it has picked up today." However, he warns that banks cannot expect instant returns, unless the Internet population itself does not reach a critical mass. Besides, he also feels that fully computerised banks, with better management of their customer base are in a stronger position to cross-sell their products through this channel. Nitin Chopra, head, consumer banking, ABN-AMRO Bank, feels that the prohibitive costs of real estate would always make Internet banking a much more viable option in the long run than physical banks. In today's environment besides their physical branches, banks need to grow non-branch delivery networks as a part of their growth strategy. ATMs are currently the hot favourite for most banks, but Internet banking definitely has the potential to leave the rest behind. Therefore, on the whole, Internet banking increases operational efficiencies and reduces costs, besides giving a platform for offering value added services to the customer, thereby fulfilling all the essential prerequisites for a flourishing banking industry.

INTERNET BANKING ON BANK

Internet technology holds the potential to fundamentally change banks and the banking industry. An extreme view speculates that the Internet will destroy old models of how bank services are developed and delivered. The widespread availability of Internet banking is expected to affect the mixture of financial services produced by banks, the manner in which banks produce these services and the resulting financial performances of these banks.

Whether or not this extreme view proves correct and whether banks take advantage of this new technology will depend on their assessment of the profitability of such a delivery system for their services. In addition, industry analysis outlining the potential impact of Internet banking on cost savings, revenue growth and risk profile of the banks have also generated considerable interest and speculation about the impact of the Internet on the banking industry. Banking through internet has emerged as a strategic resource for achieving higher efficiency, control of operations and reduction of cost by replacing paper based and labour intensive methods with automated processes thus leading to higher productivity and profitability.

However, to date researchers have produced little evidence regarding these potential changes. Nonetheless, recent empirical studies indicate that Internet banking is not having an independent effect on banking profitability, although these findings may change as the use of the Internet becomes more widespread. More recently in India too, a wider array of financial products and services have become available over the Internet, which has thus become an important distribution channel for a number of banks. Banks boost technology investment spending strongly to address revenue, cost and competitiveness concerns. For some activities, banks hope to see a near-term impact on profitability. Other investments are motivated more by a desire to establish a competitive position or avoid falling behind the competition.

The purpose of present study is to analyse such effects of Internet banking in India, where no rigorous attempts have been undertaken to understand this aspect of the banking business. The primary aim is to advance the understanding of how Internet banks are different from the non-Internet banks in terms of profitability, cost efficiency, asset quality and other characteristics by examining bank financial statements from year end 1998 to year end 2006.

The present study tests not only whether the Internet delivery channel affected the financial performance of the commercial banks in our sample, but also how these changes happened. The study examines a comprehensive set of 10 measures of financial performance that allow us to "look inside the black box" of bank performance. By developing a deeper understanding of these phenomena, we can draw more insightful inferences about the impact of the Internet on banking business strategies, production processes and financial performance. Increasing this type of knowledge is vital for both academic literature and also for bank marketers who cannot count on the initial success achieved by the Internet banking investment.

REVIEW OF EXISTING LITERATURE

A few empirical studies exist in the literature, which have examined the relative performance of banks offering Internet banking services. The table also includes the studies which have examined the financial performance of Internetonly banks that do not operate any physical branches. Egland was the first important study, which estimated the number of US banks offering Internet banking and analysed the structure and performance characteristics of these banks. It found no evidence of major differences in the performance of the group of banks offering Internet banking activities compared to those that do not offer such services in terms of profitability, efficiency or credit quality. However, transactional Internet banks differed from other banks primarily by size.

In contrast to the results of Egland, Furst found that banks in all size categories offering Internet banking were generally more profitable and tended to rely less heavily on traditional banking activities in comparison to non-Internet banks. An exception to the superior performance of Internet banks was the de novo Internet banks, which were less profitable and less efficient than non-Internet de novos. The authors concluded that Internet banking was too small a factor to have affected banks' profitability. Sullivan found that click and mortar banks in the 10th Federal Reserve District incurred somewhat higher operating expenses but offset these expenses with somewhat higher fee income. On average, this study found no systematic evidence that banks were either helped or harmed by offering the Internet delivery channel. Similar to the results of Furst *et al.*, this study also found that de novo click and mortar banks performed significantly worse than de novo brick and mortar banks. Using information drawn from banks in Italy, Hasan found that the Internet banking institutions were performing significantly better than the non- Internet groups. Additionally, the risk variables associated with the Internet group continued to be lower relative to the non-Internet group.

The asset-liability variables revealed that on average the banks in this Internet group were larger and had significantly higher trading and investment activities and less dependent on retail deposits (both demand and saving deposits) relative to the non-Internet group. The only category where the Internet group showed a lower performance was the non-interest expense category. It found a significant and positive link between offering of Internet banking activities and banks' profitability and a negative but marginally significant association between the adoption of Internet banking and bank risk levels particularly due to increased diversification. Hernando and Nieto examined the performance of multichannel banks in Spain between 1994 and 2002. The study found higher profitability for multichannel banks through increased commission income, increased brokerage fees and (eventual) reductions in staffing levels and concluded that the Internet channel was a complement to physical banking channels.

In contrast to earlier studies, the multichannel banks in Spain relied more on typical banking business (lending, deposit taking and securities trading). The adoption of the Internet as a delivery channel had a positive impact on banks' profitability after one and a half years of adoption. It was explained by the lower overhead expenses and in particular, staff and IT costs after the same period. Sathye investigated the impact of the introduction of transactional Internet banking on performance and risk profile of major credit unions in Australia. Similar to the results of Sullivan, the Internet banking variable didn't show a significant association with the performance as well as with operating risk variable.

Thus, Internet banking didn't prove to be a performance enhancing tool in the context of major credit unions in Australia. It neither reduced nor enhanced risk profile. DeYoung observed the change in financial performance of Internet community banks in U.S. during 1999-2001. The results found that Internet adoption improved community banks' profitability, particularly through increased revenues from deposit service charges. Internet adoption was also associated with movements of deposits from checking accounts to money market deposit accounts, increased use of brokered deposits and higher average wage rates for bank employees.

It found little evidence of changes in loan portfolio mix. The findings suggested that Internet adoption was associated with an economically and statistically significant improvement in bank profitability. DeYoung analysed systematically the financial performance of pure-play Internet banks in U.S. The study found relatively lower profits at the Internet-only institutions than the branching banks, caused in part by high labour costs, low fee based revenues and difficulty in generating deposit funding.

However, consistent with the standard Internet banking model, the results indicated that Internet-only banks tended to grow faster than traditional branching banks. Internet-only banks have access to deeper scale economies than branching banks and because of this, they are likely to become more financially competitive over time as they grow larger. Delgado found similar results for Internet-only banks in the EU. Nevertheless, the magnitude of technology based scale economies found in Delgado was substantially larger than that estimated by DeYoung studies.

The evidence of the impact of the adoption of Internet as a delivery channel on financial performance is mixed at both sides of the Atlantic. Nevertheless, the latest studies seem to find a positive relationship with profitability. It can be argued that as the intensity and experience in the usage of Internet increases, the financial performance of multichannel banks is likely to improve. In Indian context, many publications throw light over the importance of Internet banking and also its prospects for the Indian banking industry.

However these studies don't depict any empirical relationship between banks' profitability and Internet banking. The purpose of this paper is to study the same correlation applicable in Indian context. This paper also proposes and tests the existence of financial gaps between Internet banks and non-Internet banks in India.

DATA

The primary data set comes from the publicly available data source on bank's financial statements and income-expense reports sent to the regulators and banking associations. The Reserve Bank of India (RBI), provided the data. The data was matched with Indian Banking Associations data source, IBA Bulletin and Center for Monitoring Indian Economy (CMIE) data source PROWESS, for additional variables.

The Internet related details were drawn from a survey of commercial banks' Web sites during the period of June 2007. The banks whose home pages were not discovered despite of best efforts were assumed to be banks with no Web site. The data set is limited to the banks that are operating as commercial banks as on March end 2006. In doing so, the banks that are acquired by other banks or have closed down their operations during the period are not included. Finally, a panel data of 85 commercial banks turned out to be the sample of the study over the period 1998-2006 which represented nearly 39 per cent of total scheduled commercial banks in India.

As all the banks in sample are not observed in the entire period, the study has used an unbalanced panel data for the empirical work. The 85 banks consisted of 28 public sector banks (8 banks in State Bank of India (SBI) group) and 20 nationalized banks), 28 private sector banks (21 old and 7 new private sector banks) and 29 foreign banks. The sample includes 49 Internet banks and 36 non-Internet banks. Table reports the description of sample banks.

Table. Adoption Rates of Internet banks

Bank of Banks Banks	**Number of Banks percentage**	**Number Internet Web sites**	**Number of banks as a of banks in**	**Internet with category**
Private Sector				
Banks	28	27	17	60.7
New[1]	7	7	7	100.0
Old[2]	21	20	10	47.6
Public Sector				
Banks	28	28	26	92.8
SBI Group[3]	8	8	8	100.0
Nationalized[4]	20	20	18	90.0
Foreign Banks	29	29	6	20.7
All Banks	85	84	49	57.6

The survey results reveal that, during the period of June 2007, 84 banks in India had Web sites, of which 49 allowed transactions to be initiated through the Internet. However, the adoption rates across individual bank categories are not uniform. Adoption rates for transactional Web sites are highest in public sector and are lowest in foreign banks. Among the sub-categories, the adoption rates for transactional Web sites are highest in new private sector banks and SBI group.

DEVELOPMENT OF INTERNET BANKING

Numerous factors — including competitive cost, customer service, and demographic considerations — are motivating banks to evaluate their technology and assess their electronic commerce and Internet banking strategies. Many researchers expect rapid growth in customers using online banking products and services. The challenge for national banks is to make sure the savings from Internet banking technology more than offset the costs and risks associated with conducting business in cyberspace.

Marketing strategies will vary as national banks seek to expand their markets and employ lower cost delivery channels. Examiners will need to understand the strategies used and technologies employed on a bank-by-bank basis to assess the risk. Evaluating a bank's data on the use of their Web sites, may help examiners determine the bank's strategic objectives, how well the bank is meeting its Internet banking product plan, and whether the business is expected to be profitable.

Some of the market factors that may drive a bank's strategy include the following:

Competition — Studies show that competitive pressure is the chief driving force behind increasing use of Internet banking technology, ranking ahead of cost reduction and revenue enhancement, in second and third place respectively. Banks see Internet banking as a way to keep existing customers and attract new ones to the bank.

Cost Efficiencies — National banks can deliver banking services on the Internet at transaction costs far lower than traditional brick-and-mortar branches. The actual costs to execute a transaction will vary depending on the delivery channel used. For example, according to Booz, Allen and Hamilton, as of mid-1999, the cost to deliver manual transactions at a branch was typically more than a dollar, ATM and call center transactions cost about 25 cents, and Internet transactions cost about a penny. These costs are expected to continue to decline.

National banks have significant reasons to develop the technologies that will help them deliver banking products and services by the most cost-effective channels. Many bankers believe that shifting only a small portion of the estimated 19-billion payments mailed annually in the U.S. to electronic delivery channels could save banks and other businesses substantial sums of money. However, national banks should use care in making product decisions.

Management should include in their decision making the development and ongoing costs associated with a new product or service, including the technology, marketing, maintenance, and customer support functions. This will help management exercise due diligence, make more informed decisions, and measure the success of their business venture.

Geographical Reach — Internet banking allows expanded customer contact through increased geographical reach and lower cost delivery channels. In fact some banks are doing business exclusively via the Internet — they do not have traditional banking offices and only reach their customers online. Other financial institutions are using the Internet as an alternative delivery channel to reach existing customers and attract new customers.

Branding — Relationship building is a strategic priority for many national banks. Internet banking technology and products can provide a means for national banks to develop and maintain an ongoing relationship with their customers by offering easy access to a broad array of products and services.

By capitalizing on brand identification and by providing a broad array of financial services, banks hope to build customer loyalty, cross-sell, and enhance repeat business.

Customer Demographics — Internet banking allows national banks to offer a wide array of options to their banking customers. Some customers will rely on traditional branches to conduct their banking business. For many, this is the most comfortable way for them to transact their banking business. Those customers place a premium on person-to-person contact. Other customers are early adopters of new technologies that arrive in the marketplace. These customers were the first to obtain PCs and the first to employ them in conducting their banking business. The demographics of banking customers will continue to change. The challenge to national banks is to understand their customer base and find the right mix of delivery channels to deliver products and services profitably to their various market segments.

Types of Internet Banking

Understanding the various types of Internet banking products will help examiners assess the risks involved. Currently, the following three basic kinds of Internet banking are being employed in the marketplace:

- Informational — This is the basic level of Internet banking. Typically, the bank has marketing information about the bank's products and services on a stand-alone server. The risk is relatively low, as informational systems typically have no path between the server and the bank's internal network. This level of Internet banking can be provided by the bank or outsourced. While the risk to a bank is relatively low, the server or Web site may be vulnerable to alteration. Appropriate controls therefore must be in place to prevent unauthorized alterations to the bank's server or Web site.
- Communicative — This type of Internet banking system allows some interaction between the bank's systems and the customer. The interaction may be limited to electronic mail, account enquiry, loan applications, or static file updates (name and address changes). Because these servers may have a path to the bank's internal networks, the risk is higher with this configuration than with informational systems. Appropriate controls need to be in place to prevent, monitor, and alert management of any unauthorized attempt to access the bank's internal networks and computer systems. Virus controls also become much more critical in this environment.
- Transactional — This level of Internet banking allows customers to execute transactions. Since a path typically exists between the server and the bank's or outsourcer's internal network, this is the highest risk architecture and must have the strongest controls. Customer transactions can include accessing accounts, paying bills, transferring funds, etc.

Internet Banking Risks

Internet banking creates new risk control challenges for national banks. From a supervisory perspective, risk is the potential that events, expected or unexpected, may have an adverse impact on the bank's earnings or capital. The OCC has defined nine categories of risk for bank supervision purposes. The risks are credit, interest rate, liquidity, price, foreign exchange, transaction, compliance, strategic, and reputation. These categories are not mutually exclusive and all of these risks are associated with Internet banking.

Credit Risk

Credit risk is the risk to earnings or capital arising from an obligor's failure to meet the terms of any contract with the bank or otherwise to perform as agreed. Credit risk is found in all activities where success depends on counterparty, issuer, or borrower performance. It arises any time bank funds are extended, committed, invested, or otherwise exposed through actual or implied contractual agreements, whether on or off the banks balance sheet. Internet banking provides the opportunity for banks to expand their geographic range. Customers can reach a given institution from literally anywhere in the world. In dealing with customers over the Internet, absent any personal contact, it is challenging for institutions to verify the bonafides of their customers, which is an important element in making sound credit decisions. Verifying collateral and perfecting security agreements also can be challenging with out-of-area borrowers. Unless properly managed, Internet banking could lead to a concentration in out-of-area credits or credits within a single industry. Moreover, the question of which state's or country's laws control an Internet relationship is still developing.

Effective management of a portfolio of loans obtained through the Internet requires that the board and management understand and control the bank's lending risk profile and credit culture. They must assure that effective policies, processes, and practices are in place to control the risk associated with such loans. *See* the "Loan Portfolio Management," booklet of the for a more complete discussion of credit risk.

Interest Rate Risk

Interest rate risk is the risk to earnings or capital arising from movements in interest rates. From an economic perspective, a bank focuses on the sensitivity of the value of its assets, liabilities and revenues to changes in interest rates. Interest rate risk arises from differences between the timing of rate changes and the timing of cash flows (repricing risk); from changing rate relationships among different yield curves affecting bank activities (basis risk); from changing rate relationships across the spectrum of maturities (yield curve risk); and from interest-related options embedded in bank products (options risk). Evaluation of interest rate risk must consider the impact of complex, illiquid hedging strategies or products, and also the potential impact that changes in interest rates will have on fee income. In those situations where trading is separately managed, this refers to structural positions and not trading portfolios. Internet banking can attract deposits, loans, and other relationships from a larger pool of possible customers than other forms of marketing. Greater access to customers who primarily seek the best rate or term reinforces the need for managers to maintain appropriate asset/liability management systems, including the ability to react quickly to changing market conditions.

Liquidity Risk

Liquidity risk is the risk to earnings or capital arising from a bank's inability to meet its obligations when they come due, without incurring unacceptable losses. Liquidity risk includes the inability to manage unplanned changes in funding sources. Liquidity risk also arises from the failure to recognize or address changes in market conditions affecting the ability of the bank to liquidate assets quickly and with minimal loss in value. Internet banking can increase deposit volatility from customers who maintain accounts solely on the basis of rate or terms. Asset/liability and loan portfolio management systems should be appropriate for products offered through Internet banking. Increased monitoring of liquidity and changes in deposits and loans may be warranted depending on the volume and nature of Internet account activities.

Price Risk

Price risk is the risk to earnings or capital arising from changes in the value of traded portfolios of financial instruments. This risk arises from market making, dealing, and position taking in interest rate, foreign exchange, equity, and commodities markets.

Banks may be exposed to price risk if they create or expand deposit brokering, loan sales, or securitization programmes as a result of Internet banking activities. Appropriate management systems should be maintained to monitor, measure, and manage price risk if assets are actively traded.

Foreign Exchange Risk

Foreign exchange risk is present when a loan or portfolio of loans is denominated in a foreign currency or is funded by borrowings in another currency. In some cases, banks will enter into multi-currency credit commitments that permit borrowers to select the currency they prefer to use in each rollover period. Foreign exchange risk can be intensified by political, social, or economic developments. The consequences can be unfavorable if one of the currencies involved becomes subject to stringent exchange controls or is subject to wide exchange-rate fluctuations. Foreign exchange risk is discussed in more detail in the "Foreign Exchange," booklet of the Internet Banking. Banks may be exposed to foreign exchange risk if they accept deposits from non-U.S. residents or create accounts denominated in currencies other than U.S. dollars. Appropriate systems should be developed if banks engage in these activities.

Transaction Risk

Transaction risk is the current and prospective risk to earnings and capital arising from fraud, error, and the inability to deliver products or services, maintain a competitive position, and manage information. Transaction risk is evident in each product and service offered and encompasses product development and delivery, transaction processing, systems development, computing systems, complexity of products and services, and the internal control environment.

A high level of transaction risk may exist with Internet banking products, particularly if those lines of business are not adequately planned, implemented, and monitored. Banks that offer financial products and services through the Internet must be able to meet their customers' expectations. Banks must also ensure they have the right product mix and capacity to deliver accurate, timely, and reliable services to develop a high level of confidence in their brand name. Customers who do business over the Internet are likely to have little tolerance for errors or omissions from financial institutions that do not have sophisticated internal controls to manage their Internet banking business. Likewise, customers will expect continuous availability of the product and Web pages that are easy to navigate. Software to support various Internet banking functions is provided to the customer from a variety of sources. Banks may support customers using customer-acquired or bank-supplied browsers or personal financial manager (PFM) software. Good communications between banks and their customers will help manage expectations on the compatibility of various PFM software products.

Attacks or intrusion attempts on banks' computer and network systems are a major concern. Studies show that systems are more vulnerable to internal attacks than external, because internal system users have knowledge of the system and access. Banks should have sound preventive and detective controls to protect their Internet banking systems from exploitation both internally and externally. *See* OCC Bulletin 99-9, "Infrastructure Threats from Cyber-Terrorists" for additional information.

Contingency and business resumption planning is necessary for banks to be sure that they can deliver products and services in the event of adverse circumstances. Internet banking products connected to a robust network may actually make this easier because back up capabilities can be spread over a wide geographic area. For example, if the main server is inoperable, the network could automatically reroute traffic to a back up server in a different geographical location. Security issues should be considered when the institution develops its contingency and business resumption plans. In such situations, security and internal controls at the back-up location should be as sophisticated as those at the primary processing site. High levels of system availability will be a key expectation of customers and will likely differentiate success levels among financial institutions on the Internet. National banks that offer bill presentment and payment will need a process to settle transactions between the bank, its customers, and external parties. In addition to transaction risk, settlement failures could adversely affect reputation, liquidity, and credit risk.

Compliance Risk

Compliance risk is the risk to earnings or capital arising from violations of, or non-conformance with, laws, rules, regulations, prescribed practices, or ethical standards. Compliance risk also arises in situations where the laws or rules governing certain bank products or activities of the bank's clients may be ambiguous or untested. Compliance risk exposes the institution to fines, civil money penalties, payment of damages, and the voiding of contracts. Compliance risk can lead to a diminished reputation, reduced franchise value, limited business opportunities, reduced expansion potential, and lack of contract enforceability. Most Internet banking customers will continue to use other bank delivery channels. Accordingly, national banks will need to make certain that their disclosures on Internet banking channels, including Web sites, remain synchronized with other delivery channels to ensure the delivery of a consistent and accurate message to customers.

Federal consumer protection laws and regulations, including CRA and Fair Lending, are applicable to electronic financial services operations including Internet banking. Moreover, it is important for national banks to be familiar with the regulations that permit electronic delivery of disclosures/notices versus those that require traditional hard copy notification. National banks should carefully review and monitor all requirements applicable to electronic products and services and ensure they comply with evolving statutory and regulatory requirements.

Advertising and record-keeping requirements also apply to banks' Web sites and to the products and services offered. Advertisements should clearly and conspicuously display the FDIC insurance notice, where applicable, so customers can readily determine whether a product or service is insured. Regular monitoring of bank Web sites will help ensure compliance with applicable laws, rules, and regulations. *See* the "Consumer Compliance Examination" booklet of the, OCC Bulletin 94-13, "Non-deposit Investment Sales Examination Procedures," and OCC Bulletin 98-31, "Guidance on Electronic Financial Services and Consumer Compliance" for more information.

Application of Bank Secrecy Act (BSA) requirements to cyberbanking products and services is critical. The anonymity of banking over the Internet poses a challenge in adhering to BSA standards. Banks planning to allow the establishment of new accounts over the Internet should have rigorous account opening standards. Also, the bank should set up a control system to identify unusual or suspicious activities and, when appropriate, file suspicious activity reports (SARs).

The BSA funds transfer rules also apply to funds transfers or transmittals performed over the Internet when transactions exceed $3,000 and do not meet one of the exceptions. The rules require banks to ensure that customers provide all the required information before accepting transfer instructions. The record keeping requirements imposed by the rules allow banks to retain written or electronic records of the information.

The Office of Foreign Asset Control (OFAC) administers laws that impose economic sanctions against foreign nations and individuals. This includes blocking accounts and other assets and prohibiting financial transactions. Internet banking businesses must comply with OFAC requirements. A bank needs to collect enough information to identify customers and determine whether a particular transaction is prohibited under OFAC rules. *See* the *FFIEC Information Systems Examination* (*IS*) for a discussion of OFAC.

Strategic Risk

Strategic risk is the current and prospective impact on earnings or capital arising from adverse business decisions, improper implementation of decisions, or lack of responsiveness to industry changes. This risk is a function of the compatibility of an organization's strategic goals, the business strategies developed to achieve those goals, the resources deployed against these goals, and the quality of implementation. The resources needed to carry out business strategies are both tangible and intangible. They include communication channels, operating systems, delivery networks, and managerial capacities and capabilities. The organization's internal characteristics must be evaluated against the impact of economic, technological, competitive, regulatory, and other environmental changes.

Management must understand the risks associated with Internet banking before they make a decision to develop a particular class of business. In some cases, banks may offer new products and services via the Internet. It is important that management understand the risks and ramifications of these decisions. Sufficient levels of technology and MIS are necessary to support such a business venture. Because many banks will compete with financial institutions beyond their existing trade area, those engaging in Internet banking must have a strong link between the technology employed and the bank's strategic planning process.

Before introducing a Internet banking product, management should consider whether the product and technology are consistent with tangible business objectives in the bank's strategic plan. The bank also should consider whether adequate expertise and resources are available to identify, monitor, and control risk in the Internet banking business.

The planning and decision making process should focus on how a specific business need is met by the Internet banking product, rather than focusing on the product as an independent objective. The bank's technology experts, along with its marketing and operational executives, should contribute to the decision making and planning process. They should ensure that the plan is consistent with the overall business objectives of the bank and is within the bank's risk tolerance.

New technologies, especially the Internet, could bring about rapid changes in competitive forces. Accordingly, the strategic vision should determine the way the Internet banking product line is designed, implemented, and monitored.

Reputation Risk

Reputation risk is the current and prospective impact on earnings and capital arising from negative public opinion. This affects the institution's ability to establish new relationships or services or continue servicing existing relationships. This risk may expose the institution to litigation, financial loss, or a decline in its customer base.

Reputation risk exposure is present throughout the organization and includes the responsibility to exercise an abundance of caution in dealing with customers and the community. A bank's reputation can suffer if it fails to deliver on marketing claims or to provide accurate, timely services. This can include failing to adequately meet customer credit needs, providing unreliable or inefficient delivery systems, untimely responses to customer enquiries, or violations of customer privacy expectations.

A bank's reputation can be damaged by Internet banking services that are poorly executed or otherwise alienate customers and the public. Well designed marketing, including disclosures, is one way to educate potential customers and help limit reputation risk. Customers must understand what they can reasonably expect from a product or service and what special risks and benefits they incur when using the system. As such, marketing concepts need to be coordinated closely with adequate disclosure statements. A national bank should not market the bank's Internet banking system based on features or attributes the system does not have. The marketing programme must present the product fairly and accurately.

National banks should carefully consider how connections to third parties are presented on their Web sites. Hypertext links are often used to enable a customer to link to a third party. Such links may reflect an endorsement of the third party's products or services in the eyes of the customer. It should be clear to the customer when they have left the bank's Web site so that there is no confusion about the provider of the specific products and services offered or the security and privacy standards that apply. Similarly, adequate disclosures must be made so that customers can distinguish between insured and non-insured products.

National banks need to be sure that their business continuity plans include the Internet banking business. Regular testing of the business continuity plan, including communications strategies with the press and public, will help the bank ensure it can respond effectively and promptly to any adverse customer or media reactions.

AN INTERNET BANKING WORLD AND THE ROLE OF LOCAL BANKS

Even though fundamental competencies have not changed, in order to compete, global banks and community and regional banks can pursue different strategies in the world of Internet banking. Banking scholars have identified several strategies to deal with the technological revolution in the financial services industry. These strategies involve serving different customer segments in a variety of ways. Strategic decisions involve both operating decisions and product decisions and can be made locally on a decentralised basis or on a centralised basis.

Decentralised operating and product or service decision making has the advantage of keeping local bank decision makers in close proximity with the customer and local information. The disadvantage of this approach is that senior management may not have complete control over the operations side, while on the product or service side the bank may miss opportunities to exploit economies of scope and scale.

By default, this strategy is a natural one for small community and regional banks, given their size and/or lack of extensive branch networks. However some small banks have attempted to mitigate the disadvantages of the strategy by outsourcing back office operations and joining large electronic networks to enhance their customers' access. However, in attempting to circumvent the weaknesses of the decentralised strategy these banks may have to share a substantial proportion of the profits from their customer base with the access providers, and they also risk their customers being captured or stolen by the access providers.

Clearly the decentralisation strategy will pose significant risks and problems for small banks in the future as geographical location becomes less important in defining a bank's customer base. A strategy of decentralised operational decision making and centralised product and service decision making makes sense for banks that possess special localised knowledge about their markets, but recognise that retail customers (in all but the most remote and isolated markets) in an Internet banking world will have fairly low switching costs.

It will also be difficult for banks to make significant profits from traditional products that come to be offered on a commodity basis. Thus, it will become important for banks to offer customers a wide choice of a products and services (which emerge from a centralised product and services strategy) and to offer local or decentralised pricing differences and advice only for those products that are deemed to be of high value-added.

A strategy of centralised operational and product and service decision making recognises the growing standardisation of banking products generally, though not exclusively. Such a strategy also implies more uniformity in operations and products regardless of location, since location is less relevant in an increasingly electronic world.

Like the findings of studies on the cost effectiveness of banks using decentralised and centralised decision making more generally, it is likely that a totally centralised strategy will not be optimal for most banks. Such a strategy seems to work for the McDonald restaurant chain but it probably will not for most banks, given their special competency in local information gathering and processing.

Based on this discussion, it seems fairly obvious that a totally decentralised strategy, especially on the retail side, will become less and less profitable as we move into a more integrated electronic and Internet banking world. Customers will become more sophisticated, they will move up the learning curve, and the cost of electronic hardware and software will continue to decline, making this mode of transacting even more cost effective relative to paper and face-to-face contact. To be sure, no one knows exactly how long this will take, so the strategy may be profitable in the short run. A global strategy, on the other hand, is likely to be beyond the means of most small and medium-sized banks. For most banks, then, a strategy that exploits local market-information advantages and product synergies, scale economies and innovation seems most appropriate.

RISK MANAGEMENT PRINCIPLES FOR ELECTRONIC BANKING

The e-banking risk management principles identified in this Report fall into three broad, and often overlapping, categories of issues. However, these principles are not weighted by order of preference or importance. If only because such weighting might change over time, it is preferable to remain neutral and avoid such prioritisation.

Board and Management Oversight (Principles 1 to 3):

- Effective management oversight of e-banking activities.

- Establishment of a comprehensive security control process.
- Comprehensive due diligence and management oversight process for outsourcing relationships and other third-party dependencies.

Security Controls (Principles 4 to 10):

- Authentication of e-banking customers.
- Non-repudiation and accountability for e-banking transactions.
- Appropriate measures to ensure segregation of duties.
- Proper authorisation controls within e-banking systems, databases and applications.
- Data integrity of e-banking transactions, records, and information.
- Establishment of clear audit trails for e-banking transactions.
- Confidentiality of key bank information.

Legal and Reputational Risk Management (Principles 11 to 14):

- Appropriate disclosures for e-banking services.
- Privacy of customer information.
- Capacity, business continuity and contingency planning to ensure availability of ebanking systems and services.
- Incident response planning.

As they relate to e-banking and the underlying risk management principles that should be considered by banks to address these issues.

BOARD AND MANAGEMENT OVERSIGHT (PRINCIPLES 1 TO 3)

The Board of Directors and senior management are responsible for developing the banking institution's business strategy. An explicit strategic decision should be made as to whether the Board wishes the bank to provide e-banking transactional services before beginning to offer such services. Specifically, the Board should ensure that e-banking plans are clearly integrated within corporate strategic goals, a risk analysis is performed of the proposed ebanking activities, appropriate risk mitigation and monitoring processes are established for identified risks, and ongoing reviews are conducted to evaluate the results of e-banking activities against the institution's business plans and objectives.

In addition, the Board and senior management should ensure that the operational and security risk dimensions of the institution's e-banking business strategies are appropriately considered and addressed. The provision of financial services over the Internet may significantly modify and/or even increase traditional banking risks (*e.g.* strategic, reputational, operational, credit and liquidity risk).

Steps should therefore be taken to ensure that the bank's existing risk management processes, security control processes, due diligence and oversight processes for outsourcing relationships are appropriately evaluated and modified to accommodate e-banking services.

Principle 1: The Board of Directors and senior management should establish effective management oversight over the risks associated with e-banking activities, including the establishment of specific accountability, policies and controls to manage these risks

Vigilant management oversight is essential for the provision of effective internal controls over e-banking activities. In addition to the specific characteristics of the Internet distribution channel discussed in the Introduction, the following aspects of e-banking may pose considerable challenge to traditional risk management processes:

- Major elements of the delivery channel (the Internet and related technologies) are outside of the bank's direct control.
- The Internet facilitates delivery of services across multiple national jurisdictions, including those not currently served by the institution through physical locations.
- The complexity of issues that are associated with e-banking and that involve highly technical language and concepts are in many cases outside the traditional experience of the Board and senior management.

In light of the unique characteristics of e-banking, new e-banking projects that may have a significant impact on the bank's risk profile and strategy should be reviewed by the Board of Directors and senior management and undergo appropriate strategic and cost/reward analysis. Without adequate up-front strategic review and ongoing performance to plan assessments, banks are at risk of underestimating the cost and/or overestimating the payback of their e-banking initiatives.

In addition, the Board and senior management should ensure that the bank does not enter into new e-banking businesses or adopt new technologies unless it has the necessary expertise to provide competent risk management oversight. Management and staff expertise should be commensurate with the technical nature and complexity of the bank's e-banking applications and underlying technologies. Adequate expertise is essential regardless of whether the bank's e-banking systems and services are managed in-house or outsourced to third parties.

Senior management oversight processes should operate on a dynamic basis in order to effectively intervene and correct any material e-banking systems problems or security breaches that may occur. The increased reputational risk associated with e-banking necessitates vigilant monitoring of systems operability and customer satisfaction as well as appropriate incident reporting to the Board and senior management. Finally, the Board and senior management should ensure that its risk management processes for its e-banking activities are integrated into the bank's overall risk management approach. The bank's existing risk management policies and processes should be evaluated to ensure that they are robust enough to cover the new risks posed by current or planned ebanking activities.

Additional risk management oversight steps that the Board and senior management should consider taking include:

- Clearly establishing the banking organisation's risk appetite in relation to e-banking.
- Establishing key delegations and reporting mechanisms, including the necessary escalation procedures for incidents that impact the bank's safety, soundness or reputation (*e.g.* networks penetration, employee security infractions and any serious misuse of computer facilities).
- Addressing any unique risk factors associated with ensuring the security, integrity and availability of e-banking products and services, and requiring that third parties to whom the banks has outsourced key systems or applications take similar measures.
- Ensuring that appropriate due diligence and risk analysis are performed before the bank conducts cross-border e-banking activities.

virtually unlimited geographic territory, including across national borders. Such cross-border e-banking activity, particularly if conducted without any existing licensed physical presence in the "host country," potentially subjects banks to increased legal, regulatory and country risk due to the substantial differences that may exist between jurisdictions with respect to bank licensing, supervision and customer protection requirements.

Because of the need to avoid inadvertent non-compliance with a foreign country's laws or regulations, as well as to manage relevant country risk factors, banks contemplating cross-border e-banking operations need to fully explore these risks before undertaking such operations and effectively manage them. Depending on the scope and complexity of e-banking activities, the scope and structure of risk management programmes will vary across banking organisations. Resources required to oversee e-banking services should be commensurate with the transactional functionality and criticality of systems, the vulnerability of networks and the sensitivity of information being transmitted.

Principle 2: The Board of Directors and senior management should review and approve the key aspects of the bank's security control process

The Board of Directors and senior management should oversee the development and continued maintenance of a security control infrastructure that properly safeguards e-banking systems and data from both internal and external threats.

This should include establishing appropriate authorisation privileges, logical and physical access controls, and adequate infrastructure security to maintain appropriate boundaries and restrictions on both internal and external user activities.

Safeguarding of bank assets is one of the Board's fiduciary duties and one of senior management's fundamental responsibilities. However, it is a challenging task in a rapidly evolving e-banking environment because of the complex security risks associated with operating over the public Internet network and using innovative technology.

To ensure proper security controls for e-banking activities, the Board and senior management need to ascertain whether the bank has a comprehensive security process, including policies and procedures, that addresses potential internal and external security threats both in terms of incident prevention and response.

Key elements of an effective ebanking security process include:

- Assignment of explicit management/staff responsibility for overseeing the establishment and maintenance of corporate security policies.
- Sufficient physical controls to prevent unauthorised physical access to the computing environment.
- Sufficient logical controls and monitoring processes to prevent unauthorized internal and external access to e-banking applications and databases.
- Regular review and testing of security measures and controls, including the continuous tracking of current industry security developments and installation of appropriate software upgrades, service packs and other required measures.

Principle 3: The Board of Directors and senior management should establish a comprehensive and ongoing due diligence and oversight process for managing the bank's outsourcing relationships and other third-party dependencies supporting ebanking

Increased reliance upon partners and third party service providers to perform critical ebanking functions lessens bank management's direct control. Accordingly, a comprehensive process for managing the risks associated with outsourcing and other third-party dependencies is necessary. This process should encompass the third-party activities of partners and service providers, including the sub-contracting of outsourced activities that may have a material impact on the bank.

Historically, outsourcing was often limited to a single service provider for a given functionality. However, in recent years, banks' outsourcing relationships have increased in scale and complexity as a direct result of advances in information technology and the emergence of e-banking. Adding to the complexity is the fact that outsourced e-banking services can be sub-contracted to additional service providers and/or conducted in a foreign country.

Further, as e-banking applications and services have become more technologically advanced and have grown in strategic importance, certain e-banking functional areas are dependent upon a small number of specialised third-party vendors and service providers. These developments may lead to increased risk concentrations that warrant attention both from an individual bank as well as a systemic industry standpoint. Together, these factors underscore the need for a comprehensive and ongoing evaluation of outsourcing relationships and other external dependencies, including the associated implications for the bank's risk profile and risk management oversight abilities.

Board and senior management oversight of outsourcing relationships and third-party dependencies should specifically focus on ensuring that:

- The bank fully understands the risks associated with entering into an outsourcing or partnership arrangement for its e-banking systems or applications.
- An appropriate due diligence review of the competency and financial viability of any third-party service provider or partner is conducted prior to entering into any contract for e-banking services.
- The contractual accountability of all parties to the outsourcing or partnership relationship is clearly defined. For instance, responsibilities for providing information to and receiving information from the service provider should be clearly defined.
- All outsourced e-banking systems and operations are subject to risk management, security and privacy policies that meet the bank's own standards.
- Periodic independent internal and/or external audits are conducted of outsourced operations to at least the same scope required if such operations were conducted in-house.
- Appropriate contingency plans for outsourced e-banking activities exist.

SECURITY CONTROLS (PRINCIPLES 4 TO 10)

While the Board of Directors has the responsibility for ensuring that appropriate security control processes are in place for e-banking, the substance of these processes needs special management attention because of the enhanced security challenges posed by ebanking.

The following issues are particularly pertinent:

- Authentication
- Non-repudiation
- Data and transaction integrity
- Segregation of duties
- Authorisation controls
- Maintenance of audit trails
- Confidentiality of key bank information

Principle 4: Banks should take appropriate measures to authenticate the identity and authorisation of customers with whom it conducts business over the Internet.

It is essential in banking to confirm that a particular communication, transaction, or access request is legitimate. Accordingly, banks should use reliable methods for verifying the identity and authorisation of new customers as well as authenticating the identity and authorisation of established customers seeking to initiate electronic transactions. Customer verification during account origination is important in reducing the risk of identity theft, fraudulent account applications and money laundering.

Failure on the part of the bank to adequately authenticate customers could result in unauthorised individuals gaining access to e-banking accounts and ultimately financial loss and reputational damage to the bank through fraud, disclosure of confidential information or inadvertent involvement in criminal activity. Establishing and authenticating an individual's identity and authorisation to access banking systems in a purely electronic open network environment can be a difficult task. Legitimate user authorisation can be misrepresented through a variety of techniques generally known as "spoofing." Online hackers can also take over the session of a legitimate authorised individual through use of a "sniffer" and carry out activities of a mischievous or criminal nature.

Authentication control processes can in addition be circumvented through the alteration of authentication databases. Accordingly, it is critical that banks have formal policy and procedures identifying appropriate methodology(ies) to ensure that the bank properly authenticates the identity and authorisation of an individual, agent or system by means that are unique and, as far as practical, exclude unauthorised individuals or systems. Banks can us a variety of methods to establish authentication, including PINs, passwords, smart cards, biometrics, and digital certificates.

These methods can be either single factor or multi-factor (*e.g.* using both a password and biometric technology to authenticate). Multi-factor authentication generally provides stronger assurance. The bank must determine which authentication methods to use based on management's assessment of the risk posed by the e-banking system as a whole or by the various subcomponents. This risk analysis should evaluate the transactional capabilities of the ebanking system (*e.g.* funds transfer, bill payment, loan origination, account aggregation etc.), the sensitivity and value of the stored e-banking data, and the customer's ease of using the authentication method. Robust customer identification and authentication processes are particularly important in the cross-border e-banking context given the additional difficulties that may arise from doing business electronically with customers across national borders, including the greater risk of identity impersonation and the greater difficulty in conducting effective credit checks on potential customers.

As authentication methods continue to evolve, banks are encouraged to monitor and adopt industry sound practice in this area such as ensuring that:

- Authentication databases that provide access to e-banking customer accounts or sensitive systems are protected from tampering and corruption. Any such tampering should be detectable and audit trails should be in place to document such attempts.

- Any addition, deletion or change of an individual, agent or system to an authentication database is duly authorised by an authenticated source.
- Appropriate measures are in place to control the e-banking system connection such that unknown third parties cannot displace known customers.
- Authenticated e-banking sessions remain secure throughout the full duration of the session or in the event of a security lapse the session should require reauthentication.

Principle 5: Banks should use transaction authentication methods that promote nonrepudiation and establish accountability for e-banking transactions.

Non-repudiation involves creating proof of the origin or delivery of electronic information to protect the sender against false denial by the recipient that the data has been received, or to protect the recipient against false denial by the sender that the data has been sent. Risk of transaction repudiation is already an issue with conventional transactions such as credit cards or securities transactions. However, e-banking heightens this risk because of the difficulties of positively authenticating the identities and authority of parties initiating transactions, the potential for altering or hijacking electronic transactions, and the potential for e-banking users to claim that transactions were fraudulently altered.

To address these heightened concerns, banks need to make reasonable efforts, commensurate with the materiality and type of the e-banking transaction, to ensure that:

- E-banking systems are designed to reduce the likelihood that authorised users will initiate unintended transactions and that customers fully understand the risks associated with any transactions they initiate.
- All parties to the transaction are positively authenticated and control is maintained over the authenticated channel.
- Financial transaction data are protected from alteration and any alteration is detectable.

Banking organisations have begun to employ various techniques that help establish nonrepudiation and ensure confidentiality and integrity of e-banking transactions, such as digital certificates using public key infrastructure (PKI). A bank may issue a digital certificate to a customer or counterparty to allow for their unique identification/authentication and reduce the risk of transaction repudiation. Although in some countries customers' rights to disclaim transactions is provided in specific legal provisions, legislation has been passed in certain national jurisdictions making digital signatures legally enforceable. Wider global legal acceptance of such techniques is likely as technology continues to evolve.

Principle 6: Banks should ensure that appropriate measures are in place to promote adequate segregation of duties within e-banking systems, databases and applications

Segregation of duties is a basic internal control measure designed to reduce the risk of fraud in operational processes and systems and ensure that transactions and company assets are properly authorised, recorded and safeguarded. Segregation of duties is critical to ensuring the accuracy and integrity of data and is used to prevent the perpetration of fraud by an individual. If duties are adequately separated, fraud can only be committed through collusion. E-banking services may necessitate modifying the ways in which segregation of duties are established and maintained because transactions take place over electronic systems where identities can be more readily masked or faked.

In addition, operational and transactionbased functions have in many cases become more compressed and integrated in e-banking applications. Therefore, the controls traditionally required to maintain segregation of duties need to be reviewed and adapted to ensure an appropriate level of control is maintained. Because access to poorly secured databases can be more easily gained through internal or external networks, strict authorisation and identification procedures, safe and sound architecture of the straight-through processes, and adequate audit trails should be emphasised.

Common practices used to establish and maintain segregation of duties within an e-banking environment include the following:

- Transaction processes and systems should be designed to ensure that no single employee/outsourced service provider could enter, authorise and complete a transaction.
- Segregation should be maintained between those initiating static data (including web page content) and those responsible for verifying its integrity.
- E-banking systems should be tested to ensure that segregation of duties cannot be bypassed.
- Segregation should be maintained between those developing and those administrating e-banking systems.

Principle 7: Banks should ensure that proper authorisation controls and access privileges are in place for e-banking systems, databases and applications.

In order to maintain segregation of duties, banks need to strictly control authorisation and access privileges. Failure to provide adequate authorisation control could allow individuals to alter their authority, circumvent segregation and gain access to e-banking systems, databases or applications to which they are not privileged. In e-banking systems, the authorisations and access rights can be established in either a centralised or distributed manner within a bank and are generally stored in databases. The protection of those databases from tampering or corruption is therefore essential for effective authorisation control.

Principle 8: Banks should ensure that appropriate measures are in place to protect the data integrity of e-banking transactions, records and information.

Data integrity refers to the assurance that information that is in-transit or in storage is not altered without authorisation. Failure to maintain the data integrity of transactions, records and information can expose banks to financial losses as well as to substantial legal and reputational risk. The inherent nature of straight-through processes for e-banking may make programming errors or fraudulent activities more difficult to detect at an early stage.

Therefore, it is important that banks implement straight-through processing in a manner that ensures safety and soundness and data integrity. As e-banking is transacted over public networks, transactions are exposed to the added threat of data corruption, fraud and the tampering of records. Accordingly, banks should ensure that appropriate measures are in place to ascertain the accuracy, completeness and reliability of e-banking transactions, records and information that is either transmitted over the Internet, resident on internal bank databases, or transmitted/stored by third-party service providers on behalf of the bank.

Common practices used to maintain data integrity within an e-banking environment include the following:

- E-banking transactions should be conducted in a manner that makes them highly resistant to tampering throughout the entire process.
- E-banking records should be stored, accessed and modified in a manner that makes them highly resistant to tampering.
- E-banking transaction and record-keeping processes should be designed in a manner as to make it virtually impossible to circumvent detection of unauthorised changes.
- Adequate change control policies, including monitoring and testing procedures, should be in place to protect against any e-banking system changes that may erroneously or unintentionally compromise controls or data reliability.
- Any tampering with e-banking transactions or records should be detected by transaction processing, monitoring and record keeping functions.

Principle 9: Banks should ensure that clear audit trails exist for all e-banking transactions

Delivery of financial services over the Internet can make it more difficult for banks to apply and enforce internal controls and maintain clear audit trails if these measures are not adapted to an e-banking environment. Banks are not only challenged to ensure that effective internal control can be provided in highly automated environments, but also that the controls can be independently audited, particularly for all critical e-banking events and applications. A bank's internal control environment may be weakened if it is unable to maintain clear audit trails for its e-banking activities. This is because much, if not all, of its records and evidence supporting e-banking transactions are in an electronic format.

In making a determination as to where clear audit trails should be maintained, the following types of e-banking transactions should be considered:

- The opening, modification or closing of a customer's account.
- Any transaction with financial consequences.
- Any authorisation granted to a customer to exceed a limit.
- Any granting, modification or revocation of systems access rights or privileges.

Principle 10: Banks should take appropriate measures to preserve the confidentiality of key e-banking information. Measures taken to preserve confidentiality should be commensurate with the sensitivity of the information being transmitted and/or stored in databases.

Confidentiality is the assurance that key information remains private to the bank and is not viewed or used by those unauthorised to do so. Misuse or unauthorised disclosure of data exposes a bank to both reputation and legal risk. The advent of e-banking presents additional security challenges for banks because it increases the exposure that information transmitted over the public network or stored in databases may be accessible by unauthorised or inappropriate parties or used in ways the customer providing the information did not intend. Additionally, increased use of service providers may expose key bank data to other parties.

To meet these challenges concerning the preservation of confidentiality of key e-banking information, banks need to ensure that:

- All confidential bank data and records are only accessible by duly authorised and authenticated individuals, agents or systems.
- All confidential bank data are maintained in a secure manner and protected from unauthorised viewing or modification during transmission over public, private or internal networks.
- The bank's standards and controls for data use and protection must be met when third parties have access to the data through outsourcing relationships.
- All access to restricted data is logged and appropriate efforts are made to ensure that access logs are resistant to tampering.

LEGAL AND REPUTATIONAL RISK MANAGEMENT (PRINCIPLES 11 TO 14)

Specific customer protection and privacy regulations and laws will vary from jurisdiction to jurisdiction. However, banks generally have a clear responsibility to provide their customers with a level of comfort regarding information disclosures, protection of customer data and business availability that approaches the level they would have if transacting business through traditional banking distribution channels.

Principle 11: Banks should ensure that adequate information is provided on their web sites to allow potential customers to make an informed conclusion about the bank's identity and regulatory status of the bank prior to entering into e-banking transactions.

To minimise legal and reputational risk associated with e-banking activities conducted both domestically and cross-border, banks should ensure that adequate information is provided on their web sites to allow customers to make informed conclusions about the identity and regulatory status of the bank before they enter into e-banking transactions.

Examples of such information that a bank could provide on its own web site include:

- The name of the bank and the location of its head office (and local offices if applicable).
- The identity of the primary bank supervisory authority(ies) responsible for the supervision of the bank's head office.
- How customers can contact the bank's customer service centre regarding service problems, complaints, suspected misuse of accounts, etc.
- How customers can access and use applicable Ombudsman or consumer complaint schemes.
- How customers can obtain access to information on applicable national compensation or deposit insurance coverage and the level of protection that they afford (or links to web sites that provide such information).
- Other information that may be appropriate or required by specific jurisdictions.

Principle 12: Banks should take appropriate measures to ensure adherence to customer privacy requirements applicable to the jurisdictions to which the bank is providing e-banking products and services.

Maintaining a customer's information privacy is a key responsibility for a bank. Misuse or unauthorised disclosure of confidential customer data exposes a bank to both legal and reputation risk.

To meet these challenges concerning the preservation of privacy of customer information, banks should make reasonable endeavours to ensure that:

- The bank's customer privacy policies and standards take account of and comply with all privacy regulations and laws applicable to the jurisdictions to which it is providing e-banking products and services.
- Customers are made aware of the bank's privacy policies and relevant privacy issues concerning use of e-banking products and services.

- Customers may decline ("opt out") from permitting the bank to share with a third party for cross-marketing purposes any information about the customer's personal needs, interests, financial position or banking activity.
- Customer data are not used for purposes beyond which they are specifically allowed or for purposes beyond which customers have authorised.
- The bank's standards for customer data use must be met when third parties have access to customer data through outsourcing relationships.

Principle 13: Banks should have effective capacity, business continuity and contingency planning processes to help ensure the availability of e-banking systems and services.

To protect banks against business, legal and reputation risk, e-banking services must be delivered on a consistent and timely basis in accordance with customer expectations. To achieve this, the bank must have the ability to deliver e-banking services to end-users from either primary (*e.g.* internal bank systems and applications) or secondary sources (*e.g.* systems and applications of service providers).

The maintenance of adequate availability is also dependent upon the ability of contingency back-up systems to mitigate denial of service attacks or other events that may potentially cause business disruption. The challenge to maintain continued availability of e-banking systems and applications can be considerable given the potential for high transaction demand, especially during peak time periods. In addition, high customer expectations regarding short transaction processing cycle times and constant availability (24 X 7) has also increased the importance of sound capacity, business continuity and contingency planning.

To provide customers with the continuity of ebanking services that they expect, banks need to ensure that:

- Current e-banking system capacity and future scalability are analysed in light of the overall market dynamics for e-commerce and the projected rate of customer acceptance of e-banking products and services.
- E-banking transaction processing capacity estimates are established, stress tested and periodically reviewed.
- Appropriate business continuity and contingency plans for critical e-banking processing and delivery systems are in place and regularly tested.

Principle 14: Banks should develop appropriate incident response plans to manage, contain and minimise problems arising from unexpected events, including internal and external attacks, that may hamper the provision of e-banking systems and services

Effective incident response mechanisms are critical to minimise operational, legal and reputational risks arising from unexpected events such as internal and external attacks that may affect the provision of e-banking systems and services. Banks should develop appropriate incident response plans, including communication strategies, that ensure business continuity, control reputation risk and limit liability associated with disruptions in their e-banking services, including those originating from outsourced systems and operations.

To ensure effective response to unforeseen incidents, banks should develop:

- Incident response plans to address recovery of e-banking systems and services under various scenarios, businesses and geographic locations. Scenario analysis should include consideration of the likelihood of the risk occurring and its impact on the bank. E-banking systems that are outsourced to third-party service providers should be an integral part of these plans
- Mechanisms to identify an incident or crisis as soon as it occurs, assess its materiality, and control the reputation risk associated with any disruption in service.
- A communication strategy to adequately address external market and media concerns that may arise in the event of security breaches, online attacks and/or failures of e-banking systems.
- A clear process for alerting the appropriate regulatory authorities in the event of material security breaches or disruptive incidents occur.
- Incident response teams with the authority to act in an emergency and sufficiently trained in analysing incident detection/response systems and interpreting the significance of related output.
- A clear chain of command, encompassing both internal as well as outsourced operations, to ensure that prompt action is taken appropriate for the significance of the incident. In addition, escalation and internal communication procedures should be developed and include notification of the Board where appropriate.
- A process to ensure all relevant external parties, including bank customers, counterparties and the media, are informed in a timely and appropriate manner of material e-banking disruptions and business resumption developments.
- A process for collecting and preserving forensic evidence to facilitate appropriate post-mortem reviews of any e-banking incidents as well as to assist in the prosecution of attackers.

PERVASIVE COMPUTING: REALLY GETTING TO KNOW YOUR TOASTER

The avalanche of technologies developed in the last twenty years has conditioned consumers to expect a new wave of devices in ever-shortening cycles, yet the pervasiveness of technology is the least understood aspect, and its implications for a global society are only just beginning to come to light. Studying the application of bio-integration to the socio-economic fabric of human relationships and the interface to contemporary business has barely begun.

It is apparent that the consumer's love affair with electronic gadgetry is far from over; in fact, it could be argued that it is only just starting. The rate of technology adoption is increasing with each new generation of potential users. Although all members of society do not share this affection for technology, the pervasiveness of technology continues to impact each individual either by direct participation or as an indirect consequence. The pervasiveness of computing has many implications for financial services companies, and in some cases distracts from a clear value proposition.

Is new technology spawning a revolution in how we work and live or is our lifestyle driving the need for new technology? The architect/philosopher Richard Buckminster Fuller noted in 1980 that the time between the creation of a technology and its practical adoption by society varied by technical category and application. In his words:

My half-century experience also discovered the natural, unacceleratable lags existing between inventions and industrial uses in various technical categories, which occur as follows: in electronics – two years; aerodynamics – five years; automobiles – ten years; railroading – fifteen years; big-city buildings twenty-five years; single family dwellings – fifty years.

This commercialization time lag in technology represents the time span necessary to educate the population about the benefits of new technologies, convince society of the improvements that such new technologies bring and allow the business infrastructure to reach a point of production that will make it economically viable. Architects incorporate the practical advantages of new technology into structures that shape our behaviour, while architecture involves employing a more complex process of changing social taste. The matter of adoption of any sort of technology by individuals is an exercise in shaping the behaviour of consumers as new technological marvels emerge.

The same technological time lag can be equated to financial services products and the technologies found in the four bands in the technology spectrum (for example ATMs, credit cards, retina scanners, and the Internet) and should be a critical part of strategic technology planning. Individual technologies can be plotted along a maturity curve and compared to a similar curve indicating the level of social acceptance. The delta between the curves represents the opportunity to experiment and refine the application of the technology as well as a barometer to set the expectations of the firm on the return on investment.

Technologies mature at a predictable rate determined by the innovation of their components. However, social acceptance of technology occurs at a rate that varies from culture to culture or even within the socio-economic classes in one given culture.

For example, the use of mobile phones for banking is more popular in Scandinavia than high-tech Boston, Massachusetts. Furthermore, there is a synergistic relationship between technology, people, and how people work in the lifecycle of technology creation, adoption, impact and design. Fuller's observation on technological latency brings into question the accelerating rate at which society is adopting technology. Technological visions such as Microsoft's Home of the Future and the Halifax's Future Retail Bank are early indications that the nature of work will radically change during the next twenty years.

It can be argued that not only will the nature of work change, but where one works will undergo a transformation. For example, retail banking will need to rethink how branches are designed in order to accommodate the shift from a transaction to an advisory business, which will indeed be different in each culture serviced. Organizations such as BWA\Chiat\Day, which have radically altered the way in which people think and work by inventing work spaces that stretch beyond the conventional designs of today's business, inadvertently provided financial services firms with a glimpse into the future of financial services.

Technological gadgetry – and the pervasiveness of computing – carries with it a familiar technology banner, resembling the messages from the early twentieth-century electric companies about removing the complexity of life and enabling users greater work efficiencies, that it will provide members of our modern society with additional leisure time. Alluring words, which should be remembered as you carry your laptop, mobile phone and personal digital assistant (PDA) on your next family vacation.

Stripping away the marketing hype, pervasive computing is capable of placing the user in the centre of the technological universe, allowing the individual to control the amount of intrusion permissible by other members in the connected society.

Technology is as pervasive as you will allow it to become. Business looks at pervasive computing as a new method of interacting with consumers, whereas consumers should view it as a way of employing technology to perform tasks on their behalf. The underlying dilemma that pervasive computing brings to the surface is the new balance that individuals must strike between work, leisure and social interactions. The product of this balance is a redefinition of when, where and how people work.

A strong argument can be made that the impact of technology will be the redefinition of the socio-economic contract with business and a reexamination of the nature of work. It is not incomprehensible that the result of society embracing pervasive computing is anytime, anywhere work. Technology is redefining where and how organizations work by removing the need to be in a specific geography, at a specific time. Many financial services firms, organized under traditional hierarchical command and control structures that were established because of the need to regulate the activities of subordinates, will find moving into a matrix structure difficult unless ample investment is made in training and education.

In today's world, manufacturing, consulting and research organizations are realizing that the ability to act unfettered by work hours, geography or corporate bureaucratic structure is not creating more leisure time for employees; in practice it is enabling a freeing up of work time, resulting in additional capacity. The proliferation of technology also creates opportunities to redefine the structure of organizations and establish new functional disciplines. A new skill that individuals will need to develop is striking a balance between these two diametrically opposed forces of work and leisure. As the lines between work and play become blurred, there may be opportunities for comingled activities to occur.

For example, an employee working at home for some portion of the week can order supplies for the office and home at the same time on the same Internet site using two different payment technologies, as well as communicating with colleagues and customers on the telephone and Internet while performing many other traditional in-house tasks without commuting.

Described in a business context, pervasive technology operates within a framework which can be represented by a diagram comprising four levels of conductivity similar to concentric circles in which you are at the epicentre. Individuals can add 'layers' to their epicentre as they grow more accepting of technology and more adept at using its capabilities.

LEVEL ONE TECHNOLOGIES

The first level is composed of smart devices equipped with microprocessors, called appliances, which are attached to you and facilitate your lifestyle, including home devices, wearable computing and biometric feedback mechanisms. These devices are basically automated methods of recognizing a person based on a physiological or behavioural characteristic.

For financial services companies, these devices provide new avenues for secure transactions because of their ability to identify a single individual or entity. Level one technologies centre on the point of interaction or an interchange of value, either monetary, informational or data. Micropayments, billing data, usage information and other transactions can be used to develop a profile of customer behaviour in retail banking applications.

The same model can be applied to small businesses and other entities such as government departments, not to act as Big Brother, but to optimize operating expenses and plan future budgetary requirements.

LEVEL TWO TECHNOLOGIES

Level two technologies that represent you and perform duties on your behalf are commonly referred to as agents, including bio-enhancement, intelligent agents, robots and avatars. Intelligent agents are autonomous, adaptive computer programmes that operate within software environments such as operating systems and database networks. They assist users with routine computer tasks being tailored to accommodate individual user habits.

Avatars are three-dimensional representations of individuals in cyberspace that users may utilize to represent themselves in both form and task. At the moment, avatars are inanimate objects. However, in the near future they may be animated to further express the personality that end users wish to portray. These technologies give you the ability to represent yourself in the eEconomy, proposing the following question: When you select the physical appearance and personality of your avatar, will it reflect you or someone you would like to be?

Concerning the financial services community, level two technologies are a treasure-trove of opportunities in the development of intelligent agents that can seek out the highest yielding savings rate or the best mortgage terms to fit individual circumstances.

These agents could be employed to assess conditions on the stock market, interrogate individual securities, analyse currency rates and evaluate foreign market fluctuations. Intelligent agents will be crafted into a host of highly specialized functions that have yet to be imagined.

LEVEL THREE TECHNOLOGIES

Mechanisms on the third level are designed to keep you interfaced to the relentless stream of data generated by society by linking you to the information that is relevant to you. Technologies such as global positioning satellites (GPSs), bluetooth, wireless application protocol (WAP) and a host of new devices will act as data interchange brokers. Interface technologies are an integral part of the following example. With your smart card's stored value-chip in your mobile phone, you approach a cold beverage machine, make a selection and then transmit digital currency to it by pressing a key on the phone.

The machine accepts your token and dispenses the beverage, sends the token to the bank via its cellular modem and transmits the reduction in inventory to the beverage distributor.

In this scenario, cash has moved from your account to your card, from your card to the dispenser, and finally to the accounts receivable of the beverage company, eliminating the need for physical cash pick-up, armoured car services, lock box operations and a suite of support services.

Level three technologies present financial services firms with an opportunity to facilitate transactions across markets, suppliers, consumers, nations and all parts of the Internet. Put simply, these technologies are the tools of the twenty-first-century intermediary. The fees associated with these types of transaction will obviously be commoditized over time and command very thin margins, indicating that operational efficiency will be the key factor in sustaining long-term viability.

LEVEL FOUR TECHNOLOGIES

Finally, fourth level prescriptive technologies, called regulators, are designed to keep you within the designated limits of a process or a set of rules in society. They include radio-controlled ankle restraints, anti-theft devices for automobiles and the pet chip, an electronic dog tag that is inserted under the skin of your pet. These technologies can act both passively and actively.

The application of these technologies to financial services is in its infancy. One can imagine microsensors embedded throughout an automobile providing an insurance adjuster with the data to assess damage incurred during an accident.

DATA, INFORMATION AND EVERYDAY LIFE

Another aspect of pervasive computing is the challenge that it creates for data replication and information usability, including establishing corporate data-sharing policies to regulate the level and detail of information being passed to value chain partners.

One can speculate that if there is a direct relationship between data and value, the underlying value of information will be commoditized or worth less over time. Every piece of information has a half-life of usefulness to the individual or organization that assigns.

its original value. For example: for a stock trader, the value of up to the minute stock price information is extremely high; that same data on the following day is less valuable as a single piece of data, although it may still be valuable when plotted with similar pieces of data to form a chart or graph. Ultimately, to the stock trader, the individual stock quotation is almost valueless at some point in the future.

However, as that same element of data becomes less valuable to the trader, it increases in value to a stock analyst or fund manager. One can conclude that there is a direct relationship between information and its perceived value which is relative to who set the value on the information. This relationship between information and value is critically important to financial services organizations because of the nature of the data, received from third-party sources, passing through the business process within the firm to value chain partners.

Surprisingly, organizations are continually disappointed when they discover the often dysfunctional state of customer data that was in many cases a critical element in merger or acquisition negotiations. Often the value of the customer data is drastically reduced when the labour cost associated with bringing it up to date is applied.

Regardless of the data produced by these new technologies, it is difficult to predict how people during the next five years will use these technologies in everyday life. The more information that is collected about an individual, the greater the possibility that it can be mishandled and simply increase the cost of operations.

THE INTENT OF TECHNOLOGY

Often the purpose of a technology's initial design is derailed by the necessities of business or the way it is embraced by society. For example, the developers of television thought that its primary application was to give everyone the opportunity to receive a college education at home; however, today's television programming schedules are a long way from that ideal.

From the noble ideal of television's forefathers, its use was quickly transformed into an entertainment delivery device supported by product advertising, moving to its present state as a mechanism for selling products interrupted by entertainment programming. In order to draw a parallel between the pervasiveness of technology in everyday life, one can examine the pervasiveness of product advertising on television.

Television programming was merely supported by product commercials that provided the viewer with a view of life with the product in 10–30 seconds. Now, the products are simply integrated into the programming, noticeable as the actors or actresses in the programme strategically hold a beverage can so that the audience is able to read the label. Financial services organizations are presented with a wide range of opportunities to leverage these technologies into product offerings that supplement our everyday lives and streamline core banking services.

Pervasive technologies provide a financial services firm with the opportunity to rethink what they offer, how it is delivered and, more importantly, why a product or service offering is valuable to a customer. The long-term implications of these technologies are to change our view of technology as an asset and begin to manage it as a liability. This is not to say that technology should be treated as a liability; on the contrary, the management of technology should be as if its value declines over time.

So as to put this concept into perspective, the legacy of banking technology is rooted in the high capital equipment cost that was an investment with a useful lifespan, requiring maintenance and support personnel. Thus, the typical classification of technology as an asset depreciating over time while providing a mechanism for improved information flow. However, technology is advancing at an accelerated rate, making older technology not only less valuable, but commanding a higher cost to maintain.

Despite the rapid decay of technological value, technology is still regarded as an essential asset of the organization, one without which it cannot function. The idea of treating technology as a liability is not an oversimplification of the balance between technology investment and technology deployment; it is merely to say that the technology should be viewed and managed differently from the way in which it was managed in the past.

This can be seen in the following example: there is a fundamental difference between the strategy of an equity fund manager and a bond portfolio manager. Both specialists are managing assets with strategies that come from two very different philosophies on investing. Taking these conditions into account, the management of the technology liability will be different from core back office systems to end user or consumer devices.

If one considers that consumer retail delivery devices, such as PDAs, PCs, WAP phones and many others, will continue to experience a high turnover due to the nature of the innovation of devices and the demand for new technologies by consumers, it can be concluded that the delivery of retail banking products using these technologies will have a half-life much shorter than a core processing system. Simply, the rate of the half-life of technology is proportional to the distance to the end user. Core systems are replaced at a rate of five to ten years and retail end user technologies range from six months to four years.

The key althought to consider when treating the management of technology as a liability is that each technology should be handled according to its application to the business process that it serves and linked to a realistic expectation of a phased retirement. Again, the closer a technology is to the consumer, the faster the rate of decay and the greater the tendency to overmanage the asset. For example, a consultant was engaged to review the operating cost of the technology group within a large bank, and found an ongoing cost of warehousing a stockpile of outdated PCs because they were a depreciated asset.

The cost of warehousing these non-functioning computers, coupled with the cost of the labour associated with inventorying and tracking these assets, was greater than the new replacement value. Put simply, for the amount of money being spent on storing these outdated PCs, they could be purchasing new ones, as indeed they were.

Pervasive computing amplifies the fact that technology is ever changing. A general rule can be applied to thinking about managing pervasive technologies: the closer the technology is to the end user, the more it will be subject to change. Therefore, the key to providing pervasive technology services is a robust architecture that anticipates a continuous change of delivery platforms. The by-product of combining pervasive computing with evolving Internet technologies is to rethink core banking operations and redesign how banks work.

THE DARK SIDE OF NEW TECHNOLOGY

It is not hard to imagine a darker side to pervasive technologies as the intrusion into everyday life moves from something controlled by a consumer to an action regulated by a governing authority. Combinations of technologies have been coupled together to allowing a pet owner to pinpoint a lost pet using GPS technology.

A pet owner can elect to have this technology implanted under the skin of a cat or dog (in the case of farmers, sheep, cattle, horses) to determine where an animal is located if it becomes separated from the owner. Several organizations have discussed making this technology available to parents, allowing a similar transponder to be implanted under a child's skin to eliminate the problem of missing or abducted children. It is not beyond the range of Orwellian thinking to imagine the next evolution of this technology – a governing authority requires the insertion a GPS chip under the skin of citizens to monitor their actions and whereabouts. Regardless of the intent of these technologies, they will continue to raise questions about ethics, morality and social consciousness, creating new social responsibilities for business while redefining the relationship between technology and a diverse global population.

For financial services firms, another dark side looms in the distance. In a connected environment in which a customer's home provides massive amounts of usage data, for example lights, computer use, phone use and other data-supporting activities, the need to secure and encrypt this data arises because a criminal monitoring the data will know exactly when people are not home.

From a positive viewpoint, a variety of these GPS technologies could be employed in the physical world and cyberspace to track a variety of illegal activities, in order to reduce money laundering and drug trafficking, for example. As governments continue to develop new responsibilities for financial services providers to know the sources of depositors' funds, these technologies have an enormous potential to be used as a regulatory mechanism.

Regardless of the final evolution of the pervasiveness of technology, its potential over time to alter the social contract between employees and employer, taxpayers and governments, customer and financial services institutions is as predictable as the effect of radio, television and the PC.

The adoption of a technology will fundamentally interrupt the traditional relationships between parties and market forces, and, as has been proven, a planned design will not be able to reconfigure the way in which these relationships are maintained and executed. In conclusion, the implication to financial services is to develop a clear understanding of these trends, interpret how value can be added and create services that facilitate the transition.

8

Future Development in e-Business Technology

CAMPUS E-BUSINESS

The unprecedented flow of information across networks and between organizations, coupled with the power of computers to extract, compile, organize, and republish information, has made e-business possible. These same capabilities are also raising significant concerns and issues related to the appropriate use of institutional information and the protection of information originating or residing in college and university information systems. The developmental phase facing colleges and universities today on the road to enabling e-business as one of integration. Our progress in adopting e-business in higher education will be enabled or constrained by institutions' abilities to develop, implement, enforce, and automatc complex rules that authorize these consumers to partake of university services—for example:

- What rights will distant learners have regarding access to licensed university information resources?
- How can colleges and universities protect usage logs that record student and faculty library consumption activity for materials licensed from third parties?

The privacy, access, ownership, and security issues posed by e-business are extraordinarily complex and represent as much a set of cultural, behavioural, and policy issues as technical ones.

Colleges and universities have long—and correctly—been described as self-governing anarchies or adhocracies. Higher education's hallowed and well-established traditions of self-governance and shared governance are responsible for our remarkable history of achievement, service, and innovation. These traditions also make integration hard. In many ways, achieving the necessary level of technical integration to enable e-business is the least complex aspect of preparing the institution for e-business. Many campus chief information officers (CIOs) understand what it means to reorient systems from their current functional office views to the end-user views (student, parent, alumni, inter-enterprise) that e-business will demand. In most cases, the technical tools to achieve this kind of integration exist. In short, technical integration is a significant issue that can be addressed by vision, talent, and money. The thornier integration challenges are cultural and relate to role definitions, authority and power, and values. These issues will define the boundaries of an institution's approach to, and its likelihood of success in, implementing e-business.

THE NEED FOR A POLICY FRAMEWORK TO SUPPORT E-BUSINESS

In a farsighted article, Graves, Jenkins, and Parker at the University of North Carolina described the development of an electronic information policy framework. As e-business drives the Internet and Web from an infrastructure for storing static information to one over which much of the institutional mission is delivered, the need for such a policy framework becomes overwhelming. Although sound information policies will not guarantee entry into the world of e-business, lack of these policies will bar the door. Colleges and universities will need to develop a cohesive and consistent set of policies to guide the members of their community in a number of areas, including the following:

- Digital identity and the access to institutional technology and information resources
- Use of the institution's name and trademarks
- Acquisition, retention, and disposition of information resources
- Ownership of information in institutional systems and the management of intellectual property rights

Each of these issues is enormously complex, and colleges and universities worldwide have struggled with them for years. Digital Identity and Access to Institutional Technology

AND INFORMATION RESOURCES

In the technical context, colleges and universities must develop the means to authenticate an individual as himself or herself, recognize the individual as a member of the institutional community, and confer on or deny this individual different rights and authorities as a community citizen. In physical reality, these activities are transacted in a variety of complex formal or informal ways. We can demand photo ID cards, check signature files, or wave to the familiar librarian who regulates access to the closed stacks.

The regulation of access to institutional resources in the physical context is governed by a tapestry of policies, procedures, customs, norms, and historical happenstance that computers are not yet intelligent enough to deal with. Instead, computers depend on precise information that derives absolute answers to the following questions: (1) are you who you claim to be, and (2) are you allowed to ... [consume this service, enter this building, use this parking lot]?

Not only is this a technical challenge of enormous proportions, it is a policy quagmire that requires colleges and universities to make explicit and public distinctions about the rights and privileges that accrue to different members of the academy. What rights does the president's spouse really have? What rights do lecturers have, relative to career-ladder faculty? These policy issues will become more complex as colleges and universities move into distance education and implement cradle-to-grave strategies to create relationships with promising applicants, lifelong learners, and potential donors.

Of course, it is important to note that for public institutions, managing access to institutional information must be situated in the context of public records laws, which themselves are hard to reduce to simple rules that can be automated.

USE OF THE INSTITUTION'S NAME AND TRADEMARKS

The Internet and the World Wide Web are, among other things, a publishing infrastructure. Web browser technology is relatively simple to programme as well as to use, allowing "a thousand flowers to bloom." At nearly every college and university, a myriad of operational and dead Web pages make volumes of campus information and misinformation available to anyone with an Internet connection. Many institutions provide incoming students with sufficient disk storage to encourage their development of personal Web sites. Of course, into every flower garden will come the occasional weed, snail, or other predator. From a policy perspective, the challenge posed by the Internet and the Web is the challenge of cultural integration. Colleges and universities must specify policies that regulate the appropriate use of these very public resources. At stake in this extraordinarily complex area to govern are a variety of serious legal and public relations issues, including these:

- Pornographic materials on official institutional sites
- Sale of advertising on pages containing campus trademarks
- Creation of fraudulent sites
- Commercial use of campus resources for personal gain
- Trademark infringement
- Neglect of sites that make inaccurate, anachronistic, and obsolete information available to legislators, trustees, donors, auditors, and others

All of these issues can and will emerge within the broader policy contexts that typically respect and encourage free expression by members of the institution's community. As Graves, Jenkins, and Parker advise, "Any policy will need to balance the institution's role in protecting access to sensitive or potentially objectionable information and its role in supporting an individual's right of free expression". This difficult balancing act is hardly new, but is complicated by the levels of integration anticipated by e-business applications.

ACQUISITION, RETENTION, AND DISPOSITION OF INFORMATION RESOURCES

E-business, in much of the popular literature, begins with something called "e-tailing": the marketing of the enterprise to its existing or prospective clients. In one context, higher education institutions have been doing this for years. Each year, colleges and universities acquire the files of high school students who achieve high scores on the PSAT and shower these college-bound tenth and eleventh graders with literature extolling the virtues of their campus.

In an e-business context, smart and aggressive institutions will acquire more and more information in the competition for the "best" students. These institutions will likely develop robust profiles of students to match against the target profiles of successful applicants. Similarly, the pathologies of university hospital patients will be profiled for matching against promising experimental drugs and therapies for possible targeting of such patients for clinical trials.

These practices are entrepreneurial, effective (relative to their goals), and probably beneficial; certainly college-bound students want to be discovered and patients want access to the best modes of treatment available. However, the unprecedented ability of institutions to acquire personal information, combine this information in unique ways, and store massive amounts of this information on individuals who may, or may not, be part of the institutional community will raise significant privacy and security issues.

New policies regarding what kind of information is to be collected, how this information is to be used, and how long it is to be retained will become increasingly important. The failure to develop new standards of practice in this area will invite new regulation of this area of institutional activity. The issue of individual and institutional access to this kind of information will also rise in importance and must be dealt with explicitly in campus information policy.

In addition to developing the technologies and policies to ensure privacy and secure and protect information under institutional management, colleges and universities will need to devise and implement new policies to describe, manage, and protect related classes of information. Such classes of information include confidential information (tenure and promotion files), proprietary information (patents, trademarks, copyrights), privileged information (attorneyclient communications, counseling files), and trade information (public and private research activities).

E-business, among other things, assumes an unprecedented level of interoperation among the systems and data resources of "trading partners." In the future, campus suppliers will have access to institutional procurement systems, as will publishers, high schools, consortium partners, and others. This integration of systems and information will demand that policies and contracts regulate the acquisition, use, retention, and disposition by others in the newly extending community. This has already become a complex area of policy development at research universities, where the university values of open sharing of research findings clash with desires of private clinical research sponsors to protect information as proprietary.

A final area of concern under this broad umbrella is the management of licensed software and information resources. Campus information policy must respect the rights of authors and distributors. Evolving technologies and law will likely enhance authors' and distributors' ability to track the use of their licensed property and perhaps even to implement campuswide penalties when infringements are identified.

OWNERSHIP OF INFORMATION AND INTELLECTUAL PROPERTY RIGHTS

Information policy must seek to distinguish the ownership status of information embodied in institutionally owned digital storage and transport media from the responsibilities for managing this information. Information policies should strive to define the standards and care with which information resources must be managed, while recognizing the inherently decentralizing tendencies of networked information and resources. Most information policy frameworks that address networked information define and articulate a concept of information stewardship that allows the web of campus-related information to evolve in a fashion that balances the needs of individuals and local campus units with those of the institution as a whole.

Perhaps the most complex aspect of preparing the campus information policy environment for e-business is the set of policy issues surrounding the ownership and management of intellectual property generated on the campus. Colleges and universities have developed robust policies for the ownership and management of intellectual property protected by patents, but the rights to intellectual property developed by faculty and protected by copyright have traditionally remained with individual faculty. In fact, the total economic value of published college and university intellectual property has been small historically, and the institutional investment in the creation of this property has also been small.

The application of Internet, Web, and other information technologies to the core educational mission of higher education is changing all of this. Today, pioneering faculty are investing considerable time and energy to Web-enable their courses. Institutions in many cases are partnering with these faculty by providing grants to purchase release time from other obligations and by placing a variety of technical tools at the faculty's disposal. For the first time, faculty course materials organized in this fashion can reach beyond the confines of the classroom, hence changing simultaneously the cost structure, the investment model, and the economic value of traditional course materials. Courses created in this fashion become courseware and begin to accrue many of the attributes of books, which also are evolving to become more interactive. As the e-learning aspect of the e-business revolution evolves, institutions, their faculty, and publishers are looking at course materials as scalable economic goods that can be modularized.

New pedagogical standards are evolving in concert with new neuroscientific findings about the learning process. Institutions such as the University of Phoenix and Great Britain's Open University are investing millions of dollars in curricula for networked delivery. Faculty course notes on the Web are being reportedly pirated and repackaged for distribution by new proprietary e-business enterprises.

Clearly the new potentials posed by the integrated technologies of e-business suggest the need for new policies regarding the ownership and management of rights to faculty course materials. Such changes are, however, countercultural and could also lead to new divisions on the campus. e-business is likely to change the way institutions operate. It is a mission-critical undertaking that will challenge longstanding institutional policies and will therefore demand the careful application of change management techniques and processes.

ELEMENTS OF AN INTEGRATED POLICY FRAMEWORK

Although each institution will develop a policy that best reflects its priorities, strategies, values, and history, a framework should contain some common elements. The list that follows is offered as a starting point.

Critical Assumptions

The institution will balance the rights of individuals with the institution's responsibility to make information available to support the mission. The role of the central campus is to articulate the standards of data access and integrity and to differentiate user rights and privileges so as to achieve such balance. The following key assumption will need to be articulated:

- Under what conditions (responsibilities of resource users) and for what members of the community are access to the network, network-based services, and networked information a basic right of the campus community?

OPERATING PRINCIPLES

Policies are by definition value laden. Institutions can be well served by considering bounding the framework by principles. At the University of North Carolina (UNC), information policy is bounded by principles that do the following:

- Identify the responsibility for making information available
- Limit the institution's regulatory responsibility for information for which it is not responsible

- Assume institutional responsibility for defining access privileges to its information for classes of users

The UNC policy framework and those of other leading institutions also outline in broad terms legal, ethical, technical, governance, and economic issues for the purpose of acculturating the policy reader to the complexity of the issues and the basic values of the institution.

Information Access and Security

It will be important to establish the notion that institutional electronic information resources—including data, applications, systems,

"We don't want just anyone coming in here and making toast. Type in your password." hardware, software, and networks—are valuable. Institutional assets, including electronic information resources, must be protected according to the nature of the risk and to the sensitivity and criticality of the resource being protected. Information policy should endeavor to identify major classes of information assets requiring protection and assigning to them differential levels of protection. Information classes might include privileged information, personal information, personnel information, and public records.Areas in which security-related policies need to be addressed include the following, paraphrased from the University of California's "Business and Finance Bulletin IS-3: Electronic Information Security":

- Logical security. The policy should identify security measures to be enforced through software, network, or procedural controls (version management, and so forth), as well as communications security and reduction of risk from intrusive computer software. Various measures include end-user access controls, system administration access controls, applications software development and change control, and controls on data backup, retention, data privacy, and data transfers and downloads. Encryption policies will also need to be developed as these capabilities become ubiquitous, as will policies that specify which applications and resources must be protected by firewalls.
- Physical security. Even in an e-business environment, there are physical disaster controls and access controls (for example, check stock and other financial instruments) that must be covered by institutional policy.
- Managerial security. Although there are unique risks inherent in the management of electronic and particularly networked information resources, many of the risks remain people related. An information policy framework should attempt to integrate institutional policy related to bonding and background checking for personnel with access to sensitive and critical information. Procedures to implement such policies should also identify the processes for altering authorities when changes in duties or employment status occur.

- Responsibilities. An information policy framework must identify both those responsible for maintaining the policy and those responsible for its implementation. Ideally, policy compliance escalation procedures should be specified.
- Definitions and authorities. A policy framework should define key terms such as authorized user, disaster, and security. Information management roles such as stewardship and proprietorship should also be defined. Regulations and laws that govern an institution's access and security policies should be referenced, including public records law.
- Digital certificates. An emerging technology to meet the needs of electronic security in the networked context is the use of public key infrastructure and digital certificates. Institutions that implement certificate authorities and digital certificates also will need to develop congruent policies that identify processes for approving authorities, standards for certificates, and identification of certificates. Policies will have to be enacted that govern whether certificates are issued to individuals, servers, or certificate authorities; what the responsibilities of these authorities
- Are; and what the expiry dates of these certificates will be. Finally, policy in this evolving arena will need to describe the processes for registering and issuing certificates, maintaining a repository of certificates and public keys, revoking or renewing certificates, and managing the certificate authority's private key.

Disaster Protection

The information policy framework should describe the institution's plans, policies, and procedures for ensuring business continuity, including plans for testing critical systems periodically.The disaster recovery plan should identify emergency response procedures and specify teams of personnel responsible for responding to emergency situations.

E-MAIL

Although e-mail is not specifically a tool of e-business, its governance as a critical element of the overall campus information policy framework is critical. Institutions are advised to develop specific policies related to e-mail that establish the following elements:

- E-mail accounts as institutional property
- The institution's service commitments regarding e-mail
- The ownership of information produced and received using institutional mail accounts
- Institutional access to information in mail accounts under normal or extraordinary (emergency, investigative, and so forth) conditions

- Allowable use, including use for individual commercial gain, representations, and false identity
- Security and confidentiality of information in institutional mail accounts
- Individual and institutional responsibilities and authorities for ensuring compliance with policy

INTELLECTUAL PROPERTY

Policy related to the management and ownership of intellectual property is highly complex. For intellectual property not developed on campus and covered by copyrights, patents, licenses, or other contracts, the policy parameters tend to be straightforward:

- Software resident on institutional hardware must be used according to the terms specified under the appropriate software license agreement.
- The institution is responsible for compliance with licenses entered into by the institution on behalf of members of its community. It should maintain the right to revoke licensed privileges in cases where violations have been identified. Substantial violations of license conditions should be specified under policy, as should the process for investigating alleged misuse and for implementing remedial action.
- Information resources such as databases, books, and journal articles are governed by copyright law or by license agreements with their publisher. Institutional policy should affirm the rights of authors, publishers, and distributors to their intellectual property; define what constitutes fair use in the context of law and licenses; and identify the processes for investigating alleged misuse and for implementing remedial action.

For intellectual property developed on campus, the institution must distinguish between so-called works for hire and other works produced in the discharge of an employee's work-related roles:

- The ownership of a work for hire is generally assumed to be the property of the institution. The information policy framework should make explicit reference to the institution's assumptions about what works are considered to be works for hire and what ownership rights the institution wishes to assert. This policy should also specify what rights individuals who are creating works for hire may have (publication of a work report in a professional journal) and what the process is for securing individual access to such works.
- The ownership of other intellectual property produced by members of the campus community is more likely to fall under an institution's faculty handbook, or in policy covering patents, or even conflict of

interest and commitment. As the boundaries between course materials and published materials begin to blur, institutions will need to revisit the ownership issues as part of an integrated information policy framework.

Policy by its nature is soft, squishy, and difficult. Policy development and the policy environment are inherently value laden, and therefore there are no detailed instructions for policy formulation. Policies are for the most part context specific. A Bible college's definition of appropriate use of technology will likely differ from that of a public research university.

Policy can be integrative, and integration is the mandate that looms ahead for institutions seeking to implement e-business solutions. Colleges and universities anticipating the move to e-business must recall that e-business in many areas is not merely the application of new technology to old processes. E-business applications will open new vistas and create new risks. Extending the name and reach of your college and university can and will swell the ranks of members of your communities. As communities grow, opportunities grow. And along with opportunities come fraud, abuse, and misuse. An integrated information policy framework will be hard to institute. On the other hand, an integrated, e-business environment without a supporting policy framework will be nearly impossible to manage.

CHALLENGES OF E-BUSINESS CHANGE

One of the first challenges companies face when attempting to develop online channels is to consider how such a strategy will impact upon their 'bricks and mortar' organization. Developing a 'clicks and mortar' operation may result in a more 'virtual' form of organization in which traditional ways of working are mixed with electronic communications. It is here that a company encounters its first problem, which is usually one of technology. The particular difficulty relates to the attempt to evolve 'legacy' systems (*i.e.* the technical infrastructure that has accumulated to support the business over time) to an infrastructure that will support e-Business. Few businesses find themselves in the position where they can 'throw away' the old and introduce new, customized computer systems. Legacy systems often perform essential activities upon which daily business processes depend.

While start-up companies can leapfrog these problems, established ones face some difficult challenges. Effective e-Business solutions demand integrated front-and back-end systems, a process which may demand close co-operation between two groups (or even subcultures) with the organization. As Nigel Waterson of Gemini puts it, 'The front end has quite often been built by guys in ponytails, while the people who understand the back end are often grey haired'. System integration means that when customers interact via the Web, placing orders and purchasing goods, the stock control and financial systems also speak the same language and carry out their part of the transactions. The problem is that many such back-end systems are unlikely to be based on open Internet protocols and may even have been custom built. Nonetheless, such systems may be critical to a company's business, and include such details as bank account data and stock rotation information. As Conway points out,

IT managers are loath to replace them with something new and untested. They may not even fully understand how their legacies work any longer. The people who built the systems may well have left the company, leaving present IT experts reluctant to tinker.

Replacing or upgrading such systems also takes time, which may slow up Web developments critical to speedy e-Commerce innovation.Over and above the technological matters identified above, major *organizational* change issues must be recognized and addressed for online strategies to be realized successfully. This is because of the need to redesign business processes and structures, change organizational culture, and engage in education and training. A wide range of stakeholders may be affected, with many personnel needing to 'buy in' to the change.

There is only one way to do e-Business: fully committed. Everyone in the company must be dedicated to the effort. You can't have ten people for every thousand working on it. You can't delegate it. You have to encourage everyone to jump into the water and support them in teaching each other to swim. I'm asking for the biggest cultural change in your company's history. These issues will now be considered in turn.

Resistance to Change

There are a number of reasons why people may be unwilling to accept organizational change, as summarized below:

- Stability and security are threatened.
- Coping strategies and comfort zones are affected.
- The uncertainty of change creates anxiety.
- Imposed change reduces perceived autonomy and control.
- Job content is changed and new skills are demanded.
- Authority structures and reporting lines are altered.
- Work groups and other relationships are disrupted.
- Established routines and practices are abandoned.
- An individual's power and authority is threatened.

According to Markus (1999), workers' reactions to change vary greatly. She suggests that while some workers readily embrace new technologies, some can be hostile, and the reason for this hostility can often be attributed to poor communication and shifts in organizational power. Effective internal marketing is important here in order to segment employees into 'supporters', 'neutrals' and 'opponents' of change, and then develop appropriately customized communications in order to deal with the differing priorities of each of these groups. Implementation of change involves the disruptive transition from a current state to a future state, as a result individuals or groups can resist change. They claim that there are three types of problems encountered when an organization goes through a significant change:

- *Power*. Change can be viewed as a threat to existing power structures and it creates uncertainties, so the struggle for power escalates as individuals and groups attempt to control their environment by resisting change.
- *Uncertainty*. Anxiety is created as individuals are not sure where they stand and whether at the end of the change process they will still have a role within the organization. As a result, individuals can act irrationally, as they find it difficult to understand and interpret clearly information related to the change.
- *Control*. During the change period, it becomes difficult to maintain control because goals are changing, as are structures and roles, and certain control systems become irrelevant.

These authors also highlight the important point that within large organizations individuals usually do not openly resist change; instead, they 'subtly or passively' resist. The degree of employee involvement and participation can significantly affect the success of change. Markus claims that workers' reaction to change is dependent on

whether they have had a say in selecting the technology or the way it is introduced and used, how the new technology is communicated, how much training and support are provided, and how carefully the roll out is planned and executed.

Involving employees fully means that they become responsible for the success of the change, becoming 'owners' of the change process. IBM Global Services recommends that in order to build a successful e-Business, organizations need to challenge their employees to:

identify the cultural changes that will also be needed and to shape the processes, the linked education, learning and competency development that will be required to deliver real value in the new ways of doing business that they are proposing.

Another critical point is that organizations are bound to encounter complications in asking individuals to make changes that they are incapable of implementing. Adequate investments in training and development programmes are therefore essential, particularly, for example, if new skills in Web design are required. If individuals do not possess the skills and capability necessary to introduced planned changes, the likelihood of success is significantly reduced.

According to Buchanan and Boddy (1992), the more radical change projects are, the more open they are to organizational disruption and failure. Badham *et al*. (1997) point out that there are two aspects to radical change, as illustrated with examples in Figure 3.2. The first concerns the issue of 'breadth' - the degree to which change is central to the organization's strategy - and demands radical as opposed to incremental modifications throughout the organization. The second relates to the degree to which such modifications mark a significant departure from existing ways of doing things. Both of these certainly apply to e-Business. For example, such changes point to business process redesign, the development of cross-functional team working, and the move towards a customer-focused (instead of management-led) culture. These changes are likely to be politically controversial and threaten the interests of a wide range of stakeholders. Unlike routine change, such initiatives are also likely to be highly complex. As Badham *et al.* note, there may be a high degree of uncertainty as to what to do and how to do it; objectives may be less clear, and resource requirements will be less well known. In addition, it may be less easy to create shared perceptions of goals and build and maintain necessary commitment. For this reason, these authors suggest that more time will need to be spent ensuring effective communication to encourage flexibility, address perceptions, and generate and regenerate involvement. To illustrate the problems that can ensue in such a situation, the authors describe Merrill Lynch's move into online trading:

At the core of the change process was conflict at many levels within Merrill Lynch. There was conflict between the defenders of the brokers and their commissions and proponents of online investing. There was conflict between Merrill brokers who were concerned about losing customers to online brokers and Merrill brokers who were concerned about losing commissions. There was even conflict among Merrill executives between who favoured setting up a separate online unit to compete with the brokers and those who favoured keeping the online unit under the same executive.

Leadership

Leadership plays a crucial role in effective change management. Hunt (1998) claims that change is a learning process because people have to learn to behave differently, but in order for this process to work and for change to be successful, individuals need to be encouraged, and it is here that leadership becomes very important. Carnall also expresses the need for strong leadership; that is, 'the ability to maintain progress and a facilitative and supportive approach', and suggests that for this to happen, the leader needs to have knowledge of the change area and appropriate skills to encourage learning and change.

Some leaders use 'coercive persuasion' to force change; in other words, 'employees have no alternative but to accept the new reality because they have nowhere else to go'. Although individuals may not like the change, they have no choice, so will accept the change and accommodate the new ideas. He goes on to state that leaders need to be able to 'manipulate people's understandings of what is going on, and who are able to deliver the results quickly'. The role of the leader can be to create conditions under which success can visibly be achieved, even if only in a limited and partial way, and to rationalize and capitalize upon positive events after they have happened. Managers will instead need to be skilled in the art of leadership and corporate politics. The need to enrol and re-enrol support, neutralize dissent and resistance, and secure resources will demand networking skills and the ability to build consensus and support. They must start by gaining buy-in at the top. As Siegel puts it, 'You can have the world's greatest web strategy, but it won't work unless managers have a stake in the outcome'. To make sure they do, Siegel recommends the formation of a change team, headed by a Chief Net Officer (CNO). Furthermore, he suggests that businesses should 'Strengthen the team with managers who have good relationships with people in other divisions. The CNO will need a lot of favours, so make sure the team is credible in the eyes of the rest of the company'. If leaders recognize the type of change they are faced with, and are familiar with the sort of skills and tactics that may be employed to deal with it, the management of change is more likely to be successful.

Relationship-building and Communications

The importance of effective internal marketing to engage staff in the change process was emphasized. Increasingly, such communications are a critical aspect of external relationship building too. According to Symonds (1999a), a crucial misconception is that any business is a 'free-standing entity'. For example, in order to participate in a new development such as e-Procurement or customer relationship management, it is essential that companies involve their suppliers, partners and customers in their processes and allow each party to become familiar with each other's processes. This degree of openness and transparency is new to most organizations, and it requires significant change and high levels of trust between participants.

A genuine e-Business strategy provides electronic links in order to 'foster conversations' with staff, customers and partners. Such 'customer-led' approaches involve listening to customers in a strategic way, deepening relationships and loyalty. The importance of engaging in rich customer conversations is underpinned by a number of recent works on e-Business. The highly influential *Cluetrain Manifesto*, for instance, asserts in the first of its ninety-five theses on the new economy that 'markets are conversations'. Newell's *Loyalty.com* (2000) underlines this point, and highlights the way companies must 'leverage customer information' for the effective management of customer relationships on the Internet. Seybold's *Customers.com* (1998) makes similar points, again focusing on the need for customer-focused strategies that engage customers as parts of a community based around a company's products and personnel. Such strategies suggest something much more radical in terms of change than the mere 'bolt-on' approach of adding an online channel to market, which is often proposed as a straightforward and simple process. It calls for a re-engineering of processes and structures focused around key customer groups, rather than product or service divisions. It also implies cross-functional, team-based working. As Siegel puts it, The customer-led company has a broad interface across which all employees can get to know their customers. Employees invite customers in to collaborate on new products, support systems, and methodologies. Facilitating those interactions will take new communication skills, new tools, and the ability to move people in and out of product teams easily.

At Dell Computers, for instance, customers are brought into the product planning and manufacturing processes, with all employees encouraged to have contact with customers. Through effective collaboration across boundaries, ideas can be shared about product designs and value propositions. The result is faster and more customer-focused product and service innovation. To produce the capacity for this, considerable attention must be placed on organizational structures, processes, skills and culture - elements that may need a radical overhaul in established companies.

Role of the Change Agent

Buchanan and Boddy emphasize the importance of having an appropriate 'change agent' or 'project champion' in the successful implementation of change. The change agent should be someone who is committed to the success of the project and prepared to 'go the extra mile' in order to motivate, bully or cajole other participants as required. There is a diverse range of skills associated with performing this role; for example:

- Influencing;
- Negotiating;
- Selling;
- Inspiring;
- Commanding respect;
- Political;
- Magic and miracle working!

It is a tall order for any one individual to have all of these skills, and some will be more important than others at different stages of the project. In practice, therefore, more than one change agent may be required.

Adapting Organizational Culture

There are many ways in which the terms 'culture' and 'organizational culture' can be understood, but for our purposes we have chosen the following:

the system of meanings which are shared by members of a human grouping and which define what is good and bad, right and wrong and what are the appropriate ways for members of that group to think and behave. The pattern of learned basic assumptions that has worked well enough to be considered valid and, therefore, to be taught to new members as the correct way to perceive, think, and feel in relation to the problems of survival and integration.

Schein suggested that employee acceptance of technological change required a change in organizational culture, because practices and values tend to be built around existing technologies that have contributed to the successful development and self image of the organization. One of the strongest elements of culture he identified was the status system attached to these traditions, and the possession by individuals of critical skills. Schein claimed that innovation was a property of culture, and the potential of information technology as a competitive and strategic weapon would not be fulfilled unless innovative cultures were present or developed, enabling the organization to learn and adapt. This attitude was also noted, whose theory of 'flexible specialization' emerged from their observations that technological progress could be self-blocking, and new products were generally designed to fit existing equipment and procedures. The importance of culture was also emphasized in a study of video disk development by Graham, who found that prevailing cultural values and attitudes in the firm, based upon past experience, were inadequate when it came to dealing with an innovative product in a new market.

Although these studies pre-date the Internet era, they illustrate quite clearly how a change in organizational culture is often necessary for full advantage to be taken of the opportunities presented by new technologies. A vast literature now exists on the subject of how to change culture. As early as 1952, Lewin identified three phases of culture change, namely 'unfreezing', 'change' and 'refreezing'. 'Unfreezing' results from the questioning of norms that have led to a specific failure, thereby sensitizing employees to the need for change, which is then consolidated into new procedures or behaviours during the 'refreezing' phase. This theory seems overly simplistic and linear in its classification of the technological change process, which in practice appears invariably to be a more dynamic and turbulent series of events. Mintzberg (1979) advocated the development of a culture of 'adhocracy' that is organic and decentralized in structure, thereby avoiding the pitfalls that are usually associated with bureaucracy. He claimed that in search of innovation, such organizations minimize planning, control and the division of labour.

In practice, however, while examples do exist of individual companies, such as British Airways, that have 'created' a new corporate culture, these success stories appear to be few and far between. March and Simon, in their revised edition of a seminal text that introduced the concept of 'bounded rationality' (referring to the limited cognition of organizational members), maintained that their theory still holds true today. Despite the vastly increased resources available to the modern organization, these authors believed that potential for change would always be constrained by the conflicting agendas of employees. Green also questioned the ability of organizations to manage culture in a prescriptive way:

If culture could be levered into shape then, by now, someone would have discovered the method. The metaphors of fine-tuning and fit which abound in much of the literature on culture and strategy are altogether inappropriate for something as complex as human social systems.

He noted that while corporate cultures appear to be stable and static when studied at a particular point in time, applying a longitudinal perspective reveals that they are in fact too multidimensional and dynamic to be susceptible to manipulation by management. The key point about culture change, therefore, is that it is rarely as simple a process as is sometimes suggested when recommended as a tool for implementing projects involving new technology.

THE INTERNET

Just as the internal combustion engine (the motor car) and jet engine (aeroplane) have radically changed our lives, the Internet is beginning to do the same. In the short time of its existence the Internet has greatly affected business and society. The Internet's evolution and future development are set to continue.

The TCP/IP protocol is evolving with the development of IPv6, the next generation of the Internet protocol. The improvements in IPv6 are scalability, security and support for real-time media quality. Companies such as Ciena Corporation are working on improving bandwidth. They have a product called Wave Division Multiplexing (WDM) that moves data at the speed of 100 billion bits per second (100,000,000,000 b.p.s.). This contrasts with the standard modem's 36,600 b.p.s.

THE WORLD WIDE WEB

The Web's HTTP protocol is evolving to encompass better performance and flexible interactions between clients and servers. Companies compete in complex and increasingly competitive markets. They do so by following, for example, competitive strategies of product differentiation or cost reduction. Similarly, *relationships* are becoming increasingly important in business models.

Current developments in Web technology are best placed to enable companies to exploit their differences and build personal relationships with customers, suppliers or business partners. For example, the eXtensible Mark-up Language, the Semantic Web and other Internet developments are leading the way to providing tailoring capability in e-Business technology.

Extensible mark-up Language

The extensible mark-up language (XML) is gaining popularity over HTML with companies. XML offers companies the ability to define tags that uniquely describe their products, services or customer service culture. Companies can design XML tags to display price or product or service descriptions that cannot be done in HTML. In short, XML allows a company to tailor the feel and look of its Web site and order forms to its needs.

The Semantic Web

Semantic Web is the name given to developments in Web technology by the World Wide Web Consortium (W3C), headed by Tim Berners-Lee, who invented the Web. The Semantic Web enables communication of contextual data and information. Information makes sense to humans only when it is used in context. The Semantic Web enables such context to be captured in Web applications. The primary contribution of the Internet, the Web and associated technologies is to enable collaboration and sharing of information and knowledge among people.

The types of collaboration are numerous, ranging from intra-organizational to inter-organizational and across the boundary of the organization with the customer. Future technology development will focus on this collaborative aspect of e-Commerce and will lead to radically different organizational structures and patterns of interaction among and between businesses and their customers.

THE INTERNET AND THE WORLD WIDE WEB

Prior to the Internet, World Wide Web and its associated technologies, the impact of technology for the purposes of business transactions had been peripheral. The Internet and the World Wide Web have fundamentally changed commerce. Commerce's basic mode of communication, written and verbal communication between a business and its customer or business and its suppliers or partners, remained unchanged since Adam Smith's first observations on economic markets.

Electronic communication, in the form of digital mainframe computers and microcomputers (personal computers) connected to the Internet, has radically transformed commercial activity for customers and businesses alike. The transformation has been so fundamental that new terms such as 'e-Commerce', 'e-Business', 'e-Markets' and the 'new e-Economy' are freely used to describe the modern phenomenon of Internet-based commercial activity. e-Commerce may be described as the sharing of product and service information, developing and maintaining human commercial relationships, and transacting business over the Internet and the World Wide Web.

Technologies such as telephony have influenced business activity in the past, but their influence has not been revolutionary. Such technologies have not fundamentally changed how businesses organize themselves and how they interact with their customers, suppliers or partners. In contrast, the Internet and the World Wide Web have revolutionized business activity.

- Provides an introductory description of the current IT, Internet and World Wide Web technology underpinning e-Commerce;
- Comments on its implications for business and e-Commerce;
- Explores potential future developments in Internet and World Wide Web technology that will affect e-Commerce.

This introductory reading on e-Commerce technology should enable you to describe Internet and World Wide Web technology to enable e-Commerce. Critically, the reading should enable you to state and understand the main elements of an e-Commerce system architecture and assess e-Commerce security technology for confidentiality and payments.

Memex

The Internet's evolution has encompassed over fifty years of technological and conceptual development. The original concept of the Internet is attributed to Vannevar Bush. He worked in a team of engineers during World War II in the United States. His experience of working in an expert team of scientists led him to think about the problem of processing and sharing information among the team. His solution was the invention of a machine called Memex (MEMory EXtension). He envisaged that Memex would work like the human brain, which finds information by association. His ideas provided the conceptual framework for subsequent work on developing the technology of the Internet and World Wide Web.

ARPAnet

The Internet began in 1969 as a communications medium project of the US Department of Defence, and its associated academic and research agencies. It needed a network of computers to enable collaborative work among the different agencies. In its original form, the Internet consisted of a decentralized digital network that connected defence, research and academic mainframe computers. This network was called the ARPAnet after the agency that led the project, the department's Advanced Research Projects Agency (ARPA). The purpose of the ARPAnet was to connect various government and related computers, and in the event of disaster or war to preserve the integrity of information passing between these important government agencies. ARPAnet was privatized in 1990, and as it was gradually released to the public domain it began to be transformed into the Internet that we know today.

The World Wide Web

Around the same time, Tim Berners-Lee, a research scientist working at the European CERN physics lab in Switzerland, conceived the World Wide

Web and released it to the public domain in 1991. The problem that Tim Berners-Lee faced was how to share research knowledge among scientists who used different brands of computers and associated software at CERN. He developed the method of hypertext link for connecting information stored on different computers. In his words, his motive for inventing the Web was: 'If everyone had the same information as me, my life would be easier.

The original idea for linking electronic documents was Ted Nelson's. He coined the term 'hypertext' in the early 1960s. Marc Andreessen developed the first graphical browser for the Internet. It enabled people seeking information on the Internet to find it quickly and efficiently.

A major effect of the Internet and the Web over the 1990s was to enable executives and business strategists to develop new ways of doing business electronically. These new electronic approaches are termed e-Commerce 'business models'. Business models that combine the use of the Internet and Web technologies with fundamental business transformation are referred to as 'e-Business'.

The term e-Business is used to describe a business that shares its production or service information with customers and business suppliers or partners, fosters the development of customer relationships electronically, and enables business to be transacted from personal computers or other electronic devices, such as mobile phones or personal digital assistants (PDAs). One of the most successful e-Commerce business models is the US company Dell Computers.

It has a $14 million per day Internet-based revenue stream, or a quarter of its total revenue. Though a survey by NOP in 1999 revealed that only 15 per cent of the companies surveyed used the Internet for making online sales, Gartner Research predict that 97.5 million US users will adopt e-billing and online account management by 2005.

INTERNET AND WORLD WIDE WEB TECHNOLOGIES

The microcomputer or Personal Computer (PC) forms the basis of e-Commerce. The Internet would not have the wide reach that it has into peoples' homes in the absence of the PC. Most office PCs are linked to a computer network and PCs at home are connected to the Internet via modems or dedicated data transfer cables.

Local area Networks and Wide area Networks

PCs on local area networks (LANs) and wide area networks (WANs) are connected to the Internet. LANs and WANs are digital computer networks that connect PCs to enable sharing of information between separate computers. LANs are limited to a geographical area such as an office, whereas WANs connect computers over a wider geographical area. The computers on a LAN or WAN share information in the form of addressed packets of data. The capacity of a single computer is increased by connecting it to a LAN or WAN, as it can share computer programmes and information. A computer that is linked to a network can download and use computer programmes and share storage and printing facilities, and take advantage of network capabilities for sending and receiving data and information.

Client-server Architecture

A computer on a LAN or WAN that provides resources like application programmes or printer connections is known as a 'server'. A server provides other computers known as 'clients' on the LAN or WAN with software and other resources. This set-up is called client-server computing architecture. A server that is linked to the Internet is called a 'host computer'.

A server computer is capable of running server software, which needs to be compatible with the network operating system. The client and server are independent and perform specialized tasks to process information and run computer applications.

If you use Microsoft Word on your computer, the client, it is probable that a server will have provided the Microsoft Word software for you to use. The client-server architecture is the basis of the Internet too.

The Internet and Protocols

The Internet is the sum total connection of LANs, WANs and stand-alone computers around the world. The term 'Internet' is short for 'inter-networking' or an interconnected set of networks. It is the global network of computers, whether the computer is on a LAN in an office, or a WAN in an industry extranet, or an independent computer in a private home. An Internet-connected computer is known as an Internet host computer. The Internet is also known as the 'Net', the 'Information superhighway' or 'Cyberspace'.

The set of rules for moving information over the Internet is called a 'protocol'. The transmission control protocol (TCP) is used for sending large amounts of information between host computers on the Internet. Vinton Cerf wrote the basic ideas for TCP on the back of an envelope over lunch, and in 1983 the core protocols of the Internet transmission control protocol/Internet protocol (TCP/IP) became the standard protocol for transmitting information over the Internet.

Intranet

An intranet consists of networked internal connection of computers owned by an organization and makes use of Web technology. An intranet may be mounted on a LAN or a WAN. An intranet makes use of Internet technology such as TCP/IP, HTML, Java and HTTP to make it interoperable and to provide it with Web capability. The basic elements of an intranet are a computer network, a computer designated as a server containing server software and the Internet protocols TCP/IP.

An intranet offers several benefits to an organization: improved sharing and communication of information, open standards and cross-platform collaboration. For example, a car manufacturing company may connect its information systems on purchasing with its accounting information systems to form an intranet for sharing and processing information between two departments in the company.

An intranet is a company's own internal information transfer system that offers: e-mail, communication among different computers, connection to remote offices, a Web browser interface and special-interest news groups. For e-Commerce, an intranet is used to provide a corporate image and unified 'experience' for a customer that combines product information, ordering and customer care.

Extranet

An extranet is used for business-to-business (B2B) e-Commerce. It is the networked connection of computers of two or more companies. It is a private communication system to support trade and is used for communication and transactions between business partners, suppliers or special customers. For example, a car manufacturing company may connect its computers with its various suppliers of components for the cars it makes. Another example is the airline industry's OneWorld network, which enables customers to transfer seamlessly between airlines to reach their destinations.

Design principles

Intranets and extranets share the same design principles formulated for the Internet. The Internet design principles are:

Interoperability. There are varying operating systems that control computer functions on the many different computers on the Internet. Normally a given operating system cannot communicate with a different one. A standard to enable varying operating systems to communicate with each other was introduced by the US Department of Defence, which originally financed the Internet. Interoperability means that independent implementations of Internet protocols can work seamlessly. Consequently, operating system developers such as Microsoft or Apple incorporate software into their operating systems that enables them to operate with other computers over the Internet. Internet-compatible systems use the TCP/IP common protocol for communication. Interoperability for e-Commerce means that companies and customers do not have to purchase and upgrade software from the same vendors. Their computers will be able to communicate over the Internet because of the standard protocols.

Layering. The Internet can be regarded as a series of layers of software. The structure of the Internet is layered. It is a five-layer system consisting of: interconnect level (National Access Points, NAPs), national backbone providers, regional Internet providers, local Internet service providers, and the business and consumer market.

The bottom layers of software, interconnect and network, are concerned with operating the computer hardware. The higher layers, business and consumer market, come closer to the needs of the person using the Internet.

The most relevant layer is the layer that processes the information required by the Internet user; this is called the 'application' layer. These different hardware and application layers need to communicate with each other and they do so by using well defined interfaces. The Internet layering standard has resulted in increased reliability of Internet software and it is invisible to the Internet user.

Simplicity. The layering has resulted in simplicity of software design. Each layer is concerned only with its own functionality, making its design simpler. For example, the layer concerned with physical devices like mouse operations are hidden from the higher layers that process information. This kind of simplicity has contributed to increased software reliability too.

Uniform naming and addressing. Each Internet host computer has an Internet Protocol (IP) address that uniquely identifies it on the Internet from the millions of other computers also on the Internet. The IP address is expressed in a uniform format or 'dotted quad'. An example is: '17.10.2.3'. As the dotted quad is not meaningful to humans the domain name system (DNS) is used to provide a symbolic name for the dotted quad. An example is: 'sol.brunel.ac.uk'. The DNS is capable of translating the symbolic name into the required IP address to enable Internet operations.

End-to-end protocols. The Internet does not process information. It enables the transfer of 'packets' of information between computers. This is called end-to-end protocol. The Internet enables the transfer of information or 'content' of the packet. The transmitting or receiving computers, known as the 'end' system, do the actual processing of information.

The combined use of the Internet, intranets and extranets by companies has resulted in the term 'virtual organization' or 'networked organization'. The virtual organization is to be contrasted with the physical organization; the latter is restricted by geographical, physical space. Companies can combine computer-networking technology with information technology (IT) and information systems (IS) to develop a network of computers that can capture, process and share information and knowledge in virtual or cyberspace, where time and space are defined differently from physical time and space.

Amazon.com may be classed as a virtual organization. Virtual organizations tend to be flatter because access to information and knowledge is potentially open to all employees who have access to a PC.

THE WORLD WIDE WEB

The World Wide Web, also known as the 'Web' or 'WWW', consists of pages of information depicted as text, graphics, sound, or video clips. A Web page may contain Java applets - Java programmes that are downloaded from the server and run on the local computer.

The Web consists of over a million Web servers, and an untold number of Web browsers. What distinguishes the Web from other computer media is its ability to link Web pages dynamically; this is known as hypertext links or simply links. The Web combines computer network technology with hypertext to provide a 'global information system'.

One Web page can be linked to another by a hypertext link and the user merely has to click on the link to display related information. A link appears as highlighted on the Web page. It is this hypertext linking capability of the Web that makes it a powerful source of information. The Web is a client-server architecture system, and a Web user can access the Web servers with a Web browser such as Netscape or Microsoft Explorer.

Hypertext

A document on the Web is composed using hypertext technology. Hypertext is an electronic document system that can be read non-sequentially and interactively. The reader does not have to read it like a book, she/he can click on hyperlinks of related information. The Apollo space programme to record its documentation used a hypertext system. e-Commerce Web sites are built using hypertext documents, and other hypermedia.

Hypertext Transfer Protocol

The Web differs from the Internet by the protocol it uses to transfer information between computers. The Web uses the hypertext transfer protocol (HTTP) to connect and transfer hypertext documents stored on Web servers, also known as Web sites. All the computers on the Internet that use the HTTP protocol compose the Web.

The Web browser

A Web browser is a graphical interface for searching, accessing and viewing hypertext and multimedia files on the Web. The first browser, called Mosaic, was invented by the US company Netscape Communications, founded in 1994 by Marc Andreessen. He set himself the problem of transferring sound and pictures over the Web. His solution was the first graphical Web browser.

It allowed basic functions such as retrieving and displaying hypertext files. The growth of the Internet and the Web is largely because of the invention of the graphical browser which makes it easier for people to search and view information. Two popular browsers are Netscape Communicator and Internet

Explorer. They are more sophisticated than the original Mosaic browser and enable e-mail messaging, HTML authoring, and extensions such as scripting, plug-in and multimedia.

INTERNET SEARCH ENGINES

The Internet is unarguably the most voluminous information store in the world. Finding information on the Internet requires complex computer algorithms. These algorithms form the backbone of Internet search engines designed to help people find the information they want. Organizations need search engines to find information about customers or business competitors or partners. Search engines are computer programmes that locate specific Web pages, files or multimedia items stored on the Internet. Search engines such as Google or Autonomy use different algorithms or techniques to search for Web pages.

UNIFORM RESOURCE LOCATOR

The uniform resource locator (URL) is the address of a particular Web site on the Internet. It consists of domain names and a pathway that locates a particular host computer that is connected to the Internet. An example URL is www.yahoo.com or www.dell.com. A URL consists of the protocol that is to be used to make the Internet connection (the WWW in the examples), the name of the host computer ('Yahoo' or 'Dell') and the domain (.com). In the case of commercial companies, the name of the host computer connected to the Internet is usually the registered name of the company.

HYPERTEXT MARK-UP LANGUAGE

Hypertext mark-up language (HTML) is used to author information on a Web page. HTML documents are text files that are interpreted by a Web browser. The browser reads the HTML file and interprets the HTML instructions. The browser has to do this interpretation each time a hypertext file is loaded. A Web page can be divided into 'frames' or sub-pages.

Each frame is used to display separate but relevant information designed by the Web author. Multimedia can be facilitated by extensions to HTML or by 'plug-ins' or add-on programmes that make the Web client more versatile to deal with additional media types. An example of extension is Secure HTTP that enables sophisticated encryption and decryption algorithms for sensitive e-Commerce data like payments for transactions.

It takes time to learn to write HTML code. Authoring tools are available for automatically converting documents in Microsoft Word to HTML files, ready to load on to a Web server. Hot Dog Pro, Adobe PageMill and Microsoft FrontPage are examples. A Web site consists of one or more Web pages linked together by hyperlinks. The contents of a Web site are known as 'content'.

HTML is not capable of processing or interacting with Internet users. To process data captured through a Web form JavaScript is required.

MULTIMEDIA

Multimedia is a tool capable of providing the transfer of sound and images like pictures over the Internet. Multimedia applications require lots of memory and bandwidth - the physical capacity of data cables to carry and transfer data. For example, one minute of music requires 5 MB of data. The transfer of sound and images in real time requires special software which is added to TCP/IP and HTTP protocols. On the client end, a player is required to interpret the data and render it into sound or images.

Multimedia Internet Mail Extensions or MIME is an Internet standard for multimedia Internet e-mail. MIME enables e-mail to be cast as types consisting of HTML, text, images or video. Example MIME types are: image/jpeg, video/mpeg or application/pdf.

JAVA, APPLETS, JAVASCRIPT AND INTERACTIVITY

The Internet is popular because it is interactive. Interactivity means that the Internet user (or client) can actively request information from and provide information to the server. Such interactivity is important for e-Commerce applications. CGI script and JavaScript provide interactivity on the Internet.

Java is a programming language originally intended for programming consumer electronic devices like microwave ovens, dishwashers or electronic clocks. As there are many manufacturers of these products, Java's developer, Sun Microsystems, designed Java to be ubiquitous, meaning that it should be operable on any manufacturer's device.

Virtual Java machines that are independent of PC operating systems interpret Java, a feature that makes it ideal for Internet programming. Java programmes created for the Internet are called applets. Java applets are embedded in HTML documents.

An applet is a Java programme that is executed on the client machine. It is loaded by the Web browser and restricted to prevent security breaches. The applet is executed on a Java virtual machine in the browser.

JavaScript, originally called LiveScript, was developed independently of Java by Netscape to provide interactivity. It is used to process data captured via forms on the Internet and to create interactive Web sites, and both the server and the client side use it. JavaScript is embedded in HTML and is interpreted by a browser.

Web pages that contain JavaScript can be transferred around the Internet, because JavaScript is platform-independent or interpreted. ActiveX is a competitor of JavaScript. Scripts can be used in e-Commerce to validate service or product order form entries.

Common Gateway Interface

CGI programmes are text files that consist of line or programming code similar to JavaScript; such programmes are called CGI script. Pear is an example of CGI programming. CGI is used to create interactive Web sites that pass information from a Web browser to a server using a form, very useful for organizational needs. A form is a document that is created to interact with a user, take data from the user and send it to the server for processing, usually via a database.

ONLINE E-MALLS

In most Western countries malls have gradually become the dominant shopping location for much of what we buy. At the same time malls have become more competitive with each other and now use a variety of extra methods including promotions and entertainment to capture the highest market share. We continue to draw upon an understanding of conventional retailing in order to guide e-retailing businesses. So initially we need to identify the key principles that are important in conventional mall marketing and management. From this benchmark we can then draw lessons for e-malls.

Conventional malls are not all the same, though some have been criticized for being too similar in terms of the retailer tenants in them. Each mall is different in some respect. Sometimes it is simply a size matter, with contrasts across jumbo malls, medium to large conventional malls, down to small neighbourhood malls. In other cases they differ as to special or unusual features, with extreme examples of the wave pool or submarine ride at West Edmonton Mall in Canada or the Lego store and many rides at Mall of America.

Malls differ as well in terms of their specialization, with differences in the format. Many malls adopt the conventional format of having fashion, home and food components. But some are more specialized, such as *power centres* (a small number of large superstores, catering to bulky purchases like furniture, bedding, carpets or electrical goods) or *factory outlet centres* (giving the opportunity to buy well-known brands like Wedgwood or Nike at discount prices). Another point of difference between malls is the different emphasis given to entertainment, with some malls putting on fashion and other shows or having electronic games parlours. Careful selection of tenants could also differentiate one mall from the others, for example by grouping a lot of trendy, independent fashion designers.A recent Australian study (Sit *et al.*, 2003) has pulled together the literature on conventional malls. The study has identified four main areas which shape the image of a mall, including:

- Merchandise (types of tenants, quality, assortment, pricing);
- Accessibility (ease of access to the centre and within the centre);
- Services (including signs, escalators, restrooms);
- Stmospherics (including ambience, music, decor).

These four broad areas tend to appear repeatedly in the growing number of studies of shopping malls. The four areas thus represent a starting point for any mall owner to define what sort of brand they want to be. Notwithstanding, Sit *et al.* (2003) note that the academic studies have neglected some factors that could be important in differentiating shopping centres, namely entertainment, food and security. These authors note that entertainment and food in particular seem to be increasingly used as a method of shopping mall differentiation.

A recent British study (Dennis *et al.*, 2002), based on a study of six British malls, has provided more detailed insight into the branding of conventional malls. An interesting finding by Dennis *et al.* was that consumers were able to associate a personality with a particular shopping centre. One shopping centre studied was described as 'dull and boring and old-fashioned - lower working class or elderly'. As an animal it was like a cat or dog - not exciting, just OK. In contrast, another centre was described as like a tiger, lion or peacock - strong, vibrant, big and colourful. Dennis *et al.* conclude with some advice about active brand-management of malls. The first step is to focus on key attributes like quality, service, atmosphere and infrastructure. Second, choice of the right market positioning is important in creating a point of difference. Third, internal marketing has the potential to help. Finally, well-blended communication can develop credibility.

There is also a broad literature that focuses on how to build a good relationship between the shopping centre landlord and the retail tenant. Howard suggests that in the past too much attention has been placed by landlords on property as a financial investment, rather than investing in the relationship between the landlord and the tenant. Roberts and Merrilees empirically show that stronger cooperation between the landlord and the tenants (such as joint promotions or joint planning of tasks) can improve the performance of the mall. The same authors also show that trust is a precondition for tenants to be willing to cooperate.

LESSONS FROM CONVENTIONAL MALLS FOR ONLINE MALLS

One of the key lessons from conventional mall management that applies to online mall management is the need to manage the *business-to-business* (B2B) relationship between the online mall landlord and the e-retailer tenants. There is a need for the online mall landlord to build a trusting relationship with its online tenants. Most likely, interactivity or cross-communication may be the best way to do this, which is consistent with the Australian case study evidence (although this evidence only relates to communication between the online mall and customer/users of the mall, and not tenants per se). Additional mall management issues include things like leasing arrangements and policies. The terms of the lease need to balance the needs of both the landlord and the tenant and to provide financial incentives to expand the online tenant business as much as possible. Another lesson from conventional mall management is the need for the online mall landlord to provide appropriate and reliable services to the e-retailer tenants.

In an online context, appropriate services might include a well-designed mall, referring to the architecture, including access entrances and layout. Deck (1997) highlights the importance of navigation and other architectural design issues for successful e-malls. Second, services might also include 'decor', which in this context might mean ensuring that each e-retailer has neat and clean premises, rather than a shabby, disorganized appearance. Decor might also include the appropriate 'atmosphere', an issue that most conventional mall studies highlight. Third, traditional mall management includes 'security', which in the online context might entail a third-party guarantee (from the online mall manager, who in turn might outsource this service to a regular third-party vetting firm) that each e-retailer tenant in the online mall has secure facilities for financial transactions online.

Yet another lesson from conventional mall practices is the need to market the online mall in various ways. One way this could be done is through advertising, possibly online. There could also be a coordinated mall-wide promotion for a limited time, say a 10 per cent off deal. A further marketing tool relates to the selection of the tenant mix.

Usually the tenant mix is not accidental, but rather is planned and designed to project a particular image (brand) of the mall. Malls can be upmarket, no frills, entertainment-based and so on. Some malls are very specialized, such as factory-outlet or power centres. An onlinc mall owner can deliberately create a particular mall brand image and might be judged on how consistently they could execute this image. This is a fundamental aspect of mall marketing. Atmospherics can also be interpreted as a marketing tool, supporting the overall e-mall brand image.

MULTIPLE CATEGORY E-RETAILERS

Although not strictly an e-mall, it is interesting to consider multiple category e-retailers. Amazon is probably the best-known example in this situation, where a single-site owner sells goods across multiple retail categories, including books and CDs. In fact Amazon resembles an online department store in this respect. Perhaps surprisingly there are not many explicit online department stores. An Australian example was d-store, which had about 20 departments, though this has now ceased operating as an online department store.

Although multiple category e-retailers provide an interesting source of ideas and inspiration that may be useful for e-malls, to date there is very little academic research investigating such a format. Merrilees (2001), among other authors, has studied Amazon, but purely in terms of a single category (books) and not in terms of multiple categories. No doubt a lot of the well-known good properties of Amazon flow over to the multiple category situation, but there is still a need to ascertain how convenient and useful the site is for searching and buying multiple categories of goods on a *single* shopping trip. Further, how many users actually buy more than one category of goods from Amazon in a single trip?

SHOPPING BOTS: INTELLIGENT SHOPPER ASSISTANTS OR VIRTUAL MALL?

Shopping bots are tools that help e-shoppers identify, locate and compare products available from e-retailers (Rowley, 2000:298). There can be a consumer/ shopper perspective or an e-retailer one. In the former sense shopping bots are another tool for searching the Internet and are not very different from an online directory or a search engine. Alternatively, we can conceptualize a shopping bot from the perspective of the *e-retailer*, who forms a contractual relation (like a tenant) with the *provider* of the shopping bot (like a landlord). It is in this sense that the shopping bot can be considered as a virtual mall, which helps e-retailers present and project their merchandise to the public (Rowley, 2000). Bots tend to be either comprehensive or specialized (say books, music, CDs, gifts) in terms of product categories carried. Rowley (2000:300) lists about 20 shopping bots and suggests the following overall site for a general listing of the shopping bots: www.smartbots.com.

Category search is a common approach to moving through a bot. As an example, storesearch.com invites shoppers to select a department; the next screen displays a series of product categories in that department; then, choosing one of these categories will display a number of merchants. Rowley (2000) does address the difficulty of how the consumer might choose across shopping bots. Some shopping bots seem more suitable for certain products, but it is difficult to generalize. There is also a number of traps to watch out for, with a need for the correct level of specificity and specification. For example, a searcher might specify both the author and title of a book, but there might not be an exact match because of the way the shopping bot database is set up. Ironically, in this hypothetical case, a lower level of specification, such as only the author's name, might be more successful in locating the book. In another case, 'running shoes' might be more successful than 'shoes' or 'sports shoes'. It is hard to see how anything other than one's own experience, or praise or complaints from friends, can guide the selection of shopping bots. More academic research might help us on this matter.

PORTALS AND OTHER QUASI-E-MALLS

We have just seen that shopping bots can be considered to be a type of virtual mall. We should also acknowledge that there are many additional Internet listing and search tools or intermediaries and other third-party sites that also contribute to the world of e-commerce. Yahoo! is probably the most famous site, but there are hundreds of sites that also contribute a similar or related linking of parties through the network. We simply acknowledge this component of the e-retail sector, leaving it to other researchers to elaborate on their role.

EXAMPLES OF E-MALLS

An e-mall is sometimes referred to as a cyber-mall or a virtual mall or an e-shopping centre. It brings together a number of separately owned e-retail sites to a single virtual location, with the individual e-retailers paying rent to the centre management, as in an offline mall. A British example of such an e-mall is www.indigosquare.com.

An interesting example of an American (fashion) niche mall is www.fashionworld.com. This mall has about 100 fashion retailers in it, categorized by floor, which include Main Street and an outlet clearance floor (Hill, 2000). In the Australian case there were recently two e-malls of prominence, namely www.ozeshopping.com.au and www.sofcom.com.au. The e-mall should *not* be confused with a related system in which consumers can be guided to a particular offline (bricks) shopping centre, where they can use special deal coupons downloaded from the central system. For an American version of this latter system, see www.mysho- pping center.com.

The same sites are provided by Australian bricks malls, with similar announcements of book signings, promotions and general information about the tenants in each of the malls in the multi-mall portfolio of the mall owner. A slightly different approach has been taken by the South Australian Government, which has developed its own online mega-mall, with a category-based listing of a wide range of online vendors.

CASE STUDY: AUSTRALIAN RESEARCH INTO E-MALLS

This chapter is a little different from other chapters in that, instead of several smaller case studies, we® have one mega case study of two Australian malls. The details of the case study follow in the next section.

AN AUSTRALIAN RESEARCH STUDY OF TWO E-MALLS

The authors have developed a questionnaire based on the literature, deriving issues important to Internet users/shoppers relevant to their attitudes towards purchasing from e-malls. Respondents were asked to familiarize themselves with two predetermined Australian sites, namely www.ozeshopping.com.au and www.sofcom.com.au, and explore the two sites' features before answering a set of Likert scale-based questions.

By way of broad description, there was a difference in the overall image of the two sites. Ozeshopping was fairly close to what you might term or imagine a regular (online) shopping mall. It had an anchor store, which was an online department store (dstore), and more than 30 tenants, including many well-known Australian bricks and clicks e-retailers (such as Sanity or Strathfield). The site was fairly organized and looked like a solid upper-middle market mall. In contrast, sofcom had an entirely different image. It came across as much more variable in the types of tenants, from sophisticated to somewhat 'seedy'. Most of the tenants could be said to have a strong tourist-Australiana image, making it more of a niche mall. It had an anchor store (e-store; an electrical goods store) and had a higher proportion of pure clicks retailers.

In constructing the survey items specific to this study, prior studies were reviewed to extrapolate items examining Web usage and branding theory research. Then a survey was designed with items intended to capture the underlying multi-item constructs of e-brand attitudes, e-interactivity, e-trust, navigability and retailer-quality. Each survey item was measured on a seven-point scale of (1) disagree very strongly to (7) agree very strongly.

The current study focuses particularly on the potential roles of interactivity and e-trust *inter alia* in influencing brand attitudes with respect to e-malls. Both *interactivity* and *e-trust* have previously been shown to be powerful and central determinants of brand attitudes with respect to a particular e-retail site and the same might be expected with respect to e-malls. The study consisted of 116 Australian undergraduate marketing students from a large regional area. Given the nature of the study, only those who had indicated that they had used the Internet were selected to participate in the study. The student sample *met the minimum conditions* needed for this study in that they (1) were familiar and experienced with the Internet for information search and (2) were of an age (mostly 18-25) that comprises a major segment in the Internet buying market. Importantly, as the study focuses on purchase intention rather than actual purchase, it was not critical that respondents had previously purchased via the Internet. All respondents had access to the Internet, either privately or through university facilities. The sample consisted of an equal number of males and females with a median age of 21 years.

Modelling the Determinants of e-mall Brand Attitudes

This entailed estimating the various paths of the model, with the emphasis on a multiple regression of the determinants of e-mall brand attitude, for each e-mall separately. The regression analysis that explains e-mall brand attitude. It should be noted that the statistical fit is good, with adjusted R-squares of 0.66 and 0.57.

The main finding that both e-trust and interactivity were key determinants of brand attitude for the sample of users of the two Australian e-malls. The standardized beta coefficient on the e-trust variable was 0.5, meaning that for every additional two points of e-trust (measured on a seven-point scale), there will be a one-point increase in positive brand attitude towards that e-mall. Similarly, the beta coefficient on the interactivity variable was approximately 0.33, which means that, for every three points of interactivity (measured on a seven-point scale), there will be a one-point increase in positive brand attitude towards that e-mall. Both of these two variables were significant at the 1 per cent level, with high t-values. No other variables had a statistically significant effect on brand attitude.

Modelling the Determinants of e-mall Trust

The results of ascertaining the determinants of e-mall trust produced only one statistically significant variable, namely interactivity. There was a high beta coefficient of interactivity on e-trust for both of the e-mall sites. That is, the greater the level of interactivity, the greater the level of e-trust that was significant at the 1 per cent level.

Modelling the Determinants of e-interactivity

The perceived interactivity of each e-mall can be largely explained by a combination of both the site navigability and the quality of the retail mix in the mall.

LESSONS FROM AUSTRALIAN CASE STUDIES OF E-MALLS

The main finding of our empirical work is that both e-trust and interactivity were crucial in forming brand attitudes towards each of the two Australian e-mall sites studied. In broad terms this finding is similar to earlier research that had found the same two variables were also crucial in forming brand attitudes at the site of an individual e-retailer, CDNOW. Thus these two variables seem fundamental in explaining brand attitudes of sites that use a variety of *business-to-consumer* (B2C) business models.

However, there are some subtle differences in comparing brand attitudes across e-retailers and e-malls. With the *e-retailer site*, interactivity was the most important determinant of brand attitudes, while with the two *e-mall sites* e-trust was relatively more important. This suggests that, with the more complex and multi-retailer site, trust seems to be a bigger issue. This makes sense in that trust is more difficult to assess if there are multiple retailers and doubts can arise if trustworthy retailers are juxtaposed with less trustworthy retailers.

Trust is most likely a key factor in *any* company's reputation, whether in e-commerce or not. This seems likely because trust is akin to being reassured that the specific company will look after the interests of the user or consumer and protect them in all respects. It is a form of meta-guarantee - one that goes beyond just a product guarantee. Trust is likely to be even more important in the context of e-retailers and extremely important for e-mall owners. This is because major consumer concerns over the adequacy of credit card security or the way that privacy matters are handled could deter the completion of transactions, especially if different firms have different security and privacy policies. The issue of e-trust can also be explored by comparing the Table results across the two e-malls. The sofcom.com.au site is different from the ozeshopping. com.au site in that it has less of the large, well-known branded bricks retailers and more smaller retailers and pure e-retailers. These characteristics make it harder for the sofcom e-mall to gain the trust of users. This may be why the constant term in the sofcom mall is larger and more significant than that for the ozeshopping mall; that is, 1.81 vs. 1.30.

The study breaks new ground in explaining brand attitudes in the e-mall context. The two most important drivers of e-mall brand attitudes were *e-trust* and *e-interactivity*. These relationships were both large (that is, large regression beta coefficients) and highly statistically significant (at the 1 per cent level). Thus the model suggests that e-trust and e-interactivity are two key elements in successful Web branding of e-mall sites.

The results suggest that trust is relatively more important for e-malls compared to individual e-retailer sites in terms of developing Internet brand attitudes. This may be due to the diversity of retailers in the mall context and the inclusion of smaller retailers and pure e-retailers. Owners and prospective developers of future e-mall sites need to be cognizant of the need to develop an overall strategy of trust building. This includes the need to put in place various explicit policies and implement other mechanisms that help project confidence and trust to the consumer and other stakeholders. It also requires careful selection of online tenants, that is, those who will instil trust among e-mall consumers. Finally, and perhaps most importantly, e-mall sites need to develop interactivity, because this is fundamental to e-trust specifically and ongoing relationships more generally.

E-MALLS AS PORTS OF ENTRY FOR NEWLY STARTED BUSINESSES: THE TENANT PERSPECTIVE

It has been obvious that the main perspective that we have taken so far has been that of the e-mall owner. From this perspective we have questions like how should the e-mall be designed so as to be attractive to e-retailer tenants and to potential users or consumers of the e-mall? Although it has been implicit, another perspective is that of the tenant. This leads to a different set of questions. Do I need a presence in an e-mall for my business? If so, what would a suitable e-mall look like? Which one(s) should I become a tenant in?

An appropriate answer to some of these questions is almost certainly connected to the consumer evaluation of an e-mall. The two Australian case studies of e-malls were on the basis of users or consumers assessing an e-mall. If consumers or users rate an e-mall highly then that would be a positive cue to an e-retailer who is considering becoming a prospective tenant. However, it is not a simple matter of a prospective tenant choosing the most popular e-mall site for consumers. The reason is that the best or most popular e-malls will also have the highest rents. A prospective tenant may like to have a high-traffic, high-selling e-mall presence, but may not be able to afford it. This lesson is derived from conventional retailing. McDonald's likes to have high-traffic sites; but it has to pay a lot for them. Within a conventional mall, rents differ for different stalls (micro sites) depending on the traffic flows. The same principles apply in cyberspace.

Additional issues in how tenants might choose or use an e-mall are discussed in Hill (2000) and O'Hara (2001).

Moving on from the rent issue, the e-mall presents a great means for an upstart online organization to get a presence (Hof, 2000). Sometimes the upstarts become the main players. Hof (2000) describes the case of Indianapolis-based National Wine and Spirits Inc. wanting an online presence. Rather than potentially getting upstaged, the company formed its own e-mall (eSkye.com Inc.) that was a national marketplace for beverage makers, distributors and retailers to buy and sell online. Hall (1998) and Strom (1998) also elaborate on the idea that e-malls are a useful means not only to help launch or expand e-retailers, but in some cases to totally create the e-retailer! So one of the services provided by some e-malls is to help create the e-retailer from scratch.

E-MAIL MARKETING CAMPAIGN

- Acquire e-mail addresses (*e.g.* of people who have registered to receive information)
- Obtain permission to use the e-mail address for marketing. This is best done at the time of collection, *e.g.* registration or free samples may only be possible if the respondent checks the 'yes' box
- Select the addresses to target for the particular message
- Execute the campaign (possibly in conjunction with other communications channels)
- Respond to customer replies
- Correct and clean the e-mail list
- Track and measure the campaign performance.

Short Message Systems (SMSs) and Multimedia Messaging Services (MMSs)

While mobile phones and other mobile devices can be useful for 'distress' purchases such as paying a congestion charge (to drive into a city), the growth of m-commerce has been slow, even since the introduction of 3G. Nevertheless, even though it represents a small proportion of marketing budgets, advertising via *short message systems (SMSs)* and *multimedia messaging services (MMSs)* achieves high response rates. Because of this, spending on mobile advertising has been predicted to rocket to £6 billion over the next year or two. Mobile advertising is growing in popularity not just because of the high response, but also because mobile Web users represent an attractive demographic, with the majority being males aged 20-39 with incomes over £30,000. They are well segmented as a target for games, gambling and travel services - currently the biggest mobile advertising categories. For example, in the US, the marketing agency Mobliss has launched Snow Report (www.mysnowreport.com). Customers who have registered their interests can receive text messages detailing snow conditions at winter sports resorts. Recipients of the message can follow a link for a travel package to the resort. As with e-mail, the key to success is opt-in, with customers giving permission for these marketing activities when they register for the information service.

Viral Marketing

Viral marketing is growing as more companies use it to promote and brand their products and services. For example, the low-budget horror movie *The Blair Witch Project* owed worldwide success to a vast volume of 'word of mouse' recommendations passed around Internet chat rooms. These campaigns are becoming more sophisticated with tracking of open, click-through and success rates.

A potential problem with viral marketing campaigns is that the company is reliant on each individual in the chain to have permission to send such messages to each recipient. In many cases this is not done: viral marketing spreads much spam. The responsible marketer will be using tracking systems that can be used for follow-up of sample recipients to ensure that they do not object to such communications.

As an example of *opt-out* viral marketing, consider the hypothetical way that this book could be promoted. Prospects may initially receive an information-only message, for example an invitation to a marketing conference, ending with something along the lines of: Please forward this message to anyone else who may be interested. In the future we may want to inform you of other services and products in which we think you may be interested. If you do not wish to receive such messages, please contact the sender to be removed from the list.

Banners, pop-ups and Interstitials *

Online advertising expenditure on media such as banners and pop-ups is growing and has reached well over £150 million per year (£30 million more than cinema advertising, for example). The interstitial a pop-up that interrupts browsing to show an ad - is a much more active form of advertising than banners. Some people using the Web for a specific purpose find these irritating, though. Online advertising company RealMedia (www.uk.realmedia.com) is using a less-intrusive system called adPointer. This generates an ad when the cursor has not moved for a specific time.

Schemes that incentivize users to look at advertisements have been around for some years, but in the UK Bananalotto.com (www.bananalotto.com) has raised the stakes by offering the chance to win one million pounds as you click the banner ad. KPE, the media and entertainment consultancy, has developed around ten games for their clients. Managing Director Paul Zwillberg says:

* This section is summarized and adapted from Marketing Business e-business supplement So much of the Internet has been characterised by repurposing things that worked well in print or TV. 'Advergaming' is... a new combination that's made for the medium.... You take one of the most popular uses of interactive content and marry it with tried and tested advertising models like brand association, trial or data capture and you get something really wonderful.

Customer Relationships

The direct mail and e-mail activities described above are part of the management of customer relationships. Building on these basic communication tools, the most successful e-retailers such as Amazon (www.amazon.com) and Tesco (www.tesco.com) use various techniques of data mining, personalization and customization. For example, Amazon customizes the web page, making offers for new books, music or movies that are likely to be of interest based on past purchase patterns. Tesco likewise personalizes its communi-cations and special offers almost down to the level of the individual. These e-retailers are thus able to satisfy customers more specifically and therefore are better using the customer relationship and data mining tools.

Web Atmospherics

Web atmospherics is too important and complex a topic for this single section, in greater depth. Briefly, atmospherics includes *visual* (*e.g.* text, design, colour management, video clips, 3-D), *aural* (*e.g.* music or sound effects) and *olfactory* (*e.g.* perfume and samples) stimuli. The Edmunds (www.edmunds. com) car sales site is a good example of the use of exciting downloads of video and sound effects to illustrate cars in action. With effects like this, there is a need to avoid long download times (*e.g.* by having a separate 'click here for broadband' version for the larger memory effects). Perfume is available by e-retail, although most suppliers rely on description and well-known brands, rather than offering samples, for example Perfumania (www.mydesign erperfume.com): 'Contains citron, rose, jasmine and is accented with honeysuckle, vanilla and oakmoss making Allure by Chanel perfect for romantic use'. Atmospherics, even when fairly low-tech, have much to offer in communications mix design.

Link Popularity

Search engines use 'link popularity' in locating and ranking sites. Improving link popularity by persuading other sites to link to yours raises a site in search-engine rankings and is therefore a critical aspect of the communications mix.

Case Study: EBAY.CO.UK

The eBay site was founded in the US in 1995, originally under the name Auctionweb. The UK site was launched in 1999, growing after a slow start to become the UK's top e-commerce site measured by monthly audience numbers, with 6.8 million people (compared with Amazon's 6.1 million and Tesco's 2.7 million). In the year to March 2003, eBay's audience increased by 160 per cent, compared to Amazon's 28 per cent. Internet growth overall was only 7 per cent. The figures are 'a significant sign of the potential of [the most profitable and successful Internet players] to sell to consumers', according to Nielsen/ NetRatings (www.nielsen-netratings.com), who supplied the figures. Cheap though most individual products may be, eBay still sells over £1 billion of them per year. If eBay were considered to be an e-retailer, this would make them number one in UK market share. While many dot.coms are mainly hype, eBay is profitable, making a quarter of a billion dollars on worldwide operations in 2001. It survived the dot.com crash relatively unscathed and the share price rose from US$18 in 1998 to US$110 by 2003.Visitors to eBay spend an average of 1 hour and 11 minutes per month on the site - one of the longest of any UK site.

Visitors return to the site to check the status of items they are bidding for or selling and ebay.co.uk is one of very few e-retailers to achieve over a billion pages views per month.Many UK users are earning a healthy living as 'power sellers', taking advantage of the worldwide market to offer everything from sports utility vehicles (SUVs) to comics, records and oddments like garden gnomes, T-shirts and kettles. In the same way as the major bricks retailers are suffering increasing competition from charity shops and car-boot sales, so the established e-retailers face growing competition from online auctions.Most sellers are private individuals.

For example, Pat Austin makes £30,000 per year selling an assortment of bric-a-brac that she finds in charity shops, car-boot sales and physical auctions. She sells 1,000+ items per year and 99.9 per cent of her transactions have been positive. It is a full-time job, though, with correspondence and despatch taking up the mornings and sourcing goods the afternoons. Rosie English has a turnover of £100,000+ selling high-class women's fashion for prices of £100 to £1,000+.

She reads the fashion press to identify what editors recommend and what celebrities are wearing, then buys from sample and factory sales or direct from designers. However, eBay is not all one-person businesses, as the 'big boys' are seeing the opportunities and joining in with companies like Dell, Dixons and Sears using eBay to shift excess stock.It's a case of 'buyer beware', as auction sites do not take responsibility for deals that go wrong and offer only low insurance cover for losses. The way for buyers to identify the most reliable sellers is from feedback ratings - many regular sellers have hundreds of positive ratings.

BUILDING BLOCKS TO E-BUSINESS

Access to on-line information resources and the use of electronic transactions increasingly augment the operation of modern colleges and universities. These resources and functions are important both internally and in collaboration with external partners. To reap the full benefits that these resources and processes can offer, all members of the campus community must be able to function easily and securely throughout this rapidly growing electronic information environment. Although campuses have made great strides towards developing robust and ubiquitous communications network infrastructures, the rich information environment envisioned in Sustaining Excellence in the 21st Century will not be realized unless equally robust and ubiquitous enabling services are developed within the infrastructure of our campuses and throughout the higher education community.

I define the electronic information environment as that set of electronic information services, on-line resources, communications services, applications software, and workstations that enable us to teach and learn and work more effectively and without the M. Stuart Lynn, a colleague and friend to most of us in the information technology community, provided ideas, advice, counsel, and constraints of time or place. Within this environment, we need directories and other finding aids, credentials that can establish identity and roles for both consumer and supplier, and a myriad of other supporting services.

Infrastructure support services will enable easy and secure access to information resources, support authorized and verifiable transactions over the network, and make possible appropriate management of licensed materials and other intellectual property. With a coordinated approach, we will be able to leverage investments being made already in new applications on our campuses as well as across the higher education community.

As the electronic information environment grows and expands, it becomes necessary to acknowledge and implement certain constraints on users of these resources—the "network citizens" who navigate that environment. We must develop analogues of the administrative controls with which we are familiar in the traditional environment. These controls should be supported by generalized infrastructure services put in place and managed by the institution.

Existing access control and authentication mechanisms are largely a legacy of older centralized technology. Traditional institutional applications have been developed from the ground up, providing for all aspects of the process in an idiosyncratic way. Today we understand that many of the components of these applications have a great deal of commonality. These include a secure and reliable way to affirm that users of our resources are who they purport to be and that they are authorized to use the resources to which they seek access. There must be a source of definitive information regarding their affiliation with the campus as well as other business-related data. There must be directory services to help them find the resources they need. There must be standards and supporting services for encryption to secure data transmission and to create the digital equivalent of a personal signature. There must be efficient mechanisms to support accounting for the use of a wide variety of networkbased resources as well as services that can be supported by network communications.

Lack of common general solutions for authentication, authorization, directory services, and encryption will impede the development of a broad range of information resources, from client-server financial systems to digital libraries. If properly designed, these technical building blocks can be combined and extended to form a set of common services, or "middleware, " that will enable a wide variety of complex capabilities that are available almost transparently to the end user. These new and critical middleware services will enable members of the academic community to become true universal network citizens and roam freely and securely, without undue let or hindrance, throughout the emerging electronic information environment.

The availability and use of these and other building blocks also can form the basis for more robust and efficient management of institutional resources. Rule-based authorization processes can support distributed operation and responsibility. Well-designed and reliable support services can help the campus protect intellectual property.

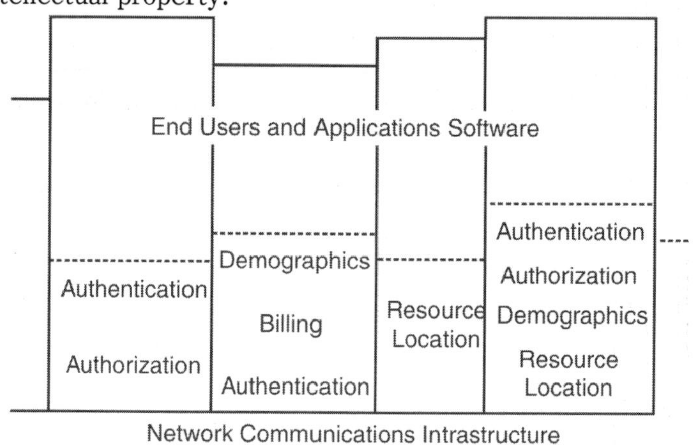

Fig. Existing Applications with Independent Solutions to the Same Set of Problems

Differences among campuses in their information environment middleware services tend to inhibit sharing of resources, a tendency that will become exacerbated as critical new shared resources such as virtual digital libraries begin to emerge. Currently a faculty member or student at one campus who is visiting another campus must make special arrangements in order to make use of many of the services at the second campus.

If the services require access control, the individual must acquire yet another password and account name. Coordinated middleware services can allow the identity and affiliations of any member of the higher education community to serve them wherever they may be working at the moment. I will continue to use the metaphor of a network citizen traveling throughout the electronic information environment to illustrate the basic middleware building blocks. It is with the goal of catalyzing the development and implementation of the best technologies to implement these services within the higher education community that we begin this management tour of the electronic information environment.

THE TERRAIN: THE ELECTRONIC INFORMATION ENVIRONMENT

The electronic information environment is an increasingly complex territory in which valuable resources can be found, but it is foreign to our usual senses. Many of the familiar problems and processes are found here but take a different form. What is our identity? What can we do here? How do we find resources? How do we traverse the environment with safety? How do we account for what we use? Do we share a common reference for time or place?

The foundation of the electronic information environment is the complex of interconnected networks (including our campus networks) known as the global Internet. Accessible from desktops both within our campuses and via the Internet are an ever growing variety of databases, information servers, vendors doing business via e-commerce, computational servers, and a panoply of applications programmes from e-mail to collaborative systems based on interactive virtual reality. E-commerce is developing rapidly in many forms and will enable reliable transaction of institutional business as well as new opportunities for individuals.

Our helpers in traveling the information environment are client software and programmes that interact with other electronic entities by means of well-defined protocols. Just as in the analogue world, these protocols provide for successful interoperation among widely differing entities. The World Wide Web is an excellent example of this concept: the same set of complex text, graphics, audio, and video can be found and viewed on almost any modern computer regardless of what kind of computer might hold them. One significant advantage of this layered approach to complex systems is that individual pieces of the environment can be built or replaced without affecting the rest of the infrastructure. Another advantage is that end-user platforms can be tailored to different user communities and application needs. This layered approach must guide us in the development of essential information environment support services.

Passports: The Authentication Service

The fundamental support service that will empower the network citizen is a universal, distributed, reliable, and robust digital credential system. Just as travelers must carry their passport when entering a different country, network citizens should carry a recognized credential when entering the electronic information environment. This credential, which can be validated by any service encountered, will ensure the authentic identity of the individual holding it.

Passports are recognized as authoritative around the world because the issuing authority is recognized by international treaty. So too should the network credential be recognized as authoritative so that network citizens can visit various sites and resources without having to resort to site-specific identification. Instead of an international treaty, there must be agreements among cooperating administrative domains to trust each other's credentials. Such agreements are based on understanding the methodology and management of the process for issuing the credentials.

The concept of a digital credential that refers to a single electronic identity is powerful because it can enable easy access to resources for the traveler. The credential itself may not carry much information about the individual, much as the traditional passport carries not much more than a picture, an address, and a passport number. However, that passport number can be the key to determining additional attributes about the holder. In an analogous way, the digital credential should have an identifier (e-ID) that is unique to the credential holder and can be used as a key to discovering further identity information.

Relying on a single credential is fraught with the potential for abuse if it is mishandled. Since e-IDs will let travelers into many places, they must be issued only with strong assurance that individuals are who they claim to be. Once the e-ID is issued, the holder must recognize that it is an extension of his or her personal identity, protect it carefully, and never lend it to another person.

Even with reliable credentials, it will be desirable in many cases for an individual to have several e-IDs to be used for different purposes. All individuals and their organizations must consider the potential impact of a compromise of the security of any e-ID. For example, the manager of an administrative computing system might have an e-ID that carries with it special privileges. That e-ID should be used sparingly and only in conjunction with that system so that compromise of the more powerful e-ID would have consequences of a more limited scope and could be dealt with more readily. The system manager would use a less powerful e-ID when doing routine work, such as checking e-mail or writing reports.

An e-ID represents an assertion on the part of a registration authority that a known individual or entity is represented by that e-ID. If the registration authority is well designed and reliable, then services in cooperating administrative domains, or realms, can be comfortable accepting those externally registered e-IDs. Thus, in the general case, the e-ID must indicate not only the individual but also the registration authority that issued the e-ID. Ultimately this concept could be extended to commercial registration authorities so that, for example, high school students registered with a local electronic notary might be able to use their own credential's e-IDs in submitting electronic applications for admission to a college or university.

Once a campus has a robust digital credential issuance and authentication service in place with reliable operational support, all of the important campus server applications should be adapted to use this system. Parts of this process could take a long time since many applications are vendor supported and vendors are not yet responding to this broader vision. Until there is a well-established generalized authentication service, each server or application has little choice but to implement its own idiosyncratic method of authentication, and the network citizen must deal individually with each one encountered.

TICKETS AND PASSES: ATTRIBUTE AND ELIGIBILITY DATABASES

Eligibility, as distinct from authentication (which warrants the identity of a particular user), is an equally important support service in the electronic information environment. Eligibility helps define what network citizens may do or that to which they may gain access. It may be based on a person's e-ID or on any set of attributes associated with that e-ID, such as the person's affiliation with or within the institution, role, or current status. Often it is desirable to separate authentication service from eligibility and attribute functions, and it may be desirable to support them on different servers.

Eligibility does not necessarily imply authorization. The network citizen may be eligible to gain access to a resource, but at the time access is requested, the service might be oversubscribed or otherwise unavailable. For example, holding an airplane ticket may not result in authorization to board that flight. Authorization is a function of the service or application based on specific business rules. These rules might take into account a variety of factors in addition to the individual's identity, such as time of day, location of the individual, or the availability of resources.

In the historical model of mainframe computing, authentication (often referred to as access control) and authorization were often closely linked. Authorization usually was determined by loose association of attributes with the user account identifier (for example, "root" or "user, group, and other" in Unix systems) or by tables of authorized users. Since each system kept its own set of authorization data, management of these data in a consistent way across a large number of servers and client platforms was problematic, although a number of projects attempted to address aspects of this dilemma. Little thought was given to generalized information environment management mechanisms until the number of different systems and services began to grow dramatically.

Today we need generalized and scalable network-based mechanisms not only for authentication but also for eligibility and attribute information. As an example of how this might be provided, suppose the network citizen requests access to a restricted database. The database server can simply query a specified attribute server, supplying the network citizen's e-ID, and receive information on the roles, affiliations, or other attributes defined for that individual. The database server then can apply a prescribed set of business rules to determine whether that particular network citizen is to be allowed access to the restricted data.

Suppose the network citizen's affiliation with the institution is "full professor and dean of the college." This might imply eligibility to view college budgetary data and approve spending plans and personnel actions, as well as to gain access to academic records and information. The same person might also be appointed to a multicampus task force on student diversity and because of that affiliation be eligible to retrieve sensitive student ethnicity and gender data. A database server that returned roles and affiliations for any given institutional e-ID would make management of this type of generalized eligibility much easier.

Such eligibility or affiliation data might be useful in transactions external to the institution as well. Appropriate individuals in any department could be given authority to submit electronic data interchange (EDI) purchase orders over the network, for example. A different set of individuals could have authority to approve payment of EDI-based invoices electronically. Workflow systems could identify individuals who need to be informed of such transactions for possible post-transaction audit.

Whereas administration of an attribute service should be hierarchical and coordinated centrally, responsibility for actual eligibility data with respect to any given service should be distributed to conform with campus management structure. This is primarily an administrative rather than a technical issue. Suffice it to say that developing and managing a database service that combines all important attributes, roles, and affiliations and allows them to be managed by the office of record would provide important generality while maintaining the institution's established administrative structure.

WHO'S THERE? THE DEMOGRAPHICS DATABASE SERVICE

One particularly vexing problem is the maintenance of accurate personal data, such as home address, campus office address, or preferred e-mail address. Today there are far too many different databases wherein the same data are entered, usually by different individuals, from separate forms that must be filled out repetitively by the person who actually "owns" the information. For example, in many cases the same individual is both a student and an employee, which means that the same personal data often are maintained by entirely separate offices. Clearly it would be desirable to have a single comprehensive database of record that would hold information about all members of the campus community and in which personal data could be maintained by the relevant individual or appropriately designated staff.

With strong authentication and a well-designed attribute service, it would be possible to build such a demographics database system. It might well be combined with a basic eligibility service so that a single database system supports both. Fields within a record would have associated rules for access or updating. All institutional applications that require use of personal data would use this comprehensive demographics database by either periodic downloading or indirect relational reference. In particular, on-line directory services for locating campus community members would use this authoritative database as their data source.

Campus network citizens could be responsible for maintaining all of their own personal data and also could check on the completeness or accuracy of other attribute data, such as payroll title or salary, status towards a degree, or the parameters of their employee benefits.

MAPS AND GUIDEBOOKS: DIRECTORY SERVICES

Information services and resources abound on campuses and beyond. The community of users changes and moves about, and the topology of the network changes periodically. How does a network citizen find anyone else or any particular service or information?

The Domain Name Service was the first widespread directory service in support of the information environment. Other common directories exist today, such as directories of people and searchable databases of information resources. Many more kinds of maps and guidebooks are needed to serve the new and complex information resources we are deploying. For example, the network citizen might want to find an on-line copy of Van Gogh's Child with Orange and the nearest colour printer that she or he is eligible to use and that is capable of high-resolution, large-format printing. New resource location services must support more complex data and search strategies.

A well-managed set of directory servers and search engines for information objects will help the network citizen discover resources and navigate easily throughout the electronic information environment.

SAFE PASSAGE: ENCRYPTION AND DIGITAL SIGNATURES

Authentication and access control alone are not sufficient to guarantee safe passage throughout the electronic information environment. Passwords can be guessed or stolen, data can be monitored in transit, and identities sometimes can be forged. The strongest defence against these challenges involves the use of modern encryption methods to ensure privacy of data transmission and create the digital equivalent of a pen-and-ink signature. Our networks are truly open systems, which is one of their strengths as well as a source of many vulnerabilities. Any transmission might be intercepted, and any data received might be questionable. Attacking computers on the Internet has become a rampant obsession among certain curious and occasionally antisocial groups. Fortunately, modern encryption technology offers potential solutions for most of these concerns. Encryption of data while in transit can protect privacy as well as the confidentiality and integrity of data. The technology required to implement data encryption has become commonplace and should be considered for all administrative or other institutional business applications. Encryption alone may not guarantee authenticity, however. We need the equivalent of a seal or at least a recognized signature associated with the contents of the document.

A digital signature must be some set of data that cannot be forged and that binds the contents of a digital document to a specific individual, role, or other entity. It must be something that only the signing entity could have created and must be verifiable by anyone in the electronic information environment.

Standards now exist for creating this type of digital signature using public key cryptography (PKC). Clearly digital signatures of this sort would enable a wide variety of institutional business to be transacted over the network with at least as reliable verification and auditability as we have now with paper forms and manual signatures.

A public key infrastructure (PKI) is critical to enabling the use of encryption and digital signatures. Fundamental to the PKI is a unique pair of very large prime numbers, generated for each credential holder, that are keys used for encryption and decryption of information. Software on the network citizen's workstation generates this pair of encryption keys and gives one of them (the "public" key) to the PKI certificate authority (CA). The other key (the "private" key) is closely guarded by the network citizen. The CA stores the public key in a directory along with the PKI certificate. Upon request, the CA or directory server provides any registered user's public key to any application that needs it.

In addition to support of the local community, a CA must have a way to find other trusted CAs on other campuses or anywhere else in the electronic information environment. This ability is part of an overall PKI and may be implemented in a number of different ways.

The basis for trusting a traditional signature is either direct knowledge or the ability to look it up in an archive maintained by a trusted authority, such as a bank. In the digital world, trust must be established through pre-established contracts based on mutual understanding of business practices, the basis for registering individuals with the CA, and the viability of the cooperating CAs.

The resulting so-called web of trust must be scalable to millions of users in thousands of locations. This can be achieved through a hierarchical model wherein a community-based CA registers subordinate CAs after verifying their viability. A consortium of college and university campuses, for example, could operate such a certificate authority and the associated services on behalf of its members. This CA in turn could register under national and international CAs to allow fully general and trustworthy access to verifiable public key directory servers anywhere in the world. A campus PKI with its root certificate authority also could register subordinate CAs for departments, the library, or special-purpose requirements. Until and unless encryption mechanisms and support services are in use, no one should send anything of value or of a sensitive nature, such as a credit card number, over the data network.

SHARING LIMITED RESOURCES: LICENSE SERVERS

The network citizen is now equipped with the basic tools for verifying identity, invoking authority, and concluding transactions safely. These capabilities enable easy and appropriate access to a wide variety of resources within our electronic information environment. Unfortunately, not all of those resources are without significant cost to the institution. A traditional library might hold five copies of a popular book or journal. Ideally this would be enough to meet the peak demand at any one time for this resource. It would not be economical to purchase one copy for every registered patron, yet we often provide software and other resources in this cost-inefficient way.

It is quite possible for software or other digital resources to be purchased by subscription, much like printed documents today. The cost of such a subscription would be based at least in part on the size of the simultaneous user community. For example, a physics department might purchase a subscription for twenty simultaneous "users" of a virtual physics laboratory software package. During laboratory classes, the students make use of the software on computers located in the facility. In the evening, when doing homework, up to twenty students could make use of the same "subscription" to run the software on their own personal computer. One way to enable this type of sharing of expensive resources is a network-based license server (NLS). The NLS serves as a clearinghouse to ensure conformance with the terms of the institution's subscription. An early implementation of the NLS concept was available with the Apollo domain computers. Macintosh and PC versions of license servers offer similar capabilities. Standardizing on an openly available NLS technology would enable publishers to develop products that could fit readily into our electronic information environment. A single NLS could moderate access to a wide variety of licensed resources, including databases and documents as well as software.

PAYING THE BILLS: AUTOMATED DEBIT THAND UNIFIED INVOICING

Much of the electronic information environment today is accessible without direct cost to the network citizen. However, as the real costs become significant, the campus may need to find efficient ways at least to account for the usage of expensive resources and possibly allocate some of the acquisition and support costs towards the end users. A building block that could help achieve this is an efficient network accounting server. Ultimately every member of the campus community, as defined in the campus's demographics database and corresponding eligibility servers, could have one or more "virtual accounts."

Transactions for services would be posted to a designated network accounting server using encrypted data flows. A wide variety of network citizen services, from print-on-demand syllabi to lunches and storehouse items, could be accounted for in this way. The network citizen should expect a single statement each month describing all services used and any costs incurred anywhere within the institution. This might include transactions with external partners as well. Eventually this monthly accounting could result in an automated debit against an external financial service, much like debit cards are used today.

WHAT TIME IS IT? THE NETWORK TIME SERVER

It may not seem obvious but many of the services we are developing need to have a common frame of reference for time. Billing information, for example, must show accurately the date and approximate time of the transaction. Network management information often needs time stamps to be accurate to within a few milliseconds. Electronic postmark or notary services must have an auditable date and time guaranteed to be within a known degree of accuracy. Thus, an important element in the set of enabling services within our information environment is the network time server.Technologies in support of network time services exist today and are deployed on most campuses. However, not all of these are synchronized with each other or with a universal time standard, such as the National Institute of Standards and Technology broadcast standard time service.Even where synchronized network time servers exist, not all essential end systems can take advantage of them yet. Campus information technology managers must understand the importance of this element of distributed systems and take appropriate steps to ensure integration of this service.Our network citizens may wish to set their own "electronic watch" from this service as well. Most modern workstations can be configured with automatic utilities to accomplish this.

WHERE TO NOW?

The building blocks I have identified are all part of a larger set of standards that comprise an information technology architecture. The basic enabling services include the following features:

- A coordinated set of authentication servers
- An attribute and demographic database server on each campus that can include a wide variety of information, including affiliation and eligibility data

- Directory and resource location servers
- PKI servers that manage certificates and public encryption keys for individual users and make possible digital signature verification
- Electronic license servers in support of site-licensed software, library materials, and databases
- Billing transaction servers that can handle a large volume of small-value debit records extremely efficiently
- Time servers and digital notary servers that form the basis for reliable and verifiable on-line content and digital institutional archives

The building blocks might relate to each other and to the communications system and applications programmes. Other building blocks might include software version control servers.

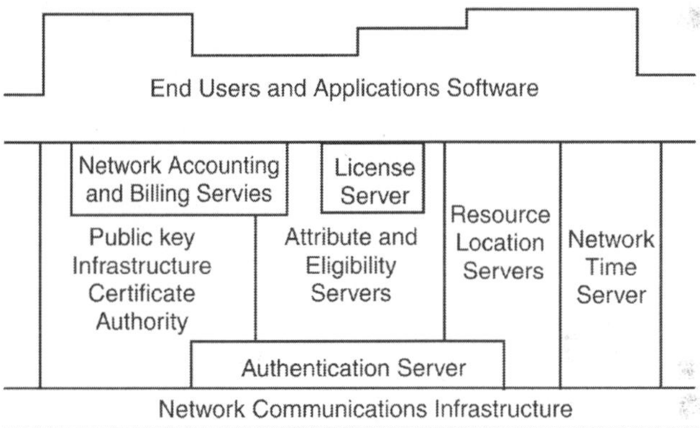

Fig. Information Environment Building Blocks with Common Interoperable Solutions for Basic Supporting Services

Campus users have access to the latest version of critical application programmes, and alias servers to support consistent mapping between e-IDs and e-mail addresses or traditional identifiers such as employee number or student ID number. Current and potential technologies behind each of the building blocks described above are in different states of development and deployment.

With persistent vision and cooperative efforts, we can refine and deploy appropriate versions of all these enabling services over the next few years. If we do not start now, it may become very difficult to develop and retrofit a coordinated set of these services later. There is much to be done before network citizens are fully empowered. Information Policy to Support

9

Banking in Rural and Agricultural Areas

INTRODUCTION

The rural population in India suffers from a great deal of indebtedness and is subject to exploitation in the credit market due to high interest rates and the lack of convenient access to credit. Rural households need credit for investing in agriculture and smoothening out seasonal fluctuations in earnings. Since cash flows and savings in rural areas for the majority of households are small, rural households typically tend to rely on credit for other consumption needs like education, food, housing, household functions, etc. Rural households need access to financial institutions that can provide them with credit at lower rates and at reasonable terms than the traditional money-lender and thereby help them avoid debt-traps that are common in rural India.

Usage of banking services by Indian households (HHs)						
Source: Census of India 2001						
	Total	No.	% of	HHs	Rural % of Total	HHs
Total No. of HHs	19.19	100	13.83	72.0	5.36	28.0
No. of HHs which use banking services	6.8	35.5	4.16	30.1	2.65	49.5

Debt profile of rural households (in %) *Source:Ministry of Labour, Ru ral Labour Enquiry Report*		
SOURCE OF DEBT	1993.94	1999-2000
Government	8.3	5.4
Co-operative Societies	7.9	13.1
Employees	11.4	6.9
Money Lenders	**27.6**	**31.7**
Shopkeepers	7.3	7.1
Relatives & Friends	12.4	15.1
Others	6.2	3.5
Banks	18.9	17.2

TABLE A

Changes in farmers reliance on the banking system

(RBI)

Year	Farmer Deposits (Rs Crore)	Farmer Borrowings (Rs Crore)	Total (Rs. crore
1992	26211	17835	273
1993	29825	19493	257
1994	36583	19669	251
1995	43341	21334	198
1996	47433	23813	194
1997	53611	27448	188
1998	57442	29442	173
1999	78881	33094	169
2000	91009	36466	162
2001	99812	43420	195
2002	108233	47430	197

CURRENT TRENDS: A POINTER TO FINANCIAL EXCLUSION

Rural Credit: The 2001census reveals the low level of banking usage among Indian households in general (35.5 per cent) and rural households in particular (30.1 per cent). This reflects on the latent demand for general banking needs in rural as well as urban segments. The debt profile of rural houscholds indicates that the major source of credit to rural households, particularly poor income working households, has been informal sector loans like money-lenders, which are usually at very high rates of interest. The terms and conditions attached to these loans impact the poor adversely. This reflects the inadequate institutional credit flow to rural areas. As on 31-3-2003, rural and semi-urban centres had a Credit/Deposit (CD) ratio of 42 per cent and 35 per cent respectively as compared to a CD ratio of 69.5 per cent and 59.3 per cent for urban centres and national level. These trends broadly indicate that despite the widespread banking network in place, there is a continued migration of rural/semi-urban savings to urban/metro centres, thereby causing a banking divide between rural and urban areas.

Agricultural Credit: An equally important concern that needs attention is the flow of institutional credit to agriculture. The progress of agricultural credit in India has depended crucially on government intervention over the years, *i.e.* package of incentives and policy measures, which the RBI and the Centre formulate and implement. The growth of commercial banks' lending to agriculture and allied activities witnessed a substantial decline in the 1990s as compared to the 1980s. Credit flow to the agriculture sector of all formal sources amounted to ₹ 70,810 crore in 2002-03 and ₹ 86,981 crore in 2003-04, much below the levels envisaged in the Tenth Plan. Agriculture's share in scheduled commercial banks' total outstanding credit as on 31st March 2005 was only ₹1,12,475 crore.

The total agricultural lending by commercial banks is lower than credit in "personal loans" which stood at ₹ 2,66,988 crore, comprising advances for housing and consumer durables. In recent years, retail advances have increased by 41.2 per cent in 2004-05 as compared to the growth of 27.9 per cent in the overall loans and advances of Scheduled Commercial Banks. As a result, their share in total loans and advances increased significantly during the year ended March 2005.

However, according to a recent study, only 15 out of 85 banks registered an increase in return on assets as at the end of 2004-05 over 2003-04. Hence, the argument that rural credit drives down the banks profits and increases NPA is not justified. NPA in rural credit are far less and the rate of retrieval of rural credit NPAs is faster than other advances. The annual growth rate of farm credit is around 15 per cent and this growth in rural advances essentially comes from advances like gold loans for agriculture and Kisan Cards. About 70 per cent of the present rural credit stock of over ₹ 115243 crore is Kisan Credit Cards spread over 4.8 crore of such card holders. This shows the narrow focus of the banks towards shortterm production loans rather than for term loans. Post reforms, the banking system has mobilised more deposits from farmers and extended less credit to a declining number of farmers.

TABLE B

Deposits received under RIDF as on 31st March 2003

Source: NABARD Report 2002-03

Year	Total (Crore)
1995-96	350
1996-97	1042.30
1997-98	1007.04
1998-99	1337.95
1999-2000	2306.63
2000-01	2653.64
2001-02	3590.72
2002-03	3857.09
Total	16145.37

These are reflected in the figures for farmer borrowings and deposits in the last decade as in Table A. Many scheduled commercial banks are shying away from agriculture and priority sector lending even though the commercial banks have an excess investments portfolio beyond the required limits of 25 per cent. Furthermore, scheduled commercial banks are resorting to the soft window option of investing in the Rural Infrastructure Development Fund (RIDF) of NABARD. Table B illustrates the growing contributions to the corpus of RIDF received by NABARD by way of deposits from Scheduled Commercial Banks against their shortfall in priority sector/ agricultural lending during the preceding year.

Policy Initiatives by Government/RBI

To meet the gap that existed in meeting the credit needs of the rural poor, the Government appointed a working group on rural credit, the Narasimhan Committee in July 1975. Based on its recommendations, Regional Rural Banks (RRB) emerged in 1975. These banks were meant to take banking to the rural masses, particularly in areas without banking facilities, make available cheaper institutional credit to the weaker sections of society, mobilise rural savings and channelize them for other productive activities in rural areas and bring down the cost of providing credit in rural areas. The number of RRBs increased dramatically over a period of time. At the end of the fiscal year of 2002-03, there were 196 RRBs spread by a network of 14,350 branches, accounting for 44.5 per cent of the total rural network of all scheduled commercial banks (including RRBs). The bulk of the loans from RRBs have been given to priority sectors, which accounted for over 70 per cent of the total. Agriculture alone took up 46 per cent of the priority sector advances. RRBs have also taken a lead role in the financing of Self Help Groups (SHG's) mostly comprising women leading to their economic and social empowerment. Cooperative banks were formed to promote the rural credit. Cooperative banks and RRBs differ in their ownership and management. Cooperative banks are state-government run banks while RRBs are managed by the sponsor bank with an equity stake of 35 per cent.

The Central Government and State Government hold 50 per cent and 15 per cent equity stake in RRBs. Since independence, the RBI has taken a number of measures to augment the flow of rural credit. It has a unique system of extending General Line of Credit-I for seasonal agricultural operations and General Line of Credit-II for the handloom sector out of the created money. The RBI has also been issuing directives for a long time now regarding 'social and development banking' like imposing a cap on the interest rates and sectoral allocation of credit and expansion of rural branches.

The RBI has also made it mandatory for commercial banks to lend 40 per cent of their advances to the 'priority sector'. The Service Area Approach was introduced by the Government in 1989, which imparted development orientation to agricultural lending. Other major innovations in the field of rural credit delivery in the 1990s were the successful introduction and implementation of Kisan Credit Cards (KCCs) and the extension of micro-finance in the form of Self-Help Group (SHG).

WHAT IS RURAL BANKING?

Rural banking in our country refers to a set up of credit institutions for economic development of rural areas. There are three streams of such institutions- the cooperative banks which were initiated with the onset of the 20th century; the commercial banks which were involved in rural banking from late sixties onwards; and, Regional Rural Banks which were especially created as a new breed of banks in 1975, further intensifying the structure of rural banking.

The expansion of the network of branches has been rather more in rural areas especially after nationalization and with the set up of Regional Rural Banks, it has now brought down the average population covered per branch to approx. 13000 from 65000 in 1969. It has reduced regional imbalances in the spread of bank's branches to a great extent. However, population per branch is still high in North Eastern States- Assam, Manipur, Meghalaya, etc. Efforts are on to ensure availability of more bank branches in these areas.

Various studies on financial flow bring out the impressive widening and deepening of India's financial infrastructure. AS on March 31st 2003, out of total 66436 branches of scheduled commercial banks, 32244 braches were functioning in rural areas, apart from 14813 branches located in semi-urban areas. The Reserve Bank of India, as per its guidelines on 24th August 1996, decided to allow the establishment of new, local banks in the private sector in order to give encouragement to rural and semi-urban savings and to provide institutional credit for viable economic activities in the local areas. Local Banks are supposed to cater to the needs of local people and to provide efficient and competitive financial inter mediation services in the areas of operation.

FARM CREDIT

The role of credit in promoting agricultural growth is to provide the wherewithal for private investment in inputs and fixed capital to enable farmers to switch over to a superior production function. A product oriented lending system advocated by the Reserve Bank of India implies providing credit for such investments on the basis of its techno-economic feasibility rather than loan collateral and focusing particularly on those farmers with low income saving base which precludes their undertaking investments without credit. The role investments without credit.The role of credit growth in indirect but positive and its productivity is no different from that of investment financed by it. Large scale financing for farm machineries and minor irrigation has greatly facilitated increased agricultural production. As a result of private investment in credit, there has been drastic increase in the quantum of farm credit.

While the movement is poised for big growth, we have to ensure that the agriculture sector attains necessary resilience to show sustained growth to sustain the same. This calls for widening of agricultural production credit, rapid increase in the capital formation in agriculture enhancing access to credit by small farmers/ marginal farmers and ensuring highest participation of farmers in the credit programmers. The economic participation of rural masses is critical to attain the equitable development of the country. The Government is also of the view that the full potential of agriculture as a profitable activity must be realized at the earliest to benefit the farmers. Among the factors that will help in realizing this potential are access to institutional credit to more farmers and appropriate quantity and quality of agricultural credit. Lending institutions must view agriculture as a sector where there are commercial opportunities to lend and earn reasonable profits. Failure to deliver adequate credit in a timely manner will be detrimental to interests of both the banks and the large community of farmers. The Government of India estimated the credit flow from all lending institutions for the year 2003-04 at ₹ 80,000 crores and plans have been prepared by lending institutions to enhance the level of flow of ₹ 1,05,000 crores for the year 2004-05. This represents a 30 per cent increase over the previous year. To double the credit in the next 3 years, an agricultural credit growth of 30 per cent by Commercial Banks, 30 per cent by Cooperative Banks and 40 per cent of Regional Rural Banks is suggested. Under a broad framework of a special Agricultural Credit plan, commercial banks will make an effort to bring into their fold on an average at least 100 new farmers at each rural and semi-urban branch during the current year. The goal is to enlarge the universe of new farmer borrowings from banks by about 50 lakhs.

STRATEGY

Each rural and semi urban branch of commercial bank on an average will take up at least two or three new investment project in the area of plantation and horticulture, fisheries, organic farming, agro processing, livestock farming, micro irrigation, sprinkler irrigation, watershed management, village ponds development and other agricultural activities. Cumulative Agency-wise all India position of progress under SHG-Bank Linkage programme as on 31st March 2004.

(₹ In Lakh)

Agency	No. of SHGs Financed	Bank Loan
Commercial Banks	538,422	225,480
Cooperative Banks	134,671	37,110
RRBs	405,998	127,820
Total	1079091	390410

(Lakh)

Agency	No. of cards Issued
Commercial Banks	13222
Cooperative Banks	24259
RRBs	3899
Total	4138

In every district on an average, all commercial banks put together will finance ten agro clinics during the current year. NABARD will finalise a programme for agro clinics.

Public sector banks have been advised to lend more to small and marginal farmers and their progress on this behalf will be monitored.

Emphasis has been laid to implement and monitor the branch credit plans.

KISAN CREDIT CARD SCHEME

Kisan Credit Card scheme primarily caters to farmers who are eligible for sanction of production credit for cultivation purposes. The scheme is implemented by commercial banks, RRBs and Cooperative banks in all states and Union Territories. The Credit extended under the KCC is in the nature of revolving cash credit and provides for any number of drawals and repayments within the limit. While fixing the limits, the bank takes into account the entire, production credit requirements of farmers for the full year. The credit card is normally valid for 3 years subject to an annual review.

As on March 2004, 4.14 crore Kisan Credit Cards had been issued.

Cumulative Agency wise All India Position of KCC as on 31st March 2004.

It is the farmers who by and large avail of some kinds of institutional credit. The other farm households have to obtain credit from non-institutional sources. Hence every effort must be made to enhance coverage of institutional credit, including through Kisan Credit Cards, in line with the higher goals of agricultural credit in the coming years. Scheduled Commercial banks have 33,029 branches (rural and semi urban). RRBs have 14,051 of such branches and these outlets have to be energized to enhance the flow of agricultural credit.

It was envisaged that by 31st March 2004 all eligible agricultural borrowers will be covered under Kisan Credit Cards Scheme. However, due to some constraints, impediments and operational difficulties, the lofty objective could not be fulfilled.

The Indian Banking system has been playing a vital role in supporting and financing small scale industries and village industries, handlooms, power looms, sericulture and rural handicrafts. Until the nationalization of banks, however, this role was quite minimal. Since nationalization, the era of regulated and directed credit stared and commercial banks were brought into the fold of priority sector lending. With the passage of time, the scope of priority sector has expanded to cover various other economic activities contributing to poverty alleviation and creation of employment opportunities.

While the small scale industrial unit is clearly defined in terms of value of investment in plant and machinery, the definition of medium industry is of recent origin. Credit assistance provided by commercial banks of SSI sector is treated as part of credit to priority sector in which banks are expected to deploy 40 per cent of their total credit. Not only is credit to SSI sector accorded priority, it is also provided at a concessional rate of interest; the element of concessionality is linked to the size of a loan and the priority accorded to it. Credit in the form of terms loans as well as working capital is one of the crucial inputs for the development of the SSI sector. The institutional structure for the flow of credit to the sector comprises of two institutions at the apex level, *viz.*, Small industrial Development Banks of India (SIDBI) and National Bank of Agriculture and Rural Development (NABARD). The primary credit institutions are commercial Banks and state Financial Corporation.

While large companies have recourse to the capital market, the SSI units because of their size and organizational structure, cannot approach this market. There is a need to formulate special schemes to assist the SSI sector units for entering high technology and high risk areas. Other measures needed to increase the flow of finance and tackle the problem of capital inadequacy are fixing norms for working capital/inter-institutional co-ordination, coordinated lending of term loans, working capital etc.

The institutional structure providing both financial and non-financial series is well diversified, ably specialized and closely integrated. With the emergence of SIDBI, the financial institutional structure has been further strengthened. In totality, there has been a phenomenal increase in the financial services to Rural Industrialization.

BANK CREDIT TO SHGS

In terms of improving the outreach of the rural formal banking system, NABARD's major success has been through the SHG-Bank linkage programme. A series of research studies indicated the needs for alternative delivery mechanism. Over the time, it has come to be known as Micro Finance. Microfinance is a useful tool in building the capacity of the poor in management of sustainable self employment activities, besides providing other financial services like savings, housing, consumption credit, insurance cover, etc. The Mission of NABARD is to link one million SHGs with the overall banking system by the year 2008, facilitating access of 100 million rural poor to formal credit system. In the context of up scaling the micro finance programmes in terms of coverage as well as innovative products, studies are going on.

The micro finance concept has captured the imagination of a wide range of stakeholders resulting in an amazingly large number of formal and non-formal bodies pertaining with NABARD over a period of last decade. The saving-led SHG-Bank Linkage Programme initiated by NABARD in 1992 as a pilot project for linking 500 SHGs to banks, has now been recognized as the largest and fastest growing microfinance programme in the world. Cumulatively, 1,079,091 SHGs have been provided with bank credit as on 31st March 2004.

The national policy of microfinance should emphasise on encouraging initiatives and participation of different type of institutions in micro finance, bringing the micro finance sector with the formal banking channels. Only study of the impact of the programme was conducted in 2002, covering 115 members from 60 SHGs in three backward states *viz.* Chattisgarh, Orissa and Jharkhand. The socio-economic conditions of the members were compared between pre and post SHG situations to quantify the impact. The findings of the study showed significant increases in the assets (30 per cent) structure. Annual savings increased from ₹ 952 to ₹ 1863 registering twofold increase. There was remarkable improvement in social empowerment of SHG members in terms of self confidence, involvement in decision making, better communication, etc. Besides, repayment performance was found to be much better.

RURAL GODOWN

Storage plays an important role in agriculture. About 8-10 per cent produce is lost during the post harvest storage. If not stored in proper and scientific way, a part of the produce goes waste. The role of rural godowns in this regard can hardly be over-emphasised. Foodgrains are stored for consumption, for payment in kind of labour, feed, seed and year to year reserves. The prime purpose in an expectation of increase in their price and supply to customers during the marketing year. Rural godowns play an important role in storage of agriculture produce. Along with the grains produced by the cultivators, the purchased produce from traders, fertilizers and cotton bales can also be stored.

Being a credit cum subsidy scheme, farmers are also attracted to it for avoiding distress sale.

Subsidy under the scheme is linked to institutional credit and is available only to such projects as are financed by commercial banks, cooperative banks and Regional Rural Banks. Loans to entrepreneurs from banks for construction/ renovation/expansion of godown etc. would have an adequate long term repayment period. Assistance under the scheme shall be a available on capital cost of construction of go down only. Banks can aggressively finance this scheme. Banks will however be free to finance in addition to storage, allied activities like consumer shops, agriclinics, weighing, grading, packaging and quality certification, warehousing etc. to meet various requirements of the farmers.

Some of the new avenues of Rural Finance which have immense potential in the countryside can be underlined as follows:

1. Minor Irrigation- Drip Irrigation and Sprinkler Irrigation
2. Land Development and Water Management
3. Farm Pond scheme
4. Plantation and Horticulture
5. Cultivation of Medicinal plants, spices and other new crops
6. Organic farming
7. Processing of fruits and vegetables

8. Processing of spices
9. Promoting Dairy Cooperatives for women.

In addition to the above, the Banks need to introduce customer-friendly products. Likewise, a line of credit against the valuation of agriculture land with flexibility to activise the same for acquiring fixed assets, working capital requirements, consumption needs, etc.

Marketing of various deposit and credit schemes by displaying posters at Panchayat Office, primary schools, government hospitals will facilitate smooth flow of rural finance. Rescheduling, the business hours of rural branches to 2 to 3 cash hours is one of the ways to create opportunities for increased flow of finance as more time can be devoted to marketing of schemes, contacting people for canvassing loan proposals, recovery, renewal of documents etc.

In the ultimate analysis, organizing village meets for creating awareness about facilities available with the bank, safety, liquidity of funds, various deposits and advances schemes can go a long way in finetuning the rural finance outlets.

ROLE OF GOVERNMENT/RBI IN MEETING THE CHALLENGES

The number of reports on the rural credit delivery system matches the population of co-operative credit institutions, is a common saying in banking circles. As the agriculture sector becomes more commercial, there would be a greater need for credit. Banks need to change their strategy towards agriculture lending, from 'directed' credit to the one that is business opportunity- led. A substantial jump in the credit flow to agriculture is envisaged in the Tenth Plan at ₹7,36,570 crore, which is more than three times of what was achieved during the Ninth Plan. The contribution by commercial banks is projected at ₹3,81,652 crore. In order to achieve this target, the Government has directed banks to double the flow of farm credit from the level achieved as on 31.03.2004 in the next three years. In this context, the Government/ RBI needs to take a number of initiatives:

Revitalising RRBs: Although, RRBs have established themselves as a strong alternative mechanism for rural credit delivery, their potential and relevance is rather neglected in the current scenario. The issue of capital infusion of RRBs assumes critical importance to enlarge the scope of RRB operations. RRBs need to be provided with adequate capital support to enable them to have a net capital adequacy ratio (CAR) of 5 per cent. The share of sponsoring institutions in the capital structure of RRBs also needs to be enlarged to make them majority shareholders. By acquiring the majority shareholding in RRB, the sponsor banks/institutions can convert them into vibrant and professional subsidiaries and area-specific special business units (SBU). In the long run, they may merge all their agricultural and rural activities under the umbrella of these SBU. The government should further amalgamate regional rural banks (RRBs) with the sponsor banks to increase the reach of PSBs in rural areas.With the merger of RRBs with sponsor banks, the latter will get a wide branch network in rural areas.In the long term, however, a single independent owner of all RRBs with exclusive focus on rural and micro-credit, would be a great step towards channelising resources for the purpose for which RRBs were established.

Increasing the scope of NABARD: NABARD has evolved over the past two decades into a strong and rural-sensitive developmental institution with a complete understanding of the complexities of the agricultural and rural sectors. NABARD should thus become an apex development bank in the rural and agricultural sectors with direct equity participation in RRBs along with sponsoring institutions With presence on the boards of all RRBs and co-operatives, NABARD is fully equipped to emerge as a strong player in the rural credit system. NABARD's promotion of self-help group (SHGs) movements reflects its immense capability in capacity building and nurturing the rural credit delivery system.

Minimum CD Ratio: In order to obviate the regional or urban/rural imbalances, the minimum benchmark CD ratio provided (for example, 55 per cent) should be envisaged in all districts of the country. That will assist broad-based and equitable credit expansion, thereby contributing enhanced economic activity. The reason urban India is reflecting enhanced economic activity post-reforms is the availability and expansion of credit for housing and consumption purposes.

Reducing cost of rural credit: A different dispensation under CRR and SLR would help in making available more resources for rural credit deployment. The rate of interest paid on CRR balances held by these rural institutions might also be marginally (100 basis points) above what is paid to commercial banks. Similarly, the Central Government and all State governments need to park their rural developmental funds with RRB to ensure cheaper flow of demand deposits. Regulation with respect to banking has been designed for delivery in urban India and distribution required more manpower to be deployed in rural areas. All rural financial institutions need special dispensation suited to their local potential and challenges.

Commodity Markets: The focus of the commodity exchanges has been confined to traditional future/derivative trading centres, and the farmers and actual commodity users are still not participating. Only traders and speculators are participating in it. Banks should be permitted to offer futures-based products to farmers in order to enable them to hedge against price or weather risk, etc. To mitigate the risk in the financing of agriculture, the Government should allow banks to operate on behalf of farmers and participate in commodity futures. Allowing banks entry into commodity futures trading will not only boost liquidity and turnover volumes but will also provide them with a protective cover against default on agricultural loans. In the new arrangement, banks can lend to farmers or cooperatives and simultaneously encourage them to sell into futures contracts. This can help reduce the risk of farmers defaulting on their loans in the event of a fall in spot commodity prices or unexpected weather conditions.

Crop Insurance: The Agriculture Insurance Company of India (AIC) should further spread crop insurance awareness level among the Indian farming community, which is abysmally low. The Union and State Governments should give time-bound subsidy on premiums of crop insurance to increase the coverage of the AIC.

Promoting Micro-finance/Micro enterprise: Micro-finance refers to the provision of small-scale savings, credit, insurance, and any other financial services to those who cannot access them from formal financial institutions. Due to issues of risk and cost associated with servicing the larger numbers of small low capital input businesses, the formal sector lending to micro enterprises is low. Banks offer a variety of potential advantages for financing micro-enterprises like commercial outlook and relatively sophisticated skills. Apart from acting as a credit provider, the banks should act as agents of change by helping people in acquiring the basic knowledge of business, policy environment, etc.

Well-defined investment policy: RBI/NABARD should also provide a well-defined investment policy for the above mentioned institutions. This will help these institutions in better deployment of surplus funds. In comparison to PSB's and Private Sector banks these institutions can't afford to have statistically sophisticated models for investment and treasury management. In that regard they seek the guidance and assistance from the supervisor in this area. Learning from other countries/ Adopting new models: Banks also need to look at the models followed by banks in other countries. For example, Bangladesh Grameen Bank model and micro-finance experience of Philippines are quite well-known. Banking Correspondents in Brazil is another successful model where banks can create a network of "banking correspondents". These banking correspondents are small outlets, which provide basic banking services, example drug stores, petrol pump, small stores in the neighbourhood, etc. The widely spread post-offices network in the country can also be used to deliver banking services. Banks and regulators need to look at these models and their feasibility in the Indian scenario to bridge the banking divide.

AGRICULTURE CREDIT IN INDIA

Agriculture credit is an important prerequisite for agricultural growth. Agricultural policies have been reviewed from time to time to provide adequate and timely availability of finance to this sector. Rural credit system assumes importance because for most of the Indian rural families, savings are inadequate to finance farmingand other economic activities. This coupled with the lack of simultaneity between income realization and expenditure and lumpiness of agricultural capital investments. The institutional credit system is critical for agricultural development and its role has further increased in the liberalized economic environment. In India a multi-agency approach comprising co-operative banks, scheduled commercial banks and regional rural banks (RRBs) has been followed to allow credit to agricultural sector.

TYPES OF AGRICULTURE CREDIT

The agriculture credit can be classified on the basis of:

- According to Tenure of Agricultural Credit *i.e.* the credit requirement based on the time-period of loans.It can of three types:
  - *Short-Term:* It refers to the loans required for meeting the short-term requirements of the cultivators.These loans are generally for a period not exceeding and repaid after the harvest. For example loans required for the purchase of fertilizers, HYV seed, for meeting expense on religious or social ceremonies *etc.*
  - *Medium-Term:* These loans are for a period up to 5 years. These are the financial requirements to make improvements on land, buying cattle or agricultural equipments, digging up of canals *etc.*
  - *Long-Term:* These loans are for a period of more than 5 years and are generally required to buy additional land or tractor or making permanent improvements on land.
- According to Purpose of Agriculture Credit: The agriculture credit on the basis of purpose for which the credit is used can be of two types:
  - *Productive:* Productive loans are the loans that are related to agricultural production and economically justified. For example purchase of tractor, land, seeds *etc.*
  - *Unproductive:* Unproductive credit are used for personal consumption and unrelated to productive activity for example loans for expenditure on marriages, religious ceremonies *etc.*

SOURCE OF AGRICULTURAL CREDIT IN INDIA

There are two broad sources of agricultural credit in India:

- Non-Institutional Sources
- Institutional Sources

Non-Institutional Sources

The non-institutional finance forms an important source of rural credit in India,constituting around 40 per cent of total credit in India. The interest charged by the non-institutional lenders is usually very high. The land or other assets are kept as collateral. The important sources of non-institutional credit are as follows:

- *Money-Lenders:* Money-lending has been the widely prevalent profession in the rural areas. The money-lenders charge huge rate of interest and mortgage the property of the cultivators and in some cases even the peasants and members of his family are kept as collateral.
- Other Private Sources:
  - *Traders, landlords and commission agents:* The agents give credit on the hypothecation of crops which when harvested is used to repay loans.
  - *Credit from relatives:* These credits are generally used for meeting personal expenditure.

Institutional Sources

The general policy on agricultural credit has been one of progressiveinstitutionalization aimed at providing timely and adequate credit to farmers for increasing agricultural production and productivity. Providing better access to institutional credit for the small and marginal farmersand other weaker sections to enable them to adopt modern technology and improved agricultural practices has been a major thrust of the policy. National Bank for Agriculture and Rural Development (NABARD) is an apex institution established in 1982 for rural credit in India. It doesn't directly finance farmers and other rural people. It grants assistance to them through the institutions described as follows:

RURAL CO-OPERATIVE CREDIT INSTITUTIONS

Rural Credit cooperatives are the oldest and most extensive form of rural institutional financing in India. Themajor thrust of these cooperatives in the area of agricultural credit is the prevention of exploitation of the peasants by moneylenders. The rural credit cooperatives may be further divided into short-term credit cooperatives and long-term credit cooperatives.

Short-term Credit Cooperatives

The short-term credit cooperatives provide short-term rural credit and are based on a three-tier structure2 as follows:

Primary Agricultural Credit Societies (PACs)

These are organised at the village level. These societies generally advance loans only for productive purposes. The main objective of a PACS is to raise capital for the purpose of giving loans and supporting the essential activities of the members such as supply of agricultural inputs at cheap price, improving irrigation on land owned by members, encourage various income-augmenting activities such as horticulture, animal husbandry, poultry *etc.* In India, around 99.5 per cent of villages are covered by PACs.

District Central Cooperative Banks

These cooperatives are organised at the district level. The PACS are affiliated to the District Central Co-operative Banks (DCCBs). DCCBs coordinate the activities of district central financing agencies, organise credit for PACs and carry out banking business.

State Co-Operative Banks

The DCCBs are affiliated to State Co-operative Banks (SCBs), which coordinate the activities of DCCBs, organise provision of finance for credit worthy farmers, carry out banking business and act as leader of the Co-operatives in the States.

Long-term Credit Cooperatives

Long-term credit Cooperatives: These cooperatives meet long-term credit of the farmers and are organised at two levels:

Primary Co-Operative Agriculture and Rural Development Banks

These banks operate at the village level as an independent unit.

State Co-Operative Agriculture and Rural Development Banks:

These banks operate at state level through their branches in different villages.

COMMERCIAL BANKS

Commercial Banks(CBs) provide rural credit by establishing their branches in the rural areas. The share of commercial banks in rural credit was very meagre till 1969. The All India Rural Credit Review Committee (1969) recommended multi agency approach to the rural and especially agricultural credit. It suggested the increasing role of the CBs in providing agricultural credit. Further, under the Social Control Policy introduced in 1967 andsubsequently the nationalization of 14 major CBs in 1969 (followed by another six banks in 1980), CBs have been given a special responsibility to set up their advances for agricultural and allied activities in the country.The major expansion of rural branches took place and CBs introduced Lead Bank scheme and district credit plans for rural areas. Banks were asked to lend 18 per cent of their total advances to agriculture within thequota of 40 per cent of priority sector lending. This expansion of rural credit remained till the late 1980s.However, during late 80's, CBs suffered huge losses due to waiving of agricultural loans by the government.The financial liberalization process with the adoption of Narasimham Committee report in 1993 hasnecessitated the banks to focus on profitability and adopt prudential norms. The proportion of bank credit to rural areas especially small borrowers has come down steadily.

REGIONAL RURAL BANKS (RRBS)

RRBs are the specialised banks established under RRB Act, 1976 to cater to the needs of the rural poor. RRBs are set-up as rural-oriented commercial banks with the low cost profile of cooperatives but with the professional discipline and modern outlook of commercial banks. Between 1975 and 1987, 196 RRBs were established with over 14,000 branches. As a result of the amalgamation, the number of RRBs was reduced from 196 to 133 as on 31 March, 2006 and to 96 as on 30 April 2007. RRBs covered 525 out of 605 districts as on 31 March 2006. After amalgamation, RRBs have become quite large covering most parts of the State. Increasedcoverage of districts by RRBs makes them an important segment of the Rural Financial Institutions (RFI). The branch network of RRBs in the rural area form around 43 per cent of the total rural branches of commercial banks. A large number of branches of RRBs were opened in the un-banked or under-banked areas providing services to the interior and far-flung areas of the country. RRBs primarily cover small and marginal farmers,landless laborers, rural artisans, small traders and other weaker sections of the rural community. However,even after so many years, the market share of RRBs in rural credit remained low and have suffered huge losses.In recent years Government has initiated reform process to improve the functioning of RRBs.

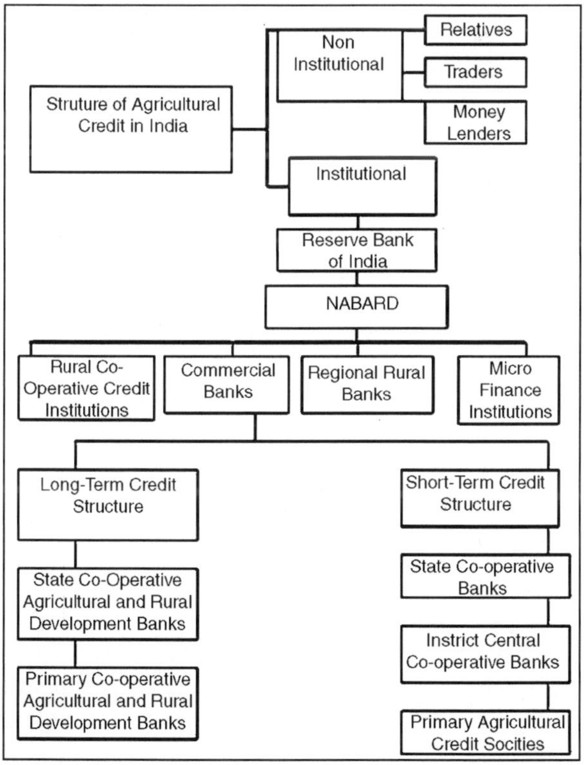

Fig. Structure of Agricultural Credit System in India

Efforts are made to increase the capital base and investible fund of these banks. The financial support is provided to improve training, technology development including computerization in these banks. The structural consolidation process has been initiated by amalgamating these banks.

This has resulted into pooling of resources including experienced workforce, common marketing efforts and thus better customer services.Further, RRBs have been able to derive the benefits of increased area of operations and enhanced credit exposure. These measures have provided remarkable improvements in the financial performance of RRBs. The number of RRBs incurring losses and the levels of non-performing assets has reduced dramatically.

MICRO FINANCE INSTITUTIONS (MFIS)

Banks offer concessional interest rates for the rural credit. However; small farmers are unable to access thembecause of borrower-unfriendly products and procedures, inflexibility and delay, and high transaction costs,both legitimate and illegal.

Thus, Non-Government Organisations (NGOs) are providing alternative means to enhance access to credit by the poor since, mid-70's. After pioneering efforts by organisations like SEWA,MYRADA, PRADAN and CDF, in 1992 the RBI and NABARD encouraged commercial banks to link up with NGOs to establish and finance self-help groups (SHGs) of the poor.

The RBI has included financing of SHGs under priority sector lending. At present, there are three groups of SHGs *viz.* SHGs formed and financed by the banks (20 per cent); SHGs formed by other formal agencies but financed by banks; SHGs financed by banks using NGOs and other agencies (8 per cent).These institutions provide small loans to the poor at low interest rates without collateral.

The experience of micro-finance scheme in India suggests that i) It is the cost effective way of financing the rural poor; ii) The repayment rate of SHGs is more than 95 per cent due to peer pressure; iii) It reduces transaction costs of borrowers as well as lenders; iv) It inculcates the habit of thrift among members and provide timely credit.

COOPERATIVE AGRICULTURAL CREDIT INSTITUTION

Agriculture contributes to the biggest proportion (about 35per cent) of the Indian national income while rural areas account for the majority of our population (about 75per cent) in the country. Majority of the economic problems, thus lie in agriculture and rural areas. For solving these problems various efforts have been made for several decades in the past and they have to be continued for several decades in future. Provision of adequate, timely and cheap finance is an important aspect for the development of agriculture and allied activities. Agriculture is a productive occupation and one of its essential input is finance or capital. This may be provided by the cultivator himself or like other enterprises, he may borrow it from some one else and repay it from the output of the field in which it has been invested. Unfortunately an Indian farmer is not able to make the maximum use of his time, labour and productive capacity of his land because of the lack of adequate credit facilities. This booklet throws some light on co-operative agricultural credit institution, which has become a main source of credit to the farmers.

MEANING AND SCOPE OF CREDIT IN AGRICULTURE

Credit has been regarded as a condition which enables a person to extend his control, as distinct from ownership of resources. It represents the borrowing power of the individual who wants to make use of certain resource during a certain period, through their temporary control, and promises to return them along with the price for temporarily using them.:

Agricultural credit is, thus essentially, an operation of securing money from one source or the other by creating the confidence that the amount of loan would be invested in productive operations so that the lender will get back the loan with interest as per agreement Agricultural credit involves extending the net cultivable area by bringing waste and fallow land under cultivation, providing manures and fertilizers, protection of land, the provision of irrigation, making large amounts of fixed and working capital available to agriculture, changing farm organisation, enlarging its share of gross national product and increasing labour return in agriculture. Adequate and timely finance enhances the withholding capacity by the producers and their bargaining position.

Right type of credit also avoids: marketing problems. Credit, thus, injects an element of healthy competition and concrete commercial calculations in farm operations. The subsistence farming gives way to commercial farming, the simple process of production makes room for mechanized operations and Latitudinal changes sweep the length and breadth of the countryside. Agricultural credit can ignite the process of managerial skills involved in the farm enterprises. Thus, the role of credit consists in laying the foundation alone of farm revolution and maintaining the structure built upon it

OBJECTIVES OF AGRICULTURAL CREDIT

The objectives of agricultural credit should be to:

- Improve the low standard of living of the agriculturists by making agriculture a business rather than a way of life;
- Increase the agricultural production and consequently strengthen the farm economy;

- Develop the resourcefulness of farming class;
- Enable the farmers to adopt technological changes with ra view to bring about improvement of agricultural production;
- Provide cheap credit for producing more through added inputs and better farm management so that recovery could be made easily;
- Inculcate the habit of thrift and savings among the farmers I through better use of capital;
- Supply credit to the farmers in adequate quantity, at a cheaper rate of interest and at the time need;
- Provide both production and consumption credit to farmers so that they are freed from the clutches of the money lenders; and
- Establish a right equilibrium between the amount granted and the degree of genuineness of the use to which credit is to be put.

ROLE OF COOPERATIVES IN PROVIDING AGRICULTURAL CREDIT

The main players in the field of agricultural credit in the formal sector include the commercial banks, the regional rural banks (RRBs), and the rural cooperatives. The rural credit cooperatives in the country are in an impaired state. Several factors have led to the impairment of the Cooperative Credit Structure, but it would be advisable to understand the magnitude of the problem first. The cooperatives once dominated the rural credit market in the institutional segment (with a share of around 65 per cent, going by the All India Debt and Investment Survey 1991), but now have a significantly smaller role.

Data for the past decade indicates a fall in the share of cooperatives in the rural credit market, from around 62 per cent in 1992-93 to about 34 per cent in 2002-2003 inspite of an increase of just under 10per cent per annum in the absolute disbursement on a compounded annual basis.

Two trends emerge from the overall flow of credit to agriculture from the commercial banking sector. The number of rural branches of commercial banks has gone down marginally as part of the branch rationalisation programme. The second trend is that even though the commercial banks almost meet their targets for lending to the priority sector, they have moved more towards larger customers. The average size of direct loans to agriculture in the portfolio of the commercial banks was ₹ 13,500 in 1997, and is ₹ 31,585 now. The average size of loans of the PACS, in comparison, is currently only ₹ 6,640 per borrower, according to the data tabulated overleaf.

Thus, in a country predominated by small or marginal land holdings, the reach of the cooperative system is much deeper than the other institutional arrangements in the rural areas.

Notwithstanding the falling share of cooperatives in the overall share of institutional credit practically in all States, it was found that in States like

Gujarat, Maharashtra, Haryana, Madhya Pradesh, Chhattisgarh, Orissa and Rajasthan, the share of cooperatives in institutional credit is currently 50 per cent or more. In States like Bihar, Jharkhand, Himachal Pradesh and Assam, their share is negligible.

The traditional banking system, the systems and procedures of which are actually designed for the urban industrial and business financing, has limitations in reaching out to the last mile. The exposures of the banks for this segment have risen, but, the rates for defaults in repayment have also gone up. Most often, this happened because banks have not applied appropriate methods for banking with the poor, by keeping in touch with the customers and applying social collaterals. Banks have traditionally worked on documentation related appraisals, rather than on trust and production related appraisals. The client group, however, needs much more support than what the banks currently provide. By implication, we need to necessarily look to the cooperative sector for delivering credit to small and marginal farmers, and those who have little or no productive assets. It is, therefore, imperative that the cooperative sector, particularly at the primary level, be revived on a priority basis.

INDIA'S AGRICULTURAL ECONOMY

In the early 1950s, half of India's GDP came from the agricultural sector. By 1995, that contribution was halved again to about 25 per cent. As would be expected of virtually all countries in the process of development, India's agricultural sector's share has declined consistently over time as seen in the table below.

Table. Share of agricultural output in India's GDP

Year	*1950/51*	*1965*	*1976*	*1985*	*1991*	*1999*
Percentage share	52.2	43.6	37.4	32.8	28.3	24.4

In the last five decades, the Government's objectives in agricultural policy and the instruments used to realize the objectives have changed from time to time, depending on both internal and external factors. Agricultural policies at the sectoral level can be further divided into supply side and demand side policies. The former include those relating to land reform and land use, development and diffusion of new technologies, public investment in irrigation and rural infrastructure and agricultural price supports. The demand side policies on the other hand, include state interventions in agricultural markets as well as operation of public distribution systems. Such policies also have macro effects in terms of their impact on government budgets. Macro level policies include policies to strengthen agricultural and non-agricultural sector linkages and industrial policies that affect input supplies to agriculture and the supply of agricultural materials. During the pre-green revolution period, from independence to 1964-1965, the agricultural sector grew at annual average of

2.7 per cent. This period saw a major policy thrust towards land reform and the development of irrigation. With the green revolution period from the mid-1960s to 1991, the agricultural sector grew at 3.2 per cent during 1965-1966 to 1975-1976, and at 3.1 per cent during 1976-1977 to 1991-1992. Acharya (1998) explains that the policy package for this period was substantial and consisted of:

- Introduction of high-yielding varieties of wheat and rice by strengthening agricultural research and extension services,
- Measures to increase the supply of agricultural inputs such as chemical fertilizers and pesticides,
- Expansion of major and minor irrigation facilities,
- Announcement of minimum support prices for major crops, government procurement of cereals for building buffer stocks and to meet public distribution needs, and
- The provision of agricultural credit on a priority basis. This period also witnessed a number of market intervention measures by the central and state Governments.

The promotional measures relate to the development and regulation of primary markets in the nature of physical and institutional infrastructure at the first contact point for farmers to sell their surplus products.

Acharya (1998) also notes that the rate of growth of productivity per hectare of all crops taken together increased from 2.07 per cent in the decade ending 1985-1986 to 2.51 per cent per annum during the decade ending 1994-1995. Similar evidence of an increase in yields, a partial measure of productivity gains given by output per unit of land area is seen below for various crops.

Table. Yield for various crops (kg/ha)

	1950/51	1960/61	1970/71	1980/81	1990/91	1995/96	1998/99
Rice	668	1 013	1 123	1 336	1 740	1 855	1 905
Wheat	663	851	1 307	1 630	2 281	2 483	2 596
Coarse cereals	408	528	665	695	900	941	1 035
Pulses	441	539	524	473	578	552	661
Food grains	522	710	872	1 023	1 380	1 499	1 611
Oil seeds	481	507	579	532	771	851	948
Cotton	88	125	106	152	225	246	240
Sugarcane	33 422	45 549	48 322	57 844	65 395	68 369	69 288

Although productivity gains were sustained in the 1990s after the liberalization process began, the yield rates for most of the agricultural products in India are far below comparable rates in a number of other countries. Except for sugarcane, tea, coffee and jute, India's yields are lower than the world average. It should be noted that India is ranked second both in area and output for sugarcane production and is the largest producer of tea and jute in the world. Although India is doing quite well in wheat production, the average yields in the Netherlands and Ireland are more than three times India's yield rates. In all other major crops, India's productivity performance seems to lag behind others.

Why Globalize?

Globalization in the context of agriculture can be best discussed in the context of three components – improvement of productive efficiency by ensuring the convergence of potential and realized output, increase in agricultural exports and value added activities using agricultural produce, and finally, improved access to domestic and international markets that are either tightly regulated or are overly protected.

These components are linked in various ways. For example, productive efficiency would enhance value added activities in agriculture through agro-processing and exports of agricultural and agro-based products. These activities in turn would increase income and employment in the industrial processing sector. Thus globalizing agriculture has the potential to transform subsistence agriculture to commercialized agriculture and to improve the living conditions of the rural community.

Ahluwalia (1996) explains that this indirectly requires an improvement in agricultural growth from between 2 and 3 per cent in the past to about 4 per cent per year. Although initially, with respect to agriculture, there was no major policy reform package in the 1990s, it was however anticipated that the opening up of the agricultural sector to foreign trade, the move to a market determined exchange rate and reduction of protection for industry would, over time, benefit the agricultural sector.

Manmohan Singh (1995), the then Finance Minister, in his inaugural address at the 54th Annual Conference of the Indian Society of Agricultural Economics, brought to notice that a policy of heavy protection of the industrial sector operated to the disadvantage of the agricultural sector when industrial prices were raised relative to world prices and thus the profitability of investing in industry was raised relative to agriculture. This would lead to a shift of resources from agriculture to industry. A policy of heavy industrial protection also led to an appreciation of the exchange rate. Ahluwalia (1996) noted that over-valuation of the exchange rate (before the Indian rupee was devalued by 18 per cent in two phases starting in July 1991) discouraged agricultural exports more than industrial exports because Indian industrial policy had sought to offset the constraints faced by industries via a system of export incentives for market support. Agricultural exports on the other hand were denied any such incentives as they did not use imported inputs.

Ahluwalia (1996) argued that in the past, the agricultural sector was negatively protected because of the above two reasons and the fact that farmers were denied access to the world markets due to trade barriers. Exports of plantation crops and a few commercial crops were free from export restriction but exports of essential commodities, particularly food products, were subject to bans, quotas and other restrictions. Interestingly, Kruger and others (1991) showed that while many developed countries continue to protect agriculture, developing countries do not do so. However, no formal attempt or theoretical framework has yet been used to assess the extent of negative protection in Indian agriculture. The implementation of economic reform in the Indian agricultural sector has been a gradual process. These include an 87 per cent cut in tariff on agricultural products, sustenance of high-yield crop varieties, removal of minimum export price on selected agricultural products, a lift on quantity restrictions on the export of some crops and various land reforms related to tenancy rights and land ceilings.

PRODUCTIVITY GAINS FROM GLOBALIZATION AND ECONOMIC REFORMS

In the wake of India's efforts towards globalization and economic reforms, the expected benefits of total factor productivity (TFP) growth can be represented using the production frontier. The production frontier traces out the maximum output obtainable from the use of inputs.

Opportunities from globalization and economic reforms can lead to:

- shift from A to B due to technical efficiency
- shift from B to C on existing frontier due to input growth
- upward shift from C to D due to technological progress

Which constitute various sources of TFP growth, can be linked with trade gains. The movement from A to B led by technical efficiency allows increases in output when inputs and technology are used to their fullest potential to obtain the greatest yield. Given that India has been involved in agricultural production for so long, there would be learning-by-doing gains that can help boost production given the expected increase in demand as India opens up. The increased production would enable a better utilization of inputs, especially that of advanced capital technology. The reduction in the tariff rate for agricultural products from 113 per cent in 1990-1991 to 26 per cent in 1997-1998 is also expected to motivate local producers into rethinking their production techniques and efficiently utilizing the inputs and technology to keep costs of production down in order to remain competitive. The optimum or efficient use of land and water resources would then allow agriculture to respond to the demand for other products such as horticulture and livestock which is expected to increase following a rising trend in the per capita incomes of both rural and urban groups.

The move from an overvalued exchange rate to that of a market determined rate would also make agricultural exports cheaper and hence boost exports. The new trading opportunities would necessitate an increased use in the quantity of inputs to boost output and this allows for the movement from B to C along the existing production possibility frontier. Increased exports would bring about economies of scale and as Verdoon's law states, output growth would lead to productivity growth.

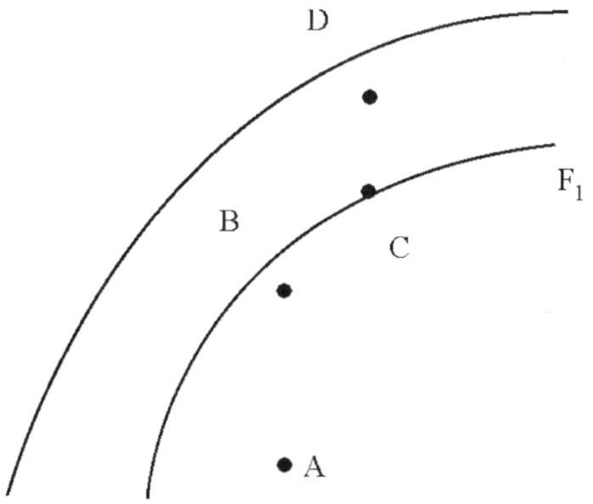

Fig. Total Factor Productivity Gains from Globalization and Economic Reforms

The scale of output under increased exports would justify the huge fixed costs underlying technologically advanced equipment and hence increase incentives to adopt high quality inputs. The use of such inputs would result in technological progress and this is represented by the shift from C to D. The reduction in tariff rates in industry from 1990-1991 to 1997-1998 range from 153 per cent to 25 per cent for consumer goods, 77 per cent to 18 per cent for intermediate goods and 97 per cent to 24 per cent for capital goods.

This means that farmers now have relatively cheaper access to imported new technology and better capital equipment as well as the option of adopting better farming tcchniques and this should lead to technological progress. In particular, the development of agro-processing as an instrument for agricultural and rural modernization will bring benefits, given its capital-intensive and technology-intensive nature.

Lower duty rates on plastics and metals also lower costs of packaging. These forms of cost efficiency should allow competitive pricing of products. In addition, external competition can be expected to motivate local producers into the production of improved quality intermediate inputs for agriculture.

The importance of technology in agricultural development was first demonstrated in the 1970s with impressive growth in yields following the introduction of new wheat and rice varieties. But this technology was limited to areas of assured irrigation as the new seeds also required heavy inputs of fertilizers and pesticides for optimal results. However, the potential for further extending this technology is not yet exhausted as there is scope for expanding irrigation further and improving the quality of irrigation in many areas. For further technological progress, genetic engineering and the biotechnology revolution provides a prospect of developing new varieties that can flourish with less dependence on water and chemical inputs. Such reduced dependence upon chemical fertilizers and pesticides is also desirable because of environmental considerations, which are an increasing concern. It must however be acknowledged that the link between trade liberalization and productivity growth is two-way as they both feed on each other. The productivity gains can be obtained from openness but to benefit from openness via increased demand for exports, agricultural products need to be priced competitively. In other words, productivity growth is necessary to lower the costs of production.

INDIA'S ECONOMIC REFORMS IN AGRICULTURE

Although India's economic reforms were initiated in June 1991, the process of liberalization was implemented gradually and thus it is difficult to assess the full impact of the liberalization measures. Nevertheless, an attempt is made to discuss what is observable in terms of agricultural growth.

One observation is that the expected increase in exports due to liberalization simply did not occur. India's share in world exports was 0.6 per cent in 1997; India has to aim for at least 4 per cent by 2005 in order to meet the growing import demands for capital goods, raw materials and crude oil as well as to meet her external financial commitments. For the last decade or so, India's share in world exports of agriculture has been between 2 per cent and 3 per cent. India is not as competitive as the other countries and calculations show that India's crop yields have increased at a slower rate over the 1990s.

In addition, the agricultural sector's output growth decreased to 2.9 per cent during 1992-1993 to 1998-1999. Kalirajan and others (2001) explain that two important reasons for the slowdown are that there was no major breakthrough in developing new high-yielding varieties during the 1990s and there was a decline in the environmental quality of land which reduced the marginal productivity of the modern inputs. What could this mean in terms of the effectiveness of the policies of reduced protection to industry, a market determined exchange rate and the opening of the agricultural sector to foreign trade?

First, although the reduction to protection of industry is substantial, there is reason to believe that the reduction was not necessarily sufficient to benefit the agricultural sector whose tariffs were also drastically reduced. Hence, the expected shift in resources to agriculture did not occur. Second, is the apparent ineffectiveness of the market determined exchange rate in boosting exports. This is however not surprising as the exchange rate may not be a key factor determining agricultural export demand for India. In general, unlike manufacturing industries, agriculture did not benefit much from these two policies because the share of imported inputs in the value of agricultural production is small. It is likely that a change in the mindset and attitude of farmers has yet to take place and there are delays or hesitation in embracing India's openness.

Third, in opening up the agricultural sector to foreign trade, India has taken major steps towards trade liberalization since 1991, partly on its own initiative and partly from its commitments to WTO. Kalirajan and others (2001) provide a detailed review of these reform procedures. But why have the benefits from trade liberalization been slow to come?

One reason is that prospects for growth in agricultural exports depend partly on domestic policies and partly on the removal of protectionist policies pursued by developed countries such as Japan and members of the European Union (EU). An OECD report (1998) estimated that the producer equivalent subsidy in the OECD countries increased by US$ 9.3 billion from 1988 to 1993 and this subsidy as a percentage of the value of production in 1997 was 9 per cent in Australia, 20 per cent in Canada, 47 per cent in EU and 70 per cent in Japan. These protectionist practices do not seem likely to come to an early end. An UNCTAD report (1999) noted that 29 member countries of the OECD spent an average of US$ 350 billion a year in agricultural support between 1996-98. Schumacher (2000) further reports that the EU provides product-specific trade distorting domestic support to at least 50 different agricultural products. The implication of these reports is that food exports from India may not show a large increase given the international environment and the still-existing restrictions on exports in the major importing markets based on the self-sufficiency argument and food security. Other macroeconomic factors, such as the recession in developed countries in 1996-98 as well as the 1997 South-East Asian financial crisis, have clouded the possibilities of increasing Indian exports.

Another problem faced by Indian agricultural exporters is the protectionist measures in the form of non-trade barriers that developed countries use to restrict market access. This is by tightening requirements of quality, testing and labeling, and anti-dumping and countervailing measures. For example, in May 1997, the EU banned marine products from India citing unhygienic processing conditions. The extra costs of meeting the standards required in export markets as well as costs associated with changes in the production mix and transactions associated with exports may well be discouraging Indian exporters.

One existing problem of India's agricultural protection is the use of input subsidies. The general argument favouring this has been that it is necessary to encourage the use of particular inputs for production for various benefits. For India, Gulati and Sharma (1995) show that the input subsidy in per cent of GDP increased from 2.13 in the triennium ending 1982-1983 to 2.73 in the triennium ending 1992-1993.

But the benefits of these subsidies have accrued to only certain classes of farmers in some regions cultivating irrigated crops. Furthermore, highly subsidized prices of inputs such as irrigation water and electricity for pump sets have encouraged cultivation of water-intensive crops, over-use of water, ground water depletion/salinity and water logging in many areas. Subsidy for nitrogen fertilizer on the other hand has resulted in nitrogen phosphorous potassium imbalance and acted as a disincentive for use of the environmentally friendly organic manure. As a result, the linkage between food crops and non-food crops, which include fodder, has been reduced.

These adverse consequences are a drain on the fiscal burden of central and state Governments. Thus, if not properly monitored, input subsidies can be counterproductive and, in this context, protection to lower costs of production should be done selectively in the course of liberalization.

In fact, Agenda 21 of the United Nations Conference on Environment and Development in 1992 stressed that there is a need for integration of environmental considerations in the pricing of natural and other resources in such a way that prices reflect social costs.

Such a pricing policy will not only lead to a more efficient use of scarce resources but also result in subsidy reductions and improvements in environmental quality. The money saved from the reduction of subsidies can be spent in the development of rural infrastructures, agricultural research, farmers' education and other forms of support for agriculture.

AGRICULTURAL GROWTH AND PERFORMANCE

While the above analysis has provided a general view of the impact of economic reforms, this chaper examines agricultural growth and performance in the states of Bihar, Karnataka, Tamil Nadu and Punjab with their attendant policy implications.

The yields for various crops in these states differ greatly. While Tamil Nadu had the highest yield in rice, oil seeds and sugarcane, Punjab enjoyed the highest yields in wheat, coarse cereals, pulses and food grains. Karnataka on the other hand is seen to do well in cotton and Bihar performed quite well in pulses and coarse cereals. Further analysis and findings by Kalirajan and others (2001) show that Punjab had made remarkable achievements on the agricultural front while Bihar had remained stagnant in the last two decades, with Karnataka and Tamil Nadu showing moderate achievement. Clearly, differences in physical endowments, climatic conditions and institutional characteristics are some of the reasons for the varying productivity performance. Thus, having across the board economic reforms is likely to work less effectively than state-specific policy measures that enable each state's agricultural yields to reach their full potential. The comparative advantage of each state's agricultural production should be determined and with inter-state restrictions removed, total agricultural output would see a very significant increase.

For example, Karnataka with less favourable soil and water resources should be given incentives to concentrate on agro-processed products and corporate agriculture in horticulture, floriculture and animal husbandry, or to undertake watershed development to help with dry land agriculture. Many studies have indicated that with watershed areas, productivity growth has been mainly due to seed and fertilizer use. Thus, this state has to be given input subsidies for high yielding seed varieties but at the same time, the farmers need to be educated on the over use of chemical fertilizers.

With Bihar, agricultural performance is problematic on many fronts. First, although demographic pressure has increased and agricultural technology has improved, most of the uncultivated land is concentrated in southern Bihar, where irrigation facilities have not kept pace and the soil is of poor quality. Given the physiography of southern Bihar, wells are also unsuitable and thus the dominant mode of irrigation has been through tanks whose expansion and maintenance has been neglected. Second, the infrastructural facilities of Bihar have been lagging as seen by the infrastructure development. Due to infrastructural bottlenecks, availability of modern goods and services has not increased or their supply remains costly or unreliable.

Third, agriculture in Bihar is dominated by small and marginal farmers and the prevalence of mass poverty is largely related to the backwardness of agriculture. Fourth and importantly, the state agricultural policies in Bihar are in dire need of review. The semi-feudal production condition still exists in rural areas and the ineffective protection of tenancy rights has hindered agricultural growth. The slow pace of land consolidation reflects inadequate financial outlays and a shortage of manpower. Kalirajan and others (2001) note that marketing and extension services in Bihar are also rather weak compared to the other states.

Punjab on the other hand, was one of the few states which enjoyed the success of land reforms and the high priority of investment in rural infrastructure. Also, the irrigation base of the small and medium sized farms was comparable to that of large farms. In addition, the Punjab Agricultural University at Ludhiana contributed to the development of new seed varieties.

However, there are clear signs of a decline in crop yields since the 1990s and this has been associated with the increasing use of fertilizers and excessive water use which have increased the unit cost of production as a result of declining soil quality. Hence, care is needed when providing further input subsidies in fertilizer and water use. Another related fact is the steep increase in wages in Punjab and in the absence of productivity increases, the cost increase has affected the profitability of farmers. With Tamil Nadu, the main crop has been rice as this state is blessed with two monsoons. But from 1992-1997, there has been a steady decline in the areas irrigated by canals and an increase in well-irrigated areas while the use of tanks remains an unreliable source of irrigation. However, major improvements in about 10 rice varieties released in the early 1990s can be expected to improve productivity growth in rice production although pests and diseases as well as imbalance in the use of fertilizers are major constraints. Thus Tamil Nadu could do with subsidies of pesticides and farmers should be educated on the more effective use of fertilizers to obtain high yields. Interestingly, the cropping pattern of late has shown increasing substitution of food crops by commercial crops but there is concern that the benefits will reach farmers only with the development of adequate infrastructure such as roads and markets. However, that Tamil Nadu has a higher index than the all India average of infrastructure.

Bibliography

A. Poshadri and Aparna Kuna : *A Handbook of Food Techno's*, New India Publishing Agency, Delhi, 2013.

Ashok K Chauhan and Ajit Varma:*Microbes : Health and Environment*, I K International, Delhi, 2007.

B.N. Dash: *Commercial Banking : Risk and Credit Management*, Arise Publication, Delhi, 2011.

Benton E. Gup and James W. Kolari: *Commercial Banking: The Management Of Risk*, Wiley, 2001.

Bijay Kumar Sinha: *Indian Banking and Economic Reforms : Problems and Prospects*, Classical Publication, Delhi, 2007.

G P Kapoor: *Commercial Banking*, APH Publication, Delhi, 2004.

Harbans Lal Sharma: *Commercial Banking Development : A Study*, Rajat Publication, Delhi, 2003.

Harmeet Singh: *Dairy Farming*, APH Publication, Delhi, 2011.

K.R. Gupta: *Economics : For UGC-NET/SLET and Other Competitive Examinations*, Atlantic Publication, Delhi, 2011.

Keshava, S R.: *Economics*, New Age International, Delhi, 2009.

Madhulika Bhatnagar.: *Encyclopaedia of Catering Technology, Food Service and Hospitality Management, Vol. I to III*, Delhi, Anmol Publication, 2008.

Manoj Negi: *Career in Dairy Farming*, Abhishek Publication, Delhi, 2010.

N. Lalitha: *Rural Women Empowerment and Development Banking*, Kanishka Publication, Delhi, 1997.

N.K. Sharma: *Economics : Theory and Practice*, DND Publications, Delhi, 2015.

P R Gupta:*Dairy India 2007: Serving the Dairy Industry Since 1983*, Dairy India Yearbook, 2007.

Poonam Vats: *Political Participation and Attitudinal Transformation of Rural Women*, Abhijeet Publication, Delhi, 2004.

Punam Kumari: *Rural Women at Work*, Classical Publication, Delhi, 2001.

R.K. Uppal: *Indian Banking : Scaling New Heights*, Kunal Books, Delhi, 2009.

R.K. Uppal: *Indian Banking and Contemporary Issues*, Kunal Books, Delhi, 2011.

R.K. Uppal: *Indian Banking in New Global Order*, Sarup Publication, Delhi,. 2012.

R.K. Uppal: *Indian Banking in the Globalised World*, New Century Publications, Delhi, 2008.

R.K. Uppal: *Indian Banking Industry : Issues Challenges and Opportunities*, Sarup Publication, Delhi, 2013.

Rajesh Pal: *Indian Banking and Globalization*, Adhyayan Publication, Delhi, 2009.

Ravishankar Kumar Singh: *Indian Banking and Financial Sector Reforms : Realising Global Aspirations (2 Vols-Set)*, Abhijeet Publication, Delhi, 2006.

Reema Mukherjee: *Rural Women Empowerment*, Adhyayan Publication, Delhi, 2008.

S. Maria John, R. Jeyabalan and S. Krishnamurthy: *Rural Women Entrepreneurship*, Discovery Publication, Delhi, 2004.

W.L. Slatter, T. Krishtofferson and D.A. Seiberling: *Manual of Dairy Industry : Training and Development of Personnel for the Dairy Industry*, Asiatic Publication, Delhi, 2012.

Index